POP MUSIC
THE TEXT BOOK
REVISED EDITION

**JULIA WINTERSON   PETER NICKOL   TOBY BRICHENO
BEN KAYE   JESSICA WINTERSON**

PETERS EDITION LTD

A member of the EDITION PETERS GROUP
FRANKFURT/M. · LEIPZIG · LONDON · NEW YORK

In memory of Alan Bricheno

Peters Edition Limited
2–6 Baches Street
London
N1 6DN

Tel: 020 7553 4000
Fax: 020 7490 4921
e-mail: sales@editionpeters.com
Internet: www.editionpeters.com

First published 2003
© 2003 by Hinrichsen Edition, Peters Edition Limited, London
New, revised edition © 2013 by Peters Edition Limited, London.

ISBN 978-1-84367-039-1

A catalogue record for this book is available from the British Library

Designed by Peter Nickol
Text and music originated by Peter Nickol
Map by David Mitchell
Cover designed by Joy FitzSimmons after an idea by Jessica Winterson
Cover photo: Sex Pistols – Glen Matlock, Johnny Rotten and Steve Jones,
Screen on the Green, 1976.
Photographs courtesy of Rex Features Limited

Contents

Foreword

In the ten years since *Pop Music the Text Book* was first published, there have been revolutionary advances in digital music technology transforming nearly every aspect of the music industry. This second edition is a major update on the original book, with an extra chapter on the 2000s, complete revision of the music business chapter, and new information added to other chapters including new and updated profiles and more examples of further listening.

This book differs from many others written about pop music in that it makes direct reference to the music throughout. It gives an overview from the 1950s to 2013, investigating the influence of each generation upon the next. It does not profess to be an encyclopaedia, and there is no attempt to catalogue every band that has emerged since the 1950s; rather, it tells a story that looks at the history, the music, and some of the significant styles and characters along the way.

The development of music technology is traced over three chapters, exploring ways in which the technology and the music have helped to fashion each other. Chapter 12 looks more closely at some of the styles and musical structures in common use, and includes a glossary of relevant musical terms. Chapter 13 examines the music industry, exploring the different roles of those who work within it and outlining the changes that have taken place in the twenty-first century.

The historical chapters are arranged by decades – though with a degree of flexibility, as changes in styles of music do not fit neatly into such divisions. Each of these decade-chapters includes profiles of some of the influential musicians of the relevant period, and there are also 'further listening' lists – which are not definitive or comprehensive, but mention important artists not individually profiled, or significant records lying outside the main historical thrust of the times.

Writing in 2013 about the 2000s is quite unlike writing about the 1950s or 60s, and the different perspective is reflected here. Some styles evolve over years; others seem to appear and disappear overnight. As time passes, the significance of some artists and developments will emerge more clearly.

THE AUTHORS

Toby Bricheno is a composition graduate, a remixer/producer and a guitarist; he earns his living from writing music for television and film. Peter Nickol is a book editor specializing in music and education, and also a composer. Julia Winterson has lectured in pop music for several years, developed course specifications in the subject, and edited several anthologies of music. Ben Kaye is a music technology graduate and DJ. Jessica Winterson is researching into subversion and dissent in popular music.

ACKNOWLEDGEMENTS

The publishers would like to thank all those who contributed their time and expertise to the development of this book, in particular Robert Attridge for his advice on all things American, Maria Bricheno for her invaluable help and Jessica Winterson for the cover idea.

Our thanks are also due to the music technology and pop students at the University of Huddersfield, Phil Brookes (Academy of Contemporary Music), Andy Collier and Adrian Hooper, DJ Steve Townsend, musicologist David Toop, Simon Warner (University of Leeds) and Tim Warner (Salford University) for their advice.

We are particularly grateful to Tom Farncombe for his help with Chapter 12, including chart transcriptions and analyses.

chapter

1

Julia Winterson

Context

In 1956 the film *Rock Around the Clock* hit cinemas across the United States and Europe. It caused a sensation.[1] The audiences were dancing in the aisles and jiving in the streets; there were unruly and sometimes violent scenes. In some places the film was banned – and it was all because of the music. Bill Haley and the Comets' song 'Rock around the clock' was the first rock 'n' roll music that many had heard. Few would have imagined the far-reaching and powerful effect it would have on its audience. It was raw and punchy, with sexual overtones. It soon became a symbol of the teenage generation. To many of the older generation it symbolized rebellion and violence.

Even the British popular music magazine *Melody Maker* condemned rock 'n' roll. The music journalist Steve Race wrote:

> Viewed as a social phenomenon, the current craze for rock 'n' roll material is one of the most terrifying things ever to have happened to popular music… Musically speaking of course, the whole thing is laughable… It is a monstrous threat, both to the moral acceptance and the artistic emancipation of jazz. Let us oppose it to the end.
>
> 4 January 1957, quoted in Rogers (1982): 18

In some churches, rock 'n' roll was denounced from the pulpit.

> The effect will be to turn young people into devil-worshippers, to stimulate self-expression through sex, to provoke lawlessness, impair nervous stability, and destroy the sanctity of marriage.
>
> Revd Albert Carter, 1957, quoted in Rogers (1982): 17

Then, as now, disapproval from the establishment made it all the more attractive to teenagers, and many millions of copies of the single were sold.

Forty years later, when we come to the biggest-selling pop single of all time, it was a different story. Far from being denounced from the pulpit, 'Candle in the wind' by Elton John owes its massive success to the fact that it was played at a uniquely significant religious occasion – the funeral of Diana, Princess of Wales. That was in Westminster Abbey, in front of a congregation which included royalty, church leaders and heads of state from around the world, as well as being broadcast to millions across the globe. On this occasion it could be said that the establishment was showing its approval of popular music.

It may seem odd that 'Rock around the clock' was seen as a threat, yet 'Candle in the wind' was accepted at every level. However, the circumstances surrounding these top-selling singles illustrate two very different contexts, and show how attitudes towards pop music have changed.

---

[1] The use of 'Rock around the clock' in the film *Blackboard Jungle* had already had an impact on audiences in 1955.

To our 21st-century ears the words and music to 'Rock around the clock' sound tame. It is hard for us to believe that the song could be perceived as threatening. (What on earth would they have made of the Sex Pistols' classic album *Never Mind the Bollocks* in the 1950s?)

> Put your glad rags on and join me hon',
> We'll have some fun when the clock strikes one.
> We're gonna rock around the clock tonight,
> We're gonna rock, rock, rock, 'till broad daylight,
> We're gonna rock around the clock tonight.
>
> When the clock strikes two, three and four,
> If the band slows down we'll yell for more...
> 'Rock around the clock' (Bill Haley and the Comets)

For us to imagine how anyone could think this song had the power to corrupt, we need to be aware that when rock 'n' roll arrived in the post-war period it came as a shock. In comparison with the squeaky-clean ballads that came before, this song seemed raunchy and frenzied, loud and sexy.

The 1950s was a decade of growing optimism in the USA. As the Second World War receded, and prosperity grew, America emerged as the dominant world economy. Unlike their parents, the new generation of teenagers knew little of war and nothing of the prewar Depression. They had freedom and spending power. Rock 'n' roll acted as a common bond between many young people – it helped to distinguish them from their parents' generation. A new youth culture emerged – even the term 'teenager' was new.[2] Pop music had a central role in the creation of this youth culture, and symbolized rebellion.

Teenagers continue to adopt a lifestyle that is often consciously opposed to that of their parents. Nowadays this is more complex; the youth generation has broken up into many smaller groups, or subcultures,[3] each having a musical identity of its own.

Pop music has eclipsed all other forms of music by any measure of popularity or economic dominance. So it is not surprising that attitudes towards it have changed. In the 1950s it would have been unthinkable for heads of state to associate themselves with pop music, but Barack Obama, born in 1961, grew up with it. When in 2009 he became the first African-American president of the United States, he chose soul singer Aretha Franklin to perform 'My country, 'tis of thee' at his inauguration. One of Queen Elizabeth's Diamond Jubilee events in 2012 was a concert with a line-up including Stevie Wonder, Robbie Williams and Annie Lennox and concluding with the ska band Madness performing 'Our house' from the roof of Buckingham Palace.

Even now, however, not all pop music is 'acceptable' in the way achieved by 'Candle in the wind'. The musicians who appeared at that Buckingham Palace concert represented the benign senior-citizenship of pop; there was no grime, dubstep, drum'n'bass, or hip-hop. Around the edges of pop – as with the edges of society – lie examples or types of music that still offend or outrage the mainstream, whether through the lyrics (perhaps sexual, perhaps political, perhaps violent or otherwise provocative) or through the music (which might be very loud, or frantically fast, or discordant or in some other way jarring to 'normal' mainstream taste).

Music is not just music – it is also what we make of it. It sends out other messages, as well as the tune. It can also act as a cultural badge that helps to show and preserve the identity of different groups of people, and to distinguish them from others. Many influences have helped to mould its creation. When we refer to the context of pop music we mean the circumstances

---

[2] The word teenager, although first coined in the 1930s, was not commonly used until the 1950s. Before then young people were regarded as either children or adults.

[3] A subculture is a group of people with a distinct pattern of behaviour and beliefs that distinguish them from larger cultures or society in general. In music this refers to different styles of music, each with an identity of its own and a set of associations, such as political beliefs or particular fashions in clothes.

Associated Newspapers/Rex Features

Teddy boys outside a cinema showing *Rock around the Clock*, 1956

surrounding it – why it was written, who it was for, where it was played and how it was disseminated. The development of music technology and the recording industry, advances in communication, politics, television, radio, fashion, festivals, drugs… they have all had a part to play, and still do.

Popular culture and high culture

When we look at pop music we cannot ignore the attitudes that others have towards it. Our taste in music is part of our identity, and by identifying with particular sounds we are making a statement which affects the way our friends and parents see us. Each has their point of view ('Turn that rubbish down!').

During the 1950s and 60s, when pop music was a relatively new phenomenon, there were debates about whether people should be encouraged to listen to it. Pop music (along with television, comics and advertising, for example) is part of what is known as popular culture. Popular culture (or mass culture) offered new art forms that reached out to more people (the masses) – this meant pop songs rather than opera, jazz rather than symphonies, television rather than theatre, comics rather than books, and so on.

Sometimes popular culture was differentiated from 'high culture'. High culture (or 'high art' or, in the case of music, 'art music') was seen as superior, more serious; popular culture or popular music as trivial, ephemeral. Art music – classical music – was written down, and encompassed masterworks by Bach, Beethoven, Mozart and other great composers of the past. Arguably, it needed education to be understood. Popular music, by contrast, was not written down in conventional notation; it was entertainment, and could easily be understood by everyone.

There were further distinctions. Classical music was performed in privileged venues, whereas pop music could be played in pubs or garages or on the street. Classical music usually demands a high level of playing technique and is listened to in silence. Pop music can be played by anyone and is heard by an audience who talk and dance or drink; it is commercial and is produced for profit rather than for art. However, there is much that can be challenged about these distinctions and their associated outlooks.

At first, then, there was a confident distinction, taken for granted, between the two styles of music, pop and classical. Today those distinctions are more blurred. Who can be confident today about judgements between art music and popular music, or between high culture and popular culture generally?

Popular music and its subcultures

Just as there are sets of associations with classical music and pop music, so too are there associations with individual styles or subcultures of pop music. Rastafarianism, dreadlocks and sound systems are inextricably linked with reggae, whereas bin liners, safety pins and spitting are seen as the trademarks of punk. Rightly or wrongly, assumptions are made about the fans of both.

Some research has also suggested that the style of pop music we listen to is an indication of our social class. In the 1970s middle-class teenagers were more likely (on average) to listen to albums of progressive rock bands, whereas working-class pupils and early leavers were more likely to listen to reggae and soul singles.[4]

A sound is not just a sound. Music is tied up with our identity. Whether we like it or not, many outside factors influence our taste in music, and what we listen to sends out messages beyond the music. The context not only affects the way that music is produced, it also affects the way we listen to it.

Pop or rock?

Someone once said that writing about music is like dancing about architecture. Music is intimately involved in our everyday experience, yet it is difficult to pin down words to describe it. Ask anyone what their favourite songs are, and they usually find it easy to answer. Ask them why they like those songs, and they may struggle, finding it difficult to convey their feelings. They may say that they like 'the beat', but what does that mean exactly? They may say that it reminds them of something in the past, or that they like the words – but that is not describing the music.

Even the words 'pop' and 'rock' do not adequately describe the two supposedly distinct styles of music. They do not cover the many styles that have sprung up since the 1950s. In a very general sense, pop music is instant, based on the singles market, and aimed at teenagers, whereas rock music is album-based and directed at adults. We might agree that Lady Gaga is pop and Kings of Leon are rock, but where would reggae fit, for example? Is it pop or rock, or is it something else?

Sometimes the word pop is used as a blanket word to cover all styles – rock, reggae, hip-hop and so on. For the purposes of this book the word pop will be used most of the time to embrace both rock and pop.

---

[4] As shown in a 1973 Schools Council Project studying the influence of the mass media on the experience of schooling. It included questionnaires and case studies exploring the meanings that various forms of pop music had for pupils.

Julia Winterson and Peter Nickol

Origins

The origins of pop music are many and various, but at the heart of the matter lie five vitally important lines of development:
1. (black) blues
2. (white) folk and country
3. (black) gospel
4. (mainly white) entertainment music
5. (black) jazz

Two basic but important points emerge from this list:
1. We are talking essentially about American music.
2. Pop music is a blend of black and white influences, with the black rather predominating.

We do not mean to suggest that these are the only styles that had an input into pop music. On the contrary, at different periods many other styles and genres have contributed something. Even so, the above five genres form the historical core that led to the development of modern pop music, and this chapter will concentrate on them.

As will be described in more detail in Chapter 3, when rock 'n' roll came into being in the mid-50s, its main ingredient was blues, the music of the urban black communities of the USA, and the secondary ingredient was country music, the music of white Southerners. These two idioms were themselves directly descended from, respectively, the black and white folksong traditions of the South. Thus pop has a folksong heritage – and it inherits from those traditions many of the practices and attitudes of folksong.

The mixing of black and white, of African and European, runs through this chapter. It defines and redefines successive eras of American popular music.

The shaping of American music – African influences

Slavery began early in the seventeenth century, serving the demand for plantation workers to produce sugar, tobacco, rice and other crops. Most slaves came from the West African coastal regions and inland savannahs. They were from many different areas and language-groups, but tribes and even families were split up on arrival in America, and the survival of their original culture was severely inhibited.

Even so, there are aspects of West African music which in a general way carried over into black American music, and later into pop. Instrumental timbre is an example. The African instrumentalist selects or constructs instruments according to a preference for fuzzy or reedy timbres, and African music makes much use of percussion instruments and devices which add to the complexity of the overall tone colour. In America, the late nineteenth century saw the formation of black marching bands, which used European instruments (including leftovers from Civil War bands) but adapted them to their own traditions through a variety of improvised mutes and other tone-distorting devices. This practice was significant for jazz, and also affected blues, perhaps helping to determine the use in urban blues of the harmonica and electric guitar.

In most types of African music, rhythm and percussion play an important role – relatively more important than in European music, more complex and sophisticated. Sometimes, several different rhythms are played at the same time, creating exciting syncopations and cross-rhythms. African music is often improvised. It makes much use of call and response, where there is a dialogue between the performers, so that the leader sings a line (the call) and is answered by a chorus (the response). The use of call and response is one feature that can be traced through a wide variety of black American music: through worksongs to blues and through gospel to soul. Its use in blues is less obvious than in gospel-R&B, but it is there in the lyric structure and also in the way an accompanying instrument, such as a guitar or harmonica, often 'answers' the singer at the end of each line.

The use of pitch is important in many African languages, and ordinary speech tends to be melodious. This in turn is reflected in the music, so that singing styles often have a recitative-like quality (half-speaking, half-singing) and move easily between singing and speaking deliveries. Instruments, too, sometimes follow vocal patterns as though they could talk – an obvious example being the 'talking drums', which copy the rhythms and intonation of speech.

Some of the contrasts between pop and classical music which were described in Chapter 1 parallel similar contrasts between African and European music. European classical music was (or is) written down by a composer, for musicians to perform to an audience who listen quietly and then applaud at the end. It forms a distinct activity, for composer, performer and listener alike. In Africa, music is central to every aspect of traditional life, from rituals to entertainment, and is mostly passed on through oral tradition – by word of mouth. It often has a clear-cut social purpose, and is often associated with dance; in place of a demarcation between performer and audience, everyone joins in singing, clapping or dancing, or just moving to the music.

This dance-function can be seen in pop. Not all pop is dance music, but there is much that makes you want to get up and dance. Pop's use for spontaneous, communal dancing is the most striking of all the differences between it and classical music.

A new American music, born in slavery

From the early days of slavery, black American music began to take on an identity distinct from its African roots. English became the language of slaves as well as of slave-owners, and the scales and harmonies of European music – through hymns, parlour ballads and military marches – were also absorbed. Through this process, black American music – as opposed to African music – came into being. As LeRoi Jones points out:

> Undoubtedly, none of the African prisoners broke out into 'St. James Infirmary' the minute the first of them was herded off the ship… When a man looked up in some anonymous field and shouted:
>   'Oh, Ahm tired a dis mess,
>   Oh yes, Ahm so tired a dis mess,'
> you can be sure he was an American.
>
> Jones (1963): x and xii

European influences

Early generations of white settlers brought hymns and folk songs. Then in the nineteenth century came an expansion of music for entertainment: marches, formal dance music (waltzes, polkas), ballads and sentimental songs.

Of all these, hymns have exceptional importance to our story, for it was through hymns, more than anything else, that black Americans came into direct contact with the major and minor scales and harmonies of European music. In a way this was the most crucial mixture of all – an African (or black American) approach to music, blended with the essential building blocks of European music.

Instrumental fusions – from marches to ragtime

In the nineteenth century, America was still largely a rural community. There was a demand in country areas for travelling entertainers, and these included skilled musicians. Music could be the road to freedom for escaped or freed slaves, and many found work as professional or semi-professional musicians. As they travelled around, African influences would filter into white music, while in turn black musicians assimilated white folk tunes into their music. At this time black fiddlers were commonly found in America, often teaming up with banjo and percussion.[1] Sometimes a double bass was added. The music that they played was often used to accompany dancing – jigs and the like. Black musicians also played in military bands, and by the end of the nineteenth century there were many all-black bands – some playing for dancing as well as marching.

In the 1870s thousands of people were drawn away from rural areas to the industrial cities of the North, and this urbanization further expanded the market for entertainment. Employment was available for black musicians in theatres, music halls, bars and brothels.

One popular format was minstrel shows. These originated when white entertainers covered their faces in dark make-up (usually burnt cork) and mimicked what they perceived as black mannerisms. Soon black performers formed their own companies and played all over the USA, sometimes even blacking up themselves. They parodied white country music, such as the jig, the reels and the hoe-down, by adding syncopation and jazzing it up (or making it 'ragged') – sounding notes before the beat and putting rests on strong beats. The music was used to accompany the cakewalk dance which, with its high-kicking steps and scraping bows, made fun of white high-society. For a while the words 'cakewalk' and 'rag' were interchangeable.

Towards the end of the nineteenth century, the syncopated ragtime style started to be notated and increasingly formalized. It became a national craze and a money-spinning business, with large profits being made from the sale of sheet music. Ragtime piano music had regular march-like rhythms in the left hand but a more complex and syncopated right-hand part. The African influence could be heard in the syncopation and subtle rhythmic shifts, with the rhythms of the right hand cutting across the left. But the harmonies and structures were conventional and European, very much in line with the marches and waltzes of the time.

The son of a former slave, black composer Scott Joplin was a key figure in ragtime. Like many other black musicians of the time, Joplin first made a living as an itinerant musician, working as a member of a minstrel troupe and playing in various orchestras before eventually settling in Sedalia, Missouri, where he was the pianist at a black social club, the Maple Leaf Club. Unlike many black musicians, Joplin had a classical music training and was able to write down his music – which meant that it could be published. 'Maple Leaf rag' went into print in 1899 and very soon sold a million copies. Other famous Joplin rags include 'The entertainer' and 'The easy winners'.

Worksongs

The worksong was one of the earliest types of black American music. Most types of music-making by slaves were discouraged, limited, or even forbidden, but worksongs – which were sung rhythmically in time with the task being done – actually helped the work. Many songs made use of call and response: one member of the gang would lead the singing with the others coming in after him. An English actress, Fannie Kemble, who married a Georgia rice planter,

---

[1] This mirrored the common Ghanaian ensemble of plucked lute, bowed lute and percussion.

observed this practice around 1838, and wrote:

> The way in which the chorus strikes in with the burden [refrain] between each phrase of the melody chanted by a single voice is very curious and effective.
>
> quoted in Oliver (1969): 9

Sometimes the words came from British folk music; sometimes they were improvised and followed an AAB form where the first and second lines were the same – a tradition followed later in the blues. Many blues singers and folk singers have recorded versions of a worksong called 'Take this hammer'.

> Take this old hammer, take it to the captain,
> Take this old hammer, man take it to the captain,
> Tell him I'm goin', tell him I'm gone.
>
> If he asks you, was I runnin',
> If he asks you, was I runnin',
> Tell him I was flyin', man tell him I was flyin'.

Slave trading was abolished from the beginning of the nineteenth century onwards. By the mid-nineteenth century there were substantial numbers of free black people in the USA, but they were still denied many of the rights enjoyed by whites. This was an important age for the worksong; there was a massive demand for labour to construct new transport systems – canals, railways, tunnels – and the black population formed a large part of the workforce. In the twentieth century, worksongs continued to be sung, particularly by workgangs in the southern gaols: writer and folklorist Carl Sandburg recounts:

> We are told of a research student who took a seat on a fence to listen to the singing of a Negro work gang on a railroad. When he finally detected their words he found they were singing lines that sounded like, 'See dat white man... sittin' on a fence... sittin' on a fence... wastin' his time... wastin' his time'.
>
> from *The American Songbag*, quoted in Van der Merwe (1989): 69

During the 1930s the American Library of Congress sent out folklorists to collect field recordings of American folk music. Two of the most famous, John A Lomax and his son Alan, toured prison farms in the southern states recording worksongs, ballads, reels and blues. A significant number of blues singers were involved including Muddy Waters and Blind Willie McTell. One of the first to record worksongs was Huddie Ledbetter ('Leadbelly'), who had been jailed for assault.[2]

Early blues

Blues music grew out of the social changes which followed the Civil War. Many ex-slaves settled on smallholdings, while others took to the road to try their luck wherever they could. Effectively they did not have that much more freedom or economic clout than before, but they had freedom to travel. With the new lifestyle came a new musical tradition of solo song, and from this, blues gradually emerged – probably towards the end of the nineteenth century.

Blues have left their mark on all areas of pop music. The words are simple and honest, raw and full of emotion. They tell of injustice, unemployment and hopelessness, and the longing for a better life. They dwell on love, drink and loneliness, and always express the personal feelings of the singer. The blues are sung with soul and passion and sometimes humour, with lyrics full of slang and double meanings. Sometimes they are pure entertainment. They have been passed on from musician to musician, largely through oral tradition, and are the driving force behind white rock music.

The guitar was a popular and suitable instrument for blues, with a flexibility rather like that of West African string instruments. The guitarist could bend notes in and out of tune by

---

[2] *Work Songs of the U.S.A* (1942), a six-song compilation by Leadbelly, included 'Rock Island Line', 'Old Man' and 'Take the hammer'.

pushing the strings sideways from their normal position, to sound almost like a vocal cry.[3] When a bottleneck was used to slide up and down the strings, the effect again had a vocal quality. 'Talking blues', sometimes a form of story-telling, likewise had common ground with African singing styles, which slip easily between speaking and singing delivery.[4] Many blues songs feature a short instrumental break after each vocal line – a version of call and response.

Sometimes blues singers made the words up as they went along. The three-line verse structure – A A B – allowed time during the repetition of the first line for the singer to make up the punch line.

From 1920 onwards, blues were recorded. The demand for records by black artists grew rapidly within the black communities, and several record companies started up their own specialist 'race-record' labels. Some of the first recorded blues artists were Bessie Smith (classic blues), Charley Patton (Delta blues) and Blind Lemon Jefferson (early Texas blues). From then on we can track more easily the different styles and sub-styles.

'Delta blues' was a reference to the Mississippi Delta, an area which produced some of the greatest country blues singers – including some, such as John Lee Hooker, Muddy Waters and Howlin' Wolf, who later re-settled in the North. The Delta was a tough area, especially for the blacks, most of whom worked in the cotton fields. One of the most famous Delta blues singers, Charley Patton, was a travelling entertainer, with a deep strong voice, who used to groan and yell in his songs, accompanying himself on bottleneck guitar. One of the songs tells of the boll weevil, a cotton-eating insect which devastated the cotton crop.

> Hey, boll weevil, don't sing them blues no more,
> Hey, boll weevil, don't sing them blues no more,
> Boll weevil's here, boll weevil's everywhere you go.
>
> I'm a lone boll weevil, been out a good long time,
> I'm a lone boll weevil, been out a good long time,
> Gonna sing this song to ease boll weevil's troubled mind.
>
> 'Mississippi boll weevil blues' (Charley Patton)

Another singer, Robert Johnson, has had a great influence on the rock musicians of today. In a short but turbulent life he recorded only about thirty songs, but they include classics such as 'Dust my broom', 'Sweet home Chicago' and 'Come into my kitchen'. Johnson recorded his songs in the 1930s, since when hundreds of versions have been made by blues and rock bands across the world.

Another style of blues, much recorded in the 1920s and sometimes called 'classic blues', was a blending of blues and song forms with early jazz. Prominent among the classic blues singers were two women – Ma Rainey and Bessie Smith – whose powerful voices and strong blues style could be heard above the loud jazz band. This was a style – in very general terms – rather more geared to entertainment, less personal than the type of solo blues sung by Charley Patton or Robert Johnson.

Country music

Country music was rooted in the folk music brought by white settlers to the USA. This in itself varied a great deal from place to place and community to community, as settlers came from different backgrounds and even with different languages. Most were very poor or even destitute; some were religious dissidents; some were servants whose contracts of servitude were scarcely better than black slavery; and some were convicts.

Folk music survived best in the settled rural areas of the South and East. In the forested hills of the Appalachian Mountains, folk songs from the British Isles were noted by Cecil Sharp on the visits he made in 1916–18.

---

[3] This is a technique used by players of stringed instruments in the savannah regions of Africa.

[4] This feature can also be found in some British folk music and on the music-hall stage.

Country music developed as a commercial genre early in the twentieth century, under the same media-led influences as affected other styles such as jazz and blues: 78rpm records, jukeboxes, radio, and the sheet-music industry. It absorbed and adapted many folk styles: narrative ballads, dances of various sorts, spirituals and blues. It became a distinctively southern style, an expression of the South's conservatism and determination to cling to its rural roots and identity.

Jimmie Rodgers became country's first big recording star. Born in 1897, he worked as a brakeman on railroad gangs until tuberculosis forced him from that work in 1925. In 1927 he made a trial recording. The success that followed showed record companies that there was a large and distinct audience for music of this sort – 'hillbilly', as they termed it. Jimmie Rodgers continued to be hugely successful with his subsequent records, but TB drained his health and earnings, and he died in 1933. Many of his records demonstrate a strong feeling for the blues, learnt from black musicians with whom he had a good deal of contact in his early life, and who also taught him guitar and banjo techniques.

Rodgers did much to set the pattern for country music. Some of his songs were sentimental, with a romantic reverence for the West and its image of carefree cowboys, and in post-war country music these tendencies became hopelessly over-emphasized. In 1930 Jimmie Rodgers – a true folk-singer still – could deliver these songs with straightforward sincerity.

> The total effect of his performances was an air of effortless informality, marked by a very personal approach which insinuated its way into the hearts of listeners, making them feel that the song was meant just for them… When his audiences of railroad workers, truck drivers, laborers, farmers, and small-town people heard his songs, they recognized him as one of their own and the deadening, bleak years of the depression were thereby made more endurable.
>
> Malone (1968): 94

This identification between singer and listener was a trademark of country music, and likewise of blues.

Country music in the 1940s remained the province of southern whites – still a limited market. In the early 50s, country songs started to make inroads into the pop charts. Hank Williams was its new star singer–songwriter, with a rasping, naturally expressive singing style, which sometimes sounded as despairing as Billie Holiday's. Other country styles included bluegrass, which continued the folk-dance traditions using fiddles, banjos, guitars and mandolins; a leading bluegrass musician of this era was Bill Monroe.

Mainstream country music subsequently became highly commercialized, centred on the Nashville recording industry and the country radio stations, led by WSM's 'Grand Ole Opry'. The old narrative folk ballads evolved into the lugubrious songs of the Nashville stars, typically focusing on deceived husbands and jilted women. In terms of expressive singing and raw emotion, Bob Dylan might be seen as a truer successor to Hank Williams than were such country singers of the 50s and 60s as Jim Reeves, George Jones or Merle Haggard – good singers though they all were.

Gospel

Some of the earliest contact between black and white music was in religious services. Slave owners converted Africans to Christianity with missionary zeal. In turn, religion offered hope to the slaves. They identified with the 'children of Israel', who would one day be led to freedom in the promised land.

In the 1730s the 'Great Awakening' brought a new surge of religious sentiment, and with it a demand for livelier hymns. Then around 1800 came a 'Second Awakening'. Massive Protestant 'camp meetings' attracted thousands of people, both white and black; in effect, these were extended religious services, taking place over several days and including a great deal of singing. A report of a camp meeting held in Pennsylvania in 1838 records the distinctive participation of the black singers:

Their shouts and singing were so very boisterous that the singing of the white congregation was often completely drowned in the echoes and reverberations of the colored people's tumultuous strains.

anonymous report, quoted in Southern (1971): 94

Camp meetings were an important part of American religious life in the early nineteenth century, and in this period the 'Negro spiritual' emerged as a distinct type of religious song. Soon these were collected and notated, and thereby semi-formalized. The Fisk Jubilee Singers (from Fisk University, Nashville) helped to promote this repertoire, touring America and Europe in the 1870s, and having considerable impact on white audiences with these fervent black hymns.

Many early white emigrants from Europe to America were Puritans. They distinguished sharply between entertainment and religion, and between secular and religious music. In accordance with African traditions, black Americans were less inclined to make this separation. Blues songs or worksongs often acquired variants with religious texts, and performers slipped easily between religious and secular songs. Even today a similar practice exists: many pop-gospel songs exist with 'inspirational' lyrics adaptable to either a secular or religious context.

At the nineteenth-century camp meetings, black participants were observed to decorate the hymn melodies, to slap their thighs and move to the music, and to extend the repertoire to take in dance-like styles. In 1899 Jeanette Robinson Murphy commented on the inadequacy of some of the printed transcriptions of black spirituals, remarking that there was nothing to show the singer:

> ...that he must make his voice exceedingly nasal and undulating, that around every prominent note he must place a variety of small notes, called 'trimmings', and he must sing notes not found in our scale... He must often drop from a high note to a very low one, he must be very careful to divide many of his monosyllabic words in two syllables... He must intersperse his singing with peculiar humming sounds... [5]

Where blacks worshipped separately – as in many churches, for instance the popular Church Of God In Christ (COGIC) – they were the more likely to adopt their preferred musical styles. African vocal style included slides and slurs, whistles, yodels, and changes in rhythm and types of sound, and these were incorporated. Call and response was used in the hymn singing; a call by a lead singer would be answered by the congregation. Singers would be encouraged to improvise, and foot-stamping and clapping with up-beat tempos were often used.

In this way the impassioned style known as gospel music evolved, particularly in response to the massive urbanization that took place early in the twentieth century. Many gospel songs were written by Thomas Dorsey, who was the son of a Baptist minister, and who had earlier worked as a composer and arranger with various jazz and blues musicians, including Ma Rainey. Many of the most successful R&B or soul singers of the 1950s, 60s and 70s started as gospel singers, and several have since reverted to gospel singing after a career in pop music.

Entertainment music

If we accept that modern pop music draws principally on the traditions of blues, country and gospel, and if we consider that these are essentially forms of folk music, carrying with them many of the performance traditions of African and European folk music, we should keep in mind that there have also been other influences. It is in the nature of America's polyglot society that different sections of that society are constantly interacting with each other. The pop music of the late 1950s contained not only blues and country music but also a good deal of Tin Pan Alley, and that in turn was the result of a variety of stylistic strands.

---

[5] 'The survival of African music in America', *Popular Science Monthly*, 1899. Reprinted in Jackson, B. (ed) (1967) *The Negro and his folk-lore* Austin: University of Texas Press: 331–2.

An early example of interaction was minstrel songs and shows, which thrived in the second half of the nineteenth century but carried over into the twentieth. These were entertainments that parodied or copied the style of black plantation songs.

One outstanding white composer worked in this genre: Stephen Foster (1826–64). He was influenced by the black songs, both secular and religious, that he heard as a child, as well as by the style of established minstrel troupes such as the Christy Minstrels. In one of his best songs, 'The old folks at home', he rises above caricature to create a melody of timeless yearning. Considering another of his songs, 'My old Kentucky home', Wilfrid Mellers writes:

> It has nothing to do with genuine Negro music, not even the Westernized forms of the plantation song, and it is not true, never was true, that the sun always shone bright on the old Kentucky home, nor that the birds made music all the day. What is true is the singer's longing for release from weariness. It is this which has preserved the tune's potency throughout a hundred progressively wearier and less innocent years.
>
> Mellers (1964): 249

Towards the end of the nineteenth century, two types of variety show for white people appeared in America.[6] These were 'burlesque' and 'vaudeville'. With their striptease and sexual content, the risqué burlesque shows were meant for men only, whereas vaudeville provided family entertainment with unconnected musical, dancing, comedy, and specialty acts.

In a parallel development in Britain, music halls sprang up in many cities. These were the first buildings devoted to popular music entertainment, aimed at the growing masses of urban working people. The audiences for both music hall and vaudeville were not expected to listen quietly; they would eat and drink and join in with the songs, and the artists worked hard to establish a rapport with their audience. The themes of the songs touched everyday lives and were usually richly sentimental, topical or humorous. Often they were bawdy, heavy with double entendre – as in Marie Lloyd's 'She sits among the cabbages and peas' or 'She'd never had her ticket punched before'. In both vaudeville and music hall, successful artists became stars and could make a fortune. The music may not bear much resemblance to today's pop music, but the entertainment was for everyone, and the audience's behaviour was certainly not like that found in the concert hall.

The popular music publishing industry was centred on New York, and came to be known as Tin Pan Alley.[7] Sheet music was big business by the mid/late nineteenth century. Much of the output was sentimental ballads such as 'I'll take you home again Kathleen', topical songs such as the 'Battle hymn of the Republic', which had grown out of the American Civil War, and minstrel songs; also waltzes and other light piano music. Soon vaudeville and music-hall songs became a big source of material for sheet music.

Keen to profit from the ragtime craze, Tin Pan Alley published a great deal of music which it sold as 'ragtime', even though some of it bore little resemblance to the original black style. Black ragtime, as made famous by Scott Joplin, was restrained and polished, with rhythmic conflict between the left and right hand, whereas white ragtime was flashy and fast with only a hint of syncopation – e.g. Irving Berlin's song 'Alexander's Ragtime Band', which has a catchy repeated melody but little syncopation. Whenever a new form of African-American music became popular, the greater financial rewards often went to the white artists who adopted (or unscrupulously exploited) the broad outlines of the style, producing a watered down version for the white market.

Irving Berlin, who came from a Russian-Jewish immigrant family, became the prime example of a Tin Pan Alley songwriter, adept at the 'common touch' and at finding the right

---

[6] The blacks had their own variety shows and were booked into their theatres by the Theater Owners' Booking Agency (TOBA). Black artists received lower pay than white artists and TOBA was often referred to as Tough On Black Artists or Tough On Black Asses.

[7] Tin Pan Alley was so named because of the jangle of sound coming from the open windows of music publishers in Union Square where dozens of professional songwriters hammered away at piano keys.

blend of humour and sentiment in a wide range of styles. Following growing success with individual songs, he turned increasingly to Broadway musicals, and became the first-established of the 'big five' – the others being George Gershwin, Jerome Kern, Cole Porter and Richard Rodgers.

The Broadway musical was a successor to vaudeville but was rather more sophisticated, influenced by European operetta. By the early 1930s, the piano had been eclipsed as the main source of home entertainment. Many white Americans either listened to the radio or went to the movies for their entertainment. Hollywood immortalized the stars of the great musical shows on celluloid. Tin Pan Alley was soon to lose some of its hold, but it had been important in the development of pop music in that it had provided light entertainment for all ages and social classes, and had spread white American popular music across the world.

Jazz

The origins of jazz have long been the subject of speculation, and it is beyond the scope of this book to explore the different theories. Suffice to say:

- Towards the end of the nineteenth century, it seems that black influences were felt more strongly in the marching bands, as the musicians began to jazz up the marches, adding syncopated rhythms, bending notes and improvising on the melodies.
- New Orleans, whether or not it was the 'birthplace of jazz' (as has been debated), was certainly an important early centre, and the place where jazz first became prominent.

Turn-of-the-century New Orleans was the ideal place: a large, thriving port, and a meeting-point for many cultures – not only the black and white American of the Mississippi Delta, but also French and Spanish and Creole.[8] In the nature of the place, its transient population spent much free time in search of wine, women and song, and these could be found a-plenty in Storyville, a red-light area of New Orleans where brothels, dance halls and cabarets flourished. Here there was plenty of work for professional musicians. Jazz bands played in the dance halls and cabarets, and blues and jazz pianists played in the brothels. Jazz bands usually had six members – typically cornet, clarinet, trombone, banjo or piano, double bass and drums.

After Storyville was closed down in the clean-up of 1917–18, many jazz musicians travelled north in search of alternative opportunities, especially to Chicago. And it was in Chicago that some of the earliest New Orleans-style jazz was recorded in the 1920s – notably by King Oliver's Creole Jazz Band, which at one time included the trumpeter Louis Armstrong. Armstrong introduced new varieties of tone to the instrument, making it talk and sing. Listen to 'West End blues', universally regarded as one of the outstanding jazz records.

The Original Dixieland Jazz (or Jass) Band made jazz popular with white audiences. Their first recording ('Dixieland jazz band one-step'/'Livery stable blues') sold over a million copies. Jazz, like ragtime, came under fire from sections of the establishment, who saw it as a threat to classical music. But the youth of America liked it.

Towards the end of the 1920s small jazz groups gave way to larger commercial dance bands and jazz orchestras, and in jazz history the 1930s is the 'swing era'. Swing bands had fifteen or more players divided into brass, reeds, and rhythm section. This left little scope for improvisation in the loose manner of New Orleans jazz; instead, bands played arrangements – notated or memorized – with spaces allowed for solo improvisation. Radio was a crucial factor in building the audience for swing music, and for the dance-crazes on which the swing bands thrived. Their audience was mainly young – the beginning of an age-differentiation which increased greatly after the war.

---

[8] A term variously used, but in this context usually meaning a mixed-race descendant of French or Spanish settlers and black slaves.

Other big bands played a wider range of music than the specialist swing bands. Leading the field were Duke Ellington, whose compositional range expanded to the point where he is now regarded as a 'serious' composer and orchestrator in classical music terms, and Count Basie, whose band, based in Kansas City, was famous for its tight, bluesy style.

After World War II, jazz developed – fractured, even – in a way that could not have been foreseen. Most jazz musicians continued as before, entertaining their public and earning their living for better or worse. An influential minority, led by Dizzy Gillespie, Charlie Parker and Thelonious Monk, turned in a different direction. They sought a more complex, more exploratory style, which at the time acquired the name 'bebop' (or 'bop'). This involved a reversion to smaller groups, and a turning away from the commercialized and increasingly white-dominated world of the swing bands. Bop was artistically conscious, and in its first decade a minority interest, but it set the tone for all subsequent 'modern jazz' and eventually proved a vastly influential development.

Jazz was a more urban music than blues, less down-to-earth and more geared towards entertainment. As such it was closer to Tin Pan Alley, and there was a considerable overlap in terms of repertoire. Ella Fitzgerald was a great jazz singer, but also one of the best interpreters of Broadway songs.

Jazz plays a curious part in the story of pop music. Like country (though in a somewhat different way) it has a separate life of its own, and yet it also plays a vital role within pop. In all the above – very brief! – summary-account of jazz, the nearest thing to a point of contact with rock 'n' roll is probably the Count Basie Band. The Kansas City style of band blues – for instance as it was sung by Jimmy Rushing (with whom Basie played and recorded many times) or by Joe Turner – was an interface between jazz and city blues, and was a precursor of the type of R&B that won the hearts of white teenagers in the early 50s. The tenor sax solos that can be heard in many rock 'n' roll and R&B records lie essentially in that tradition.

There's another way, too, in which the influence of jazz can be felt. Blues guitarists like B B King or Buddy Guy improvised over the 12-bar structure, and rock guitarists like Jimi Hendrix followed suit. Many rock groups follow the format of stating a melody and then improvising over the chord structure of that melody. The music is rock, but the form and spirit resemble jazz.

Urban blues

Compared with other black American folk forms, the blues were peculiarly resilient. The songs reflected the harshness of life for African Americans, and, crucially, blues proved adaptable to urbanization. That is really how blues came to be so important to pop: it was the development of urban blues that created the immediate musical context for modern pop music.

Indeed, the amplified blues band determined the essential sound and line-up. It was necessary to play loudly to make any impact over the rough hubbub of the clubs and bars and dance-halls, but one might also hear in the music a reflection of the general harshness of city life for African Americans. In LeRoi Jones' words:

> Rhythm and blues singers literally had to shout to be heard above the clanging and strumming of the various electrified instruments and the churning rhythm sections. And somehow the louder the instrumental accompaniment and the more harshly screamed the singing, the more expressive the music was.
>
> Jones (1963): 171

If we consider blues in the 1940s and early 50s, two principal strands were emerging:

1. The more down-home, earthy styles, closely related to country blues even if played on electric instruments and in urban settings
2. The more citified styles

In the first category came musicians such as Muddy Waters, Howlin' Wolf and others who had recently converged on Chicago, bringing with them the down-home sound of Delta blues. Both men led harsh-sounding but powerful bands, recording many classic songs for the Chess label: 'Hoochie coochie man', 'Got my mojo working', 'Smokestack lightning'. Another example was Elmore James, whose taut-sounding slide guitar playing was derived from Robert Johnson; and another was John Lee Hooker, based in Detroit but internationally successful, who had a primitive, compelling boogie style. Still others had the 'down-home' sound but a more relaxed style: for instance Lightnin' Hopkins (who worked mainly in Texas and on the West Coast) and Jimmy Reed (Chicago-based). Similar to Jimmy Reed, but based in Baton Rouge, Louisiana, were Slim Harpo and Lightnin' Slim, who made a number of successful records for the Nashville-based Excello label.

The second category, sometimes called 'city blues', encompassed a wide range of styles. Dance-hall band blues came to be known as 'rhythm and blues'. This was blues for entertainment and dancing: prominent performers included Louis Jordan, Ike Turner, Big Mama Thornton and Fats Domino, but there were many others. A style of hard-swinging blues evolved in Kansas City and St Louis: one influentially successful record was 'Roll 'em Pete', recorded in 1938 by pianist Pete Johnson and singer Joe Turner.

Another style, influenced by the fluent electric guitarist T-Bone Walker and further developed by B B King, Freddie King, Buddy Guy and Otis Rush, placed more emphasis on the guitar as a solo instrument with a front-line role, even ahead of the same person's role as a singer. The guitar was played not with a slide or bottleneck (common in country and down-home styles) but melodically, high and continuous, with a ringing, sustained tone, improvising over the 12-bar structure. It was a more jazz-like aesthetic, and led to the rock concept of the solo lead guitar.

All these styles were hugely influential on the new wave of white pop music which started in the mid 50s. Rock 'n' roll drew on dance-hall blues, and indeed many black singers and writers had some success under the banner of rock 'n' roll.

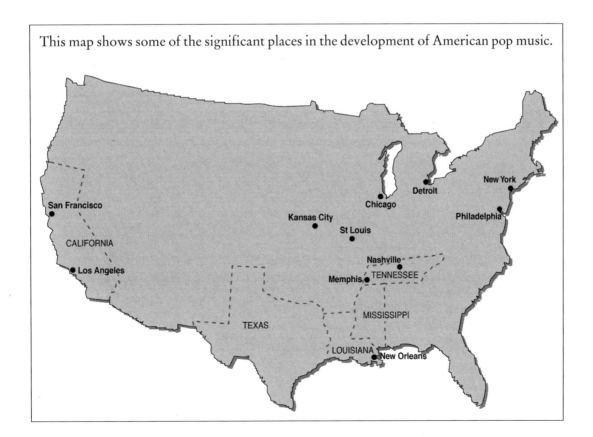

This map shows some of the significant places in the development of American pop music.

Chicago blues and the other down-home styles were a bit too harsh, and too remote from the white audience, to have much impact on rock 'n' roll; even within the black community they appealed mainly to the most recent migrants from the South. By about 1960, however, white teenagers who were already attuned to Little Richard and Fats Domino were looking for something even earthier, and eventually down-home urban blues came to be as important to rock as the city blues styles. In Britain, teenage enthusiasts seized on such blues records as were available, favouring especially the Chess label (whose material was extensively issued in Britain in the early 60s by Pye) and Excello. They formed groups which played almost exclusively material copied from these records. In that way, through groups like the Rolling Stones (who took their name from a Muddy Waters record) and the various bands led by Alexis Korner and John Mayall, the urban blues performers exerted a tremendous influence on the whole development of pop music. British writer and singer George Melly was vocalist through the 1950s with Mick Mulligan's jazz band, and performed regularly at Liverpool's Cavern Club, where he observed one of pop music's turning-points:

> Towards the end of the decade… we noticed that the management was no longer hiring a local jazz band to play during our interval. Instead we returned from the pub to find the small stage cluttered with amplification equipment, and in place of a three-piece front line playing the reassuring, if stereotyped, Negro dance-music of the 1920s, there were these young men with electric guitars playing and shouting the modern Negro urban blues at what seemed to us a quite unnecessary volume.
>
> George Melly, writing in the *Observer*, 8 September 1968

B B King's guitar-playing was the last of these blues styles to make its mark in pop/rock, but eventually it did so in a big way. As the guitar took over from the vocal as centre of attention, this arguably represented a decline in vocal lyricism relative to earlier styles, but perhaps suited young white musicians who could not sing like their blues idols, but who could develop a good guitar technique. By the mid-60s guitarists like Eric Clapton and Mike Bloomfield had emerged, to be followed by many more.

PROFILES

Leadbelly

The son of a farmer, Huddie Ledbetter (1885–1949) was born in Louisiana. He acquired his first 12-string guitar when he was a teenager and earned money busking, sometimes acting as a guide for Blind Lemon Jefferson, also then in his teens. Leadbelly was a violent man and spent more than one spell in prison. In 1917 he was arrested for murder and spent seven years in a Texas penitentiary. It is here that he probably got the name 'Leadbelly'. After a few years working as a wandering musician he was imprisoned again, this time for assault with intent to kill, and was sent to Angola State Prison. In 1933 the folklorists John Lomax and his son Alan spent four days making field recordings at Angola prison for the Archive of American Folk Song, and Leadbelly's talent as a folk-blues singer and 12-string guitarist was recognized. 12-string guitarists are unusual among blues musicians, but Leadbelly's ringing guitar style utilized its greater sound capacity. Songs recorded in these early sessions include 'The Western Cowboy', 'Angola Blues', 'Frankie and Albert', 'Take a Whiff on Me' and 'Irene'.

Lomax was so impressed that on Leadbelly's release he hired him to travel round state penitentiaries acting as a driver and assistant for more recording sessions. Leadbelly's old country blues and worksongs were no longer fashionable with black audiences but his folk blues style became increasingly popular with whites. Under Lomax's wing, Leadbelly went on to make a long series of public performances as part of the urban folk revival movement, alongside American folk artists such as Woody Guthrie, Burl Ives and Pete Seeger. In 1949 he set out on a continental tour to capitalize on European enthusiasm for blues and early jazz, but died later that year. His songs have been recorded by, amongst others, Pete Seeger, Lonnie Donegan, the Fall, the White Stripes and Nick Cave.

Blind Lemon Jefferson

One of the most influential early Texas blues musicians was Blind Lemon Jefferson (1893–1929). Like many early blues singers, he was born into poverty. As a child he sang for coins in the streets and then began to make a living as a wandering street musician. He gained a good reputation and, in 1925/6, became one of the first country blues musicians to gain a recording contract, joining the 'Popular Race Records' label which was part of Paramount. In all he recorded 81 tracks – mostly blues but also including ragtime, spirituals, and the hymn 'See that my grave is kept clean', famously covered by Bob Dylan on his eponymous debut album.

The Texan blues style was more relaxed and less African-based than some other styles. Its European influence can be heard in the Western chord progressions used by Jefferson. Part of Jefferson's individual style was to use the guitar as more than just an accompaniment, frequently answering the vocal phrases with guitar fragments, sometimes imitating the vocals, sometimes picking arpeggios. The prominence he gave to the guitar part later influenced B B King and T Bone Walker.

With his new-found affluence, Blind Lemon Jefferson was able to buy a car and hire a chauffeur, but he spent most of his money on women and drink. While only in his thirties, Jefferson froze to death in a snow storm, having had a heart attack. His early recordings went on to have a big influence on rock musicians. They include such songs as 'Mean jumper blues', 'Black snake moan' and 'Matchbox blues', and have been covered by many including Bob Dylan, the Grateful Dead and Counting Crows.

Robert Johnson

Robert Johnson was born into poverty in Mississippi in 1911. As a boy he worked as a cotton picker and learnt guitar by watching and listening to Son House and Charley Patton at local dances. At 17 he married, but his wife died during childbirth. For the rest of his life he travelled extensively and was often absent for long periods working as a street musician. Few hard facts are known about him, but several legends persist. One of the most famous is a version of the Faust legend: that he met the devil at a crossroads, the devil took Johnson's guitar, tuned it and handed it back to him; in exchange for his soul Johnson became the king of the Delta blues singers. The truth is more prosaic: Johnson was a talented and disciplined musician readily able to absorb influences from those he admired, such as the unrecorded Ike Zinneman, and Delta blues man Lonnie Johnson. He soon developed a technically proficient style which used the guitar as another voice rather than merely an accompaniment.

Johnson enjoyed little commercial success during his lifetime, but in 1936–7 he completed two recording sessions for American Recording Company (ARC). Since then hundreds of versions of his songs such as 'Rambling on my mind', 'Crossroad blues', 'Hellhound on my trail' and 'Sweet home Chicago' have been recorded. The songs have colloquial lyrics intensified by subtle pitch inflections, and are often laden with sexual innuendo, but each of them seems to be a carefully structured composition, rather than an improvised blues. Johnson had an original and wide-ranging guitar style coupled with great technical facility. As a travelling musician he would have been expected to play beyond the blues repertoire, and some eclectic influences can be heard in his playing alongside the country bottleneck and picking styles normally associated with the blues. 'Dust my broom', for example, has a boogie bass line, at that time normally only heard on the piano.

He died in poverty aged 27 from drinking poisoned whisky, reputedly administered by a jealous husband. His music has had a profound effect on many musicians, not least Eric

Clapton, Keith Richards, Jimi Hendrix, Led Zeppelin, Bob Dylan, Canned Heat and Fleetwood Mac.

FURTHER LISTENING

Negro Prison Blues and Songs, recorded by Alan Lomax
Listen to 'Rosie' and 'Black woman', two worksongs recorded in 1947 by Alan Lomax at the Mississippi and Louisiana State Penitentiaries. These powerful performances are both by inmates accompanied only by the rhythmic thud of their picks as they hit the ground.

A good example of an American folk song is 'Stagger Lee' (the title also known in variants such as 'Stackolee'). The story is based on the murder of William 'Billy' Lyons by Stagger Lee Shelton in St Louis, Missouri in 1895. John Lomax received a partial transcription in 1910 and the Lomaxes went on to make several field recordings of it in prisons across the southern states. Since then it has been recorded many times, notably by Mississippi John Hurt, Bob Dylan, Woody Guthrie, and Bill Haley and the Comets.

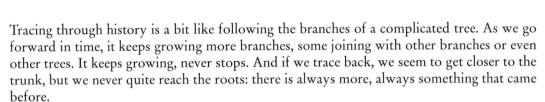

chapter

3

Peter Nickol

Fifties

Tracing through history is a bit like following the branches of a complicated tree. As we go forward in time, it keeps growing more branches, some joining with other branches or even other trees. It keeps growing, never stops. And if we trace back, we seem to get closer to the trunk, but we never quite reach the roots: there is always more, always something that came before.

The history of pop music is easily traced back to the mid-1950s, to rock 'n' roll. That was the start of modern pop. The whole pop scene of the 60s onwards fanned out from that point in the mid-50s when rock 'n' roll emerged.

But what happened immediately before that? Where did rock 'n' roll come from? It seemed to burst on the scene as if from nowhere, something new and exciting, galvanizing a generation who immediately saw it as the starting point of a new pop music. Why such an upheaval? Rock 'n' roll cannot really have come from nowhere. What happened in the mid-50s to give pop music such a shake-up?

Ready for something new

To discover the answer, we should look first at the pop charts for the preceding years. (Bear in mind that 'pop charts' is not a precise term. Popularity was originally measured by sheet-music sales, before attention shifted to record sales. There has never been a completely reliable or accurate way of measuring the popularity of songs or records.)

These are a few records that were successful in the early 50s:

- 'Auf Wiederseh'n sweetheart' (1952) by the British singer Vera Lynn, a hit on both sides of the Atlantic
- 'Here in my heart' (1952) by Al Martino, a ballad delivered in somewhat operatic style
- 'Sunshine cake' (1950) by Bing Crosby and Carole Richards. Bing Crosby came from a swing-jazz background, but sang generally in a smooth, sentimental style: a 'crooner'. 'Sunshine cake' is a lighter, more up-tempo song.
- 'Mockin' bird hill' (1951) by Les Paul and Mary Ford, a successful duo whose records – mostly light ballads or novelty songs – featured Les Paul's guitar playing

Look out for these or other pre-1954 hits on CD compilations. Other successful artists of the period include the Andrews Sisters, Nat King Cole, Perry Como, Teresa Brewer.

These records, far from shedding light on the origins of rock 'n' roll, belong to a different world – a rather sugary world of sentimental ballads and cute novelty songs. They have an air of artifice, of light entertainment. Even the better, jazz-influenced, Tin Pan Alley songs had something of the same artificiality, and these were in any case rarities in a mainly insipid collection. ('Tin Pan Alley', referring to the New York street where many of the popular music publishers had their offices, was a shorthand term for the pop industry of the 50s and before.)

There was something lifeless about this music. Its escapism served those who had experienced World War II, and before that the Depression of the 1930s, but it had little appeal for the young. In his autobiography *Clinging to the Wreckage* the British writer and lawyer John Mortimer recalled the sense of frozen time that afflicted this period:

> Public life in the decade after the war now seems to have been curiously muted; habits of obedience persisted, and demonstrations and marches, everyday events in the sixties, were unknown in the bland, forgettable decade that stretched between VJ Day and the Suez adventure. Severely shaken by the Blitz, the assured middle-class world into which I had been born remained intact until the mid fities; then, like the ceilings in our Swiss Cottage house, cracks and fissures began to be noticed and, in no time at all, the plaster was falling. Those who had been children in the war, and so had not been called upon to declare their patriotism, had found their voices.

When rock 'n' roll came along, it was raw, raunchy, aggressive, loud, and strongly rhythmic. It appealed to a teenage audience – something that previously had not really existed – and many older people reacted to it with distaste.

The 1950s were a period of unprecedented power and prosperity in the USA – clearly now the world's leading economy, and soon to become culturally as dominant. With prosperity came teenage affluence, and this was a new phenomenon. At first it had nowhere to go; there was nothing specifically teenage to spend on. But in the 50s teenage culture took shape – around cars or motorbikes, dance and fashion, and especially music.

With teen culture came also teen disaffection, teen rebellion, and occasionally teen violence. There wasn't really much of that with rock 'n' roll, but the music attracted plenty of disapproval for its sexuality and its noise. Thereafter the generation gap would wax and wane in phases, finding expression through a variety of subcultures: mods, then hippies, punks and so on.

The origins of rock 'n' roll

So where did rock 'n' roll come from? We need to look in another direction – or rather two different directions, at two other types of music that existed in the early 50s. They were not widely known, they practically never got into the pop charts, and in fact they were not really looked on as pop. One was blues, the other country music.

A good record to listen to at this point is 'Rocket 88' by Jackie Brenston, an R&B hit in 1951. (Get hold of it on a CD compilation if you possibly can.) Its good-timey feel and celebration of the motor car later became the stuff of Chuck Berry's songs, while the up-tempo swung-rhythm bass riff (on a classic 12-bar pattern) and pounding piano invite a rush for the dance floor. Stylistically the relationship between 'Rocket 88' and rock 'n' roll is clear. 'Rocket 88' is, in a sense, a rock 'n' roll record – except, crucially, that it came out several years earlier and so was aimed only at the black audience.

For blues, at that time, was not only music *by* black people but almost exclusively *for* black people, in the sense that R&B marketing took place wholly within the black community. In 1951 few white people liked that sort of music, or had much awareness of it. In the context of the wider record industry blues records were called 'race records' – not so much a pejorative term as an assumption about the market.

Country music was a parallel case. This was the music of southern whites – an essentially rural community and culture, independent in accent and outlook, largely poor. The country music audience was almost as clearly demarcated as the black audience for blues records. Like blues, country music was little known and poorly regarded by the (supposedly) more sophisticated white audience of the North.

To hear the link between country and rock 'n' roll, listen to 'Move it on over' by Hank Williams, recorded in 1947. This novelty song, in which the singer is relegated to sleeping in the dog-house after coming home late, is like an easy-going pre-echo of 'Rock around the clock'. The rhythm, melodic shape (starting with the same upward repeated triad), tempo and harmonic scheme (12-bar based) are strikingly similar to Bill Haley's record of seven years later, while the slapped string bass and male vocal group interjections also anticipate mid-50s rockabilly. The stylistic link is clear, but, like 'Rocket 88', this was an earlier record, aimed at a more limited market.

Blues and country music both had their own radio stations and record companies, mostly on a very local basis. Nowadays blues riffs are heard everywhere, and country music is hugely popular worldwide. It is hard for us to realize how segregated these musics were in the early 50s, and how limited their audiences were to the communities that created them. The respect that we nowadays give to 'foreign' musics – musics from cultures other than our own – was not then the norm.

Another good example of a blues record that shows its close relationship with rock 'n' roll is 'The fat man', recorded in New Orleans by Fats Domino in 1949. Later, Fats became very successful as a rock 'n' roll singer, selling millions of records. But 'The fat man' was an R&B hit: it sold only within the R&B market, to black people. Fats Domino made many more records within the R&B market, very successfully, before he broke into the pop charts for the first time, selling to white people and becoming a rock 'n' roll star.

The record that achieved that breakthrough in 1955 was 'Ain't that a shame', and like most of his subsequent rock 'n' roll hits it was in much the same style that he had used all along – and indeed the same as other New Orleans R&B singers who never made it into the white market.

So we arrive at our first notion of what rock 'n' roll was: not, in fact, a new type of music at all, but rather a new audience for a type of music that had existed for some years.

Johnny Otis, leader of the Johnny Otis Show, an R&B revue, describes this transition:

> Primarily they were black audiences until here in California in '55 and then they began to change... When I got on the radio and TV with my rhythm & blues or rock 'n' roll show, that is when I saw the audiences turn white. The blacks were still there but you couldn't see them anymore... If we had 500 black kids, well, that was our audience. Once I got on the radio, though, 2000 whites would show up and maybe 800 Mexicans. Then it looked like a white audience.
>
> *Rolling Stone* 97, 9 December 1971

The word 'blues' might suggest something sombre or anguished, but a good deal of R&B – e.g. Johnny Otis, Wynonie Harris, Fats Domino, Louis Jordan and many others – was dance music, entertainment. Increasingly during the early 50s, white teenagers turned towards this type of music; it had so much more energy than staid Tin Pan Alley. A radio disc jockey, Alan Freed, famously started broadcasting his *Moondog's Rock and Roll Party* in 1952, and the following year organized a stage show at the Cleveland Arena featuring R&B bands – initially postponed after chaotic oversubscription mainly by white teenagers, but later successfully staged. Rock 'n' roll was taking shape.

This R&B-band style, with its strong back-beat, solid bass riffs and raucous tenor sax solos, was the magic ingredient that brought success to Bill Haley. He started as a straight country singer and bandleader, but gradually introduced R&B elements into his style, eventually arriving at the heavily rhythmic and somewhat crude style that brought him huge success with 'Rock around the clock', 'Shake, rattle and roll' and other songs. The use of 'Rock around the clock' in the soundtrack of the film *Blackboard Jungle* helped to establish the widespread association of rock 'n' roll with teenage rebellion.

The R&B/country combination can also be heard in the earliest records of Elvis Presley, the ones he made for the Sun label in his home town, Memphis, before he became famous. Listen especially to his very first release, 'That's all right'. It is a blues, originally recorded by Arthur 'Big Boy' Crudup some years before, and recorded by Presley in July 1954. Presley's recording, along with his other Sun recordings, is widely available on compilations, and is essential listening. The accompaniment (guitar and bass) has a light, relaxed touch – more country than blues, especially in the instrumental break – but Presley's effortless, fluid singing simply rolls country and blues into a single style. Each of Presley's five Sun releases coupled a blues on one side with a country song on the other, but essentially the style is uniform, in effect showing how close the two idioms really were.

If black rock 'n' roll was simply rhythm and blues with a new white audience, white rock 'n' roll was a fusion of blues and country, and this was typified in the 'rockabilly' style of the Sun recordings – not only by Elvis, but also Carl Perkins, Jerry Lee Lewis and several other white singers. The early Presley tracks were recordings of already-recorded songs, but Carl Perkins wrote his own songs, using a style that inextricably blended blues and country. In 'Honey don't', 'Matchbox', or 'Blue suede shoes' the guitar licks and vocal lines are bluesy, yet also carry a light country tinge. The song structures are closely derived from the 12-bar blues – but that was true of many earlier country songs. The rhythmic energy makes these records typical rock 'n' roll, and it is hard to identify exactly which elements belong to blues and which to country. One can hear the subtle blend, and is reminded again that the two idioms had been interacting for many years.

Rock 'n' roll's southern roots

The historical relationship between black and white in the southern states might lead one to question how these two musics could come together. Yet, although blues and country music were quite distinct idioms, they were nevertheless largely compatible. The two idioms grew up side by side, and there was always some degree of overlapping. Country music had much more in common with blues than with the rather artificial, manufactured pop music of Tin Pan Alley. Although the South was the home of slavery, and subsequently of segregation, interaction between black and white ran deeper in the South than it did in northern cities where black communities were gathered in separate ghettoes, despite the supposedly more liberal attitudes of northern whites.

The South was more rural than the North; many migrants moved from the southern countryside to northern cities in search of work. Blues and country recordings made in the South in the 1920s and 30s sound truly like rural folk songs. Even in the 50s and later, something of this folk-nature remained in the South.

Many post-war blues recordings, for instance those from Chicago and Detroit, while stylistically not that different from pre-war blues, began to acquire urban trappings – drums and electric guitars – and the harder edge that seems so expressive of urban life. Recordings from the South, however – e.g. from Louisiana, Texas, Mississippi – still tended to have a more relaxed feel, an easy lyricism flowing from that 'folk' past.

Something of this folk-like naturalness pervades Presley's Sun recordings, with their light, airy vocal style and Scotty Moore's well-matched guitar accompaniment. It is surely significant that all the best white rock 'n' roll singers were from the southern states: Elvis Presley, Carl Perkins, Jerry Lee Lewis, Buddy Holly, Gene Vincent, Roy Orbison. With country music in their blood, they could bring natural lyricism to blues or rock 'n' roll.

Elvis in decline: from folk to pop

Elvis Presley made his first five records for Sun, starting as a complete unknown but with rapidly growing success. His Sun records are still treasured as his best. He sings with an extraordinary and unconscious freedom – natural, direct, expressive and exciting.

Then in 1956 he signed for one of the big national record companies, RCA. His first record for them was 'Heartbreak Hotel', his first international hit; other early records for RCA included 'I want you, I need you, I love you' and 'Don't be cruel' (both 1956). Listen to these tracks, and to slightly later ones like 'Stuck on you' (1960), all available on hits compilations.

How do these differ from the Sun records?

- Where Elvis's voice had been light and natural, now it has become mannered. He is still a good singer, but is singing more 'for effect'.
- The songs on the Sun records were simple blues and country songs. The RCA songs are not in a vastly different style, but are a little more contrived, relying on neat little hooks or some catchy aspect that gives each song its identity.

The effect is that these records seem more artificial – more like pop music and less like folk music.

Folk music is the 'natural' music of a community. The blues and country music of 1950–55 might or might not be considered 'pure' folk music, depending on one's definition, but they certainly had a strong folk element. Popular or commercial music, even when similar in style, is created in a more calculated way – with the deliberate aim of making money. The development from Elvis Presley's Sun records to his RCA records was from folk music (or something akin to folk music) to commercial pop music.

The comparison between Sun and RCA can be broadened. In the early 50s, Tin Pan Alley artists were recorded by the six 'majors' – RCA, Columbia, Capitol, Decca, MGM and Mercury – whereas most blues and a good deal of country were recorded by 'independents' like Sun. Naturally enough, the recording and business processes were rather different – calculated and controlled for the majors, much more casual for the independents. The musical effect was that the majors' pop products tended to sound contrived – like commercial 'products', in fact – whereas music from the independents was relatively natural, unaffected, spontaneous.

The rock 'n' roll years 1955–59 were boom years for the record industry, and a lot of the success went to independents such as Sun, Imperial, Specialty, Chess, Atlantic and others, reflecting the discovery by white teenagers of a music that they liked, and the independents' greater success in satisfying that market. Independents were doubtless just as interested in profit as the majors were, but their owners and producers (often the same person) were more at home with the easy, casual music-making styles of R&B and country, and with the raucous aggression of some rock 'n' roll.

What happened to Presley's musical style following his success was paralleled elsewhere. When rock 'n' roll became a commercial concern on a national scale, the majors tried to increase their involvement – in doing so, exercising a more controlling approach, as was their style. Many independents also tried to adopt similar tactics. Musically the principal effects were:

- A smoothing of any rough edges; a more polished product
- A move away from country-tinged white voices like Carl Perkins towards smoother-voiced singers like Ricky Nelson
- A move away from local styles or sub-styles towards a more general formula
- As with Elvis Presley's records, a move away from straight blues and country songs towards pop songs constructed with a distinctive hook or catchy chorus

During the late 1950s the mass-produceable varieties of pop song that had dominated the early 50s – sentimental songs and novelty songs – reappeared in a new guise, stylistically derived from rock 'n' roll, lyrically aimed at the teenage market, and often sung by established rock 'n' roll singers. Ricky Nelson's 'Sweeter than you' (1959) and David Seville's 'Witch doctor' (1958) exemplify these two typical forms. The wilder, more raucous varieties of rock 'n' roll, as exemplified by Little Richard or Jerry Lee Lewis, faded from prominence, at least for the time being. The scene was set for dramatic new developments in the following decade.

Other 50s developments in brief

In the story of pop music, the most significant thing about the 50s was the arrival of rock 'n' roll, and that has been the focus of this chapter. However, Tin Pan Alley was not killed off; it just no longer dominated in quite the way it did before. Rock 'n' roll became increasingly commercialized, and lost its rebellious edge, and there came into being a 'middle of the road' pop music which had stylistic links with rock 'n' roll but was created and marketed in the ways that Tin Pan Alley and the major record companies had evolved.

On the other hand, the black-music genie had been released from its bottle. If rock 'n' roll as a distinct style went 'soft', its spirit continued in the stylistic expansion and ever-growing influence of rhythm & blues.

Much up-tempo entertainment blues became part of the rock 'n' roll scene, especially if it was fairly slick, but the more intense urban blues of such artists as Muddy Waters, Elmore James and John Lee Hooker maintained a separateness that protected it from the commercialization that drained much of the raw energy of early rock 'n' roll.

Gospel-influenced R&B thrived and diversified: listen for instance to the 1950s recordings by the (original) Drifters;[1] also to early recordings by Ray Charles, Jackie Wilson and Sam Cooke. The Drifters, with outstanding lead singer Clyde McPhatter, headed the growing field of R&B vocal groups. This style eventually led to the soul music of the 1960s, and a number of singers who were successful in the R&B charts in the 50s eventually expanded their success into the pop charts in the 60s. 1959 was a pivotal year, with success for 'What'd I say' by Ray Charles, 'Lonely teardrops' by Jackie Wilson and 'Shout' by the Isley Brothers.

Jazz, in the 50s and early 60s, was at its most distant from pop music. Modern jazz developed in the 50s as an art music, led by the 'bebop' players Dizzy Gillespie, Charlie Parker and others, turning its back on the commercial world. Only later did modern jazz and modern pop start speaking to each other again. Meanwhile 'mainstream' jazz continued as a separate strand, only gradually and reluctantly absorbing the influence of bebop. Many of the tunes played by jazz musicians were (and are still) 'standards' from the Tin Pan Alley and Broadway repertoire. Likewise many singers – for instance Ella Fitzgerald, who clearly belonged to the jazz world – worked in the style-continuum between jazz and the show tunes. Frank Sinatra's success was huge in the 50s and continued into the 60s, symbolizing the way mainstream jazz and Tin Pan Alley overlapped confusingly with the more modern world of rock 'n' roll.

Britain

In Britain, teenagers – especially the distinctively-clad 'teddy boys' (so called because of the Edwardian aspect of their uniform) – followed their American counterparts' taste for rock 'n' roll. Home-grown imitations were led by Cliff Richard, whose first record, 'Move it' (1958), remains one of his best.

Musically the main British contribution to mid-decade developments was skiffle. Originally this emerged from the 'trad' jazz bands (a British phenomenon despite their exclusive focus on an American style), but skiffle's repertoire leant towards folk blues (e.g. Leadbelly) and other American folk styles, and its instrumentation was based around guitar, double bass and washboard (providing a simple but effective percussion accompaniment). The resultant style was in some ways more akin to early rock 'n' roll than to New Orleans jazz; with its accessibility and emphasis on home-made instruments, skiffle effectively became a bridge to rock 'n' roll. The leading skiffle performer was Lonnie Donegan, a powerful and expressive singer.

Britain was to play a hugely important part in the history of pop, and the seeds for this were sown in the rock 'n' roll era. But the British influence would not emerge until later.

PROFILES

Elvis Presley

Of all incidents in the history of pop, few carry such potent significance as the tale of Elvis Presley walking into the studios of Sun Records in his home town of Memphis to make a record for his mother's birthday. Whatever the exact truth of that story, it led to his making some proper recordings, accompanied by Scotty Moore (guitar) and Bill Black (bass), under the supervision of Sam Phillips, owner of Sun.

---

[1] For discussion of the early-60s version of the Drifters see page 34.

Rex Features

Elvis Presley in *Jailhouse Rock* **(1957)**

That was in 1954. Elvis was 19, working as a delivery driver. His recording sessions for Sun, which produced five singles and some other tracks, still stand as rock 'n' roll's keystone. The conventional wisdom is that they are the best records he ever made. He sings without affectation, or the exaggerated style which was to develop in his later work. Tracks like 'That's all right', 'You're a heartbreaker' and especially 'Mystery train' are relaxed and vibrant, flowing with a surge of energy, and with the vitality of the folk musics from which the style evolved.

In 1956 he was bought out by RCA, recording many of his biggest hits for them later that year: 'Heartbreak Hotel', 'Blue suede shoes', 'Hound dog'/'Don't be cruel', 'Love me tender'. He was the 'King of rock 'n' roll'.

Later in the 50s, as fame and wealth accumulated, his style and image softened. Initially he was seen as a 'baddie' – mainly because of the sexy hip-swivelling which was part of his performing style from the start – but his dutiful response to his army draft (he served from 1958 to 1960) turned him into a national darling. Under the manipulative but unmusical management of 'Colonel' Tom Parker, the focus of his career switched to Hollywood movies, and he turned out a succession of weak soundtrack albums.

The British beat boom and subsequent rise of 60s rock left Elvis musically lagging behind, though his unmatchable status ensured that he would never lack attention. At the end of the 60s his career revived, and for a while he toured and recorded productively, before slipping into reclusiveness and declining health. He died in 1977, aged 42.

Chuck Berry

While Presley's qualities and impact lay in his singing, along with the enormous magnetism of his performing persona, Chuck Berry by contrast was multi-talented: a showman-performer, and a good blues singer when he tried, but above all a songwriter and guitarist – which is where his lasting influence lay. His songs have a unique celebratory quality, expressed in words and music alike: hit after hit captured the essence of teenage culture, its burgeoning prosperity and new-found energy.

> Sweet little sixteen, she's got the grown up blues
> Tight dresses and lipstick, she's sporting high-heeled shoes
> Oh but tomorrow morning she'll have to change her trend
> And be sweet sixteen and back in class again
>
> 'Sweet little sixteen' (Chuck Berry)

> You know my temperature risin', the jukebox blowin' a fuse
> My heart beatin' rhythm and my soul keep a-singin' the blues
> Roll over Beethoven, tell Tchaikovsky the news
>
> 'Roll over Beethoven' (Chuck Berry)

Alongside these joyous lyrics lay classic guitar patterns that imprinted themselves indelibly on the musical language of pop. Berry's famous line in 'Johnny B Goode' – 'but he could play a guitar just like a-ringing a bell' – could not have been more apt for the man himself.

Berry recorded for the Chicago-based Chess label, which was otherwise mainly a blues label with a powerhouse roster of artists led by Muddy Waters and Howlin' Wolf. His first record, 'Maybellene' (1955), was a top-ten hit, somewhat different in style from his later output but featuring several Berry trademarks. One is struck first by its harsh instrumental sound: a pungent, clanging guitar flourish, then a fast and furious drum-dominated beat, with a country-rock feel emanating from the bass line. The verses are high-speed narrative, delivered with typical descriptive detail, but in the chorus he stretches his voice into something more lingering and expressive, bringing out the bluesy side of the song.

'Memphis' (1959) is another song that illustrates how Berry could capture and adapt the spirit of the blues. His gentle reading of the plaintive melody lies over a subtle, unusual backing. 'Deep feeling' (1957) is an instrumental equivalent; even without employing his skills as singer and lyricist, he comes up with a strange and beautiful piece.

Unlike Elvis Presley, Chuck Berry did not soften or modify his style after his initial success – a measure of his independent character, but also of the uncompromising recording style of Chess Records. (The same applied to Chess's other rock 'n' roll star, Bo Diddley, who did not have quite the versatile talent of Chuck Berry but generated a distinctive and earthy guitar-based sound.) On the other hand, Berry did not add new songs of substance after the mid-60s. His greatest influence lay in his fast songs and their celebratory guitar intros – typically in 'Roll over Beethoven' and 'Johnny B Goode', two of the classics of their era. This style was taken up by the British rhythm & blues groups of 1963–5, led by the Beatles and Rolling Stones, thereby ensuring Berry's continued currency.

Buddy Holly

The influence of Texas-born Buddy Holly complemented that of Presley and Berry. His music and general image were both much milder than other rockers'; he had none of the outrageousness of Presley or Little Richard, and even his toughest performances, like 'Rave on', were meek compared with 'Hound dog' or 'Long tall Sally'. But his songs formed a bridge from the rhythmic power of rock 'n' roll to a more inventive, more wide-ranging type of pop songwriting.

Like Chuck Berry, he was guitarist, singer and songwriter; his early hits were as a member of the Crickets, but his prominent role within the group soon pushed his name forward. As a Southerner, Holly had the singing ease of blues and country, but his songs shift away from those traditions. Instead, they are diatonically tuneful,[2] mostly built on the AABA song form,[3] and in that sense as close to Tin Pan Alley as to rock 'n' roll. His singing, too, tended to cross the barrier between the two idioms, sometimes highly individual (as in 'Not fade away' or 'Peggy Sue') but later tending towards sweetness and sentimentality.

Holly started out singing rock standards; it was his manager-producer Norman Petty who steered him along a more original course. Petty harnessed Holly's singing and guitar playing to the Crickets' backings and to a repertoire of songs written by various combinations of Holly, Petty and the Crickets' drummer Jerry Allison. This method of building up a record out of several independently effective elements was ahead of its time; it separated Holly from the other rock 'n' roll singers, and subsequently served as an ideal model for Lennon and McCartney in the 60s. Songs like 'Listen to me', 'Everyday' or 'Well all right' are melodic and satisfyingly proportioned. They have their distinctive hooks, but without being gimmicky, and they seem to express straightforward emotions.

---

[2] 'Diatonic': fitting the major/minor scales (mostly major), rather than modal (folk) or blues scales.

[3] See Chapter 12, 'Style and Structure'.

Buddy Holly was killed in a plane crash in February 1959. With his bright but plaintive voice he has remained a much-loved figure. His wistful recording of a Paul Anka song, 'It doesn't matter anymore', which was climbing the charts at the time of his death, served without undue incongruity as a reflection on his passing and our loss.

FURTHER LISTENING

Fats Domino 'I'm ready', 'Be my guest' (both 1959) and many others
Fats played and sang New Orleans rhythm & blues: good-humoured, easy-going, with an infectious rolling rhythm. As his music gained currency with the white teenage audience he became one of the first rock 'n' roll stars, and was consistently successful right through the 50s, recording for the Imperial label under the guidance of producer and bandleader Dave Bartholomew.

Little Richard 'Rip it up' (1956), 'Lucille' (1957)
A frantic version of dance-band R&B that caught the spirit of rock 'n' roll at its most exciting. Little Richard pounded the piano and sang with a high-pitched, gospel-tinged delivery that carried all before it.

Jerry Lee Lewis 'Whole lotta shakin' goin' on' (1957), 'Great balls of fire' (1957)
Jerry Lee Lewis evolved his own rock 'n' roll piano style, his left hand pounding out a rock-solid boogie pattern while his right hand played the high keys with flamboyant flourishes and glissandi. He was an electrifying live performer with a wild reputation, sometimes leaping onto the piano and playing with his feet. In some ways like a white version of Little Richard, yet with a curiously different feel – cool, detached, almost mocking. Jerry Lee Lewis was a good, natural country singer, but unlike Carl Perkins he did not write his own material. His records remain highly favoured by rock 'n' roll aficionados.

Carl Perkins 'Blue suede shoes' (1955)
Equally effective as singer, songwriter and guitarist, Perkins has already been discussed in the body of the chapter. He wrote 'Blue suede shoes' and had a big hit with it before Elvis Presley covered it with even bigger sales. In straight country vein, Perkins sings a beautiful, lingering line on 'Forever yours', while on 'Turn around' he captures Hank Williams' spirit of despair.

Johnny Cash 'Folsom Prison blues' (1955), 'I walk the line' (1956)
Country singer Johnny Cash (1932–2003) was originally from Arkansas, the son of a poor cotton farmer. These are two of the earliest hits from the 'man in black', released by Sun Records at a time when country music was starting to appear in the pop charts. Cash went on to have a long string of country hits and was largely unaffected by contemporary trends, although his last big hit, 'Hurt' (2003), was a heart-rending cover of the Nine Inch Nails song.

Gene Vincent 'Be bop a lula' (1956)
'Be bop a lula' was his biggest hit, and is representative of the strong recordings he made in 1956 with his backing group the Blue Caps. After that his career went into decline. He could be a superb singer, but his life was a patchwork of false starts. He died in 1971, aged only 36.

Bo Diddley 'Bo Diddley' (1955)
Like Chuck Berry, Bo Diddley recorded for the Chicago-based Chess label, and had a number of rock 'n' roll hits for them. He was a musical maverick, most celebrated for the two-bar 'Bo Diddley' rhythm which featured on a number of his records (see page 169). This is essentially a drum pattern with a powerful, ritualistic character; the rhythm is similar to the

clave rhythm found in much West African and Latin music. Some of Bo Diddley's records were more orthodox blues (e.g. 'I can tell'), and some had an affinity with down-home folk blues ('She's fine, she's mine', 'Down home train'). Still others, e.g. 'Mumblin' guitar' and 'Give me a break', were unconventional sound-creations. Bo Diddley – again like Chuck Berry – had a big influence on British groups (especially the Rolling Stones) in the early 60s.

The Chords 'Sh-Boom' (1954)

Essentially a vocal group novelty song, this was one of the first black records to be picked up by the white teenage market. The vocal group style partly stemmed from groups like the Ink Spots and the Mills Brothers, but in 'Sh-Boom' a standard chord sequence for vocal group ballads (I VI II V) was turned into rock 'n' roll: fast, rough and exciting. In 1954 the Chords' version was outsold by a white cover version (by the Crewcuts), as happened also to many other black groups. Fats Domino's 'Ain't that a shame' was initially outsold by Pat Boone's version in 1955, before Fats himself was fully accepted by the white audience.

The Drifters 'Money honey' (1953)
Ray Charles 'I've got a woman' (1955)
James Brown 'Please, please, please' (1956)

These songs exemplify the rise of gospel influence. Whereas the Chords' 'Sh-Boom' has a fairly meaningless conventional lyric, given novelty value through a string of nonsense syllables, 'Money honey' is sly and humorous, its qualities expressively brought out by lead singer Clyde McPhatter.

Ray Charles's 'I've got a woman' has the chord changes, riffs and sax solo typical of band blues, but again adds a vocal with a strong gospel tinge. His later 'What'd I say', built on gospel-style call and response, broke into the pop charts in 1959, but on the whole gospel-R&B remained outside the general pop charts until the 60s, when the British blues groups helped to catalyse a general shift in taste. James Brown's impassioned 'Please, please, please' was a big hit in the R&B charts in 1956, but only much later did he become a favourite with the white audience as well.

Jackie Wilson 'Reet petite' (1957)

Jackie Wilson was important in the transition from R&B to soul and 'Reet petite' has elements of both, as well as a touch of rock 'n' roll. As a member of Billy Ward and the Dominoes, Wilson was a well-known R&B performer before he became a soloist in the 1950s. 'Reet petite' was co-written by the then little known Berry Gordy Jr. The song's financial success helped Gordy to launch his new soul music label, Motown.

Julie London 'Cry me a river' (1955)

Julie London was an American singer and actress with a smoky, sensual voice. Her most famous single, the jazzy blues ballad 'Cry me a river', is a classic 'torch' song in a bluesy jazz-influenced style. The song became popular after she performed it in one of the first rock 'n' roll movies – *The Girl Can't Help It* (1956).

Johnny Kidd and the Pirates 'Shakin' all over' (1960)

Although US rock 'n' roll artists predominated in the UK, there were a few home-grown groups including Cliff Richard and the Shadows, Billy Fury, Marty Wilde – and Johnny Kidd and the Pirates, one of the first bands to dress up on stage wearing pirate outfits complete with eye-patches. 'Shakin' all over' with its riffing twangy guitar became one of the UK's first rock 'n' roll classics.

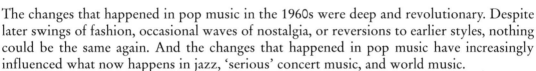

Sixties

The changes that happened in pop music in the 1960s were deep and revolutionary. Despite later swings of fashion, occasional waves of nostalgia, or reversions to earlier styles, nothing could be the same again. And the changes that happened in pop music have increasingly influenced what now happens in jazz, 'serious' concert music, and world music.

None of this was apparent at the beginning of the 60s. About five years earlier there had been the rock 'n' roll upheaval and the rise of teenage culture, but by 1960 the aggressive edge of early rock 'n' roll had worn off. Commercialization tended to even things out, and most white pop music was fairly bland. Teenage buying power, however, continued to increase, so that teenage taste remained a determining force in music and fashion.

From pop to art

What happened next was surprising, though it was in some ways similar to what had happened to jazz in the late 40s: pop became a seriously considered art-form. In 1955 rock 'n' roll was relatively close to its folk roots in blues and country, but by 1960 pop seemed well and truly to have left those roots behind, to have become pure commercial music. In the decade to come, musicians started creating pop music with artistic rather than commercial purpose. Not all pop music followed this path – much that was produced in the 60s was purely commercial – but the fact that it happened at all changed the face of pop, and subsequently of other musical styles.

Three strands of development combined to produce this revolution in the status of pop, and we will look in some detail at each of them.

Quality pop

As rock 'n' roll lost its hard edge towards the end of the 50s, it became more of a medium for songwriters and record producers; we see this in the case of Buddy Holly and Norman Petty, or with Elvis Presley and his RCA producer Steve Sholes. Straight country or blues-styled songs featured less; pop songs with catchy hooks and vocal harmonies relatively more. Other songwriters who thrived in the late 50s included Boudeleaux and Felice Bryant (who wrote for the Everly Brothers), and Jerry Leiber and Mike Stoller (who wrote for Elvis Presley, e.g. 'Jailhouse rock', and had a string of hits with the Coasters, then worked increasingly as producers, notably with the Drifters).

The Everly Brothers' early records illustrate the elements that combine to make a good pop record:
- Perfect pacing: even the slowest songs never suffer from a lack of flow
- Vocal harmonies: harshly nasal in the Everlys' case, but always perfectly balanced
- Hooks: each record is built round a simple instrumental figure like a drum roll or short guitar motif, and a simple but distinctive phrase to carry the song's title.

The combination of these factors turned simple material into minor masterpieces: 'Bye bye love', 'Claudette', 'Crying in the rain', 'Til I kissed you', 'Since you broke my heart', 'Cathy's clown', 'So sad'. The creativity that made these records so good lay less in what happened during the actual performance than in the concept that already existed before the performance – in other words, the written song plus the arrangement plus the producers' notion of the sound they were aiming it, the effect they were after. This is what distinguishes the Everlys' music from, say, Elvis Presley's Sun recordings.

With composers and producers more influential, the focus swung somewhat away from solo singers towards vocal groups. Leiber and Stoller worked during the 50s with various groups including the Drifters and the Coasters. In 1959 the Drifters re-formed with a completely new line-up, including first Ben E King on lead, then Rudy Lewis. This version of the Drifters was even more successful than the original group, with such hits as 'There goes my baby', 'Save the last dance for me', 'Sweets for my sweet', 'Up on the roof', 'On Broadway', 'Under the boardwalk' and 'Saturday night at the movies'.

To R&B purists these tracks are slick and superficial compared with early Drifters recordings such as 'Money honey', 'Such a night' or 'Honey love' (all recorded in 1953), in which lead singer Clyde McPhatter sings with individuality and gospel-influenced freedom. The comparison exactly parallels that between Elvis Presley's Sun recordings – unaffected, spontaneous – and his later, much more contrived and controlled RCA hits.

But the later Drifters hits, like the best of Presley's recordings from the same period (1959–63), had qualities of their own – craftsman-like qualities, comparable with the Everly Brothers' records. They were not hits for nothing.

This was the great period of the Brill Building, a now-legendary block in New York where songwriters such as the husband-and-wife teams Gerry Goffin and Carole King, Barry Mann and Cynthia Weil worked, contracted to a publishing company, Aldon Music. It was a sort of teenage Tin Pan Alley, a 'hit factory'.

> We each had a little cubbyhole with just enough room for a piano, a bench and maybe a chair
> for the lyricist – if you were lucky. You'd sit there and write and you could hear someone in
> the next cubby hole composing some song exactly like yours.
>
> Carole King, quoted in Millar (1971): 73

And the hits poured out: for the Drifters, Goffin/King's 'When my little girl is smiling' and 'Up on the roof', Mann/Weil's 'Saturday night at the movies' and 'On Broadway'. Many other black groups recorded Aldon songs: Goffin/King's 'One fine day' (recorded by the Chiffons), 'Will you still love me tomorrow' (the Shirelles), 'Chains' (the Cookies), Mann/Weil's 'Walking in the rain' (the Ronettes) and 'Uptown' (the Crystals). This was a middle ground between true gospel-R&B and the more synthetic white pop idiom.

The Brill Building's 'hit factory' nickname reflects how commercial this music was assumed to be, in style and intent. Clearly, a great deal of skill was involved; the songs and the records are perfect creations that people still love to hear. But the criterion for success was commercial.

An active figure here was Phil Spector. An ambitious teenage entrant to the pop scene in 1958, he immediately struck gold with 'To know him is to love him' by the Teddy Bears, a soft-voiced vocal group. Arguably 'To know him is to love him' is sugary and trite, lacking emotional depth, and as far as can be from the vibrancy of early rock 'n' roll. On the other hand it is neat, perfectly crafted, and produced in a way that maximizes the clarity of the musical texture – already a marker for his later records.

In the years ahead, Spector worked mainly as producer, leaving the songwriter's role to others. He, more than anyone else, evolved a comprehensive creative role for the producer: imagining which songs would be suitable for which artist, how the arrangement would complement the song, how the engineering would complement the arrangement. At the heart of his output during 1962–64 was a succession of hits for the Crystals and the Ronettes, mostly using songs by Mann/Weil and yet another husband–wife partnership, Jeff Barry and Ellie Greenwich. His productions gradually became more lavish, incorporating layer upon layer of densely textured instrumental sound, fading and echoing away into infinity. Yet they also had an effective simplicity, arising from his clear vision of how each record would strike the listener; often his lead singers (Lala Brooks of the Crystals, Veronica Bennett of the Ronettes, Darlene Love) would cut through with strong individual clarity, despite the complexity of the sound behind them – the famous Spector 'wall of sound'.

It was common practice for record companies to release singles as fast as they could make them, in the hope that one or two might become hits. Spector concentrated his energies on just a few records, one at a time, working relentlessly until every detail was right. He was the first record producer to surpass his artists in fame and prominence (and remains one of the few to do so). A publicity-attracting image and personality contributed to his fame, but more so the brilliance of his records: 'He's a rebel', 'Da doo ron ron' and 'Then he kissed me' by the Crystals, 'Be my baby', 'Baby I love you' and 'Walking in the rain' by the Ronettes, to mention some of the best.

In May 1966 he released another powerful single, 'River deep – mountain high' by Ike and Tina Turner. It was a pretty big hit in Britain but flopped in the States. Spector had considered it his best yet, and took exceptional umbrage at this rejection by the American public (or at least by the disc jockeys and the rest of the industry network that combined to help a record on towards success). He retired flamboyantly, withdrawing from the business and to a great extent from public view. It was a showbiz gesture from a colourful character. On that level, there was no great significance to Spector's 1966 'retirement'; it was just another display of artistic temperament – or arguably of childish pique – generally in keeping with his paranoia and cultivated weirdness.

On another level, though, we can now see it as a significant event – an indication that pop was not just commerce but something to be valued for itself. There were finely graded judgements of quality to be made, irrespective of a record's commercial performance. This was obvious enough to some pop fans but not, at that time, to classical musicians or arts commentators.

Commercial music was (and is) different from 'art music'; it was made with a different purpose. But in Spector's hands it wasn't *completely* different. He showed us that in the making of a pop record there were artistic as well as commercial criteria. Phil Spector was a commercial operator, with no shortage of recognition or financial success, but also an artist, and his 'artistic temperament' was exercised as of right.

Forty to fifty years earlier, classical musicians had recognized the artistic qualities in jazz. The pop music of 1954–62, by contrast, had little 'highbrow' recognition – neither the rough-hewn qualities of early rock 'n' roll nor the more calculated craft-skills of Carole King or Phil Spector. Through the 60s this was to change, and the 'quality pop' of Phil Spector, with its attention to detail and its striving for perfection, was one of the three strands that achieved that shift in perception.

British beat

The second strand also concerned critical awareness of quality, regardless of commercial considerations.

Rock 'n' roll had caught teenage imaginations through its energy, aggression, beat. For some of its British fans – the musically interested ones – it also opened up the world of black music, R&B. They could hear that many of the best records came from black performers – Chuck Berry, Little Richard, Fats Domino, and others who had less success. They heard white cover versions, and preferred the black originals.

These listeners felt most keenly a sense of decline as rock 'n' roll 'went soft' in the late 50s, and they also were not content to accept weak British imitations. They compensated by seeking out new R&B records, even though these had little or no success in the pop charts and could be quite difficult to obtain in Britain. Immediately this marks a shift of aesthetic: these listeners did not necessarily like what the record companies and radio stations were offering, nor what the charts were indicating as most popular; they were exercising a minority taste.

Some were led to pastures new – styles of blues too harsh and raw to have been absorbed into the rock 'n' roll world: powerful urban blues from Muddy Waters, Little Walter, Buddy Guy, Elmore James; boogie-blues from Jimmy Reed, Lightning Hopkins, John Lee Hooker; gospel-soul from James Brown, Solomon Burke, the Isley Brothers and Barrett Strong. They picked up on these styles, seizing on newly imported discs, passing them around like a new faith, and most importantly learning to play this style of music themselves.

This was the beginning of British R&B. At first these groups worked at a local level – clubs and dances – and some of them underwent an extensive apprenticeship (not least the Beatles, with years of work in and around Liverpool, plus spells in Hamburg). From 1962 they began to emerge, the Beatles leading the way followed closely by the Rolling Stones, the Animals, Manfred Mann, the Spencer Davis Group and many others. Alexis Korner and John Mayall led dedicated blues groups which served as apprentice grounds for a number of younger musicians who later shifted towards more original material – for instance in Cream.

John Lennon and Paul McCartney were already writing their own songs by then, and it was these that brought them their unprecedented success, including a rapid breakthrough into the American market. Even so, the Beatles, just as much as the Rolling Stones and other groups, originated as an R&B group; their first LPs included covers of several gospel-R&B songs ('Chains', 'Twist and shout', 'Please Mr Postman', 'You really got a hold on me') as well as Chuck Berry's 'Roll over Beethoven'.

When those British teenagers preferred Chicago blues or early Motown to more sentimental or trivial white pop records, they were exercising a musical choice. Artistic judgement was seen as something separate from commercial success, and an aura of anti-commercialism hung around many of the British R&B groups (especially the ones most dedicated to deep urban blues), despite the heavily ambitious pressures of the music business. If a group was judged to have softened its sound in search of a hit, the accusing cry of 'sell-out' would be heard.

Like Phil Spector, the British groups operated with a sense of artistic purpose. One more developmental strand was needed to turn pop into art; it came from a different direction, almost a different world.

Bob Dylan

That 'different world' was the world of folk clubs and 'urban folk' campus concerts – an unlikely source of inspiration, purveying a somewhat self-conscious variety of music, drawn from rural folk traditions but imbued with an aura of preservationism. All-white, earnest, left-wing.

The folk scene, which centred on New York's Greenwich Village, embraced songs of social protest. At the forefront were singer–songwriters such as Woody Guthrie and 'Rambling' Jack Elliott. Woody Guthrie was the senior figure, with a catalogue of powerful political songs including the anthem 'This land is your land'. Northern interest in American folk song had also been stimulated by the fieldwork of folklorists like John and Alan Lomax, and this helped to bring campus popularity to singers such as Big Bill Broonzy, Leadbelly, and Josh White.

Urban folk burgeoned in the late 50s, partly because of the relaxation of McCarthyite repression[1] and partly in reaction to rock 'n' roll – a reaction on snobbish foundations. Pop music was looked down on as trite and ephemeral, while folk was supposed to be artistic and upstanding, anxious about social injustice and generally oozing with integrity.

But a new power was rising on the folk scene, in the person of Bob Dylan. Arriving in New York in January 1961, heavily influenced by Woody Guthrie and with a vividly poetic style of songwriting, he rapidly established himself, hitting success with his early albums *Bob Dylan* (1962) and *The Freewheelin' Bob Dylan* (1963). The former had mainly non-original

---

[1] Left-wing ideas had been heavily suppressed in the early 50s, in a movement led by US Senator Joe McCarthy.

material, but by early 1962 he was writing prolifically; a flood of songs poured out, and his fame grew and grew. By mid-1963 he had achieved something like superstar status, riding on the Peter Paul & Mary version of 'Blowin' in the wind', a tour with Joan Baez, and his triumphant appearance at the 1963 Newport Folk Festival.

However, Bob Dylan was not to be confined. His interests and tastes went beyond the acoustic folk style (he had played rock 'n' roll before coming under Woody Guthrie's influence), and the imagery and poetic range of his songs were also breaking existing moulds. Also, he was feeling oppressed by the pressures of success, and began building a defensive wall about himself, retreating to manager Albert Grossman's house at Woodstock, and taking drugs.

Early in 1965 he made his move into rock, using electric instruments to support him in the sessions for *Bringing It All Back Home*, and again in May to record 'Like a rolling stone', and then for the first time on stage at the Newport Folk Festival in July. The film *Festival* includes a few vivid minutes of the Newport appearance, Dylan combining with Mike Bloomfield and other members of the Butterfield Blues Band on 'Maggie's Farm'. The electric guitars and drum kits offended some folk purists, but Dylan was irresistable, and the central albums in his output – *Bringing It All Back Home*, *Highway 61 Revisited* and *Blonde on Blonde* – are his classics, soaked in a strange combination of desperate, antagonistic feelings with visionary poetic imagery.

Dylan's influence had become pervasive; he carried literary seriousness and political awareness into the pop mainstream. The very idea of having lyrics with some sort of poetic value was virtually unheard of before he came along. What he had to say, and the way he used his songs to say it, had a tremendous impact in the mid-60s, affecting musicians and listeners alike. Of course the industry continued to produce plenty of trivial pop songs, but pop as a whole could never be the same; it was available as a vehicle for serious songwriting.

Whatever you want to do

Highway 61 Revisited came out in 1965. From then on anything was possible. The previous frontiers of pop were swept aside, made to look like trivial convention. Bob Dylan, the Beatles, Phil Spector came from very different angles, but recognized the qualities in each other, and were mutually affected.

All through the following year, 1966, examples sprang up of pop musicians working in this newly opened-up territory, making records which would have been inconceivable two or three years earlier. Listen, for instance, to some of the following tracks:

- 'Signed DC' by the Los Angeles group Love, from their first album. Loneliness and despair find voice in this ballad by the group's leader, Arthur Lee.

> Sometimes I feel so lonely
> My comedown I'm scared to face
> I pierced my skin again Lord
> No one cares for me
>
> 'Signed DC' (Love)

- 'Love you to' by the Beatles, from *Revolver*. A George Harrison song, with Harrison playing sitar and Anil Bhagwat on tabla. This was one of a number of songs displaying the burgeoning interest in Indian classical music.

- 'Tomorrow never knows', also from *Revolver*. This remarkable John Lennon song marks a crucial point in the Beatles' development, opening up the magical sounds explored in their recordings of the following year ('Strawberry Fields', *Sgt Pepper*, etc.). 'Tomorrow never knows' re-uses a rhythm from an earlier song, 'What you're doing' (from *Beatles for Sale*), but surrounds it with surges of strange, exotic sound while Lennon's distant voice calls on us to lay down our thoughts and 'surrender to the void'. Not only Indian music but Indian religion – or more generally Eastern spiritual thinking – was attracting much attention. While the interest was mostly superficial, it indicates how far pop had moved in a short time.

- 'Eight miles high' by the Byrds. Their earlier hit 'Mr Tambourine Man' was one of the first pop treatments of a Bob Dylan song, and caught the imagination with its brightly-coloured new sound. 'Eight miles high' was written by group members Roger McGuinn, David Crosby and Gene Clark, and features a driving rhythm and distinctive Indian-flavoured fractured guitar. With its West Coast accent and vocal harmonies, it is a record of its time, capturing the heady, breathless excitement of new things happening.

- 'Hey girl' by Them. This may not be an easy recording to get hold of, but is an interesting precursor to Van Morrison's later and highly successful albums. Them was Morrison's group from 1963 to 66, originally an R&B group from Belfast but by 1966 in a state of disintegration. 'Hey girl' is a sensual, sensation-exploring lovesong, of a type that became typical of Morrison.

- 'Who are the brain police' and 'It can't happen here' by Frank Zappa's group, the Mothers of Invention, from their album *Freak Out*. If groups like the Byrds and the Beatles were enthusiasts for the way forward, for new meanings, new possibilities, the Mothers provided a more cynical commentary. Zappa's use of large-scale musical planning and avant-garde sounds showed some of the musical possibilities that had been opened up by the discarding of commercially-dictated confines; the calculated weirdness and frequent satirical slant provide a conceptual equivalent. Nowadays Zappa's music has been taken into the repertoire of several new-music ensembles.

67–70: the hippy era

The mid-60s was an opening-up period, a time of creativity and rising awareness. Pop music could be anything people wanted it to be, and the years 67–70 saw a great diversity of styles, and the taking of different style-strands to their extreme ends. This was the time of the first moon landing, and pop music was determined to explore in every possible direction.

In Britain, music colleges remained wedded to classical (or contemporary-classical) music; not until much later was any common ground or possibility of interaction widely acknowledged. Art colleges, however, were quicker to understand the artistic growth of pop music and interact with it; many art students doubled as pop musicians. In New York a striking art/music collaboration took place between Andy Warhol and the Velvet Underground, the former lending his name and involvement to the latter's first album, released early in 1967. The Velvet Underground's first three albums form a coherent whole, containing some beautiful as well as some intensely harsh music, mostly written by the group's leader, Lou Reed.

Jimi Hendrix, in the meantime, was taking guitar sounds into unknown territory. In essence an improvising blues guitarist in the tradition of Buddy Guy and Otis Rush, he brought to bear an extraordinary unfettered oneness with his guitar, so that wherever his imagination led him, it would somehow find expression in his music. The results varied with his state of mind and the day-to-day vagaries of a drug-fuelled three years of stardom, but he was constantly playing, constantly recording – with the support of his engineer, Eddie Kramer, who helped him to realize his more technologically-demanding multi-tracked visions – and left an enduring legacy in a too-short career.

No other improvising musician had quite the impact or importance of Jimi Hendrix, but this was the time when long guitar solos became commonplace. At the same time, the rift between pop (or 'rock' – the preferred term for its followers) and modern jazz began to lessen. Miles Davis and his player-colleagues gained broader acceptance, and a number of groups worked in a 'jazz-rock' style; this cross-fertilization increased during the following decade.

Rock, at this time, increasingly differentiated itself from 'pop'. It tended towards albums and live performances, 'serious' lyrics, and sometimes long improvisations. Pop, by contrast, concentrated on the commercial three-minute single (7-inch 45rpm record). Not everyone accepted the distinction as valid. It was largely promoted from the rock side, as a way of distinguishing itself, and became a somewhat debased currency due to the overblown seriousness and grandiose style of many rock groups in the late 60s and early 70s.

Songwriting remained the principal medium for pop creativity. Most songwriters – like Lennon and McCartney – worked in the context of a group: Ray Davies with the Kinks, Pete Townshend with the Who, Brian Wilson with the Beach Boys. Towards the end of the 60s there was a trend towards solo acoustic performance, rather in the manner of Bob Dylan before he turned electric. Joni Mitchell was a leading figure among these singer–songwriters, a type of performer that greatly flourished in the 70s.

The musical opening-up of 1966 onwards was catalysed by several extra-musical factors – drugs were a big influence, and so was politics.

Drugs were not new on the music scene, but they had remained in the background – part of day-to-day life for many musicians, but usually not a direct or creative influence on the music. In the 60s marijuana and then LSD became fashionable features of youth culture, and the 'mind-expanding' or 'psychedelic' properties of these drugs were experienced by many musicians as a creative stimulant. Drug experiences were discussed more openly than before. Experimentation was easier, and was widely looked on as an adventure – there was a touch of glamour associated with it. Drug-taking as a general activity was less common in the 60s than it is now, but among pop musicians it was widespread. It accorded with the spirit of the time – a spirit of openness and exploration.

Woodstock Festival, 1969

SIPA Press/Rex Features

Politics, too, though hardly a new phenomenon, came onto the pop agenda in a new and forceful way. With the escalation of the Vietnam War through the middle and late 60s came a huge anti-war movement, and with it a generally left-leaning and alternative youth culture which wore its idealistic leanings on its colourful sleeve. A few years earlier, politics and idealism had crept sideways into pop music from the urban folk movement of Greenwich Village and campus concerts, but that was nothing compared to the huge burgeoning of hippy culture with its avowed creed of 'peace and love'.

Many musicians who came through the British R&B scene became prominent figures in the rock groups of the late 60s, and role-models to the hippy generation. Leading the way were the Beatles and the Rolling Stones, but by the time *Sgt Pepper* was released – hugely influential though it was as an album – the Beatles were no longer a cohesive force, and broke up at the end of the decade. The Stones continued to tour and record, becoming reliable stalwarts of the rock scene in the 70s.

California – especially San Francisco and the Bay Area – was a major centre for hippy culture, and several of the era's leading groups emerged there. Jefferson Airplane were one of the first to align themselves openly with the psychedelic experience and to express it in their music. The Grateful Dead, even more, became emblematic of hippy culture, espousing it in their image, their lifestyle and their independence from the commercial establishment. They were in their prime at the end of the decade (and into the early 70s); their extended live performances highlighted Jerry Garcia's lead guitar improvisations, but the studio albums were compact and economical, with well-crafted songs.

The Doors, from Los Angeles, could hardly have been more different. Their impact was channelled through the theatrical qualities of their performances, heavily focused on lead singer Jim Morrison, and they cultivated a certain darkness of image which gave them enduring romantic appeal.

As rock music became more and more flamboyant in the late 60s, more extreme and sometimes self-indulgent, it moved away from its roots in black music (urban blues, rock 'n' roll, gospel R&B) and became mainly a music for white youth. This rootlessness did not go unnoticed, and one response was an injection of country music influence, which affected particularly several of the West Coast groups including the Byrds and the Grateful Dead. The 'country rock' style, as exemplified in the Byrds' 'Turn! Turn! Turn!', was a counterweight to the overcomplexity of some rock, but rather degenerated in the 70s, becoming the bland prototype for 'adult oriented rock', as the American radio industry termed it.

The whiteness of some late 60s rock thus became a weakness, and ran counter to its origins. It also contained a political paradox. Widening political awareness and the anti-establishment ethos was allied with the rise of the civil rights movement and Black Power, but it was a slightly uneasy alliance: white Americans' hair, grown long, became the flowing tresses of hippy flower-power, while black Americans' hair, grown long, became the Afros of an assertive Black Power movement. The white counterculture broadly supported the black struggle, but cultivated an increasingly separate music.

Among musicians, Jimi Hendrix was the main exception to the rule. Others who bridged the gap included Sly and the Family Stone, whose records in the period 1968–70 stand out as highly original, yet without recourse to extreme effects.

60s soul

As described above, the evolution of pop from a purely commercial music to one which encompassed all manner of artistic aspiration was mainly a white concern. In a sense, black music had already made its bid for artistic freedom in the immediate post-war years, when bebop broke away from mainstream jazz, starting the modern jazz movement and in doing so turning its back on mass popularity.

By the early 60s, however, in the wake of the British blues boom, blues and gospel-R&B had achieved widespread appreciation, and the 60s saw a flowering of pop-oriented R&B or soul music. Berry Gordy's successful Tamla/Motown group of labels was notable for being black-owned, unlike most of the earlier independent R&B labels. Detroit-based Motown achieved an extraordinary catalogue of hits by such artists as the Supremes, the Temptations, Smokey Robinson and the Miracles, the Four Tops, Marvin Gaye, Martha and the Vandellas, and others.

Motown aimed for the (white) pop charts. Its hit-making, rather like the earlier Brill Building successes, was achieved by a quasi-industrial production-line approach, and some people considered that the records sounded correspondingly mechanistic. But the Motown producers and songwriters, like Phil Spector, brought great skill and artistic judgement to bear on the business of producing catchy, danceable three-minute masterpieces.

Particularly successful was the team of Brian Holland, Eddie Holland and Lamont Dozier. During the mid-decade they were rarely out of the charts, through their work as writers and producers for the Supremes, the Four Tops, Martha and the Vandellas, and others. Their effectiveness – again, like Phil Spector's – lay in their ability to work with a dense musical texture and yet allow the important elements to shine through unimpeded. Motown's own studio musicians, including a string orchestra, helped to produce the distinctive sound. There was always a massive emphasis on the rhythm section; drums were supplemented by hand-claps or tambourine, cutting through the texture, and every record was irresistably danceable. Motown artists, dressed in their suits or glitzy evening dresses, included choreographed dance steps as part of their act. Diana Ross and the Supremes came to epitomize the glamorous Motown sound and image. In 1964 they had the first of a string of American No. 1 singles with 'Where did our love go'.

Smokey Robinson was another very skilful writer and producer for various artists, as well as being the light-as-air lead singer of the Miracles. To the poised grace of his songs he added lyrics with a light, fanciful touch, and in 'The tracks of my tears' (1965) he achieved one of the great songs of the decade.

Motown were at first reluctant to get involved in the political and artistic aspirations (or, sometimes, pretensions) of the white rock scene, but in the early 70s Stevie Wonder and Marvin Gaye struck out in more individualistic directions, in each case after renegotiating their contracts to allow them more personal control. Another (non-Motown) soul writer and singer, Curtis Mayfield, travelled a similar route from his 60s records with the Impressions to his solo albums from 1970 onwards.

Other independent labels producing high-quality danceable soul records included Stax and Atlantic, with such singers as Aretha Franklin, Otis Redding and Wilson Pickett. These records – and those from smaller independents – tended to be more intimate, with smaller ensembles rather than the power-sound of Holland-Dozier-Holland's Motown productions. Stax was promoted via black radio and aimed at the rhythm and blues audience. This style was marked above all by expressive gospel-tinged vocals, supported by incisive, clean arrangements for rhythm section and (often) brass and saxes.

Stax had their own house band – Booker T and the MGs – who backed singers on hundreds of recordings as well as releasing their own instrumentals, most famously 'Green onions' (1962). The Stax sound was raw and emotional, with close links to gospel and blues. Compared with Motown, they allowed singers to take more chances, leaving more room for improvisation. Songs were usually recorded in few takes, and all the instruments were cut together. Otis Redding's heartfelt songs owed much to their improvisational nature. 'I've been loving you too long' (1965) is characterized by its free improvisation, rising in intensity to an impassioned climax redolent of a fervent preacher. The backing is sparse: broken chords on the guitar, punctuated by a few horn stabs. The interest instead focuses on the timbre of the sounds, and most of all on Redding's soul-baring voice, with its note-bending, vibrato and tremolando.

Stax suffered a huge blow in 1967 when Otis Redding and four members of his band died in a plane crash.

Just as Redding was dubbed the King of Soul, Aretha Franklin was often referred to as the Queen. The daughter of a Baptist preacher, she started out as a gospel singer in her father's church, learning from some of the great gospel singers of the time, including Mahalia Jackson. Her use of melisma, where several notes are sung to one syllable, stemmed from her days singing in church, and was a precursor of 1980s R&B. She signed to Atlantic in 1966 and soon became their main female artist. With her powerful, wide-ranging vocals she had an impressive run of late 1960s soul hits including 'Chain of fools', 'I never loved a man' and 'I say a little prayer'. In Franklin's hands the song 'Respect' became both a feminist anthem and the soundtrack to the American civil rights movement.

The new sound of Jamaica

Most Caribbean popular music, broadly speaking, falls outside the scope of this book, and had little impact outside Caribbean communities until, in the 1980s, 'world music' became an acknowledged umbrella term – since when there has been a great expansion of cross-cultural music-making of every conceivable sort.

Jamaican music, however, has to be an exception – too influential on mainstream pop to leave out of this account.

Early 60s Jamaican pop, 'ska', fused American dance-blues with local idioms. Jamaican record labels proliferated, various styles and sub-styles grew and transmuted, and through the West Indian communities in London and New York these musics filtered through into wider British and American awareness. Ska and rocksteady tracks began to make inroads into the pop charts, and from 1968 onwards reggae – a term which started with a narrow stylistic meaning but became more general – emerged strongly. In the 1970s, reggae was for a while the principal black influence and invigorating force in pop music, especially in Britain.

The middle and late 60s: a bird's-eye view

This chapter has concentrated on the far-reaching development in the mid-60s of art-awareness in pop. This came from the confluence of three strands:

- The 'quality pop' of producers and writers like Phil Spector
- The British R&B groups, whose respectful reinterpretations of black American blues and gospel-R&B represented a discriminating anti-commercialism
- The 'urban folk' movement in New York's Greenwich Village and on the university campuses, with its political awareness and literary approach – a movement brought to bear on pop through the influence of Bob Dylan

This major development was bound to change pop's relationship with other types of music, and with other artforms, but those changes mainly lay ahead.

All this made the 60s a particularly fruitful decade for pop music. By the end of the decade the pop scene was far more diverse than it had been at the start, and it is impossible to mention all the significant styles or artists here. By 1970 the art-music side of pop stood alongside soul music, which still retained some of the natural expressiveness of its folk origins, and also alongside commercial pop, which occasionally succeeded but mostly failed to match the standards set by Phil Spector. Reggae was beginning to emerge as a new force. Jazz continued to be quite separate from pop throughout the decade, until at the very end it showed signs of a convergence which gathered pace in later decades.

PROFILES

Phil Spector

Phil Spector was born in 1940 in New York but spent his teenage years in California, taking a considerable interest in music and learning to play several instruments. His early musical activity is difficult to reconstruct with any certainty, but it seems that he was fascinated from the start by the business of creating records, and wrote 'To know him is to love him' in 1958, apparently adapting the title from the epitaph on his father's gravestone. He made the record himself, finding a local girl singer, Annette Kleinbard, to sing lead, but overdubbing all the background vocals himself and probably playing some or all the instruments. He called the group the Teddy Bears, and then found a small Los Angeles record company, Dore, who were willing to issue the record – which promptly became a No. 1 hit. Before his eighteenth birthday, Spector had worked out this Svengali-like control of process which was to be his trademark.

For about a year, Spector toured and performed as a member of the Teddy Bears. Then, in 1959, he moved to New York and made contact with Jerry Leiber and Mike Stoller (whose work he already knew well). He became contracted to them, based at the Brill Building. This was the time of Leiber and Stoller's most productive work with the Drifters, and Spector certainly attended some of their recording sessions, even though it is not clear exactly which ones or what his involvement was.

For the next two years Spector worked for a number of different record companies and artists, accumulating experience and managing to have hits with Ben E King (as co-writer of 'Spanish Harlem'), Curtis Lee, Ray Peterson and Connie Francis. In 1961, together with LA-based businessman Lester Sill, Spector formed Philles Records and started working with the Crystals. From then on, he had his own outlet for his own creations, which he could shape without responsibility to anyone else. The rest is history – but living history, in the sense that Spector's early 60s records continue to live, still unsurpassed even in this 21st-century age of high-tech multi-track infinite-possibility sound manipulation.

In his book about Phil Spector (1974) Richard Williams comments that whereas many American pop producers regarded the Beatle-led British invasion of the early 60s as a threat (which indeed it was, sweeping aside tired old formulae in favour of a vibrant, fresh style), Spector was excited by the British groups and welcomed their arrival, recognizing in the Beatles and Rolling Stones a youthful energy which he shared, unlike the established industry businessmen. Even so, the more artistic-oriented and anti-commercial aesthetic that came in on the back of the British invasion was somewhat foreign to Spector's own approach.

Since the 'River deep – mountain high' debacle Spector has never quite captured the form of his best records. He re-emerged after a couple of years to make some records for A&M, and in the early 70s worked with John Lennon and George Harrison, following controversial post-production work on the Beatles' last album, *Let It Be*. After that he produced a handful of albums, notably Leonard Cohen's *Death of a Ladies' Man* (1977) and the Ramones' *End of the Century* (1980). Both received some praise, though not universal acclaim.

Spector's private life continued to be controversial. His behaviour was often wild and eccentric, with stories abounding of gun-wielding aggression. He spent many of his later years as a recluse and was rarely seen in public. In 2003 a B-movie actress, Lana Clarkson, was shot and killed in his Los Angeles home. Although he repeatedly denied his involvement, in 2009 Spector was eventually convicted of her second degree murder and sentenced to a minimum of 19 years in the California state prison system.

David Magnus/Rex Features

Phil Spector and the Ronettes

Harry Goodwin/Rex Features

Bob Dylan:
portrait of a legend in the making

Bob Dylan

Bob Dylan's boyhood was spent in the small Minnesota mining town of Hibbing. His interest in music focused first on country music, then rock 'n' roll; apparently he led a high school band, playing frantic Little Richard-style piano as loudly as possible. In 1959–60 he spent a year in Minneapolis, ostensibly as a student at the university there, hanging out in coffee bars and mixing with the 'beats' – the radicals or bohemians of the time, and forerunners of the hippies.

At this time he switched from rock 'n' roll to 'urban folk', turning on to Woody Guthrie in a big way. This served to focus his style and sound, providing his harsh-sounding voice with a type of song suited to it, and giving him an urge to travel east and visit Guthrie, who was then a permanent patient at Greystone Hospital in New Jersey, suffering from Huntington's Chorea. (He died in 1967.)

Dylan arrived in New York late in January 1961, heading straight for Greenwich Village, and visiting Guthrie at Greystone within a few days (and many times afterwards). There was a magnetism about Dylan, and despite roughnesses and incongruities he quickly impressed those who heard him singing in clubs or coffee bars – which he did as much as possible. Jack Elliott recalled:

> He was trying to sound like an old man who bummed around eighty-five years on a freight train, and you could see this kid didn't even have fuzz on his face yet. But I was charmed by it... His voice, he didn't have much control over it. He just aimed for a note – but he aimed for a lot of *good* notes and it was far out, because folk singers weren't doing that kind of thing.
> quoted in Scaduto (1972): 58–59

In his crucial first three months in Greenwich Village, Dylan worked his way into the folk scene, got to know a lot of people, got an important two-week engagement at Gerde's Folk City, and generally kept moving up. Later in the year, as he got better and his reputation grew, he began to get into the recording studios, doing sessions with Harry Belafonte, Victoria Spivey, Big Joe Williams and Carolyn Hester – through whom he met producer John Hammond, a meeting which led quickly to a recording contract with Columbia and then to his first album, recorded in three or four sessions late in 1961.

Dylan's success escalated from that point. Having started with great determination to make his mark, manipulating people and situations on the way, he now found himself surrounded by people determined to manipulate him, and the collisions were many and painful. The detailed story is documented elsewhere, notably in the books by Scaduto and Shelton (see Bibliography, page 216), and is fascinating to follow, for Dylan achieved an almost godlike status during that period.

His albums are his own document, and they form a sort of narrative, like those of other artists whose recordings reflected their artistic or personal development. The second and third contain powerful protest songs, but in the fourth, *Another Side of Bob Dylan* (1964), he turns away from outside politics and protest, concentrating on personal songs – love songs, perhaps, but including some with a bitter tinge. Already at this stage he was using his songs to express his resistance to pressures – or people – he did not like. Anger and revenge infused many of his songs of this period.

Two great albums followed, *Bringing It All Back Home* and *Highway 61 Revisited*. Next came *Blonde on Blonde*, recorded in Nashville early in 1966 – somewhat less harsh and more introverted. Then in July 1966, Dylan suffered a serious motorcycle crash, which served as the signal – or excuse – for a complete withdrawal from performance and from public life. Almost 15 months later, in October 1967, he returned to Nashville to record his next album, *John Wesley Harding*, released in January 1968. This was a considerable reversal and generally a surprise. Gone was the vengeful bitterness of *Highway 61*; in its place, a warm, reflective album, simple in texture (in marked contrast to the then-fashionable complex super-albums that followed in the wake of the Beatles' *Sgt Pepper*). And then, after another year, came *Nashville Skyline*: mellow, contented country music.

Dylan's albums since 1970 continue to reflect his personal changes, but these fall outside the scope of this brief survey. His big influence on pop music took place during the 60s; it left him revered in a way that was difficult for him to live up to.

The Beatles

Their albums, too, form a narrative. But unfortunately the first chapter is missing: only fragmentary recordings exist of their raw, early club performances. The later chapters also seem unsatisfactory, with messy personal disharmony ending the group collaboration, and the death of John Lennon in 1980 abruptly curtailing much that might have been. In between, they recorded some magical albums, and gave pop an infusion of vitality and creativity that inspired many others.

Three-quarters of the Beatles were together from early 1958; John, Paul and George all came from musical families. Their gradual improvement and consolidation was rewarded in August 1960 with an offer of an engagement at Hamburg, where several clubs had already established a practice of using English groups and singers. This was the first and most important of their five visits. The work was much harder than anything they had experienced before, playing long hours, seven nights a week. The engagement was given several extensions, eventually ending late in December 1960 after nearly five months. The heavy workload produced a tremendous improvement in their playing, and helped to give them the group identity on which their success was built a few years later.

Their German rocker audience was tough and their own working conditions harsh, and the circumstances bred a wild stage manner which was much liked. This success continued during their second visit, April to July 1961, and in Liverpool their style of performance generated similar enthusiasm. *Please Please Me* was still two years away, but it may well be that this period saw their best live performances:

> Our best work was never recorded… in Liverpool, Hamburg and other dance halls. What we generated was fantastic, when we played straight rock, and there was nobody to touch us in Britain. As soon as we made it, we made it, but the edges were knocked off…
>
> John Lennon, in an interview with *Rolling Stone*, 7 January 1971

Following *Please Please Me* and *With the Beatles*, their third album was *A Hard Day's Night* (1964). This marked a new phase, a 'middle period'. In a sense it was a new phase for pop music generally, with attention swinging for the first time from singles to albums. It contained only Lennon/McCartney songs, and developed the line of quieter, more melodic songs that had already appeared in, for instance, 'Thank you girl' and 'All I've got to do'. Now, however, the style was tighter, with not a note wasted, a distillation that suited the more intimate nature of the LP medium and marked their transition from live performers to a studio group. Two good examples are 'Things we said today' and 'I'll be back'. In 'Things we said today', a static, minor-mode opening, dry and understated, is set off by four bars with surprise modulations and a gently chromatic melody, and then by a more angular 'middle eight'.

Gradually through 1965 the Lennon/McCartney songs become more reflective and less exuberant, as heard in *Rubber Soul* (released in December 1965). In 1966 the group stopped touring, found time to rest and think, and started leading more individual lives, with new interests. This was the next transition for the Beatles, to a 'third period' – songs of experience and awareness – beginning with *Revolver* (1966) and continuing into the rich, expansive sounds of their 1967 recordings.

1967 marked a flamboyant peak. *Sergeant Pepper's Lonely Hearts Club Band* was a startlingly unified album, but from then on the force of the group's impending disintegration played an ever-growing role. *Let It Be* was originally intended to be a 'live' album, imperfections included, and with matching film. The whole scheme got bogged down in troubles and confusion, though paradoxically the LP that eventually emerged from the debris did contain some of the group's all-time best performances, including 'Get back', 'I've got a feeling' and 'Across the universe'.

The Beatles' last recording sessions, resulting in *Abbey Road* (1969), swung the emphasis back to the carefully produced side of their work. Side 2 is a unified sequence of ten short song-sections, rising in three broad sweeps to a final climax. George Harrison's 'Here comes the sun' starts the sequence, and his solo guitar comes to the fore as each main section builds in pace and intensity.

Jimi Hendrix

Like Bob Dylan and Phil Spector, Jimi Hendrix was devoted to his music from early on. He probably acquired his first guitar in 1958, aged 15, and is remembered for his attachment to it and its successors, and for his love of learning and demonstrating new guitar tricks. As time went on, this attachment became almost literal; he is remembered as carrying it everywhere, playing it constantly, sleeping with it, playing it in bed. And from this attachment grew the immediacy of expression with which he played.

Hendrix was born in Seattle in November 1942. He enlisted in the army (airborne division) in 1961, but left in '62. Always he sought opportunities to play, and 1963–4 saw him travelling around, especially in the South. In 1964 he toured with the Isley Brothers' band, and in '65 with Little Richard. By this time he had already developed some of the idiosyncratic tricks – playing with his teeth, etc. – for which he later became famous.

He was also beginning to look 'weird' – not like most black Americans, but with freaky clothes and long hair. Musically, too, his tastes went beyond the R&B circuit; he loved Bob Dylan's music and was also drawn towards the British groups (his version of the Troggs' 'Wild thing' was an early favourite, as was Dylan's 'Like a rolling stone'). When Bob Dylan first arrived in New York he was making a career move, playing the role of hobo–folksinger and heading straight for Greenwich Village. Ironically, Hendrix was the more genuine guitar hobo – always on the move, basically homeless and aimless, culturally as well as geographically. He first came to New York in March 1964 (it was there that he picked up the Isley Brothers gig), kept coming back, and increasingly spent time in the Village.

All the time he was experimenting, forging his own style, full of tricks and techniques unencumbered by tradition, sometimes born from sheer showmanship, but all contributing to his overall vocabulary.

From around June 1966 he was playing in Greenwich Village as Jimmy James and the Blue Flames, and on 5 July was seen by Chas Chandler at the Café Wha? Chandler had been bass-player with the Animals, but was planning to get into record production. During his last month in the Village, Hendrix played with John Hammond Jr, but Chandler was seriously interested in what he had seen, and after necessary preparations he brought Hendrix to England, on 24 September 1966. From then on, his career took off like a rocket. Sadly, his three years of superstardom were messy, increasingly mired in drugs and dissolution, culminating in his death in Sept 1970 in London. He was ill-served by many of those around him.

The legacy of his recordings is complex. He released few approved albums – basically three, plus a fourth that arose from contractual obligations:
- *Are you Experienced* (1967)
- *Axis: Bold as Love* (1967)
- *Electric Ladyland* (1968)
- *Band of Gypsies* (1970)

But he also left a large quantity of unreleased material, and much has since appeared, with no absolute certainty as to what his intentions might have been. In his short career he played and recorded a great deal, sometimes loose and 'live', sometimes alone in the studio, recording take after alternative take.

His performance recorded at the Woodstock Festival in 1969 shows something of the expressive range of his playing. Much of Hendrix's music was spiritually related to Bob Dylan's. Both men suffered under the pressures of success, and both used music to express personal pain and despair. In the 'Star spangled banner'/'Purple haze' sequence recorded at Woodstock, Hendrix's guitar flows on and on in an apparent stream of depression, going far beyond the instrument's conventional stylistic limits. Then, halfway through the quiet blues which briefly follows 'Purple haze' and ends the sequence, he goes into another world, transcending the surrounding anguish as for twelve bars the music floats on a new and profound level.

His studio-recorded version of the 'Star spangled banner', as released posthumously on *Rainbow Bridge*, is strikingly different from the Woodstock version. Instead of the wrenchingly painful downward bomb-like screams there are glittering upward swirls and cascades of light, a glowing firework display. The comparison demonstrates Hendrix's versatility, his ability to be an improvising live performer but also, in partnership with his engineer Eddie Kramer, a manipulator of sounds in the studio.

FURTHER LISTENING

Faced with the stylistic explosion that was 60s pop music, this chapter has concentrated on certain all-important strands of development and the artists that activated them. The following list – not in any way comprehensive – mentions some of the significant artists and records that would otherwise be omitted.

The Beach Boys *Pet Sounds* (1966)
The Beach Boys transcended their early surfing-and-girls image to make some inventive and, by pop standards, complex records. Together the Wilson brothers created an original sound characterized by its close vocal harmonies, catchy melodies, slick production and lush inventive arrangements, some using sound effects and unusual instruments. Tracks include 'Wouldn't it be nice', 'God only knows' and 'Sloop John B'.

The Kinks 'Sunny afternoon' (1966), 'Waterloo sunset' (1967)
The Yardbirds 'Shapes of things' (1966)
The Rolling Stones 'Paint it black' (1966), 'Ruby Tuesday' (1967)
The Small Faces 'All or nothing' (1966)
Like the Beatles, many other groups who emerged from the British R&B/beat movement gradually shifted from cover versions to doing their own songs. 1965–7 saw a wealth of exciting and unusual songs such as the above.

The Who 'My generation' (1965), 'Substitute' (1966)
These two blistering songs – one of teenage rebellion and the other of class rage – were written by guitarist Pete Townshend. Both have a spontaneous, energetic sound fuelled by Townshend's riffs, Keith Moon's explosive drumming and John Entwistle's nimble bass work. 'My generation' opens with a series of power chords and builds up in intensity with a crescendo of feedback – one of the first such uses of this effect.

John Mayall and the Bluesbreakers *Bluesbreakers with Eric Clapton* (1966)
Mayall formed his Bluesbreakers band in 1963. He was something of a talent-spotter, and the band's ever-changing line-up introduced such future rock heroes as Peter Green, Mick Taylor and Mick Fleetwood. This seminal album of blues standards was Clapton's first album as a blues guitarist and helped to cement his godlike status.

Cream *Disraeli Gears* (1967), *Wheels of Fire* (1968)
Cream comprised Eric Clapton (guitar), Jack Bruce (bass) and Ginger Baker (drums), arguably the first rock supergroup, and responsible for Clapton's meteoric rise to fame. The band was famous for its live performances and long improvised solos. Some accused them of self-indulgence (*Wheels of Fire* includes a 15-minute drum solo), but they were revered by many others. Blues-rock album *Disraeli Gears* features classic songs such as 'Strange brew' and 'Sunshine of your love', which opens with one of the most famous riffs ever recorded.

The Lovin' Spoonful 'Do you believe in magic' (1965)
An East Coast equivalent of the Byrds, the Spoonful were one of the first American groups to emerge in the wake of the Beatles. This, their first hit, captures the infectious excitement of the period.

Pink Floyd 'Arnold Layne' and 'See Emily play' (1967)
Strange, heady, imaginative songs by Syd Barrett from the earliest period of this group. After Barrett's departure, their 1968 album *A Saucerful of Secrets*, including songs such as Roger Waters' 'Set the controls for the heart of the sun', signalled a more grandiose future style.

Janis Joplin *Pearl* (1971)
The strength of Janis Joplin's voice never wavers in this posthumous album. Joplin was a blues-rock performer of huge range and power; the album contains soulful ballads alongside raucous and raunchy songs.

Captain Beefheart and his Magic Band *Trout Mask Replica* (1969)
One of the most innovative rock musicians of his generation, Captain Beefheart recorded albums unlike any others, with surreal lyrics, complex rhythms and an experimental style that juxtaposes R&B, free jazz, blues and the avant-garde. *Trout Mask Replica* is usually regarded as his masterpiece. The album was produced by Beefheart's friend Frank Zappa, and features the extraordinary Magic Band: Zoot Horn Rollo, Antennae Jimmy Semens, the Mascara Snake, Rockette Morton and Drumbo. Highlights include 'China pig' and 'Moonlight on Vermont'.

The Doors *L.A. Woman* (1971)
The Doors' brooding, unsettling lyrics and psychedelic sounds, and the unpredictable behaviour of their charismatic singer Jim Morrison, helped to make them one of the most notorious bands of the era. *L.A. Woman* was released in the same year as the mysterious death of Morrison, aged 27.

Nick Drake *Five Leaves Left* (1969)
This influential album is a gently poetic work of world-weary melancholy. With Drake's understated singing backed by acoustic guitar and exquisite string arrangements, it comes somewhere between folk music and the singer-songwriter genre. Although few copies were sold during the reclusive Drake's lifetime, *Five Leaves Left* attracted a cult following in the years after his death from an overdose of anti-depressants at the age of 26. Countless rock musicians have cited Drake as an influence.

James Brown 'Papa's got a brand new bag' (1965), 'I got you (I feel good)' (1965)
With a career going back to his first hit 'Please, please, please' in 1956, James Brown maintained an uncompromising line in dance-hall R&B/soul. His style changed little from one song to another during this period, but a rock-solid beat ensured continuing popularity with his hard-core fans. He went on to play a significant role in the evolution of funk.

The Contours 'First I look at the purse' (1965)
Martha and the Vandellas 'Dancing in the street' (1964), 'Nowhere to run' (1965)
Three of the best, most powerful Motown tracks of the mid-decade.

Otis Redding 'Mr Pitiful' (1964), 'Respect' (1965), 'Try a little tenderness' (1966)
Southern Stax soul at its tightest and most expressive.

Nina Simone 'I put a spell on you' (1965), 'I wish I knew how it would feel to be free' (1967)
Singer, songwriter and civil rights activist Nina Simone created her own distinctive style of music characterized by a bluesy jazz feel, hypnotic soulful singing and complex piano parts. Her ambition to become the first black concert pianist was thwarted when she failed to win a place at the Curtis Institute of Music for what she believed were racial reasons. She once wrote 'My music was dedicated to the fight for freedom and the historical destiny of my people.'

Nina Simone, 1969

Gladys Knight and the Pips 'Letter full of tears' (1961), 'Just walk in my shoes' (1968)
The early hit 'Letter full of tears' is a passionate, committed performance of what on paper appears a naive lyric. In 1966 the group signed with Motown, and Gladys's performance of 'I heard it through the grapevine' (1967) preceded Marvin Gaye's massively successful version. Gladys Knight was one of Motown's less favoured artists but remained a high-quality singer. In 1968 'Just walk in my shoes' was a hit in Britain: its typically hard-driving beat supports a wrenching, bitter vocal performance.

Dionne Warwick 'Don't make me over', 'Anyone who had a heart' (1963), 'Walk on by', 'You'll never get to heaven' (1964), 'Do you know the way to San Jose?' (1968)
Burt Bacharach was a songwriter who liked to go outside the conventional confines of pop songs, in terms of form, time signatures, phrase structure, instrumentation and other parameters. He emerged from the Brill Building system of the early 60s, and found in Hal David the ideal lyric-writing partner. As a songwriting team they produced hits for many artists, but the heart of their work, in every sense, is represented by their records with Dionne Warwick, whose singing matched the delicate precision of Bacharach's orchestrations.

The Shangri-Las 'Remember (Walkin' in the sand)', 'Leader of the pack' (1964), 'Past, present and future' (1966)
Phil Spector, influential and brilliant though he was, worked with a style of teen-oriented pop song that was in decline in the mid-60s. Its final extravagant flourish can be heard in the extraordinary records of the Shangri-Las, produced by George 'Shadow' Morton, who was a sort of heir-without-a-throne to Spector. 'Remember (Walkin' in the sand)' and 'Leader of the pack' were sizeable hits; other Shangri-Las records are less well known but worth seeking out. 'Past, present and future' is one of the most extreme: melodramatic soap-opera spread thickly on a layer of the 'Moonlight' Sonata.

Prince Buster 'Al Capone' (1967)
A big figure on the Jamaican sound system scene in the 60s, Prince Buster was a forerunner of the 'toasters' (Jamaican-style rappers) of the 70s. 'Al Capone' was a big ska hit, and helped open up the British market for Jamaican-made records.

chapter

5

Julia Winterson and Toby Bricheno

Seventies

GOODBYE TO THE SIXTIES: THE CORRUPTION OF IDEALS?

The 1970s rock critic Lester Bangs once said:

> The essential misapprehension about popular music is that it is anything other than a totally capitalist enterprise. In fact, it has absolutely nothing to do with anything except making money and getting rich. Some popular musicians start out with revolutionary rhetoric, but all they want is cars and girls and champagne.[1]

Does this contradict the previous chapter, which describes how pop became art in the 60s? Pop *did* become art, and musicians *did* care about the quality of their music and what it expressed. Many continued to do so even through the grossness of 70s rock, and many still do. But musicians are human; they want success. If it comes, who can resist its temptations and rewards?

During the 1960s, styles of pop music became more diverse and this trend continued into the 1970s. Some styles evolved, others came about as a reaction to what had gone before, but one thing was certain: pop music was big business.

By the mid-1960s, those aged 25 or under accounted for almost 50% of the population in North America and the UK, and they had huge spending power. The fact that half a million had revelled in the upstate New York mud bath that was the Woodstock Festival could not have escaped the attention of the pop-music moguls.[2] The rock establishment of the early 70s invested in vast high-tech studios, filled huge stadiums with record-buying fans, and sold millions of records. The bands became ever more distant from their audiences – mere dots on the stage. The Rolling Stones, who had epitomized 1960s rebellion, now used a private plane for their massive money-making tours.

In part, the 1960s had been a decade of cultural and artistic protest, an idealistic, innocent time with a dream of a better society. In 1970 more than half a million made their way to the Isle of Wight and what was to be the biggest rock festival ever held. It was a coming together of like-minded people, who enjoyed the music in a haze of drugs and optimistic idealism, but there were sour undertones that were to herald the end of the 60s' innocent hedonism. Small groups of underground activists were determined to have the festival declared a free event, but by now the counter-culture was being drawn into the economic mainstream; while they protested outside, pulling down fences, the bands were haggling over their fees backstage.

---

[1] Quoted in Palmer & Medlicott (1976): 287. Lester Bangs was an American rock critic who contributed to *Rolling Stone* and *Creem*. He lived the rock 'n' roll lifestyle and died from a drug overdose when he was 33.

[2] Woodstock was a three-day festival in 1969 which (unexpectedly) had 500,000 visitors. Also unexpected was the heavy rain. The line-up included Jimi Hendrix, Janis Joplin, the Grateful Dead, John Sebastian, Joe Cocker and the Who. The festival can be seen in the film of the same name.

Hippy hedonism was about to fall out of style. Only weeks later, Jimi Hendrix was to die by choking on his vomit: one of a series of tragic deaths, many drug-induced, in the chain of self-destruction which seemed to typify this era. The search for new sounds and the air of rebellion that had permeated 1960s rock music largely disappeared. The underground had become staid, tried-and-tested styles dominated, and much of the creative spirit seemed to give way to the get-rich-quick philosophy.

A good illustration of this was the transformation of the cult hippy band Tyrannosaurus Rex into T Rex. In the late 1960s, the folk duo Tyrannosaurus Rex played Eastern-influenced acoustic sets to a cult following, mainly on the UK university circuit. The words were Tolkeinesque, and the songs were peopled with mystics, elves, witches and magicians. The title of the 1968 album *My people were fair and had sky in their hair... But now they're content to wear stars on their brows* says it all. The turning point came in 1970 when the band went electric and abbreviated their name to T Rex. They had a string of No. 1 hits and were soon filling stadiums. Some accused T Rex's singer, Marc Bolan, of 'selling out', but he went on to become one of the richest and biggest British rock stars of the 70s and a revered figure in glam rock. Listen to the earlier song 'Debora' (1968) with its colourful imagery of 'stallions' and 'galleons' set against a background of acoustic guitar and bongos, and contrast it with the electric boogying of 'Bang a gong, get it on' (1971),[3] with its rock clichés and twelve choruses of the title, to appreciate the two different styles.

The early 1970s was the era of the supergroups. Huge publicity machines rolled into action to promote tours. Posters and merchandising began to have a more important role. Millions of albums were sold, and sales-records were broken. Bands such as Fleetwood Mac, the Grateful Dead, Pink Floyd, Supertramp, Deep Purple, the Eagles and Led Zeppelin played to crowds of 100,000 and more.

Ever-increasing importance was attached to 'image'. Some would argue that the visual dimension became more important than the sound. Flashy clothes, long permed hair, platform-soled shoes, light shows and live props were the norm. Alice Cooper's macabre theatrical props included an electric chair, live snakes and a guillotine.

And what of the sound? This was the heyday of the guitar hero, the era of the extended guitar solo where improvisation hit new heights – or depths – and artistic exploration was at times replaced by ponderous pretension. Rock music splintered into a series of mutants, amongst them being folk rock, jazz rock, progressive rock, and heavy metal.

Heavy metal

Of all the styles spawned during this era, heavy metal has probably been the most popular and the most enduring. With its roots in the British blues movement, the music of bands such as Deep Purple took on a new, tougher personality. First dubbed as hard rock or heavy rock, heavy metal was built on high volume and electric guitar distortion. It featured screaming vocals, driving rhythms, high-decibel ultra-fast guitar solos, and a machismo image. The look, copied by many of the fans, was important: studded leather and denim, logos and crucifixes, tight jeans, boots and long hair. Favourite colour: black.

Led Zeppelin were hugely influential in the development of heavy metal. Ex-Yardbird and guitar hero Jimmy Page formed the band in 1968 along with the singer Robert Plant, and went on to record a stream of rock classics which include 'Dazed and confused', 'Communication breakdown', 'Whole lotta love' and their theme song, 'Stairway to heaven'. Page's guitar playing was virtuosic and imaginative. His lengthy, complex solos sometimes featured the use of a violin bow on the strings, and he made famous the double-necked guitar. Led Zep broke box-office records on tour in the US and UK, and were infamous for their bad-boys-on-the-road image.

Another ex-Yardbird and guitar hero, Jeff Beck, went on to form the Jeff Beck Group, featuring vocalist Rod Stewart, rhythm guitarist Ronnie Wood and (later) drummer Cozy

---

[3] 'Get it on' was the title in the UK, 'Bang a gong' in the USA.

Powell. The band had an important influence on the emergence of heavy metal in the 1970s.

The definitive heavy metal band Black Sabbath made their debut in 1970 with the album *Black Sabbath*. Fronted by the deranged vocals of 'Prince of Darkness' Ozzy Osbourne, the leaden, crunching guitar riffs played at mind-numbing volume and the lyrics' obsession with the darker side gave the music a sinister malevolence, aided and abetted by Osbourne's stage antics. (Could anyone ever beat biting the head off a live bat?) Guitarist Tony Iommi had to adapt his playing technique after a work accident where he lost the tips of two fingers. He made thimbles for the fingers, used lighter strings and tuned the strings down to make the playing action easier. This resulted in a darker, heavier sound. The classic heavy metal song 'Paranoid' (1970) is typical of early Black Sabbath with its driving rhythms, menacing vocals and distorted power chords.

Heavy metal has been consistently popular and still has legions of fans. Since the 1970s there have been many offshoots – from death metal to metalcore, hair metal to punk metal – all tied together by high-energy guitars, angst-ridden lyrics and aggressive rhythms.

Folk rock

When Bob Dylan went electric, the infamous cry of 'Judas' was heard at the Royal Albert Hall, but Dylan was unrepentant and his decision was influential. Folk clubs were still going strong in the UK in the 1960s, and towards the end of the decade folk rock emerged. Folk rock brought traditional songs into the pop repertoire, and combined traditional folk instruments such as violin and mandolin with the amplification and drum kits of rock. For its inspiration it looked to the West Coast and bands such as the Byrds. Fairport Convention was the epitome of folk rock. Important figures in their ever-shifting personnel included Sandy Denny (vocals), Richard Thompson and Ashley Hutchings (guitars) and Dave Swarbrick (fiddle). Their 1969 album *Liege and Lief*, arguably folk rock's most important album, took the listener into a world of pastoral songs of love and death. For typical examples of folk rock, listen to the psychedelic arrangement of the traditional folk song 'Reynardine' or to Traffic's acoustic arrangement of the English folk song 'John Barleycorn' on the album *John Barleycorn Must Die*.

Folk rock of a different kind was also a significant movement in the USA, focusing on singer–songwriters such as Joni Mitchell, James Taylor and many others, who sang mostly about their personal experiences. Their music was lyrical, reflective and literate, and was usually for solo voice accompanied by acoustic guitar. Listen to James Taylor's laid-back singing style and accomplished finger-picking on *Sweet Baby James* (1970) and *Mud Slide Slim and the Blue Horizon* (1971). Canadian Joni Mitchell, originally a 60s folk singer, had a string of successful albums during the 1970s, including *Blue* (1971), *Court and Spark* (1974) and *The Hissing of Summer Lawns* (1975). The music is characterized by Mitchell's confessional lyrics, her eclectic, sometimes jazzy influences, and above all by her voice – pure in tone, with a wide range, weaving distinctively around the evocative imagery.

Jazz rock

Jazz rock is a confusing blanket term used to cover various types of music that fuse elements of jazz and rock. It ranges from serious jazz improvisers (such as Miles Davis, Joe Zawinul and John McLaughlin) to high-energy rock bands (such as Chicago and Blood, Sweat and Tears) whose only nod in the direction of jazz is an expanded horn section. The best examples of jazz rock, which truly fuse the complexity and improvisation of jazz with elements of rock style, are probably those by trumpeter Miles Davis on albums such as *In a Silent Way* (featuring John McLaughlin, Chick Corea and Herbie Hancock) and *Bitches Brew*. Davis's attraction to the sounds explored on *Bitches Brew* was in part a reaction to the music of Jimi Hendrix and James Brown, and in part a desire to reach a bigger and younger audience, to play big shows, and ultimately to start making money comparable to the super-enterprises of the mammoth rock tours.

The most commercially successful jazz rock band (or jazz fusion as it was sometimes known) was Weather Report. They played together for 16 years during the 1970s and 80s, combining elements of free modal jazz, rock, funk, and world music. They even produced a hit album *Heavy Weather* (1977). The band was co-led by keyboard player Joe Zawinul and saxophonist Wayne Shorter, who had both played with Miles Davis. Over the years it included bass players Jaco Pastorius and Alphonso Johnson, and drummer Peter Erskine. Their early music could be described as collective free improvisation but they later moved towards a more structured groove-based style as heard in their hit single 'Birdland' (1977), which went on to become a jazz rock standard.

Jazz fusion also embraces a mixture of funk, soul and R&B with jazz and rock. Herbie Hancock's *Headhunters* (1973), a massive seller, was partly inspired by Hancock's love of Sly Stone's music.

Progressive rock

Progressive rock became a commercial force in the 1970s. Too diverse to define exactly, it encompassed a wide variety of rock bands from Traffic and Soft Machine to Emerson, Lake and Palmer, and Yes. 'Prog rock' could be seen as an attempt to elevate rock music onto a higher intellectual plane, to be taken seriously as an art-form. It was an album-based style, with large-scale compositions and extended doodling solos. Following in the footsteps of *Sgt Pepper*, many albums were concept-based, telling epic stories or embracing over-arching themes. Keyboards player and ex-Yes member Rick Wakeman was an enthusiastic protagonist of the style. He was well-known for his flamboyant solo stage shows: *The Myths and Legends of King Arthur and the Knights of the Round Table* (1975), was performed live on ice.

One of the most significant early prog rock albums was King Crimson's *In the Court of the Crimson King* (1969). Led by guitarist Robert Fripp, King Crimson looked beyond the boundaries of rock music and married wild poetic lyrics with electronic sounds, jazz, classical music and experimental rock. Many progressive rock bands used synthesizers and electronic sounds; central to the pioneering King Crimson sound was the mellotron (see pages 145–6). The album features the classic heavy metal sounds of '21st-century schizoid man'. Dominated by a solid main riff, the song alternates verses, swirling psychedelic production, and a complex middle section of up-tempo jazz-rock. Robert Fripp's extended guitar solo uses different amplification effects and adventurous, dissonant melodic lines.

Pink Floyd's album *Dark Side of the Moon* (1973) was to bring the band huge commercial success. This epic concept album combined lush production with sound effects and an eclectic musical style, creating a dark, atmospheric world. The album is renowned for its brilliant sound quality and use of contemporary recording techniques including tape manipulation and multi-track recording. 'Money', a satire on greed and avarice, opens with a cash register tape loop and has the unusual time signature of 7/4. The performance through a massive PA system at the 1975 Knebworth Festival was heralded by Spitfires flying overhead – a typical 1970s flamboyant gesture. This kind of show led to a sub-category of progressive rock: symphonic rock.

Symphonic rock

This was a time when progressive rock bands were keen to show off their classical credentials. Bands such as Yes, the Moody Blues and Genesis attempted to infuse their music with a symphonic sound. Several of Emerson, Lake and Palmer's albums featured rock arrangements of classical music; one was an adaptation of Musorgsky's *Pictures at an Exhibition*. Keith Emerson was an accomplished, classically-trained pianist; he was brave enough to take early synthesizers, and even at one point a classical orchestra, on the road. In 1974 the band embarked on a world tour, under the heading 'Welcome back my friends to the show that never ends'. The spectacular, over-long arrangements and self-important title invited symphonic rock's alternative title: 'pomp rock'. Other bands, from Supertramp and Genesis in the UK to Styx and Kansas in the US, were to fall prey to this style. Even Deep Purple recorded a concerto with symphony orchestra, a sorry attempt which arguably proved to be neither good rock music nor successful classical music.

There was, however, one spectacularly successful marriage of rock style with classical techniques: Mike Oldfield's *Tubular Bells* of 1973. It is an instrumental work of symphonic proportions, opening with the eerie theme subsequently made famous in *The Exorcist*. A vast array of electronic, keyboard and orchestral instruments build up to a climax, developing themes over changing time signatures. It sold more than 16 million copies worldwide, went to No. 1 in virtually every country of release, and provided Richard Branson with a financial foundation on which to build the Virgin empire.

By the mid-1970s, the heyday of prog rock was coming to a close, and it was not long before punk stuck two fingers up to it. The commercial machine also had its sights set on the younger section of the market in the early 1970s. Bands such as the Osmonds, Sweet and the Bay City Rollers were all designed to appeal to the 'teeny bopper' age group. The need for simple forms of pop music was partly a reaction to over-elaborate rock styles. The result was slick, polished and unashamedly catchy – disposable 'bubblegum' music.

Party time – glam rock

Glam rock emerged as an antithesis to the serious aspirations of late-60s rock music. The music was simple and catchy, silly and fun, a mishmash of 60s-based styles. But what mattered most was the image: glitter and glitz, sequins and platform soles, make-up and ambiguous sexuality. Concerts became fashion shows for the audience as well as the performers. It was largely a British phenomenon; perhaps the gender-bending prevented it from catching on in the US.

Loosely speaking, there were two types of glam rock. The disposable music of bands such as Sweet, Gary Glitter and T Rex – sometimes known as glitter bands – formed one category. Eye-liner and silver Lurex were the order of the day, and the lyrics rarely strayed far beyond Sweet's 'Ho-chi-ka-ka-ho Co-Co'.

But there was another, more esoteric side to the movement, in which artists such as David Bowie and Roxy Music appealed to an older and cooler audience. The emphasis here was still on style, but the music had ambitions too. With their art-college background, Roxy Music cultivated sophistication and elegance and applied it to every aspect of their image, from clothes to album covers. The early albums *Roxy Music* and *For Your Pleasure* were well-crafted and individual, combining the creative synthesizer playing of Brian Eno (who went on to work with ambient and experimental music) with the oboe and saxophone playing of Andy Mackay and the detached lounge-lizard crooning of Brian Ferry. This unique instrumental combination combined straight rock with more adventurous elements, such as the unexpected textures and atonal turns which are found throughout 'Bogus man'. The lyrics, too, include abstruse or surprising touches ('Do the Strand', for example, includes references to Lolita and Guernica). The albums juxtapose verse-and-chorus rock tracks with imaginative free forms – as in 'In every dream home a heartache', which opens with several verses of restrained, menacing couplets against a background of swirling synthesizers, a sound reminiscent of Velvet Underground, until it suddenly breaks out into ecstatic, spaced-out jamming.

Possibly the only influential US group who could fall into the glam rock category were the New York Dolls, who made cross-dressing part of their act. However, a new brand of party-time, fun music was developing in America, founded on two strands of black music: Philadelphia soul ('Philly soul', as it was widely known) and funk. These two styles came together to form a music that achieved enormous worldwide popularity – disco.

GOOD TIMES: THE DISCO BOOM

Disco was born in New York's discotheques – after-hours and private clubs where the music was for dancing. Many of these catered predominantly for a black or gay clientele. The gay club scene had been growing in the early 70s, partly in response to the Stonewall Riots,[4] which led to demands by gays to be able to congregate without police harassment.

Tony Cummings describes the atmosphere of the early disco clubs:

> The 'sound'… is the sound of a 20,000 dollar DJ system with three turntables, immense coffin-shaped speakers and tweeters hung separate from the woofers enabling discs with a lot of highs to propel the human body into perpetual motion. You'll find such sound systems in night clubs who've ditched live music for the disco action, in warehouses converted into party palaces with a system and some strobes. … but you'll find it at its most hectic and frenetic in the whirling crystal ball world of New York City. [5]

Disco's uplifting music, and escapist lyrics about dancing, love and sex, struck a chord and soon found a wider audience, especially following the release of the 1977 film *Saturday Night Fever*, whose accompanying soundtrack album became one of the best-selling of all time. Glamorous and decadent, with much emphasis on looking good, disco's 100% feel-good spirit had an enduring influence on dance music.

> He wears the finest clothes, the best designers heaven knows
> Ooh, from his head down to his toes
> Halston, Gucci, Fiorucci
> He looks like a still, that man is dressed to kill
> 'He's the greatest dancer' (Sister Sledge)

Origins: Philly soul and funk

Philly soul was notable for its lavish productions, featuring strings and soulful vocals, both of which were to feature heavily in disco. 'If you don't know me by now' (1972) by Harold Melvin and the Blue Notes is typical of the Philly sound, with its close harmony and lush string arrangements. The O'Jays' 'Love train' from 1972 (1973 in the UK) combines vocals and strings to uplifting effect. 'The sound of Philadelphia' by the Three Degrees was another well-known song featuring up-tempo brass, string-laden arrangement and off-beat hi-hat part – all of which later became trademarks of disco. However, these tracks lack the distinctive 'four-on-the-floor' bass-drum part and chunky drum sound that are so typical of later disco.[6]

'Funk' was an offshoot from soul music, born in the 1960s. Although similar to soul, it had a grittier, harder sound and made little or no use of orchestral backings. Conversely, the bass, guitar and drums became more important. One of funk's earliest and most famous proponents was James Brown. Already influential in the transition from 50s R&B to 60s soul, he was also instrumental in developing funk's harder, less melodious sound. A tight, funky guitar part, along with Brown's trademark clipped, energetic vocals, are evident on 'Hot pants' and 'Get up (I feel like being a) sex machine', both early 1970s tracks.

The funky sound was energetic and raucous, with punchy horns, long jams and driving rhythms. The drum break on Brown's song 'Funky drummer' has probably been sampled more than any other. Synonymous with the funk sound were the brothers Bootsy Collins

---

[4] In June 1969, the New York City police raided a Greenwich Village gay bar, the Stonewall Inn. The street erupted into violence and several nights of protest followed. The 'Stonewall Riots' marked the beginning of the gay liberation movement.

[5] Tony Cummings, 'Gloria Gaynor and the Disco Boom', *Black Music*, June 1975, quoted in Chambers (1990): 165.

[6] So called because the bass drum plays on each beat of the bar. In 4/4 time there are four bass-drum notes per bar, or 'four on the floor'.

(bass) and Catfish Collins (guitar). Both started in James Brown's band and later joined the other godfather of funk, George Clinton, in his collectives Funkadelic and Parliament. The lyrics were sexy, the vibe was uplifting and the flamboyant outfits – Bootsy's star-shaped glasses, extra-wide bell bottoms and Clinton's rhinestone-studded platform soles – all added to the party atmosphere.

Another pioneering group, Sly and the Family Stone, managed to bridge the far-apart worlds of funk and white rock music. The band combined black and white, male and female musicians, ignoring musical boundaries and incorporating elements of pop and rock, soul, funk and jazz. The funk influence can be heard in their 1970 track 'Thank you (falettin me be mice elf again)', which features the repetitive clipped riffs and brass interjections typical of funk, with strong emphasis on the flat seventh (the note below the key-note). The band influenced many later musicians, including Prince and the Red Hot Chilli Peppers.

Early days of disco

The lush sounds of Philly soul combined with the earthier sounds of funk with its emphasis on drums, funky guitar and groove, resulting in the classic disco sound. One of the earliest disco hits was 'Never can say goodbye' by Gloria Gaynor in 1974. Although its uplifting mood and soaring strings revealed its Philly soul roots, the relatively fast tempo and driving drums placed it firmly in the disco genre. Gaynor worked with the legendary producer and mixer Tom Moulton on the *Never Can Say Goodbye* album.[7] He extended three tracks – 'Honey bee', 'Never can say goodbye' and 'Reach out, I'll be there' – so that they filled the first side of the album in a non-stop mix, thereby creating the first album made specifically for club use. Gaynor is probably best known for her 1979 hit 'I will survive'.

One of the most celebrated partnerships in disco was that of American singer Donna Summer and Italian producer Giorgio Moroder. Summer's 1975 (1976 in the UK) hit 'Love to love you baby' was one of the first disco songs to feature breathy moans and sighs – the idea came to Summer after hearing the infamous 1960s Jane Birkin and Serge Gainsbourg song 'Je t'aime... moi non plus'. Initially 'Love to love you baby' was not a hit, but Neil Bogart from Casablanca Records, an important specialist disco label, became interested in it and asked Giorgio Moroder to do an extended mix. Moroder agreed, and the resulting 17-minute version, with its sexually charged vocal and sweeping, luxuriant strings, was a big hit in the clubs.

Golden age

In 1977 Summer and Moroder collaborated on a song which many consider the most important disco track ever – 'I feel love'. Combining Moroder's famous incessant synthesizer bass line, swirling chords and programmed drums with Summer's ecstatic, blissed-out vocal, the song was to serve as a blueprint for house and techno. Perhaps more than any other song, 'I feel love' shows disco at its sophisticated and sensual best, a world away from its multi-coloured Afro wig image portrayal in the 90s disco revival.

The other big name in disco was Chic, formed by the production team of guitarist Nile Rodgers and bassist Bernard Edwards. They had a string of hits throughout the late 70s including 'Good times' whose bass-line later featured on Sugarhill Gang's 'Rapper's delight'. Rodgers and Edwards later went on to write hits for Sister Sledge and Diana Ross.

With disco at its zenith, the infamous club 'Studio 54' opened in New York in April 1977 and quickly became host to a legion of celebrity party-goers including Elizabeth Taylor, Andy Warhol and Bianca Jagger – who once entered the club on a white horse led by a naked man. Studio 54 became notorious for decadent behaviour, a reputation it embraced; one of the club's walls featured a man in the moon apparently snorting cocaine from a spoon!

---

[7] Moulton pioneered the 12-inch single, which offered longer playing times and allowed louder, bassier mixes to be cut.

From the point of view of the record industry, one problem with disco music was that it was played almost exclusively in clubs rather than at home, so that unit sales were relatively low. However, the release of the film *Saturday Night Fever* in 1977 changed disco from a relatively underground New York scene to a worldwide phenomenon. The theme of a working-class Brooklyn boy escaping the drudgery of normal life by strutting in the disco struck a chord with the public. The film shot the Bee Gees to the height of their fame with songs like 'Night fever' and 'Stayin' alive'.[8] Until this point, disco had been seen as mainly black or gay, but its central role in a blockbuster film (with, ironically, a white group providing the soundtrack) propelled it to mainstream acceptance. Clubs opened across the US and Europe, playing the music people had heard in the film, and dance classes taught the moves of John Travolta, the film's star, to an eager public.

Disco in decline

At the turn of the decade disco's popularity began to wane – probably due to two main factors, one musical, the other extra-musical. As with so many artistic movements, disco was innovative at first but ended up being a parody of its former glories. Too many records began to sound formulaic – a disco beat with a sing-a-long chorus grafted on top. Rock artists also tried for a piece of disco's success, with drastically varying results. Blondie's 1979 hit 'Heart of glass' added an ice-cool aloofness, but other attempts were less successful. Perhaps the final death knell for disco was the series of 'Stars on 45' singles from the early 80s: medleys of popular artists' songs – for instance Beatles or Abba – over an unimaginative and clichéd disco beat.

The other factor concerned social attitudes. Sylvester's 1978 hit 'You make me feel (mighty real)' was the first mainstream disco hit to be performed by an openly gay performer. This, coupled with a strong disco following among the black, Hispanic and gay communities in the US, started a ground-swell of anti-disco sentiment among more conservative elements, culminating eventually in the 'disco sucks' campaign and the infamous 'disco demolition night' at a baseball stadium in Illinois, where thousands of disco records were burned and destroyed. Ironically, around the same time, the Village People had worldwide hits with 'YMCA' (1978) and 'In the Navy' (1979). They were kitted out as gay stereotypes and singing anthems to the gay lifestyles, but many people seemed not to notice.

Disco's legacy

Disco still retained a loyal following in the gay clubs, especially in Europe. In the early 80s a faster, more synthesizer-orientated mutation of disco appeared – high energy (or HiNRG as it was known by its fans). It had a less soulful sound than disco and took a lot of its inspiration from the work of Giorgio Moroder, making extensive use of frenetic synthesizer bass lines and drum machines. Its most memorable star was probably the outrageous American drag-queen Divine, with tongue-in-cheek songs like 'You think you're a man', which was produced by the emerging pop production team of Stock, Aitken and Waterman (who would dominate the European pop charts of the late 80s and early 90s).

Hard on the heels of HiNRG came the revolution that was house music. The pounding four-on-the-floor bass drum, syncopated hi-hat patterns and electronic bass-lines of 1980s house music can be traced directly back to disco and HiNRG. Disco also became a happy hunting-ground for the 1980s and 90s dance producers, whose samplers were hungry for loops and samples with an authentic 70s 'feel'. The vast majority of samples used in 80s and 90s dance music were taken from funk and disco records of the 60s and 70s. The opening bars of Rose Royce's 1979 hit 'Is it love you're after?' formed the basis of S'Express's 1988 UK hit 'Theme from S'Express'. Loleatta Holloway's 70s disco single 'Love sensation' was sampled and used (without permission!) on Black Box's 1989 smash hit 'Ride on time'. The number

---

[8] The soundtrack to the film was essentially a Bee Gees album fleshed out with a few other disco artists.

of drum loops that have been sampled from this era is anybody's guess. In the late 90s, 'filtered house' made extensive use of whole sections of 70s disco, looped and filtered.

Disco did not die; it evolved. The story continues in the 80s, with house and techno.

REBELLION: REGGAE, PUNK AND AFTER

After the protests of the 1960s, it seemed that Western pop had moved away from politics altogether, and had entered a slick world of fantasy, theatre and escapism. But during the second half of the 1970s two musical styles were to change that. Youth rebellion was reclaimed by anti-establishment, anti-everything punk music; and Jamaican reggae became the voice of protest and social comment throughout the world. By the end of the 1970s both punk and reggae bands were to perform on the same bills at massive Rock Against Racism rallies in the UK, demonstrating against rising xenophobia and racism fuelled by organizations such as the National Front. RAR was the first political pressure group to be led by pop music.[9]

60s Jamaican music, from ska to rocksteady to reggae

Reggae has its home in the small, impoverished island of Jamaica, making all the more remarkable the worldwide influence it was to have from 1970 onwards. It has been described as the first world music. Just as blues stemmed from hardship, so too did reggae. Its roots were in mento and blues – especially the dance-hall R&B style popular in nearby New Orleans, with its jumpy, relaxed rhythms and jazzy horn sections. Mento, Jamaica's calypso-style folk music, was the dominant sound in Jamaica until the 1940s, when radios became more affordable and Jamaicans discovered American radio stations and R&B. People started travelling to America and buying exclusive pressings to play back through home-made box speakers – hence 'sound systems'. Sound systems were a crucial development in Jamaican music, and later were indirectly to give rise to other musical offshoots such as rap, scratching and dance music. As early as the 1950s, DJs would talk over the sounds, 'toasting' and chatting in rhythm with the music. Toasting was later to have a bearing on the rise of rap in the US. Several of Jamaica's most influential and powerful producers started as sound-system operators, among them Clement 'Sir Coxsone' Dodd, Duke Reid and Prince Buster.

In the early 60s ska developed as a distinctive Jamaican style, derived from New Orleans R&B but with a characteristic fast, jumpy rhythm:

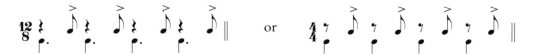

For examples of ska, listen to 'Guns of Navarone' by the Skatalites, 'Al Capone' by Prince Buster or 'Phoenix City' by Roland Alphonso. The Skatalites, led by trombonist Don Drummond and including saxophonist Roland Alphonso and pianist Jackie Mittoo, comprised the cream of Jamaica's instrumentalists; many of their records featured jazzy solos riding on the ska rhythm.

Around 1966 a new Jamaican style evolved: rocksteady. Much slower than ska, the jerky off-beat quavers gave way to an ultra-steady, bass-dominated 4/4. Ska's jazzy horn lines faded from prominence, the bass grew more important, and the rhythm guitar (and maybe piano or organ) gave a strong off-beat emphasis to the second and fourth beats – the rhythm that was to become reggae. Good examples include 'Rock steady' by Alton Ellis, 'Judge Dread' by Prince Buster or 'Feel like jumping' by Marcia Griffiths.

---

[9] Formed in 1979, RAR-USA was the North American extension of the UK movement.

Musically the transition to reggae was not a precise thing; rather, rocksteady rhythms became more diversified, sometimes faster, and the term 'reggae' gradually and retrospectively came to refer to all of them, and hence to Jamaican music in general. 'Do the reggay' by the Maytals (1968) was an early use of the word, and a good example of this group's exciting, powerful music; listen also to their later albums *Funky Kingston* (1973) and *Reggae Got Soul* (1976), both recorded after reggae in general and the Maytals in particular had built up a white audience.

Jamaica became independent in 1962, and people flocked from the countryside into Kingston, seeking work and settling in fast-growing shanty towns such as Trench Town. With high unemployment, the phenomenon of the Jamaican 'rude boys' – disaffected youths on the street – arose, and became regular subject-matter for the rocksteady and reggae songs of the late 60s; 'Rudy a message to you' by Dandy (Robert Thompson) (1967) was an early example.

'Rude boy' songs displayed a mixture of attitudes. Many were critical of the youths who caused considerable disorder within their own ghetto communities, and attempted to call them to order, but other songs expressed sympathy or identification with the rude boys. This was in line with a growing political and social awareness, and sense of protest, and a willingness to voice such themes through songs.

Another theme that began to emerge in reggae songs around this time was Rastafarianism – a religion which draws on Christian ideas, standing strong against the wicked forces of Babylon and looking towards repatriation to Africa. It advocates the use of ganja (cannabis), which is seen as an aid to enlightenment, and the wearing of dreadlocks as symbolizing a natural way of life. Rastafarians regard Haile Selassie, emperor of Ethiopia from 1930 to 1974, as their spiritual leader. When Haile Selassie visited Jamaica in 1968, there was a huge growth in Rastafarianism, with many reggae artists adopting the religion – most famously Bob Marley, who became a spokesmen for millions of young blacks. Rastafarianism was also to find a home in the inner cities of the UK and the US, helping to promote black identity in the face of racism.

Reggae in the 70s

Before the 1970s, reggae was little known by the white audience, though it made some successful forays into the British pop charts: 'My boy Lollipop' by Millie Small in 1964, 'The Israelites' by Desmond Dekker in 1969, 'Wonderful world, beautiful people' by Jimmy Cliff in the same year, and 'Young, gifted and black' by Bob Andy and Marcia Griffiths in 1970.

In 1973 the hard-hitting film *The Harder they Come* was released, starring Jimmy Cliff. Reggae music provided both the soundtrack and the plot. Songs such as 'You can get it if you really want' and the title song introduced reggae to a worldwide audience. Around the same time Island Records boss Chris Blackwell had committed himself to recording and promoting an album by Bob Marley and the Wailers; *Catch a Fire* was released in 1973. When Eric Clapton released a cover version of Bob Marley's 'I shot the sheriff' in 1974, reggae was set to take the music scene by storm. Bob Marley's songs – Rastafarian, and often political – became famous internationally, and he became the first Jamaican artist to have worldwide fame.

'Africa', by the Mighty Diamonds (1976),[10] has many features that are typical of reggae. The bass drum plays on the second and fourth beats of the bar, reinforced by rim shots on the snare drum. The drums, bass and guitar play a repetitive accompaniment to the vocals, which deal with the Rastafarian theme of a return to Africa.

> Africa is the land of home
> Africa is the land where I and I come from
> Africa our fathers' land is calling us home

---

[10] Included in Winterson (2002b).

So long we have been a slave and no more will we roam
So I hope and pray that the day will come
When we see the rising sun

'Africa' (the Mighty Diamonds)

Many of these features are also found in Delroy Washington's 1976 hit, 'Freedom fighters'.[11] The guitar plays one of the hallmarks of reggae, repeated off-beat quaver clipped chords, and the bass, one of the most important instruments in reggae, plays the same four-bar pattern throughout.

Various lines of development followed the explosion of worldwide interest in reggae in the mid-70s. Engineer-producers such as King Tubby and Lee 'Scratch' Perry worked with 'dub' recording techniques – essentially remixing without the vocal tracks (or with the vocals occasionally dropping in and out), changing volume levels in the mix, bringing instruments up or down, and adding reverb and echo effects. Remixing was not a new invention; rock engineers, such as Eddie Kramer working with Jimi Hendrix, had become used to spending long hours on alternative mixes. But these were subservient to the performing group or artist; dub reggae was the beginning of remixing as a distinct art with its own final outcomes – instrumental dub 'versions'.

Another use for dub versions was as backings for 'toasters' – DJs who spoke or chanted over the music in the rhyming manner that later, in the hands of black Americans and over a different style of music, was called 'rapping'. DJ-toasters such as U-Roy, Big Youth, I-Roy and Dillinger built on the early example of Prince Buster to develop the toasting style. Many records were issued with the same backing track on both sides: with vocal on one side, and a dub instrumental or toasting version on the other.

Straight songs in this period – late 70s – tended to fall into two broad categories. Gregory Isaacs, Delroy Wilson and Dennis Brown were the big singing stars in the sweet-sounding style labelled 'lovers rock', while groups like Culture and the Mighty Diamonds kept Rastafarian faith with 'roots reggae'.

The British poet Linton Kwesi Johnson, influenced by Jamaican DJs such as Big Youth and U-Roy, combined his poetry, spoken in Jamaican patois, with reggae dub backings. In many cases the words were strongly political, dealing with police brutality and racist violence. 'Sonny's lettah' is a powerful political song about the perils of the 'sus' law.[12]

when all of a sudden a police van pull up
out jump tree policemen
de whole a dem carryin baton
dem walk straight up to me and Jim
one a dem hold on to Jim
seh dem tekin him in

'Sonny's lettah' (Linton Kwesi Johnson)

In Britain, the late 1970s saw a revival of reggae's precursor, ska. One of the key bands was the Specials, whose keyboardist, Jerry Dammers, formed his own label, Two Tone, to promote the ska revival. The ska bands had a punky, aggressive edge as well as multi-racial line-ups which were uncommon at that time. Strong anti-racist sentiment was expressed in songs like 'Racist friend'. The Specials' biggest hit was the political, pro-birth-control anthem 'Too much too young' (1979). With bands such as the Selecter, the Beat and Madness (who went on to have a successful mainstream pop career), the ska revival enjoyed a number of UK hits at the turn of the decade, and later influenced numerous US punk/ska bands of the 90s, e.g. Rancid and Less Than Jake.

---

[11] Included in Winterson (2002a).

[12] England's infamous *Suspicion of Loitering with Criminal Intent* law (a.k.a. 'sus') gave the police wide discretionary powers to stop and search anyone they regarded as suspicious. There was a widespread feeling that these were used unduly against the black community.

Punk

In mid-70s England, college campuses were awash with the escapist and fantastical sounds of Genesis, Yes, Deep Purple and Led Zeppelin. Meanwhile, early disco was making its presence felt on the airwaves. Neither of these genres reflected what it was like to live through the three-day week and high unemployment of the time. They did not reflect what it was like to be young in Britain with no prospects and no future. What was the point of working hard at college only to find yourself having to 'sign on' for unemployment benefit at the end of it? It was all a far cry from the glamour of disco or the fantasy world of progressive rock.

However these factors were precisely the conditions needed to spawn a totally new movement based on anger, nihilism, teenage angst and hatred of 'rock dinosaurs' – punk. Punk's DIY 'anyone can do it' ethos, coupled with short, aggressive 'three-chord thrash' songs, were in part a reaction against the virtuoso musicians (or 'musos') and lengthy 'concept' albums produced by the arena rock bands.

Prog rock albums were created in the studio – a long process of lush production – and were then taken on the road to be performed to huge arena crowds. Punk reversed this tradition: bands established themselves by performing live in pubs and clubs, and any subsequent recordings were deliberately given a live, immediate feel. Prog rock solos were long, designed to show off the technique of the instrumentalist; new material would often be introduced and improvised upon. Most solos found in punk music were short breaks, often paraphrasing the melody or simply embellishing a chord.

The typical punk line-up of singer, two guitars and drums eschewed the electronic instruments often found in prog rock. The typical punk guitar player produced a sort of buzz-saw sound, with rhythm chords, distortion and feedback creating an impenetrable wall of sound. Bass playing was often a continuous series of repeated eighth-notes. The music was fast and urgent.

Gone, too, was the transatlantic accent adopted by so many pop singers, abandoned in favour of a vernacular British (often London) accent. The typical singing style was declamatory – a sort of sneering recitative, half way between singing and talking, or more aptly shouting.

Origins of punk

Although it was a British phenomenon, punk was heavily influenced by US artists. The Velvet Underground, a New York-based band from the late 60s and early 70s, were one of punk's ancestors, having a similar lack of interest in musical virtuosity. The simple, repetitive chord structure and insistent ensemble rhythm of 'Waiting for the man' (1967) exemplifies this. Another forerunner band, who displayed the aggressive attitude and shock tactics which typified punk, were the Stooges, hailing from America's Midwest. The Stooges' music was more brutal and less 'arty' than that of the Velvet Underground. Stooges vocalist Iggy Pop said of the Velvet Underground's first album 'I heard other people who could make good music – without being any good at music. It gave me hope.'[13]

Often referred to as the 'Godfather of Punk', Iggy Pop was renowned for his outrageous stage antics, including smearing himself in peanut butter, and various acts of self-mutilation. His lyrics underlined this out-of-control stage persona, and also summed up the nihilism and boredom felt by many teenagers. The Stooges' raw, elemental style is best captured on the *Funhouse* album (1970). Stand-out tracks include 'Down on the street', 'Loose' and 'TV eye'. Their uncompromisingly hard sound continues to influence many bands today.

The band which would be the bridge between the US and the UK were the New York Dolls. Though musically not as ground-breaking as the Stooges (they had more parallels with the Rolling Stones and glam rock), their attitude definitely foreshadowed that of punk. The Dolls' audacious behaviour, which involved onstage baiting of their audience and flirtation

---

[13] *A History of Punk* by A S Van Dorston at www.fastnbulbous.com/

with Nazi imagery, caught the eye of English entrepreneur Malcom McLaren. McLaren briefly managed them and embraced their provocative image, including draping the stage with communist flags before American audiences. The Dolls split up in the mid-70s and McLaren returned to the UK to become manager of perhaps the greatest punk band ever – the Sex Pistols.

Some would argue that the first punk rock band was the Ramones. While bands such as the Stooges and the New York Dolls set the stage and aesthetic for punk in the States, the Ramones laid down a musical blueprint, cutting the songs down to their bare essentials – simple chord progressions coupled with a catchy tune, all played at blinding speed. 'Blitzkrieg bop', their first single, was released in 1977. A two-minute song based on three easy chords, it has a raw and chaotic sound with a raucous half-shouting style of singing. Their first four albums are usually regarded as their best work, and include such songs as 'Judy is a punk', 'Sheena is a punk rocker' and 'Teenage lobotomy'.

It has also been argued that another trailblazer of the anarchic punk genre was Patti Smith. Her lyrics had more in common with Beat and Symbolist poetry than with the romantic love songs which had predominated in women's pop. Her music is hard to catego-rize: stream-of-consciousness performance art moving between speaking and singing, it could be loosely described as 'art rock'. One of her greatest contributions was in changing the image of women in rock. The cover of her 1975 debut album *Horses* is a shot of Smith taken by the American photographer Robert Mapplethorpe, showing her dressed in a simple white shirt and skinny tie with unkempt hair and a defiant expression. This potent image demonstrated her refusal to be objectified as a woman, and paved the way for other women in pop to play with the concept of femininity.

The class of 76

1976 was year dot for punk. Punk was initially a London-centric, rather incestuous movement,[14] and in September 1976 the capital's 100 Club played host to a two-day punk festival. The line-up reads like a Who's Who of punk – the Buzzcocks, the Clash, the Damned, the Sex Pistols and Siouxsie and the Banshees. The festival was swiftly followed by the appearance of the first punk single – 'New rose' by the Damned. Its tribal drums and simple, almost Neanderthal riffs encapsulated much of what was to follow.

The following month 'Anarchy in the UK' was released by the Sex Pistols. The sound was very different to that of the Damned's single. Its multi-tracked guitars and accomplished production went against punk's low-budget ideals, but the end result was so powerfully overwhelming that few complained. Vocalist Johnny Rotten's snarling vocals and vitriolic lyrics laid out an iconoclastic agenda.

During the promotional campaign for 'Anarchy' the Sex Pistols did a live TV interview with interviewer Bill Grundy. Grundy unwisely baited the band, who responded with a string of profanities. There was an outcry in the following morning's tabloids, rocketing the Pistols to overnight fame.

The Pistols' outrageous public persona and cutting-edge music inspired many bands to form, including the Clash, who supported the Sex Pistols on their 1977 tour. The Clash's eponymous debut album was released to critical acclaim the same year. Taking a more political stance than the Sex Pistols,[15] Joe Strummer's disillusioned, heartfelt lyrics struck a chord with many a disillusioned youth.

---

[14] Some of the 'Bromley contingent', a collection of fans from South London, went on to be in important bands themselves, e.g. Siouxsie Sioux (Siouxsie and the Banshees) and Billy Idol (Generation X). McLaren's girlfriend, Vivienne Westwood, a fashion designer, contributed greatly to punk's look. Jamie Reid, who designed the Sex Pistols' distinctive covers, was a friend of McLaren's.

[15] The Damned's Brian James once said about the Clash's Mick Jones: 'He's into changing the political system. I want people to enjoy themselves and forget politics'.

Punk in decline

Punk's culture of resistance seemed to sum up the frustrations of a generation. It was opposed to the rock establishment, and for a time there was a genuine movement where bands played in pubs and dives all over the place, tickets were cheap, and no longer did you have to pay over the odds to sit through a never-ending guitar solo. There was an air of anarchy and rebellion, and it felt as though things were going to change. But there was no unified political message. Bands vied with each other and fought among themselves. Punk burned brightly for two years, but its decline was swift. Bassist Glen Matlock, a key part of the Pistols' song-writing team, was ousted in favour of Rotten's friend John Ritchie, better known as Sid Vicious.[16] The Sex Pistols' US tour of 1978 was plagued with problems, culminating in Rotten leaving the band. He was briefly replaced by train-robber Ronnie Biggs, in a transparent effort to cash in on Biggs's infamy. The result was a parody of the Pistols' former glory. Vicious died of a heroin overdose in 1979 and the Pistols disintegrated. The Damned also split the same year, though they would later reform. The Clash's style moved away from straight punk, and they enjoyed considerable success in the US until their split in 1986.

By 1980 the originators of punk had either died, given up or moved on, leaving only imitators in their wake.[17] It was time for America to take over, in the form of bands such as the Dead Kennedys, Black Flag and the emerging 'hardcore' scene.

Punk's legacy

Punk took rock 'n' roll back to its basics. It stripped away artistic pretensions, did away with prog rock's excesses and the pomp of concept albums such as Yes's *Tales from Topographic Oceans*. Instead of the endless guitar solos of bands like Led Zeppelin and Deep Purple there were three-minute, three-chord hits of anger and energy. Punk inspired countless bands. The Fall, Joy Division and U2 were all born out of punk's 'anyone can do it' ethic. Without punk there would have been no US hardcore, no Nirvana, no nu-metal. The short, sharp, shock of punk – the aggressive, distorted guitars, belligerent, harsh vocal style and confrontational lyrics – are clearly evident in these sub-genres. Its spirit is also present in the dance revolution of the 80s, where people with no traditional instrumental skills began to make new and innovative music with whatever ability and equipment they could muster.

Punk, pop and the new wave

Punk's vitality and energy rubbed off on non-punk musicians, and on both sides of the Atlantic a hybrid of punk and pop surfaced – new wave.

Though they hailed from the same period as punk and had an aggressive sound, New York band Blondie never displayed the nihilistic or political attitude that typified true punk. Blondie's guitar-driven, pop-oriented songs were successful in both the UK and US, due in no small part to their photogenic singer, Debbie Harry. Fellow Americans the B-52's developed a completely different style, with oddball 1960s imagery and sounds, including bouffant-haired girl singers, cheesy organs and surf-like guitars. The B-52's transmuted punk's anger into good-time dayglo wackiness, typified on 'Rock lobster' from their debut album, *The B-52's*.

Meanwhile, a young Irish band, the Undertones, combined punky power and simplicity with tuneful songs concerning adolescent joys and fears. Their best known hit, 'Teenage kicks' (1978), showcases nasal vocalist Feargal Sharkey's talents in a joyful celebration of

---

[16] He was also sometimes known as John Beverly.

[17] At the time of writing several of the surviving originators of punk have reformed their bands, notably the Sex Pistols and the Clash.

what it is to be young. Also in Ireland in the late 70s, a group of Dublin school friends formed U2. Their anthemic, melodic style soon found an audience, and they went on to be one of the biggest acts of the 80s and 90s. The distinctive, chiming style of their guitarist, the Edge, influenced many other players.

Contemporaries of the Sex Pistols, the Jam had a sound which bridged punk and new wave.[18] The aggressive guitars and political lyrics were reminiscent of punk, but the highly melodic vocals of Paul Weller harked back to English mod bands of the 60s such as the Who and the Small Faces; their sharp, besuited image was also derived from the 60s mod look. Indeed, Weller's political, highly England-centric lyrics may have contributed to the band's lack of Stateside success. The Jam had many UK hits from the late 70s to early 80s, including the atmospheric 'Down in the tube station at midnight' and their big hit 'Going underground', featuring Weller's trademark clipped vocals and Pete Townshend-like guitar power chords. Weller split the band in 1982 to form the more soul-oriented but still political Style Council, before finally going solo in the early 90s. The Jam's short, punchy and melodic songs influenced many key UK bands of the 80s and 90s including the Smiths and Oasis. There were other mod revival bands, concerned with recreating mod's former glories, but the Jam added some of punk's bile to an otherwise retro movement.

One band that made a startling transition from punk to pop were Adam and the Ants. Initially a punk band with a sado-masochistic image, Adam and the Ants were transformed into pop warriors par excellence after drafting in the infamous Malcom McLaren for an image and musical makeover, during which McLaren retained vocalist Stuart Goddard but replaced the rest of the band with new musicians. The resulting hybrid American-Indian/pirate image and African Burundi-style drumming proved highly successful in the UK during the early 80s, where the band had a number of hits including 'Ant music', 'Stand and deliver' and 'Prince Charming'.

Three of the surplus Ants from the original line-up went on to form Bow Wow Wow, also under the supervision of McLaren. Bow Wow Wow provoked outrage when mohicaned 15-year-old Burmese lead singer Annabella Lwin appeared half-naked on the cover of their first album. The colourful combination of Lwin's bratty voice, sexually-charged lyrics with African-inspired guitar and tribal drumming was most original and, along with the revamped Ants, was one of the first examples of the use of 'world music' in a pop context.

The fusion of punk and pop proved to be a fruitful one, energizing pop from the bland doldrums of the mid-70s. Manchester's Buzzcocks did it more successfully than most, with hummable tunes and witty, sincere lyrics alongside powerful, driving guitars. Though mainly active in the late 70s, their brand of punk pop showed the way forward for many bands of the early-80s' new wave. Their biggest hit was the teen-angst anthem 'Ever fallen in love with someone (you shouldn't've)'. However they were not afraid to show their punk roots with songs like 'Orgasm addict' and 'Oh shit'.

Elvis Costello is often included in the new-wave movement, mainly due to his punky sneer, and lyrics which often tackled difficult and controversial subjects, including wife-beating, mercenaries, and most memorably the Falklands war in 'Shipbuilding'. He went on to be a prolific singer–songwriter, achieving success in both the US and UK, and operating in a wide range of genres, from soul to country to classical.

US punk

As punk spluttered and mutated in the UK, it was taken up in the USA, evolving into US hardcore. Hardcore was so named deliberately to segregate it from the new-wave scene. Emergent new-wave bands in the UK had rediscovered melody and a new sense of stylistic experimentation. The US hardcore bands went in the opposite direction, with a harder

[18] 'In the city', their first single, even shared the same bass-line as the Sex Pistols' 'Holidays in the sun'.

sound, faster tempos and an unmelodic, shouting vocal style, effectively intensifying the more extreme attributes of punk. The crop of new independent labels like SST, Discord and Alternative Tentacles provided a home for these earnest, defiantly anti-commercial bands to flourish.

The California-based band Black Flag released their debut EP, *Nervous Breakdown* in 1978, the first record to be released on SST. Their sound was darker and harder than previous punk, and had a great influence on the hardcore scene. Fellow Californians the Dead Kennedys featured highly political, outspoken frontman Jello Biafra, who frequently targeted large corporations, the American administration and far-right political organizations in his lyrics. The Kennedys' first album, *Fresh Fruit for Rotting Vegetables* (1980) received critical acclaim in both the US and UK, and is regarded as one of the first hardcore albums. 'Holiday in Cambodia' demonstrates how hardcore was moving away from the English punk sound, with its incorporation of nightmarish lyrics and darkly chromatic guitar. When the Kennedys split in 1986, Biafra remained politically active, running for mayor in San Francisco.

Not everything was based in California however – Minneapolis's Hüsker Dü were a hardcore band who evolved a more melodic sound which influenced Nirvana and later 90s bands such as Green Day and Sum 41.

One of hardcore's most notable inventions was not musical at all, but a way of living known as 'straight edge'. Named after a song by Minor Threat, straight edge was a negation of the nihilism of British punk. No drink, no drugs: plain, utilitarian T-shirts and jeans were the order of the day. However, hardcore shared UK punk's DIY ethic and strong distrust of anything corporate.

The period following punk's decline was one of great musical experimentation. People who had never dreamed of starting a band now had a go. Many movements came and went – the ska and mod revivals, Goth, futurist, New Romantic, as well as a perplexing array of hard-to-classify 'post-punk' acts.

PROFILES

David Bowie

David Bowie was hugely influential during his peak in the 1970s – with effortless cool, sexual ambivalence and ever-changing images, he achieved cult status. Others bands had an image and stuck to it; Bowie reinvented himself at every turn, cultivating ambiguities of husband/homosexual, singer/actor and leader/loner. How he was packaged was as much an aspect of his art as what the package contained. He had a commitment to stylishness, and set up a number of visual precedents in terms of personal appearance. With his make-up and dyed hair, he created a new sexually ambiguous image for youth to copy. In doing so he opened up questions of sexual identity (often referred to as gender-bending) that had previously been repressed or ignored in youth culture. (The hit 'Rebel, rebel' includes the line 'Rebel, rebel – got your mother in a whirl, She's not sure if you're a boy or a girl.') These fashionable metamorphoses were much copied, and every concert attracted a host of look-alikes.

With an air of ironic detachment, Bowie placed himself in the world of art and fashion, counting amongst his influences Andy Warhol, Philip Glass, Jacques Brel, Lindsay Kemp and Jean Genet. Bowie worked with Lindsay Kemp's mime troupe in the late 1960s and has always had a simultaneous acting career. His first substantial film role was as an androgynous alien in *The Man Who Fell to Earth* (1976). He is one of the few pop stars with real acting skills, and has always brought showmanship and theatre to his gigs.

After a number of earlier albums, Bowie's major breakthrough came with *The Rise and Fall of Ziggy Stardust and the Spiders from Mars* (1972). As Ziggy Stardust, Bowie played the first of a series of characters that have peopled his career. The songs on *Ziggy Stardust* set the

Ilko Musto/Rex Features

David Bowie as Ziggy Stardust, Earl's Court, London, 1973

tone for the next few albums – solid rock with a relentless beat and generally pessimistic lyrics, not short of hooks and riffs, often rising to melodramatic climaxes. Mick Ronson's guitar-playing, fleshed out with a string orchestra, was a vital element of the sound. On stage Bowie and Ronson made a vibrant duo – and Ziggy made Bowie an international star. When Ziggy retired in 1973 he was replaced by *Aladdin Sane*, a concept work centring on global destruction. This saw Bowie head-to-toe in white grease paint. Musically, the style remained more or less the same, another string of good pop songs, decorated with the sometimes bizarre, sometimes jazz-influenced flourishes of pianist Mick Garson. The doom-laden *Diamond Dogs* (1974) followed. With ideas borrowed from the writer George Orwell, it told of a world of dictatorship and oppression.

During the late 1970s, Bowie lived in Berlin and worked with ex-Roxy Music member Brian Eno. They experimented with electronic music and produced some innovative work, including the 1977 album *Heroes*, where on the song 'Moss garden' Bowie plays Japanese koto to Eno's electronic accompaniment. Later reinventions included Philadelphia-style soul man on the 1975 album *Young Americans* and experimental-music composer on *Low*, another collaboration with Brian Eno.

Bob Marley

On Thursday 21 May 1981, Kingston, Jamaica, came to a complete standstill for the funeral of Bob Marley. Edward Seaga, the Prime Minister, spoke of Marley's songs to the ten-thousand-strong crowd, saying:

> 'Trenchtown rock' – the symbol of his life; 'No woman no cry' – for his comforting hand of compassion; 'One love' – for his vision of peace and unity; and 'Rastaman vibration' – for his deep mystical faith.

Three years earlier Marley had brought together the two Jamaican political leaders, Seaga and Michael Manley, at the 'One love' concert, in an attempt to encourage peace between the two political camps, whose followers had been pursuing their conflict using ever more violent tactics.[19] The event immediately acquired symbolic significance in Jamaica, and the song became known all over the world for its noble aspiration, and the ideal of reconciliation.

Bob Marley was born in Nine Miles, Jamaica, in the heart of the so-called 'ganja parish'. His mother was a young black servant and his father, whom he rarely saw, was a white ex-British army officer from Liverpool. Marley spent his youth in the Trench Town ghetto, where he soon joined forces with Bunny Wailer (originally Livingstone) and Peter Tosh to form the Wailers. From early on, the group identified with the underprivileged and rebellious youth of Trench Town:

> We come from Trench Town
> Lord we free the people with music
> That's what they say, Trench Town
> Say we're the underprivileged people
> So they keep us in chains

'Trench Town' (the Wailers)

Their first song, 'Simmer down', recorded for Studio One producer Clement Dodd, was an instant hit in Jamaica. They went on to produce a string of records – mainly cover versions – but split from Dodd's label in 1967, and two years later started working with Lee Perry, who recognized their potential and encouraged them to produce their own material, putting them together with the drum and bass duo Carlton and Aston Barrett (who formed the heart of his studio band, the Upsetters). By this time Marley had already written 'Lively up yourself', 'Trenchtown rock' and a number of other songs which were later re-recorded for Island.

In 1972 Chris Blackwell, Jamaican entrepreneur and owner of the Island label, heard Marley's latest songs and was impressed by them, and decided to sign the Wailers, recognizing their potential to be marketed to rock fans. Blackwell's interests were twofold: he supplied reggae records on the Trojan label to the Jamaican market in Britain, and also developed new rock acts for the Island label. Marley was the first reggae artist to achieve international recognition in the popular market, beginning with the album *Catch a Fire* in 1973. With his stage charisma, vocal tenderness and songwriting skills, Bob Marley had rock-star appeal.

Catch a Fire contained original material written by Bob Marley and Peter Tosh. The sound was off-beat strummed guitar chords, electric guitar solos (for most of his career Marley used a Gibson Les Paul) and electronic sounds, alongside the traditional Afro-Caribbean percussion section. Purists argue that the arrangements conceded too much to the unsubtle demands of rock, but the powerful lyrics and magnetic performances placed Jamaica and reggae on the world map. The sound is intimate, with mainly sparse instrumentation and mantra-like reggae rhythms. Several songs, such as 'Concrete jungle' and 'Slave driver', have politically charged lyrics; others, such as 'Stir it up', are love songs. 'Stir it up' builds from the opening off-beat guitar strumming, instruments entering one

---

[19] At the time of the concert the roles were reversed: Manley was Prime Minister and Seaga was opposition leader. Manley led the People's National Party (PNP) and Seaga the Jamaican Labour Party (JLP).

by one, adding to the laid-back seductive rhythms over a repeated bass-line. It is notable for the psychedelic organ and guitar sounds and the long imaginative improvisation towards the end.

In 1974 Peter Tosh and Bunny Wailer left to be soloists and the band added a trio of female backing singers, the I-Threes (including Marley's wife, Rita Marley). A big commercial breakthrough came in 1975 with the *Natty Dread* album. This album, potent both lyrically and musically, is full of rallying songs of political and social commentary such as 'Them belly full (but we hungry)', warning that 'a hungry mob is a angry mob', 'Revolution' and 'Rebel music' as well as the hit ballad 'No woman no cry'.

Marley became a symbol of rebellion and protest worldwide, from the Zimbabwean independence movement to white punks in Europe. This also made him a target in politicized Jamaican society. He was nearly assassinated in the election year of 1976 when seven armed men broke into his home on the eve of an electioneering concert – but he sang at the concert all the same. Marley died of cancer in 1981, and Peter Tosh was shot dead in 1987 in mysterious circumstances. Bob Marley's body lies in a mausoleum in Nine Miles, attended by dreadlocked guards.

The Sex Pistols

The Sex Pistols' story goes back to 1974 when guitarist Steve Jones and drummer Paul Cook were in a band called the Strand in London. They met Malcolm McLaren at his clothes shop Sex. McLaren introduced Cook and Jones to his shop assistant, Glen Matlock, a bass player and talented songwriter. Green-haired teenager John Lydon (better known as 'Johnny Rotten' because of the poor state of his teeth) was recruited on vocals, and the Sex Pistols were formed. His head still full of the decadence and dirty glamour of the New York Dolls (whom he had previously managed), McLaren wanted to form a UK equivalent. Despite legendary animosity between the two bands,[20] Johnny Thunders, guitarist with the New York Dolls, had a definite influence on the playing style of Steve Jones.

McLaren's art-college education had brought him into contact with the 'situationist' movement. The situationists' anti-work/anti-bourgeois sloganeering used in the Paris riots in May 1968 had a great impact on McLaren. Situationist slogans found their way onto many of the clothes sold at his shop and were subsequently worn by the Pistols and their fans. One slogan – 'a cheap holiday in other people's misery' – was used by Rotten in the Pistol's 'Holidays in the sun'. A photograph from the French riots, of a girl with a safety pin (one of punk's most enduring icons) through her lips, inspired the cover of the Sex Pistol's single 'God save the Queen', which featured the Queen with her lips fastened together in the same way.

T-shirts with Nazi swastikas, naked breasts and sado-masochistic imagery, along with the bondage pants that were found in McLaren's shop, defined the punk look. Their shock value was proved when punks were actually arrested for wearing such outfits on several occasions. Hair was also styled to shock – dyed and spiked in a style that perfectly complemented the confrontational clothes.

The combination of McLaren's intellectual posturing and cultural savvy, Rotten's persona, appearance and acerbic lyrics, and Matlock's songwriting talents, was fortuitous to say the least. It is probably fair to say that the Sex Pistols would never have happened if any one of these three key people had not been involved. It is also often overlooked that Cook and Jones were fine musicians in their own right, as is clearly evident on the Pistols' recordings. McLaren's famous statement, 'A band that can't play is better than a band that can', was a memorable sound-bite, but was far from the truth in the Sex Pistols' case.

Their first single, 'Anarchy in the UK', released by EMI in December 1976, with its torrent of guitars and Rotten's trademark sneering voice, is probably punk's most famous

---

[20] The Sex Pistols song 'New York' was a thinly veiled attack on the New York Dolls. Johnny Thunders later reciprocated with the song 'London Boys'.

**Johnny Rotten:
portrait with safety pins**

artefact. Despite being banned by the BBC it reached 38 in the British charts. The Bill Grundy incident had whipped the press into a frenzy. The Pistols' provocative stance and outlandish appearance, coupled with their audience's growing reputation for violence,[21] meant that many of their gigs were cancelled by terrified councils and promoters. EMI baulked at the torrent of bad publicity and promptly dropped the Sex Pistols from their label. More seriously, Glen Matlock was replaced by the stylish but talentless Sid Vicious on bass guitar. The band were subsequently signed up by A&M Records in March 1977. As a publicity stunt, the record contract was signed in front of Buckingham Palace. However, the following week A&M dropped the Pistols,[22] even though they were in the middle of pressing the band's second single 'God save the Queen'.

The next (and final) record label to sign the Pistols was Virgin Records. 'God save the Queen' was released in June 1977, coinciding with the Queen's silver jubilee celebrations. Despite being banned by daytime radio for its anti-royalist sentiments, the song reached No. 2 in the official UK charts.[23] To promote the single the Pistols chartered a boat down the Thames and played a short set, only to have several members of the 'cruise' (including McLaren) arrested on disembarking. Worse was to come in the form of attacks on members of the band and their entourage. In separate incidents Johnny Rotten had arm tendons severed in a razor assault, and Paul Cook needed stitches after being attacked by a group of thugs with an iron bar.

The next single, the less inflammatory but still abrasive 'Pretty vacant', was followed by their album *Never Mind the Bollocks – Here's the Sex Pistols*. A predictable tabloid outrage

---

[21] Audience fighting was not uncommon. Sid Vicious (at that point only a fan) allegedly blinded a girl in one eye after throwing a glass on the second night of the 100 Club punk festival. Additionally, the style of dancing called 'pogoing', which involved jumping up and down whilst knocking into other members of the audience, was very popular.

[22] This followed Rotten's arrest for drug possession and Vicious' trashing of A&M's toilets.

[23] Many shops would not stock the record or even display its position in the chart, instead leaving the No. 2 spot as a blank. Others, such as HMV in Oxford Street, sold the record but kept it hidden under the counter. 'God save the Queen' was kept off the No. 1 spot by Rod Stewart, even though allegedly it outsold Stewart's song by four to one.

(and a court case over the use of 'bollocks' in the title, which the band won) ensued, and the album went to No. 1 in the charts.

Since Sid Vicious' bass-playing was at a very elementary level, Jones was charged with recording the bass parts on the album. Not an experienced bassist, he simply doubled the root note of his guitar part on the bass, giving the Sex Pistols their distinctive, slab-like sound.

In the autumn of 1978 the Pistols commenced a tour of Europe and America. It was not a success. The band's spiralling drug problems and internal frictions (the members had split into two camps – Cook/Jones and Rotten/Vicious) were further compounded by playing to hostile audiences in unsuitable venues. Rotten left the band after a disastrous gig in San Francisco, and later formed Public Image Limited.

Cook and Jones were encouraged by McLaren to take part in his *Great Rock 'n' Roll Swindle* quasi-documentary. Vicious had become a heroin addict, spurred on by his American girlfriend, Nancy Spungen. After Spungen was found stabbed to death in a New York hotel room, Vicious was charged with her murder. Released on bail, he died of a heroin overdose on 2 February 1979 in New York. He was 21 years old.

The remnants of the band limped on, releasing a few uninspired singles with various vocalists before calling it a day. With original bassist Glen Matlock, they reformed for the aptly-named 'Filthy Lucre' tour in 1996.

Abba

This Scandinavian pop outfit shot to fame after winning the 1974 Eurovision song contest with 'Waterloo', and went on to be the most successful pop band of the 70s.

All four members had been involved in various projects prior to Abba. Bjorn Ulvaeus and Benny Andersson worked together as a production and songwriting team, while singers Agnetha Faltskog and Anni-Frid Lyngstad had careers as solo artists. The girls had sung backing vocals in a previous incarnation of the band, the awkwardly named 'Bjorn & Benny Agnetha & Anni-Frid'. Manager Stig Anderson suggested making the band's name an acronym of their first names, and 'Abba' was born. Ulvaeus and Faltskog were romantically paired, as were Andersson and Lyngstad; these relationships provided lyric material before eventually disintegrating in very public break-ups.

Abba's kitsch dress sense and goody-goody image led to the group's not being taken seriously in some quarters, and following the initial success of 'Waterloo', which was a worldwide hit, the group's popularity waned. However, the many critics who tried to write them off as one-hit wonders had seriously underestimated the songwriting and production talents of Andersson and Ulvaeus, the visual appeal of singers Agnetha and Anni-Frid, and – perhaps most importantly – the way the two girls' voices, although very different individually, blended together perfectly.

Abba's next hit, 'SOS', was a lavish production, a winning and dynamic combination of a tense minor-key verse dramatically contrasted with the huge Spector-esque sound of the chorus, complete with baroque-like keyboard flourishes and multi-layered vocals.

Imaginative instrumentation and arrangements abounded in Abba's music: the a cappella start to 'Take a chance on me'; the ethereal layered keyboards on 'Eagle'; the throbbing synthesizers on 'Does your mother know'; and the strange waltz time and hard rock combination of 'I'm a marionette', which is somewhat reminiscent of Kurt Weill. All the songs, however, shared the irresistible and instantly recognizable Abba vocal sound, which many producers of the girl/boy bands of the 90s and 2000s strove to emulate.

Abba attempted world domination with *Abba the Movie* (1978), a thinly veiled promotional tool for the accompanying soundtrack *Abba the Album*. Abba subsequently jumped on the disco bandwagon with *Voulez-Vous* (1979), though the change of style was mostly cosmetic, with the songs retaining their trademark big vocal harmonies.

The previous year Ulvaeus and Faltskog had divorced, followed by Andersson and Lyngstad only two years later. The break-up of their personal relationships was unflinchingly mirrored in songs like 'One of us', and perhaps most movingly in 'The winner takes it all' from *Super Trouper* (1980), where, in perhaps her best ever performance, Agnetha's soaring voice quivers with emotion.

The strain of working together following their divorces proved too much, and the band stopped collaborating, although they did not formally split up. Andersson and Ulvaeus went on to work with lyricist Tim Rice on the successful musical *Chess*, while the two girls pursued solo careers, with some success, though nothing to compare with their time in Abba.

In 1995 the Australian film *Muriel's Wedding* was released, prominently featuring Abba songs in the soundtrack. The film helped to bring Abba's music back into public consciousness, and sparked a host of tribute bands. Then in 1999 a musical, *Mamma Mia*, containing almost thirty of Abba's most popular songs, was staged in London and was an immediate success, demonstrating the enduring popularity of the band and their songs. The stage show is now running all over the world, and a hugely successful film adaption broke box office records in 2008.

FURTHER LISTENING

The more forward-looking trends in 70s pop were disco and punk, but much of the decade's music explored territory opened up in the 60s, as reflected in most of the following list.

Carole King *Tapestry* (1970)
This quiet, reflective album stayed in the charts for more than six years and includes, among other well-crafted songs 'You've got a friend' and 'I feel the earth move'. Part of the attraction of the album is King's unfussy vocal style and the incisive lyrics.

Simon and Garfunkel 'Bridge over troubled water' (1970)
A powerful but measured song about friendship and self-sacrifice which went to No. 1 on both sides of the Atlantic.

Lou Reed *Transformer* (1972)
After the Velvet Underground disbanded, Lou Reed achieved chart success with his second solo album, *Transformer*. David Bowie and Mick Ronson produced a collection of cool, laid-back songs which included 'Walk on the wild side', 'Perfect day' and 'Goodnight ladies', with lyrics of drugs, decadence and sexual ambiguity.

Stevie Wonder *Talking Book* (1972), *Innervisions* (1973), *Songs in the Key of Life* (1976)
Stevie Wonder had a sequence of outstanding albums in the mid-70s. His songs address racial, social and spiritual issues as well as themes of love. Originally a child prodigy in the Motown mould, Stevie Wonder has embraced many styles from soul to rock 'n' roll, jazz to reggae, and more. His music is characterized by his unique voice and melodic gift, coupled with often complex arrangements and contrasting textures.

Elton John *Goodbye Yellow Brick Road* (1973)
Elton John was at first marketed as a singer–songwriter, but soon proved that he could embrace more than one musical style. This album, penned with lyricist Bernie Taupin, opens with the progressive rock epic 'Funeral for a friend'. It includes the ballad 'Candle in the wind' (which went on to become the biggest-selling single of all time), and changes mood with the rock song 'Bennie and the jets'. This versatility, coupled with his kitsch theatricality, helped him to become one of the biggest pop superstars of the early 1970s.

Carly Simon *You're so vain* (1972)
Her biggest hit, with its famous line 'I bet you think this song is about you', prompted much speculation.

Queen 'Bohemian rhapsody' (1975)
With their enormous, visually spectacular tours, Queen (with Freddie Mercury) were unsurpassed at stadium rock. The pompous but inimitable single 'Bohemian rhapsody' (1975) is notable for its wildly ambitious, quasi-operatic style, its dense layers of overdubs (which made it difficult to perform live) and its length (nearly six minutes). Its pioneering promotional video was made on a shoestring budget of £4,500 in only four hours.

Cozy Powell 'Dance with the devil' (1973)
A legend on the British rock scene, Powell's heavy-hitting style helped to shape the early metal sound. He alternated between session work and stints in major rock bands including Whitesnake, Jeff Beck, Rainbow and Black Sabbath.

Ian Dury *New Boots and Panties!!* (1977)
Dury's pithy humorous lyrics are delivered in mock-Cockney slang to a tight stylish backing. Following his death, the album was remade with the title *Brand New Boots and Panties* (2001). Vocalists who joined the Blockheads on the new album include Robbie Williams, Madness, Billy Bragg and Shane MacGowan.

Bruce Springsteen *Born to Run* (1975)
'The Boss' was another stadium filler. *Born to Run* was much hyped beforehand but did not disappoint. The huge sound, enhanced by high-quality production, has been compared with Phil Spector's 'wall of sound'. Even after repeated hearings, the high-energy title track still has the power to make your hair stand on end.

Meatloaf *Bat Out of Hell* (1978)
Another exuberant performer, Meatloaf achieved worldwide success with this album. Written by Meatloaf's mentor Jim Steinman, this grandiose concept album has camp excesses of rock, heavy metal and opera. Strong melodies and powerful vocals are enriched by top quality production and full orchestra.

John Lennon 'Imagine' (1971)
The title track of John Lennon's 1971 solo album *Imagine* has become, like Bob Marley's 'One love', an anthem of aspiration, hope and trust.

The Eagles *Hotel California* (1977)
This album epitomized the laid-back West Coast sound, with its accessible songs, harmony vocals, and Joe Walsh's guitar, all based around the theme of coping with the LA rock style.

Van Morrison *Astral Weeks* (1968), *Moondance* (1970), *His Band and the Street Choir* (1970), *Tupelo Honey* (1971), *Saint Dominic's Preview* (1972) and *Veedon Fleece* (1974).
Van Morrison's haunting intense masterpiece *Astral Weeks*, worshipped by the critics, was the start of a creative period for Morrison. The music veers between soul, Celtic rock and jazz with intense, often melancholic, lyrics.

Dr John 'Such a night' (1973)
Dr John is best known as a boogie and blues pianist with a distinctive growling voice. His idiosyncratic personality and eccentric stage presence attracted a cult following, most of whom were unaware of his New Orleans session pedigree. 'Such a night' is taken from the album *In the Right Place*, recorded with the funk band the Meters.

Al Green 'I'm so tired of being alone' (1971), 'Let's stay together' (1972), 'I'm still in love with you' (1972)
Classic, soulful love songs from a gospel-influenced singer who went on to be a preacher. The early and mid-70s were his most fruitful period, with a series of albums produced in

Memphis by Willie Mitchell. Green's fluid and expressive voice is set off by tight rhythmic backing and terse, effective arrangements for strings and brass.

Max Romeo *War ina Babylon* (1976)
Powerful roots reggae with a social–political message, produced to perfection by Lee Perry. Max Romeo first made his name in 1968 with 'Wet dream', a song rude enough to earn a broadcasting ban, but re-emerged in 1971 as a committed Rastafarian.

Funkadelic 'Maggot brain' (1971)
A searing nine-minute guitar solo by Funkadelic's Eddie Hazel. At the recording session, George Clinton famously told his lead guitarist to 'play like your mother just died'.

Tom Robinson Band '2-4-6-8 motorway' (1978), 'Sing if you're (glad to be gay)' (1978)
'2-4-6-8 motorway' is an infectious single with a raucous sing-along chorus. Tom Robinson has been a political activist throughout his life and many of his songs have political themes. On its release, 'Glad to be gay' soon became a British gay anthem.

6

Toby Bricheno

Eighties

The 1980s saw a further splintering of musical styles, as independent labels sprang up during punk and its aftermath, and music technology progressed (especially MIDI and sampling), enabling new genres such as house and techno to exist. In what would be a decade of variety and experimentation in underground music, the 80s also witnessed considerable cross-fertilization between styles and genres.

Song structures increasingly moved away from the traditional pop templates: 12-bar blues and verse/chorus. One of dance music's innovations was the abandonment of traditional song structure in favour of a freer, more fantasia-like form.

The different styles of the decade can broadly be categorized into three areas:
- Post-punk guitar music
- Technology-influenced styles, especially in the dance-music revolution that followed house and techno, but including also rap
- Pop styles

This chapter follows these broad categories – though of course there are always groups and singers who do not fit the pattern; some of these are discussed towards the end of the chapter.

The 80s saw the rise of club culture, not only for dance styles but also to cater for a growing audience of fans of post-punk and indie music, who wanted a safe haven where they could listen and dance to the music they loved.

POST-PUNK GUITAR

Goth

The post-punk generation of pale, contemplative youths, who were too young to have been involved in the punk scene, admired its power and originality, but were deterred by its degeneration and by the skinhead-dominated burgeoning 'Oi' movement.[1] Goth began as a sub-genre of punk, but moved away from punk's simple raw power in a more considered and experimental direction. Gone were the non-stop chain-saw guitars (though they occasionally reappeared), thrashy rock drumming and political anger-laden vocals. In came angular, discordant guitars, tribal, tom-heavy drums and wailing, doom-laden singers. As the goth movement evolved, these earlier, more experimental attributes were replaced by a more conventional, rock-oriented sound. The vocal histrionics and decadent image of Ziggy-period

---

[1] Sometimes known as 'street punk', and much beloved by skinheads, Oi was an attempt to return to punk's imagined working-class roots, and was recognizable by its sing-along football-terrace-style songs and basic, everyday lyrics. A good example would be Sham 69's 'Hurry up Harry'.

Bowie were also influential; the biggest hit by goth band Bauhaus was a cover of Bowie's 'Ziggy Stardust'.

One band that bridged the gap between punk and goth were Siouxsie and the Banshees. Their earlier material, such as 'Love in a void', was straight-ahead punk. However, later tracks such as 'Playground twist' and 'Happy house' introduced chiming guitars, lurching, tribal drums, doleful bells, wailing vocals and disturbed, obsessive lyrics. While retaining elements of punk's energy and attitude, the resulting sound had a darker, more morose feel, which, coupled with Siouxsie Sioux's striking morbid palor and heavy, almost Egyptian eye-makeup (inspiring a legion of look-alike fans), laid the foundations for goth.

The Banshees were plagued with personnel problems, and at one point temporarily recruited a guitarist from another well-known goth band, the Cure. Although the Cure were more often classified as post-punk, they changed with the release of 'A forest' from their second album, *Seventeen Seconds* (1980). With its chorused, brooding guitars and anguished vocals, 'A forest' remains one of the defining songs of the goth œuvre. Then, following perhaps their bleakest album, *Pornography* (1982), the Cure took an increasingly quirky, pop-oriented direction and became a popular stadium band in the late 80s and 90s.

Bauhaus, named after the German art-movement, were probably the first band that could be described as pure goth. Formed in Northampton in 1978, they released 'Bela Lugosi's dead', a highly original nine-minute epic based around bossanova drums, which were used to trigger delays in a dub-like fashion. Nervy guitars, a doomy bass-line and singer Peter Murphy's vocal dramatics added to a tense, ghostly atmosphere. Their ground-breaking debut album, *In the Flat Field* (1979), was full of stark, discordant guitars and obliquely sexual, nightmarish lyrics that were far-detached from the by-now-foundering punk scene. 'Double dare', the first track on the album, was possibly the first song ever to feature distorted bass guitar. Daniel Ash's guitar-playing often made more use of noise than melodies, and, along with U2's the Edge and the Smiths' Johnny Marr, he was one of the most influential guitarists of the 80s. Bauhaus's live shows were also starkly innovative – the made-up, spiky-haired, black-clad performers, with only white lights, a TV monitor and a strobe added, made for an almost expressionist sense of theatre.

Sheila Rock/Rex Features

The Siouxsie Sioux look, 1982

Along with Bauhaus, the Sisters of Mercy were, if not the most original, then definitely the most imitated goth band. Initially accused of copying Joy Division, the band soon evolved a harder, rockier sound while maintaining a dark, brooding edge. The use of a drum machine in place of a drummer, paired with singer Andrew Eldritch's low, shuddering, often monotone voice (along with copious amounts of dry ice), set the precedent for many of the goth bands that followed. Likewise, the Sisters' dress code of motorbike jacket and dyed black hair was much emulated by fans. 'Alice' (1982) and 'Temple of love' (1983) both showcase the band's trademark drum-machine barrage alongside relentless single-string riffing and Eldritch's deep howl. Their most successful album, *Floodland* (1987), showed a change of direction, with keyboards becoming more prominent. Always keen on the grand gesture, Eldritch had recruited famed Meatloaf producer Jim Steinman, with predictably grandiose results, including the New York Choral Society performing on the track 'This corrosion'.

Even more than punk, goth was a complete lifestyle. As well as music, there was goth fashion (based on Siouxsie, Sid Vicious and Victoriana). Horror and occult literature (especially vampire literature, with its subtext of dark sexuality) was also influential, e.g. the fantastical and macabre H P Lovecraft and Edgar Allan Poe, as well as Neil Gaiman's *Sandman* graphic art novels. There were even goth holiday destinations, such as Whitby (linked to Bram Stoker's *Dracula*). Goth's phantasmagorical realm was a perfect refuge for the inward-looking, angst-ridden teenager, seeking to escape a drab and dull world. Though its popularity waned through the 90s, goth had a great influence on the industrial scene and its offshoots, including Marilyn Manson and Nine Inch Nails, especially in terms of image and lyrics.

The birth of 'indie'

Though its musical importance was declining, punk's 'have a go' philosophy was still being enacted. People started small record labels, independent of the majors, and began putting out the kind of records that they wanted to hear. In time, the word 'indie' not only referred to these small labels but also to the kind of music their bands played. In the UK, focus moved from London to the industrial cities of the North. Manchester in particular was to be of prime importance. Away from the capital's media glare, bands had more time to experiment, and three wildly differing groups emerged – the Fall, Joy Division and the Smiths.

Almost unclassifiable in any genre, the Fall formed in early 1977 in Manchester and are still active today, despite many personnel changes. Their cantankerous frontman Mark E Smith became well known for his caustic, cryptic lyrics, humorously laconic delivery and so-straight-it's-weird man-in-the-street dress sense. Influenced by the Velvet Underground, Can and the obligatory Sex Pistols, their almost shambolic music was challenging from the start, but found a champion in legendary BBC Radio 1 DJ John Peel (the Fall were his favourite band). Their early, idiosyncratic sound is captured on the album *Live at the Witch Trials* (1979), recorded in only two days. *This Nation's Saving Grace* (1985) has a tighter, more controlled sound, influenced by Smith's wife at the time, guitarist Brix Smith. *The Infotainment Scam* (1993) showed the Fall moving in a more commercial, dance-oriented direction, and remains perhaps their most accessible album.

Joy Division (then called the Stiff Kittens) formed in 1976 after being inspired by a Sex Pistols gig. They soon evolved a darker, more stripped-down sound than many of their contemporaries, more akin to the Velvet Underground. Singer Ian Curtis had an unusual, almost crooning voice, which when combined with his dark and troubled lyrics sounded light-years away from many other vocalists of the time. Bass player Peter Hook had a distinctively melodic style which would be emulated by many bassists of the 80s. Though they released only two albums, the influence of Joy Division on the post-punk bands of the 80s is almost impossible to overstate. The combination of Curtis's individualistic voice and the band's sombre sound virtually kick-started the goth movement, and the influence can be heard in countless bands including Echo and the Bunnymen and the Sisters of Mercy.

After receiving praise for their first album, *Unknown Pleasures* (1979), the band were about to embark on their first US tour when tragedy struck. On 18 May 1980, Curtis, who had struggled with illness and depression, hanged himself in his Macclesfield home. He was 23. Less than two months later, their second and final album, *Closer*, was released, and the band had a top-twenty hit with the non-album single 'Love will tear us apart'. The song has since being covered many times by artists as diverse as Paul Young, P J Proby and U2.

The remaining members went on to form the very successful New Order. Their biggest hit, 'Blue Monday' (1983), was an early example of the combination of dance and rock music which became increasingly popular in the late 80s and early 90s. 'Blue Monday' remains the UK's biggest-selling 12-inch single to date.

Impresario Tony Wilson signed Joy Division to his Manchester label, Factory Records. Wilson had previously hosted a Granada TV new-music programme called *So it Goes*, which featured up-and-coming bands.[2] Factory was very design conscious, and catalogued everything; flyers, badges, even TV programmes, had a catalogue number. The highly idiosyncratic Factory signed various weird and wonderful acts, including the unruly Happy Mondays.

Another Manchester band, the Smiths, signed with the London-based Rough Trade label.[3] The volatile songwriting partnership of singer Morrissey and guitarist Johnny Marr proved to be extremely fruitful, if not particularly successful commercially. Despite having only three top-ten UK hit singles, the Smiths gained a legion of adoring fans and masses of critical acclaim until their split in the late 80s. (See the profile at the end of the chapter.)

The guitar hero returns

Despite the explosion of new, innovative bands that appeared in punk's wake, many stadium bands such as Queen, Genesis and Aerosmith continued to have widespread success. Van Halen and Canada's Bryan Adams were popular with people deterred by the often challenging and uncommercial music made by the post-punk bands, or with those from an older generation who mourned the passing of the 70s 'rock gods' such as Led Zeppelin. Meanwhile, a younger generation was preparing to resurrect the 'guitar hero'.

Virtuosic rock guitarist Steve Vai set new standards in technical ability. His playing makes use of rapid scales and arpeggios with extensive exploration of effects, processors and the tremolo arm. The Van Halen brothers – guitarist Eddie and drummer Alex – formed Van Halen in the 70s but had their biggest success in the 80s with their melodic hard-rock sound. Eddie Van Halen's 'Eruption', an almost two-minute guitar solo full of lightning-fast playing, squeals, tapping and divebombs,[4] heralded the return of technical virtuosity on the guitar. Van Halen's advanced palette of techniques inspired a whole new generation of guitarists to practise away in their bedrooms, and many similar bands, such as Bon Jovi and England's Def Leppard, enjoyed considerable success. The tight spandex trousers and generally archaic attitudes of some of these bands were cleverly parodied in the mock-documentary film *This is Spinal Tap* (1984).

The obsession with image eventually brought about 'glam metal' (a.k.a. 'hair metal') in the mid-80s. Mostly centered on Los Angeles, bands like Poison and Mötley Crüe played a brand of melodic metal, replete with over-coiffured hair, make-up and dandyish clothes, the accent being more on looks than music.

A rawer, harder-edged form known as 'speed metal' was also evolving, influenced by the new wave of British heavy metal bands such as Motorhead as well as by the US hardcore

---

[2] Including, in their day, the Sex Pistols and the Buzzcocks.

[3] Rough Trade started as a shop specializing in reggae and punk, and then expanded into an indie record label and distribution network, releasing records by the Fall, Stiff Little Fingers, Cabaret Voltaire and countless other indie bands of the 80s.

[4] Tapping is a technique whereby the guitarist taps the neck with the strumming hand, enabling very fast playing. Divebombing allows drastic changes of pitch obtained via the locking tremolo arm.

scene.[5] Highly technical and somewhat difficult to master, speed metal ran at furiously fast tempos, but it soon mutated into a genre known as 'thrash metal', which featured extreme changes of tempo and dense, doubled-tracked guitars. Thrash mainly hailed from the US West Coast (Metallica, Slayer) and New York (Anthrax). Both Anthrax and Metallica (and their offshoot Megadeth) went on to be incredibly successful bands, selling millions of records. Their belligerent, pummelling sound and angry, quasi-punk attitude proved very popular with US youth. Megadeth acknowledged the influence of punk on their sound with a cover of 'Anarchy in the UK' on their platinum-selling album *So Far, So Good... So What!* (1988). Their influence on the nu-metal movement of the late 90s and early 2000s can be heard in the dense textures and high degree of proficiency.

A band that had the tough attitude of thrash, but with a more traditional hard-rock sound and a touch of hair-rock glam were Guns N' Roses. Though founded in LA, they were a much more hard-hitting and decadent proposal than the hair-metal bands. The original cover for their debut album, *Appetite for Destruction* (1987), featured a girl being raped by a robot, and was quickly replaced with less offensive, rather bland artwork, echoing the infamous 'Smell the glove' scene from *This is Spinal Tap*. Despite the large amount of publicity it generated, the album did not sell in large numbers until the video for the single 'Sweet child o' mine' received frequent rotation on MTV.[6] The album then went multi-platinum and continues to sell well to this day.

TECHNOLOGY TAKING HOLD

Synthesizer bands

Guitars did not have it all their own way in the 80s. Encouraged by the falling price of technology, and new instruments such as programmable drum machines becoming available, a new genre emerged which was later named 'Futurist', after an Italian art-movement of the early twentieth century which was fascinated with the emerging technology of the time (such as the car). The original futurists proposed, for instance, making music from unconventional sources such as car horns and klaxons. The roots of pop futurism go back to the 70s, when the highly experimental, dadaist-influenced Cabaret Voltaire formed in 1973 and employed tape loops and experimental techniques,[7] which had more in common with 'serious' composers like Stockhausen than with pop music. Cabaret Voltaire's 'Nag nag nag' (1979) fused punk's aggression and attitude with harsh filtered synthesizers and drum machines to make a genuinely new sound. (Developments in music technology are discussed more fully in Chapters 10, 11 and 12.)

Probably the biggest influence on futurism was the German band Kraftwerk ('power station' in English). Formed in 1970, Kraftwerk eschewed guitars in favour of synthesizers. The band's technology-infused lyrics and cool, detached sound covered such non-traditional areas as radioactivity, robots and the (then hi-tech) pocket calculator. In addition, the vocals were often treated by a vocoder, further increasing the synthetic feel of the music. This instrument combines two sounds (commonly that of a voice and a synthesizer) and uses one to modulate, or affect, the other, resulting in a highly synthetic, robotic sound. The vocoder became very popular in 80s and late 90s dance music.

The image of the robot is very important to us... we always found that many people are robots

---

[5] A new style of heavy metal suffused by the energy of punk, with Deep Purple-style vocals, including bands such as Iron Maiden and Praying Mantis.

[6] A television station launched in the 80s which was then totally committed to pop music.

[7] Dada was an anti-art movement, bordering on the surreal and challenging traditional notions of what art should be. It emerged early in the twentieth century, born out of the horror of World War I, and of disdain for the bourgeoisie.

without knowing it. In Paris, the people go in the Metro, they move, they go into offices, 8 o'clock in the morning – it's like remote control.

Kraftwerk's Florian Schneider in the late 70s.

Interestingly, their UK hit 'The model' was the only song written about a human on their album *The Man Machine* (1978). Notoriously tight-lipped, giving very few interviews or photo sessions, Kraftwerk evolved a uniform image, with all four members often identically dressed. Highly influential on such acts as New Order, Beck and especially David Bowie, Kraftwerk's often repetitive music was also to be an influence on both electro and techno.[8]

Kraftwerk's dispassionate, almost dehumanized style was evident in bands such as Ultravox and Tubeway Army (named after a gang who used to beat up tube passengers at random). The latter's singer and mainstay, former glam-rock obsessive Gary Numan, dressed in a similar way to the members of Kraftwerk, in utilitarian black clothes. Though Tubeway Army began life as a punky guitar band, Numan was inspired after experimenting with a synthesizer left behind at a band rehearsal. The band's sound gradually became more reliant on synthesizers and electronic percussion, while Numan invented a ghostly android-like persona with lyrics conjuring up a future nightmare world to match. The outlandish image, eerie music and cold, detached lyrics proved to be a commercial success, and the band had a No. 1 UK hit in 1979 with 'Are "friends" electric?'. Numan subsequently embarked on a solo career, having several hits including 'Cars' and 'Complex' before fading from the public eye. His career was resuscitated when Armand van Helden sampled 'Cars' for his 2000 hit 'Koochy', and 'Are friends electric?' was used as the basis for the Sugababes' 2002 hit 'Freak like me'.

Almost the antithesis of punk's bile and fury, the combination of futurism's somewhat dark, alienated lyrics and stark, unnatural image meant that there were similarities with the goth movement, but as a whole futurism was a more dispassionate affair compared to goth's obsession with sex and death. Initially, the Human League, with ominous synthesizers and synthesized drums on the proto-electro 'Being boiled', were included in the futurist canon. But following the departure of two of their members and the recruitment of two girl singers (spotted dancing in a Sheffield nightclub by frontman Phil Oakey), the band headed in a more pop-oriented direction, though still using synthesizers as the basis of their sound. The resulting album, *Dare* (1981), is notable for doing away with the distant, icy futurist sound and replacing it with hummable tunes and boy-meets-girl lyrics. The album achieved enormous success, charting at No. 1 in both the US and UK, and included the hit single 'Don't you want me baby'. With *Dare*, the band had made the transition from futurist to synth pop. As punk combined with pop to give birth to new wave and punk pop, the futurist sound similarly married to a pop sensibility, with jaunty tunes. The synthesizer now ruled much as the guitar had done in previous decades. More and more synth-pop bands and artists appeared – Orchestral Manoeuvres in the Dark, Thomas Dolby, Howard Jones, Soft Cell, and of course the synth-pop band *ne plus ultra* – Depeche Mode.

Initially pop-lightweights with breezy songs like 'Just can't get enough', Depeche Mode changed direction drastically following the departure of their main songwriter, Vince Clark, in 1981. The band evolved a darker sound which, although heavily synthesizer-oriented, also made use of emerging digital technology (such as the sampler) to capture harsh 'industrial' sounds. The content of the lyrics also followed an increasingly melancholic direction, addressing such subjects as religion and sado-masochism. Depeche Mode's harsh, gloomy sound and subject matter began to generate interest in the goth world. The combination of technologically driven sounds and goth sensibilities became a big influence on the industrial scene of the late 80s and early 90s, and on bands such as Nine Inch Nails, Skinny Puppy and Ministry.

After its peak in the early 80s, synth pop cross-pollinated with synthesizer-heavy Moroder-influenced disco and the HiNRG scene to produce a more dance-oriented sound.

---

[8] Seminal electro artist Afrika Bambaataa famously sampled two Kraftwerk tracks on his 1982 hit 'Planet rock'.

The Pet Shop Boys were an intriguing combination of a reedy-voiced ex-music-journalist and a technical boffin. They brought witty, ironic lyrics, glamour and grandiose arrangements, courtesy of producer Trevor Horn.

Horn, more than any other producer, defined the mid-80s sound – chunky, funky drums and lashings of Fairlight samples, producing enormous soundscapes of pristine sound-quality. Probably two of the best examples are 'Close to the edit' (1984) by Horn's band the Art of Noise and 'Two tribes' by Frankie Goes To Hollywood.

Frankie Goes To Hollywood were spotted by Horn playing 'Relax' on the UK music programme *The Tube*. Despite a rather rough-and-ready performance, Horn saw the potential of a mixed gay/straight band dressed in quasi-S&M gear singing the lyrics 'Relax, don't do it, when you want to come'. After Horn's pounding tech-disco makeover, the song was banned by the BBC for the offending lyrics, thereby guaranteeing success (it went to No. 1 in the UK charts in 1983).

Hip-hop culture, electro and rap

Though punk ruled the roost of the white urban underground in the UK in the late 70s, it provoked little interest in the urban black areas of the USA. They had their own under-ground culture – hip-hop. The term 'hip-hop' refers to US urban black culture of the late 60s onwards: DJ-ing, graffiti art, breakdancing, MC-ing and 'rap'. The term 'rap' was retrospectively imposed onto hip-hop music by record companies. However, it is widely synonymous with hip-hop, and we will use the term 'rap' from here on.

There were similarities with punk; hip-hop music, like punk, was an underground movement, largely unsupported (and unrecognized) by the major labels of the time. One major difference, though, was that while punk used nothing but live bands, hip-hop was *unthinkable* without DJs. It was in the hip-hop community that the idea of DJs as artists in their own right, combining and manipulating existing recordings into something new, first took root.

Rap was born in the Bronx area of New York in the 70s, though its vocal origins lie in the Jamaican 'toasting' tradition. Toasting is a vocal technique – a cross between talking and rhythmic chanting – that was originally practised by Jamaican MCs. Since its birth, rap has always focused on rhythm rather than melody and harmony – a hint, perhaps, of African origins, as tribal African music can be highly complex rhythmically without recourse to melody.

Black DJs such as Afrika Bambaataa, Barbados-born Grandmaster Flash and the Jamaican-born 'father of hip-hop', Kool Herc, extended the drumming sections (or 'breaks') from records by mixing between two identical copies of the same record. Some of the DJs emulated the Jamaican 'toasting' style over the top of these breaks, announcing their presence at the parties and clubs and generally proclaiming their mixing skills. Short phrases became longer, and the DJs who did this became known as emcees (or MCs). This practice of 'MC-ing' over the breakbeat section of records was the origin of rap. Graffiti art became part of the hip-hop lifestyle, and the dangerous procedure known as 'tagging', whereby scrawled signatures were sprayed in ever more difficult-to-reach places (such as subway trains and bridges) became widespread. A highly skilled style of dance also evolved called 'break-dancing' (so called because dancers hit the floor during the extended break sections played by the DJs), incorporating martial arts moves and gymnastics as well as head- and back-spinning, and was even featured in the mainstream 1983 film *Flashdance*. Breakdancing 'battles' occurred when rival gangs of dancers (or 'crews') tried to outdo each other with feats of technical skill.

Initially the only available recordings were cassette bootlegs of the DJs' live performances at clubs and 'house' or 'block' parties. These tapes were played by fans on the street on large portable stereos which became known as 'ghettoblasters'. However, the potential market was recognized, and Sugarhill Records was founded to put out the kind of music heard at the clubs and parties. In 1979 the label released 'Rapper's delight' by the Sugarhill Gang, which appropriated the bass-line and drums from Chic's 'Good times'. It was a smash hit far beyond its home territory of black inner-city New York, putting rap on the map and crossing racial and cultural boundaries, as well setting a precedent for hip-hop and rap artists to do raps over other artists' well-known records.

Grandmaster Flash was a highly accomplished technical DJ, scratching and mixing together Queen and Blondie along with funky breakbeats on his 1981 release 'Wheels of steel', the first record to capture live scratching. In collaboration with rapper Melle Mel (who was credited with writing the first full-length raps, as opposed to the short phrases which were prevalent at the time) he produced the 1982 hit 'The message' – a no-holds-barred depiction of life in the ghetto. A far cry from the boasting and bragging of previous rappers, it set the tone for many a rap. They also worked together on the anti-cocaine anthem 'White lines'. Both records used programmed rather than 'live' drums, showing the influence of the burgeoning electro scene.

A recording by four white Germans – Kraftwerk's *Trans-Europe Express* – was having an enormous impact on black American dance music. Kraftwerk's cool, precise music was combined by Afrika Bambaataa and producer Arthur Baker with the earthy rhythms of hip-hop to make Bambaataa's 'Planet Rock', ushering in a new genre called electro-funk – or 'electro', as it became more widely known. Electro also incorporated the robotic bleeps of the arcade video-game machines that were popular at the time.

As electro grew more popular, non-hip-hop artists began to get in on the act, most memorably jazz musician Herbie Hancock in his collaboration with Bill Laswell and Zulu DJ Grandmixer DST on 'Rockit'. Full of computer bleeps, scratching and tight, programmed drums, 'Rockit' took electro from a New York underground movement to mainstream acceptance, winning a coveted Grammy award. The Rock Steady Crew, a breakdancing collective, were spotted by the ever-curious Malcolm McLaren performing at a Bow Wow Wow gig. McLaren was inspired, and recorded 'Buffalo gals' with Trevor Horn and the World Famous Supreme Team, resulting in a UK top-ten hit in 1982. With further releases such as 'Soweto' and 'Double Dutch', McLaren incorporated Zulu musicians, anticipating Paul Simon's use of African musicians on *Graceland*.

More and more labels were springing up, Def Jam being of prime importance; on its roster were artists such as Run-DMC, Public Enemy and the first white rap group, the Beastie Boys.

Run-DMC were not from a deprived background, but a more comfortable suburban area of New York. The stripped-down sound of their first album, *Run-DMC*, contained probably the first ever rock/rap track, 'Rock box'. This combination was further explored on their second album, *King of Rock*, which brought a harder edge to rap. The connection between rock and rap had its first hit when the band collaborated with Aerosmith on a re-make of the rock band's 'Walk this way', resulting in a worldwide hit that resurrected Aerosmith's faltering career. As a consequence of this cross-over appeal, the album went platinum and Run-DMC were the first rap outfit to be played on MTV.

The Beastie Boys were no strangers to guitars, having started as a mediocre hardcore band before evolving into a raucous, rap outfit. Shunning the James Brown samples of black hip-hop, and initially apolitical,[9] the band plundered the music that reflected their white, affluent upbringing, sampling rock bands such as AC/DC and Led Zeppelin on tracks like 'Fight for your right (to party)'. In no position to sing about racist oppression, the band instead chose to sing about what they knew – being young, rebelling against parents, and hell-raising in general. Their penchant for wearing Volkswagen pendants caused a rash of car-badge thefts. Initially dismissed as one-hit wonders, the band later became more experimental. On their second album, *Paul's Boutique* (1989), the Dust Brothers production team infused the Beastie Boys' sound with 70s funk. Now located in California, the band made an album that can be read as a love letter to the Beasties' native New York, full of in-jokes and

---

[9] Later, one member, Adam Yauch, converted to Buddhism, and the band have since held various benefits to raise consciousness over China's annexation of Tibet.

references to their home city. Though not a commercial success, the album has a chopped-up, almost psychedelic sound that can be heard as an influence on the music of 90s hip-hop misfit Beck.

Supporting on the Beastie Boys' 'Licence to Ill' tour were black hip-hop outfit Public Enemy. A very different proposition to the Beastie Boys, Public Enemy have been described as the 'black Sex Pistols', and became the most influential hip-hop act of their time. Unlike the misogynistic, violence-obsessed lyrics of gangster rap, those of Public Enemy's Chuck D railed against the white establishment, while fellow-rapper Flavor Flav brought light relief.

Their 1988 album, *It Takes a Nation of Millions to Hold Us Back*, is a ferocious collage of James Brown samples, saxophone squeals and brutal beats, with Chuck D's anti-establishment polemic balanced by Flavor Flav's tomfoolery. The following year, Richard Griffin, Public Enemy's 'Minister of Information', was ejected from the band following comments made to the *Washington Post*.[10] More controversy arose from the band's endorsement of controversial Muslim activist Louis Farrakhan. In addition, their entourage of dancers – Security of the First World – were dressed in military uniforms reminiscent of the black supremacist movement the Black Panthers. The collaboration with metal band Anthrax on a reworked version of 'Bring the noise' was critically well received and a commercial success, pointing the way forward for the metal/rap cross-over artists of the 90s such as Rage Against the Machine and Limp Bizkit.

By the mid-80s, rap had crossed the continent and a West Coast scene was beginning to emerge. With more emphasis on a funk feel, this was where gangster (or 'gangsta' rap) first took hold, with hard-hitting lyrics about violence, guns and drugs.

Los Angeles was the birthplace of NWA (Niggers With Attitude), whose dynamic, aggressive sound, controversial lyrics and confrontational attitude marked them out for media attention. The expletive-laden title song from their *Straight Outta Compton* (1988) album is NWA at their toughest and rawest – a break, a one-note horn sample, raps and very little else. Ironically, NWA's audience was predominantly white, no doubt impressed by NWA's profane language, tales of violent ghetto life and gun-toting stance, which was in stark contrast to the poodle rock and fading hardcore scene of the time. Their most controversial song was 'Fuck tha police' which resulted in a warning to their record label from the FBI. Ice Cube, possibly their most talented rapper, left shortly afterwards, briefly guesting with Public Enemy whilst NWA slowly disintegrated.

The lurid cover artwork and often violent and profane lyrics of rap were attracting increasing interest in the US from the likes of the infamous Parents' Music Resource Center (PRMC), an organization of self-appointed moral guardians fronted by Tipper Gore. The PRMC successfully lobbied for the 'parental advisory' warning sticker that by 2001 adorned three out of five rap albums. Wal-mart refused to stock recordings sporting a parental advisory sticker, causing many acts, including Public Enemy and Busta Rhymes, to do 'clean' versions of their releases with the offending words and/or artwork replaced, specifically to sell at such stores. Miami outfit 2 Live Crew were particularly notorious; their album *As Nasty As They Wanna Be* was banned in six states, mainly over the lyrical content of the track 'Me so horny'. Rap was not alone in attracting the attention of the PRMC; rock and pop artists such as Marilyn Manson, Madonna, Prince and even John Denver came under scrutiny.

Rap continued to grow in popularity in the 90s, and, with less controversial acts such as the slick and squeaky-clean MC Hammer, rap gained mainstream acceptance. However, all was not rosy in hip-hop's garden: inter-gang troubles and East Coast / West Coast rivalry bubbled over into murder. West Coast rapper 2Pac Shakur and the Notorious B.I.G. from New York were killed within six months of one another in 1996. Another victim of violence was Run DMC's Jam Master Jay, who was shot dead in his studio in 2002.

---

[10] Griff was quoted as saying, 'Jews are responsible for the majority of wickedness that goes on across the globe,' to *Washington Post* journalist David Mills.

HOUSE AND TECHNO

From any perspective, house owes its existence to disco – the four-on-the-floor bass drum, syncopated hi-hats and soulful vocals can all be traced back to disco. What *was* new was the way that 80s technology had opened up different ways of creating music. The introduction of MIDI in the early 80s enabled one musician to control many different electronic instruments (by using either an internal or external sequencer) with ease, and affordably. The short, repeating patterns of house music were facilitated, even encouraged, by the technology available, which initially did not allow long patterns to be programmed.

House

The origin of the word 'house' in a musical context goes back to the Warehouse club in late-70s Chicago, where a New York DJ, Frankie Knuckles, played disco, funk and soul to a mainly gay audience. By the early 80s, however, new releases in these styles were becoming increasingly rare, forcing Knuckles to find new ways of keeping the crowd happy:

> I had to re-construct the records to work for my dancefloor, to keep the dancefloor happy, as there was no dance music coming out! I'd take the existing songs, change the tempo, layer different bits of percussion over them, to make them more conducive for the dancefloor.
>
> Frankie Knuckles quoted on www.jahsonic.com

European acts such as Kraftwerk, and producers such as Giorgio Moroder, were very popular in the US Midwest cities of Chicago and Detroit. Their electronic sounds were wedded to disco and funk cuts to produce a sound that was harder than disco and more danceable than Kraftwerk.

More and more clubs sprang up, and it was in these that house's defining attributes took shape. Knuckles began to employ the equipment available to him – a reel-to-reel tape recorder to lengthen and alter the mixes and a Roland 909 drum machine to emphasize the four bass drums to the bar that defines house. Another DJ, Ron Hardy, used two versions of the same record to prolong the mixes (much as New York DJ Kool Herc had done previously), as well as introducing harder, almost industrial sounds into the mix. This new, tougher sound appealed to members of the straight black community in Chicago.

Postal worker Marshall Jefferson heard Hardy DJ-ing and, despite having no traditional musical skills, felt inspired to create some tracks himself. His resulting hit, 'Move your body' (1986), became one of the most sampled Chicago house tracks ever. Jefferson could not play keyboards, so he wrote the keyboard riff directly into the sequencer. The resulting unusual chord sequence was to a have an enormous influence, especially on acid house.

As a producer, Jefferson would also play a part in the release of the first Chicago house track to utilize the soon-to-be-legendary Roland TB-303. Initially made to replace a human bass-player, the 303's quirky, unrealistic sound doomed it to failure when first released. However, it was precisely that idiosyncratic nature (and affordability, due to many unwanted 303s being put up for sale) which later made such an indelible mark on the evolution of dance music. Chicago DJs Pierre, Spanky and Herb Jackson were searching for a bass sound for a new track when DJ Pierre started twiddling the knobs of a 303 while a sequence was actually playing, instead of leaving them static. The resulting squelching, ever-changing sound was unlike anything they had ever heard. Lasting a marathon eleven minutes, 'Acid trax' uses only the 303 and a drum machine,[11] with interest generated by the dub-like dropping in and out of the drum machine's instruments, and especially the constantly filtering 303. It was a move away from the other house music of the time, featuring no vocals and no 'hooks' other than the disjointed 303 riff. The track was a quantum leap in dance music – no 'live' performers are involved, apart from twiddling the 303's control knobs. The final studio version

---

[11] The origin of the word 'acid' in a dance music context is unclear. Whether it refers to the way the 303 bassline 'burns' into the track, or to the hallucinogen LSD (a.k.a. acid), widely available in clubs in the mid-80s, has never been determined.

of the track was subsequently produced by Marshall Jefferson, and two years later, in 1987, 'Acid trax' by Phuture was finally released on the Trax label.

Early house tracks were often played on tape machines in the clubs. The new electronic-based sound soon gained massive popularity, and demand for vinyl versions of the tracks grew, resulting in what is generally agreed to be the first ever house record, 'On and on' by Jesse Saunders and Vince Lawrence, which was released in 1983. Saunders' reworking of an old Isaac Hayes song, 'Love can't turn around', in collaboration with Farley 'Jackmaster' Funk became the first international house hit in 1986. After a fairly innocuous start, with male vocal and tinkling programmed hi-hats, the track explodes in a maelstrom of pum-melling drum machine, orchestral 'stab' samples and a furious snare-drum roll. Such features became staples of house for many years.

Meanwhile in New York, a different style was emerging: garage, named after a club called the Paradise Garage. Though it played a wide range of music, the venue became known for a more traditional, gospel-inflected sound, with more emphasis on singing ability than in house. The classic early garage track 'Don't make me wait' by the Peech Boys is reputedly one of the most sampled recordings in history.

Techno

With Chicago the birthplace of house, Detroit is the original home of techno. The story begins in the late 70s when Detroit DJ Charles Johnson (a.k.a. 'Electrifying Mojo') played a wildly eclectic selection of music on his radio show, ignoring the generally racially segregated programming which was prevalent at the time. One of his favourite albums was Kraftwerk's *Computer World*, which he often played in its entirety, alongside black acts like Parliament and Funkadelic. The innovative combination of black funk and white electronica was not lost on Johnson's listeners, in particular black high-school friends Derrick May, Juan Atkins and Kevin Saunderson. The 'Belleville Three', as they became known, invented the sound known as 'Detroit techno'. While bearing similarities to house, its leaner, less exuberant sound is clearly evident in Detroit techno's defining moment: 'No UFOs' by Juan Atkins (in the guise of Model 500). Released in 1985, 'No UFOs' is a mesh of backwards electronic sound effects and chattering chords over an ominous synthesizer bass-line. Unlike many house records, it is devoid of soulful vocals and generally has a colder, less uplifting feel.

Derrick May gave techno its first mainstream success in 1989 with Rhythim is Rhythim's 'Strings of life'. Although a smoother, jazzier track than Atkins' effort, its mechanistic, syncopated sampled strings reveal its Detroit lineage.

House was generating interest across the Atlantic, and many European DJs and producers came to Chicago eager to find out more. Being close to Chicago, Detroit was also explored. As a result, techno began to take off in Europe, especially Britain and Germany, while remaining very much an underground phenomenon in the US.

By the early 90s, techno was hugely popular in Europe, despite being sidelined by the Americans, who were still rather suspicious of anything with a direct link to disco. From its Afro-American roots in Detroit, techno became a white, European concern.

House and acid house in the UK

By 1987, UK DJs were playing house and techno. Soon British artists were coming up with their own versions. The main differences between the US and UK scenes were:

- Drugs – LSD ('acid') and the mild hallucinogen MDMA (a.k.a. Ecstasy) were closely linked with the emergent dance culture in the UK. Ecstasy is a psychedelic ampheta-mine that promotes strong feelings of well-being, empathy and connection to others. It was originally used to treat psychological problems.

- Sampling – UK dance producers had a more cavalier attitude to sampling than their US compatriots. Also, technology was becoming cheaper and more powerful, allowing longer samples to be taken.

- Race and sexual orientation – Although a mainly gay scene at first, the advent of home-grown house tracks and the rash of clubs that sprang up in London led house and techno to became a mixed black/white, straight/gay phenomenon.

Two of the first UK house tracks (known as 'tunes' by the UK dance music fraternity) to chart were 'Pump up the volume' by M/A/R/R/S (1987) and 'Theme from S'Express' by S'Express (1988). Both tracks made heavy use of the increasingly omnipotent sampler, with 'Pump up the volume' taking a cut-and-paste approach, jumping between different breaks, and an eclectic selection of samples, including what sounds like Arabic wailing and guitar feedback. S'Express cheekily plundered the intro synth and brass hook from Rose Royce's disco classic 'Is it love you're after' and laid them over a house loop interlaced with kitsch vocal samples. Both records made No. 1 in the UK, demonstrating how house was becoming a mainstream genre there.

The Spanish island of Ibiza had been a haven for hippies and people seeking an alternative way of life since the 70s, and a club scene that would explode in the 90s had already taken root in the 80s. Ibiza DJs in clubs like Amnesia and Pasha were playing such disparate artists as U2, Penguin Café Orchestra and Nitzer Ebb, alongside house and techno. This 'grab bag' philosophy of mixing together different genres became known as the 'Balearic sound' or 'Balearic beat'.[12] The ready availability of Ecstasy on Ibiza fuelled the easy-going attitude and lack of self-consciousness which was to typify the dance scene in the UK in the coming years.

DJs and club-goers alike wanted to recreate the vibe and sounds of Ibiza back home in the UK. DJ Paul Oakenfold flew the originator of the Balearic sound – Argentinean DJ Alfredo – from Ibiza to play at Oakenfold's new club in London in 1987. The handful of Ibiza veterans set the tone:

> The look was a weird mix of Mediterranean beach bum, hippy and football casual – baggy trousers and T-shirts, paisley bandanas, dungarees, ponchos... – loose-fitting, because the Ecstasy and non-stop trance dancing made you sweat buckets.
>
> Reynolds (1998)

Soon a new sound began to emerge, based on the array of different sounds heard at these clubs: acid house. One of the earliest acid house releases was Baby Ford's sample-intensive 'Oochy koochy'. A discordant, burbling 303 reminiscent of 'Acid trax' is combined with a house loop, deep synthesizer bass, piano, and a grainy, Detroit techno-like riff to create a disorienting, psychedelic but highly funky web of sound.

A key difference between the late-80s dance culture and that of the late 70s was that disco clubs were about dancing well, dressing sharp and *being seen*. The acid-house clubs were all about 'letting go', dancing with people you did not know, to music you did not know, spurred on by the bonding effects of Ecstasy. The image of the 'nightclub' of 70s Britain – playing Jeff Beck's 'Hi ho silver lining' to a crowd of boozed-up, leering office workers – was being replaced by a new image of late teens to early 30s dancing quite literally *all night* to innovative electronic music, with not a fight in sight.

POP TRENDS

New romantics

In Britain in the early 80s, a new type of sound arrived – a combination of new wave and synth pop with more traditional 'straight' pop. It started in London clubs such as Billy's and later the Blitz, where DJs played a mixture of 70s glam and disco alongside the emerging electronic acts of the time such as Gary Numan and the ubiquitous Kraftwerk. Almost as important as the music in these clubs was the dress code. The idea was to look as glammy as possible – the more outrageous the better, with the boys trying to outdo the girls in every

---

[12] Ibiza is one of the Balearic islands.

area, including make-up. Several bands emerged from these clubs, including Visage (who had a hit in 1980 with the synth-pop track 'Fade to grey') and Spandau Ballet. Picking up a statement by Spandau Ballet's producer, Richard Burgess, the press adopted the term 'New Romantic' to describe these bands.

Dressed in frilly romantic period costumes and kilts, Spandau Ballet had their first hit with 'To cut a long story short' in 1980. The song was a combination of a speeded-up disco groove overlaid with white funk guitars and a nagging synth riff, topped by the powerful voice of Tony Hadley. Later they honed their sound: Hadley adopted a smoother, almost crooning style, which the band complemented by moving in a slick, more soul-oriented direction. This change of style brought the band top-ten hits in the US and UK, winning them a legion of young female fans.

Not all of the new romantic bands were spawned from London clubland. Again taking disco, synth pop and new wave as their starting point, Birmingham's Duran Duran became one of the movement's highest-profile bands, and were one of the first bands to exploit the music video as a way of marketing their music. Their early videos, such as 'Girls on film', caused controversy in the UK over the band's use of sexual imagery. Videos for later songs such as 'Rio' and 'Save a prayer' featured exotic locations around the world, lending the band a glamorous, jet-setting image. Duran Duran's music became more polished, if less adventurous, and they ruled the charts in the UK in the early/mid 80s, with ten top-ten hits from 1982 to 1986. With their mainstream audience they became, like Spandau Ballet, teen idols.

New romantic's gender-bending look was taken to an extreme by former Blitz cloakroom attendant George O'Dowd (better known as Boy George) and friend/rival Marilyn, both of whom were frequently mistaken for girls when they first appeared on national TV. Boy George's band, Culture Club, became successful almost immediately, thanks to George's heavily made-up, cross-dressing image coupled with the band's polished, soul-influenced pop sound. Their first hit, 'Do you really want to hurt me,' went to No. 1 in the UK and was swiftly followed by six consecutive top-ten hits, as well as comparable success in the US. Culture Club was one of the first post-new-wave bands, in that their sound and image had nothing to do with the punk explosion of the late 70s. Indeed, as Boy George himself said, it was as if 'punk never happened'.

'Pure pop'

In contrast, UK two-piece Wham! were down-the-line pop – no frills, just generally up-tempo, feel-good songs covering such teen-oriented subjects as unemployment and jealous girlfriends (despite lead singer George Michael's being gay). Wham! achieved great success in the mid-80s on both sides of the Atlantic and was one of the first Western pop acts to tour in China. Their brand of carefree pop set the stage for the likes of British boy-band Bros and the deluge of similar acts that followed in the 90s.

One common factor in many mainstream pop acts of 80s Britain was the production trio of (Mike) Stock, (Matt) Aitken and (Pete) Waterman. In total the trio racked up more than 140 hits for artists such as Kylie Minogue, Jason Donovan,[13] Sonia, and Rick Astley.

Stylistically a cross between HiNRG, white soul and sugary hook-laden pop, S.A.W.'s rather formulaic brand of pure pop was loved and loathed in equal measure. The songs were easy to sing: a definite advantage given the non-musical origins and limited technique of many of their vocalists, but also making them popular with an audience who could sing along with the records. Most of the songs were breezy, with lyrics about love (requited or unrequited), and were lapped up by the target audience – which was, at least initially, mainly young girls and gay men.

In the early 90s the trio split, with Waterman going on to repeat his earlier success with the five-piece Steps, adding a healthy dash of Abba-like melodies to his usual formula.

---

[13] Both Minogue and Donovan were originally stars of the Australian soap opera *Neighbours*. Due to the programme's popularity throughout the 80s in the UK, both were groomed for pop stardom by S.A.W. The UK pop world has since become the home for many an Antipodean ex-soap star.

SOLO ARTISTS

There were a number of very successful solo artists in the 80s who do not fall neatly into one of the previously mentioned genres.

Whitney Houston

Most successful of all was Whitney Houston, who by the late 1980s became America's highest-earning black female singer, winning power and influence that had eluded others before her. She broke the Beatles' record for the number of consecutive No. 1 singles (seven), her soundtrack for the film *The Bodyguard* (1992) became the biggest-selling soundtrack of all time, and she was the first black female artist to break through the unspoken colour bar at MTV.

Houston was born into a family that was steeped in soul and gospel music: her mother Cissy Houston was a soul and gospel singer, she was the goddaughter of Aretha Franklin, and her cousin was the singer Dionne Warwick. She began singing with a gospel group at the age of 11, and soon started work as a backing vocalist for Chaka Khan and Lou Rawls, while still a teenager. At the same time she won a modelling contract and went on to become only the second black model to appear on the cover of the American magazine *Seventeen*.

Arista's influential president, Clive Davis, recognized her potential and signed her to his label in 1985, overseeing the recording of her first album and grooming her for success. Her slick debut album, *Whitney Houston* (1985), introduced a new brand of smooth, sophisticated soul music and included three No. 1 hits: 'Saving all my love for you', 'How will I know' and 'Greatest love of all'.

Over her next albums *Whitney* (1987), *I'm Your Baby Tonight* (1990) and *The Bodyguard* soundtrack (1992), she became famous for her passionate power ballads, often gravitating to emotionally-charged songs with lyrics about triumphing over the odds – such as the rousing soul number 'The greatest love of all'.

Central to Houston's singing was her mastery of melisma – a technique rooted in gospel singing where a run of notes are sung to one syllable. A prime example can be heard in 'I will always love you' (1992), where renditions of the words 'I' and 'you' are spun out over several notes. This prominent use of melisma eventually developed into what became known as urban R&B – a virtuosic singing style incorporating flashy melodic embellishments. Houston's ubiquity on radio and television paved the way for other African-American R&B singers such as Mariah Carey, Beyoncé and Destiny's Child.

Houston spent most of her last years mired in a drug addiction that shattered her voice and her image. In 2012 she was found dead in a Los Angeles hotel room. Her total record sales by that time had exceeded 170 million.

Madonna

A former dancer, Madonna (Madonna Louise Veronica Ciccone) signed to Sire Records in 1983 as a pop/disco starlet. However, on her second album, *Like a Virgin* (produced by Chic's Nile Rodgers), Madonna showed she had a yen for controversy, with the video for the title single showing her slinking around Venice, wearing a crucifix and pursued by an amorous lion. A sexually charged performance on UK's *Top of the Pops* added fuel to the fire. The religious connotations of her name combined with her sensual image and lyrics caused quite a stir in the early 80s.

'Material girl', the second hit single from *Like a Virgin*, neatly encapsulated the materialistic, 'greed is good' spirit of the 80s mainstream, with Madonna being showered with expensive gifts by choreographed suitors in the accompanying video. Madonna's go-getting attitude had turned her into a role model for aspiring girls all over the world. 1989 saw another controversial moment with her video for 'Like a prayer', which had her worshipping and kissing an icon of a black Jesus and dancing in a field of burning crucifixes.

Madonna's albums were by now guaranteed hits, but not everything she touched turned to gold. Her chequered film career is well documented, containing such turkeys as *Shanghai Surprise* and *Swept Away*. Despite this, Madonna's great achievement in the 80s was her skilled manipulation of the media, especially the way she used her videos and sexuality to this end.

Like many mainstream stars of the 80s, Madonna was more innovative in terms of image and marketing than she was musically. Her 80s recordings were almost exclusively straight-down-the-line pop, occasionally tinged with other influences, as on the Latin-influenced 'La isla bonita'. Later on she embraced house on songs such as 'Vogue', and gained critical acclaim for her collaboration with British musician William Orbit on her album *Ray of Light*, which combined elements of the UK dance scene, giving her a more contemporary and inventive sound.

Bruce Springsteen

Another 80s American icon, known for his energetic live performances, is Bruce Springsteen. Forever synonymous with no-frills rock anthems and heartfelt ballads about life in small-town America, he cut his teeth as a singer-songwriter in New York's Greenwich Village. He wrote about the hopes and dreams of a young man growing up in his native New Jersey, with the themes of escape and the road constantly recurring. In 1984 he released the bombastic *Born in the USA*. Misread by many (including Ronald Reagan) as a tub-thumping celebration of the American Dream, the album was in fact partly a critique of the US and partly a celebration of working-class spirit, covering various issues including the Vietnam War. He went on to tackle more difficult subjects. AIDS was treated with great sensitivity in the title song for the film *Philadelphia*, and the aftermath of 9/11 on the album *The Rising*.

Prince

One of the US's most capable and controversial musicians in the 80s was the multi-instrumentalist Prince, the diminutive sex-machine from Minneapolis. Growing up in an overwhelmingly white city, Prince needed grit and determination to break into the music business. He was signed at the age of twenty by Warner Brothers in 1978, and given almost unprecedented artistic control over his output – from his first album onwards he was allowed to write, play and produce.

The rather bland pop funk of his earlier albums was eclipsed by his attention-seeking, overtly sexual image and controversial lyrics. On the cover of his third album, *Dirty Mind*, Prince poses in a pair of bikini briefs and trench coat, looking for all the world as if he forgot to put his trousers on. The album's controversial lyrics, including those dealing with incest ('Sister'), were retained at the cost of radio play.

However, the album *1999* (1982) rocketed Prince to star status, selling more than three million copies. Continuing his theme of sexual freedom, Prince created a wall of bombastic electro-funk, probably best exhibited on the title track. The follow-up album, *Purple Rain*, was even bigger and contained some of his best-known work, including the songs 'Purple rain', 'When doves cry' and 'I would die 4 U'.

Prince continued to comment on such burning issues as AIDS, drug abuse and gang violence on the 1987 double album, *Sign o' the Times*. The striking title song – stripped-down funk, melodically similar to Donovan's 1968 hit 'Hurdy gurdy man' – deals with the worldwide spread of AIDS.

Like Madonna, Prince made several ill-advised forays into the world of film. Likewise he got into trouble with the PMRC over the lyrical content of 'Sugar walls', the song he wrote for Sheena Easton which addressed the theme of female masturbation. The 1987 album *Lovesexy* sold poorly in the US, but his faltering career received a temporary boost with the success of his sample-laden *Batman* soundtrack. The follow-up album, *Graffiti*

Bridge (1990), also did poorly commercially. The 90s were generally not a happy time for Prince, with record-company troubles and patchy albums which saw his popularity wane to some extent, as he perhaps let his exclusive artistic licence get the better of quality control.

PROFILES

Michael Jackson

The self-proclaimed 'King of Pop', Michael Jackson, was born into a musical family on 29 August 1958, in Gary, Indiana. His domineering, allegedly abusive father pushed the obviously talented Jackson into the entertainment industry at an early age along with his brothers. The Jackson Five were quickly snapped up by the Motown label, and in 1970 achieved a No. 1 hit with their first single 'I want you back', a feat repeated by their next three songs. Their energetic funky, soul-tinged pop was a change from Motown's more mature previous output, but it was a big hit with audiences, leading to the act's own animated TV show. Despite a few solo releases, Michael remained very much a part of the Jackson Five, later renamed the Jacksons.

His first adult solo release was *Off the Wall* (1979), recorded with veteran producer Quincy Jones. A well-rounded combination of up-tempo funky disco, soul and dewy-eyed ballads, it shot him to stardom and provided four hit singles. Michael continued to be an active member of the Jacksons, but his solo work was now becoming a high point of their live shows.

His next album, *Thriller* (1982), was to eclipse anything he or the Jacksons had achieved so far. Clocking up an astounding 24 million copies sold, the album stayed at No. 1 for 37 weeks in the US. The title song was made into a lavish 30-minute promo directed by John Landis, who was responsible for the film *An American Werewolf in London*. Other promotional videos from the album, such as 'Billie Jean' and 'Beat it', received heavy airplay on MTV. Jackson was now a superstar, famous for his expressive singing voice and gliding 'moonwalk' dancing. However, the media soon began to pick up on his more unusual characteristics, such as his ever-present white glove, constantly lightening skin-tone and helium-like speaking voice.

Increasingly reclusive through the mid-80s, Jackson bought a ranch which he kitted out like a funfair, inviting children to come and stay. He dubbed this fantasy world 'Neverland'. His follow-up album, *Bad*, did not sell as well as *Thriller*, and was viewed by the media as a dip in form. Although Jackson's next album, *Dangerous*, again reached the No. 1 spot, it was unceremoniously booted off by Nirvana's *Nevermind*, showing the depth of change that was occurring in the US public's taste. Jackson's behaviour was becoming increasingly eccentric, with his obvious plastic surgery operations increasing the media interest even more. All-out scandal hit Jackson in 1993 when he settled out of court after he was accused of sexual misconduct with a teenage boy. Subsequent public appearances almost always featured strange and sometimes alarming behaviour, naturally attracting massive media attention.

Although his career slowly recovered with the release of two more studio albums, *HIStory* (1995) and *Invincible* (2001), worse scandal was to come, and in 2003 he was arrested on further charges of child abuse. Jackson was tried and acquitted in 2005 but by now his musical talent was overshadowed by his bizarre and notorious private life. In 2009 an ambitious London concert series, *This Is It*, was planned. During the long rehearsal period, Jackson died as the result of taking a lethal amount of prescription drugs. His death was ruled as a homicide and his personal doctor was convicted of involuntary manslaughter.

The Smiths

If any band defined the UK indie style of the 80s – jangly guitars, thoughtful lyrics, unglamorous image – it was the Manchester-based four-piece the Smiths. Despite having very few top-ten hits, they received critical acclaim and continue to have an ardent fan-base.

Before the arrival of the Smiths, the UK independent scene was ruled by the dressy, decadent goths, a handful of staunch punks, and the highly mannered, synth-heavy pop of the new romantics. The Smiths' sound refuted the then-dominant goth scene, rejecting gloomy baritone vocals and brooding, angular guitars in favour of Morrissey's tragi-comic, occasionally falsetto croon and the sophisticated, melodic guitar style of Marr. The increasingly fashionable synthesizer was also shunned by the band.

The Smiths' plain, thoroughly English name was reflected in the band's everyday dress code. Morrissey's idiosyncratic anti-image – adorned with NHS hearing-aid and spectacles, with a spray of gladioli in his back pocket – was a denial of traditional 'he-man' rock imagery.

The songwriting team of singer Stephen Morrissey (better known simply as Morrissey) and guitarist Johnny Marr began in 1982. Both had a deep knowledge and love of older music, especially 60s pop. The line-up was completed with the recruitment of bassist Andy Rourke and drummer Mike Joyce.

The shy, self-deprecating Morrissey was fascinated by 60s working-class England, and his lyrics featured whole lines from books and films of the period. He was well read, with a particular fondness for Oscar Wilde. His lyrics were far removed from the normal rock canon – literary but colloquial, sometimes heartbreaking (for instance in 'Last night I dreamt that somebody loved me'), and frequently humorous (as in 'The Queen is dead'). Morrissey covered subjects such as vegetarianism on the album *Meat is Murder*[14] and, more controversially, the UK 'moors murders' of the 1960s, in the song 'Suffer little children'.[15] However, his lyrics were mainly concerned with shyness and unrequited love in everyday England.

The Smiths' first single, 'Hand in glove', was released in 1982 on Rough Trade Records to critical approval but public apathy. Their follow-up single, 'This charming man', reached the UK top 30 in 1983, and the next single, the bleak 'How soon is now', did better still. The song's lyrics painted a picture of unbearable loneliness, which along with Morrissey's mournful voice earned him a 'miserablist' tag which he never really lived down. Several months later Morrisey and Marr acknowledged their love of the 60s with a new release of 'Hand in glove' with 60s icon Sandie Shaw taking over the vocals.

The Smiths finally cracked the US top 100 with the release of their album *The Queen is Dead* in 1986. It covered a wide range in music and lyrics, from the anthemic and acerbic anti-monarchist title track to the amusing ditty 'Frankly Mr Shankly'.

Despite continued success in the UK and US, Johnny Marr grew increasingly disenchanted with the band, especially the increasingly capricious Morrissey. Rourke's heroin use was an additional problem. Within weeks of the release of their final album, *Strangeways Here We Come* (1987), Marr left the band. Despite a half-hearted attempt to continue without him, the Smiths disbanded soon afterwards.

Marr guested on guitar for other bands before collaborating with New Order's Bernard Sumner and the Pet Shop Boys' Neil Tennant in Electronic. Meanwhile, Morrissey embarked on a successful solo career. Unfortunately neither musician succeeded in recreating the chemistry that had existed in their former partnership. However, the Smiths' music was an inspiration for countless British bands. Morrissey's sensitive, thoughtful lyrics and mournful voice, combined with Marr's intricate, lyrical guitar style, showed how far the Smiths had moved away from punk, and also set the tone for the 80s indie style.

---

[14] Always strongly opinionated, Morrissey let fly at various targets during interviews, including meat-eaters in general and UK Prime Minister Margaret Thatcher in particular.

[15] Ian Brady and Myra Hindley murdered four children during 1963 and 1964 and buried their bodies on Saddleworth Moor, near Manchester in northern England.

U2

U2's epic sound and often political lyrics have made them one of the most popular bands in the world. Bono in particular has never lacked conviction, but his sweeping statements and religious and political tub-thumping have proved attractive to some listeners and a real turn-off for others. If ever there was a band who thought that their music could change the world, it was U2.

Formed in 1978 by four school friends – vocalist Bono, guitarist the Edge, bassist Adam Clayton and drummer Larry Mullen – U2 were initially a post-punk band. However, the Edge's strident guitar sound blurred the distinction between lead and rhythm guitar and was something new, as can be heard on 'I will follow' from their debut album, *Boy*, released in 1980.

Bono's big, powerful voice is well showcased on the passionate and fiery 1983 album *War*. The album featured the anthem 'Sunday bloody Sunday', which addressed the events in Londonderry in 1971, when unarmed civil rights demonstrators were fired upon by the British military, leaving 14 people dead. Bono further addressed civil rights issues on the follow-up album *The Unforgettable Fire*,[16] on which he sang about Martin Luther King in the song 'Pride (in the name of love)':

> Early morning, April 4
> A shot rings out in the Memphis sky
> Free at last, they took your life
> They could not take your pride
>
> 'Pride (in the name of love)' (U2)

A characteristically intense appearance in the 1985 Live Aid charity concert increased U2's growing reputation.[17] Even greater success was to come with the release of their 1987 album *The Joshua Tree*, which went to No. 1 in both the US and UK and also provided hit singles in 'With or without you' and 'I still haven't found what I'm looking for'. The band were also featured on the front cover of *Time* magazine, an honour previously bestowed on only the Beatles and the Who.

Following the explosion of dance culture in Britain in the late 80s and early 90s, the band went in a more eclectic and electronic direction with the album *Achtung Baby*. The accompanying 'Zoo TV' tour made extensive use of enormous video screens and suspended East German Trabant cars, as well as pranks such as Bono's phoning up celebrities live on stage. After further flirtations with dance music, the band returned to a more rock-oriented sound on *All That You Can't Leave Behind* in 2000. The album was a huge commercial success, as were all that followed. In 2006 U2 Ltd moved most of its tax affairs to the Netherlands in response to the Irish government's decision to cap the tax-free exemption on royalties at €225,000. The move was criticized in the Irish parliament. U2 continued to make highly lucrative tours including the 360 Tour, which featured the largest concert stage structure ever and in 2011 became the highest-grossing concert tour in history.

FURTHER LISTENING

Iron Maiden *The Number of the Beast* (1982)
The much-imitated Iron Maiden spearheaded the new wave of British heavy metal with this album of aggressive hard-riffing songs.

---

[16] Named after a photographic exhibition about the bombing of Hiroshima in World War II, visited by the band during a tour of Japan.

[17] Live Aid was a huge benefit concert organized by Bob Geldof to help the starving people of Ethiopia. It was broadcast across the world, and featured Dire Straits, Queen, David Bowie, Madonna and Simple Minds among others.

Talking Heads 'Once in a lifetime' (1980)
Following their first hit, 'Psycho killer' (1977), New York band Talking Heads made a series of critically acclaimed albums in the 70s and 80s. With vocalist David Byrne and sometime producer Brian Eno, their albums (notably *Fear of Music* 1979 and *Remain in Light* 1980) were intelligent and thought-provoking. The band experimented with different styles of music, sampling African and Eastern sounds and combining these with sometimes funky, sometimes poppy, guitar rock. One of their few singles, 'Once in a lifetime', features intricate, polyrhythmic percussion with recited abstract verses breaking out into an exuberant chorus. The song features in the 1986 film *Stop Making Sense* (a recording of a live concert), arguably one of the best rock movies ever made.

Tom Waits *Swordfishtrombones* (1983)
This uncompromising album is dominated by percussive sounds and complex rhythms accompanying the croaking, gravelly voice of self-styled Bohemian Tom Waits. The surrealism of the album also owes something to the unusual recording techniques and the song lyrics, which are set in a world of misfits. Tom Waits has maintained a cult following since his earliest albums in the 70s.

Paul Simon *Graceland* (1986)
Paul Simon broke the UN anti-apartheid boycott to make this controversial album, recording with black South African musicians including Ladysmith Black Mambazo, Miriam Makeba and Hugh Masekela. Songs such as 'Homeless' and 'Diamonds on the soles of her shoes' blended rock and African sounds and rhythms.

Dire Straits *Brothers in Arms* (1985)
Dire Straits were one of the most successful British bands of the 1980s; this album was a multi-million seller. The laid-back sound centres on Mark Knopfler's rough vocals and fast-flowing Fender Stratocaster guitar solos. Songs include 'Money for nothing' and 'Walk of life'.

R.E.M. 'The one I love' (1987)
In a 1988 interview, guitarist Peter Buck's description of a typical R.E.M. song included the terms 'minor key', 'mid-tempo' and 'enigmatic'. All of these could be applied to 'The one I love'.

Pretenders 'Back on the chain gang' (1982), *Learning to Crawl* (1984)
The Pretenders combined the creative songwriting energy of the mid-60s mod groups with some of punk's stripped-down directness and the depth of sound of 80s recording techniques. With a sound dominated by singer/guitarist Chrissie Hynde, and songs written by her, this album is a model of rhythmic precision and clarity.

Cyndi Lauper *She's So Unusual* (1984)
Writing much of her own material, Cyndi Lauper hit the charts with her first solo album *She's So Unusual*, which includes both the feminist anthem 'Girls just want to have fun' and the hit single 'Time after time'.

Soft Cell 'Tainted love' (1981)
'Tainted love' is included on Soft Cell's album *Non-Stop Erotic Cabaret* (1981). It is a synth-pop cover of Gloria Jones' 1965 northern soul classic.

Pet Shop Boys 'It's a sin' (1987)
This dance-pop track features splendidly orchestrated electronic sounds, layers of keyboards, organ, wordless choirs, samples of church services and the Latin mass, all with lashings of reverb.

Level 42 'The sun goes down (living it up)' (1983)
Funky jazz rock band Level 42 are probably best known for Mark King's dexterous bass work – a percussive slap technique giving a distinctive driving groove to songs such as this top-ten hit.

Fine Young Cannibals 'Johnny come home' (1985)
Much of the character and appeal of this infectious single lies in Roland Gift's unique soul-influenced voice.

Joan Jett and the Blackhearts 'I love rock 'n' roll' (1982)
Renegade Joan Jett's raucous cover of an obscure B-side by the Arrows.

chapter

7

Toby Bricheno

Nineties

Three main strands run through 90s pop:

Rock and indie
Following the innovative 80s, many guitar bands chose to look backwards. With exceptions, the 90s will not be remembered for inventive guitar-based music.

Dance
By contrast, dance exploded into myriad innovative sub-genres, just as post-punk guitar music had done in the previous decade. The ever-evolving technology provided the opportunities and the tools.

Manufactured pop
This was also an era of 'manufactured bands' such as Take That or the Spice Girls, whereby a vocal group would be assembled, usually by a manager or production company, signed to a record company, and then heavily promoted through TV, radio and the press.

By the end of the decade, US/UK domination of pop was being challenged increasingly by groups from mainland Europe and Japan, and by growing awareness of the pop musics of other cultures and languages.

Selected artists are profiled at the end of the chapter, and, as in other chapters, there is a Further Listening list which includes a number of records lying outside the main narrative.

ROCK AND INDIE

Grunge

Generally centred around Seattle in America's North West, 'grunge' was a combination of the Stooges, early-70s heavy rock (especially Black Sabbath), and punk. However, the spiky haircuts of punk were replaced by heavy rock's long, lank locks, and punk's political agenda was also largely ignored. To some extent, grunge was a rebellion against the pouting, preening LA rock scene. Grunge's defining characteristics were the use of heavily distorted, fuzzy guitars, and a strongly anti-'muso' stance, with guitar solos being a distinct rarity, the focus instead on heavy 'riffing'.

Bands like Mudhoney and Nirvana took the bare basics of metal, added a dash of punk attitude and aggression and made it cool again. (No mean feat.) Mudhoney was one of the first grunge bands to achieve success. The song 'In and out of grace' from their 1988 *Superfuzz Bigmuff* EP (named after the famous distortion pedals of the 70s) was probably their finest moment – a wild rip-roaring 'slacker' anthem,[1] with an unhinged atonal twin guitar section as well as a drum solo that actually sounded cool. Mudhoney were signed to the small local independent Sub Pop label, which subsequently signed Nirvana.

Nirvana's 1989 debut album *Bleach* was a hit on the US college radio circuit and a significant success for Sub Pop. Major labels became interested, and the band signed with DGC Records and in 1991 released the grunge album that made the world stop in its tracks – *Nevermind*. Less fuzzy and distorted than *Bleach*, and with a more polished sound, *Nevermind* still packed a heavy punch, especially on the opening song (and MTV favourite) 'Smells like teen spirit', which became a worldwide hit, much to the astonishment of the band. 'Teen spirit' started off with a clean guitar tease, exploding via a drum fill and a hail of distorted guitars into what became the grunge anthem. The difference between Nirvana and the rest of the grunge bands was that *Nevermind* possessed a healthy dose of pop mixed in with heavy guitars, pummelling drums and singer Kurt Cobain's intense, almost hoarse vocals, thereby giving the album appeal to a wider audience.

The success of the band and subsequent media hysteria began to take its toll on the sensitive Cobain. The band's tortured follow-up to *Nevermind*, *In Utero* (1993), was originally titled *I Hate Myself and I Want to Die*, perhaps giving an insight into Cobain's mental state at the time. *In Utero* was less commercial than *Nevermind*; the band drafted in veteran noise-rock producer Steve Albini in an attempt to recapture the sound (and possibly the vibe) of their pre-DGC releases. Despite the less radio-friendly sound, the album sold very well.

On 8 April 1994 Cobain was found dead from a self-inflicted gunshot wound. The two remaining members went their own ways, with drummer Dave Grohl forming (and singing for) the Foo Fighters, to all intents and purposes a more corporate-sounding, toned-down Nirvana, who have enjoyed great success with their radio-friendly sound. Grohl also guested on drums for Queens of the Stone Age, probably the band most justifiably able to claim to be a Nirvana for the twenty-first century. In 2009 Grohl formed the supergroup Them Crooked Vultures with Led Zeppelin's John Paul Jones and Josh Homme from Queens of the Stone Age. Nirvana were a double-edged sword for US rock – they unwittingly brought American 'indie' out of its ghetto and into mainstream culture, but at the same time spawned hundreds of sound-alike bands that caused much of US rock to stagnate in the mid-90s.

Fusions and revivals

A lot of 90s bands grew up listening to funk and rap from the 70s and 80s as well as rock, punk and indie, and many bands incorporated a mix of genres into their music. A fusion of rock, rap and funk can clearly be heard on 'Give it away' (1991) by California's Red Hot Chilli Peppers. The slower, funky tempo and guitars are coupled to powerful rock drums, guitar (partly recorded backwards) and a quasi-rap lead vocal.

Another West Coast band with the same idea were Jane's Addiction,[2] who showcased their own hybrid style on songs such as 'Been caught stealing', which utilizes a dance-like drum pattern and a tempo closer to rap than to conventional rock, while still having rock guitars and a solo. One of the differences between these bands and the grunge acts was the greater degree of technical musicianship involved.

Rage Against The Machine had a harder, more metal-influenced edge, displayed on 'Killing in the name', which begins with powerful thrash-like riffing that develops into a funkier riff while singer Zack de la Rocha performs a political anti-establishment rap. They were more sonically experimental than some of their peers, as heard on their 1992 song

---

[1] Slang for uninterested, activity-shirking youth, much used in the early 90s, probably named after the film *Slacker* (1991).

[2] In 1991 Perry Farrell of Jane's Addiction set up a touring music festival, Lollapalooza, which went from city to city featuring alternative bands. The first line-up included Jane's Addiction, Siouxsie and the Banshees, Living Colour, Nine Inch Nails and Ice-T.

'Bullet in the head'. The opening bass-line's funk origins are evident, while the heavily effect-laden guitar sounds more akin to hip-hop DJ scratching. In the chorus, however, a more conventional rock guitar sound takes over.

The fusion between rap and rock proved fruitful, and was the basis for much of the nu-metal scene of the late 90s. The sound was intensified, the guitars and basses detuned for a heavier sound,[3] and the hip-hop quotient was increased, often including a DJ in the band's line-up, to give us 'rap rock' and its very close relative 'nu-metal'. Catering to a white teenage male audience, the dress style incorporated such elements as baseball caps and baggy shorts.

Korn laid the foundation for later bands. Influenced by grunge as well as rap and metal, their uncompromisingly brutal music and angst-ridden lyrics are much in evidence on their 1994 debut album *Korn*, with the two guitarists' seven-string guitars adding extra depth and punch. Singer Jonathan Davis's varied vocal delivery – alternating between singing, whispering and a throaty growl – is reminiscent of Trent Reznor from Nine Inch Nails.

Korn were soon followed by nine-piece outfit Slipknot, known for their mask-wearing antics as much as their music. With less emphasis on hip-hop and more on metal, Slipknot recall grindcore bands,[4] such as Bolt Thrower and Napalm Death on tracks like 'People=shit' from *Iowa* (2001).

A well-known band in this genre were Limp Bizkit. Loud, brash and ever keen to offend moral guardians, they got their break when their loud-mouthed singer, Fred Durst,[5] passed a demo tape to Korn, who were impressed and gave Limp Bizkit a support slot, leading to gigs with other established bands. The band were often criticized for Durst's sub-Beastie Boys, annoy-your-parents lyrics, which were littered with expletives (as on 'Hot dog' from *Chocolate Starfish and the Hot Dog Flavored Water*). Complete with the obligatory DJ who scratched records while the band were playing, Limp Bizkit's raucous combination of rap and metal is probably best experienced on their debut album *Three Dollar Bill Y'All*. Their later output became more formulaic, as perhaps did the nu-metal genre in general.

Punk made a reappearance of sorts in the 90s, albeit in an altered form. Californian bands like Green Day, Blink 182 and the Offspring took the fast tempos and simple guitar chords of punk but left behind the politics, bile and style. Adding catchy tunes and tongue-in-cheek humour, their brand of good-time punk/pop was very popular on both sides of the Atlantic. Three-piece Green Day were hugely popular in the 1990s and are widely credited with popularising punk rock in the US. They started out as members of the punk underground, but in 1994 their major label debut album *Dookie* introduced them to a much wider audience and included the hits 'Basket case', 'Longview' and 'Welcome to paradise'. By 1995 they had become superstars and the Californian grass-roots punk scene turned away from them.

The underground legacy of the New York alternative scene, along with the rough-and-ready US garage rock of the 60s, was combined with the British punk and indie sound, resulting in bands like New York outfit the Strokes. The gritty, simple production and uncomplicated approach on their debut album *Is This it?* (2001) heralded a return to the basics of rock, and a great contrast to the heavily produced sounds of nu-metal.

The Stroke's stripped-down sound was taken even further by bands such as the Yeah Yeah Yeahs and the more bluesy White Stripes, both of which did away with a bass player altogether, the White Stripes being a mere two-piece group.

UK rock and indie

From bright beginnings in the innovative 80s, the UK indie scene gradually followed an increasingly retrospective direction. In 1986, UK music paper NME gave away a free cassette

---

[3] Guitars and basses with an extra, lower string were also manufactured.

[4] A British phenomenon from the early 80s: an extreme mix of punk, metal and guttural, caveman-like vocals. Napalm Death were known for the brevity of their songs, the shortest being one second long.

[5] Durst was a professional tattooist, and had tattooed some of Korn's musicians.

entitled *C86* and single-handedly created a sub-genre of indie. Many of the bands on the cassette, such as the Pastels and Talulah Gosh, were strongly influenced by the chiming, sensitive sound of the Smiths, adding a nostalgic dose of wistful 60s, Monkees-like pop. Perhaps the most important song on the *C86* cassette was 'Velocity girl' by Primal Scream. The Marr-like jangly guitars, and soft, rather fey vocal, laid the foundations for a surge of retrospective music.

The jangly sound of *C86* was mainly but not purely a British phenomenon – R.E.M. from Georgia in the United States ploughed a similar furrow throughout the 80s and 90s, to critical acclaim and widespread success. The thoughtful, reflective lyrics of singer Michael Stipe were sympathetic to left-wing concerns, endearing R.E.M. to college radio-listeners, with whom they initially found success. R.E.M. truly entered the mainstream with the singles 'Shiny happy people' and 'Losing my religion' from the 1991 album *Out of Time*. The following year they repeated this success with their album *Automatic for the People* (1992), which included the hit single 'Everybody hurts' – a message for people in doubt or despair which has since been used by various charities. In 2010 the song was released as a charity single, 'Helping Haiti', in order to raise money for the victims of the 2010 Haiti earthquake.

Madchester

The so-called 'Madchester' scene (named after a song by the Happy Mondays) was the sound that allegedly got the indie kids *dancing* rather than 'moshing' (a frenetic style of en masse dancing by audiences at gigs, derived from the punk 'pogo'). It was a loose conglomeration of Manchester-based bands, some of whom had introduced elements of the burgeoning dance scene into their sound. The use of Ecstasy (usually associated with the dance scene) was also a common factor among bands, and the favoured clothing style gave rise to an alternative label for the Madchester scene: 'Baggy'. The defining musical features were vague-sounding vocals over 'funky drummer'-type drums and 60s-sounding guitars, a good example being 'The only one I know' by the Charlatans.

A focal point of the Madchester scene was the Hacienda, one of the first major clubs to play house music outside London. Co-owned by New Order, it was home to many indie bands including the Smiths, the Happy Mondays and the Stone Roses. After finishing last in a 'battle of the bands' at the Hacienda, the Happy Mondays signed to Factory Records. The influence of the emerging house and acid-house scene can be heard in the hypnotic and repet-itive groove of 'Wrote for luck' from their first album, *Bummed*. The Mondays developed a habit of incorporating other artists' work into their own, and based two of their songs on Beatles classics, much to the displeasure of the copyright owners. One of their biggest hits, the jaunty, piano-driven 'Step on' (1990), was a cover/reworking of John Kongo's 'He's gonna step on you again' (1970). A similar approach was adopted by Oasis, who based a number of their songs on past models.

The Stone Roses' blend of melodic, jangly psychedelia, sung with a northern English accent, had a more tenuous dance connection, but was included in the Madchester movement mainly due to geography and the band's druggy image. However, some songs did contain a dance element – demonstrated in the combination of funk and rock on the last half of 'I am the resurrection' from their eponymously titled debut album (1989), and the ten-minute funky-drummer workout on the 12-inch version of 'Fool's gold' (1992). The Stone Roses' main stock-in-trade was a dreamy reverb-laden vocal over a heavily Byrds-influenced backing, in evidence on most tracks from the first album. Such tripped-out vocals and chiming guitars were to be a big influence on Britpop's Oasis.

Though not directly involved with the Madchester movement, Primal Scream similarly dabbled with a hybrid of dance and indie. Singer Bobby Gillespie was a former member of Scottish indie outfit the Jesus and Mary Chain, whose nihilistic combination of soft-focus vocals and vicious guitar feedback was very popular in the 80s and 90s, best exhibited on the album *Psychocandy*. Primal Scream collaborated with DJ Andy Weatherall on the hit single

'Loaded' in 1990. While its lazy, stoned groove showed how far the band had come from their *C86* roots, 'Loaded' also bore a resemblance to the Rolling Stones' 'Sympathy for the devil'. On their dubby, gospel-inflected album *Screamadelica* (1991), the band hired former Stones producer Jimmy Miller to recreate the 60s sound on songs such as 'Movin' on up' and 'Damaged', while also incorporating more contemporary sounds courtesy of Weatherall.

Primal Scream's record label, Creation, was the label of choice for many indie bands in the late 80s and 90s, including such diverse artists as rock-traditionalists Oasis and the ground-breaking My Bloody Valentine. My Bloody Valentine were famous for their sonic experimentation, and the fact that their *Loveless* album (1991), which took seventeen different recording engineers and almost two years to complete, reputedly almost bankrupted Creation. Nevertheless, *Loveless* became an important album for left-field, experimental indie, due to its invention and cutting-edge recording techniques – exemplified in the mesmeric, blurred sound of the closing track, 'Soon'.

Britpop

Britpop was generally a nostalgic movement, consciously looking back to the heyday of British music in the 60s and 70s, perhaps as a reaction to the experimentalism and innovation of the 80s. (It was sometimes known as 'dad-rock', due to its popularity with teenagers' fathers, because it sounded so similar to the music of their youth.) Bands like the Kinks, the Who and especially the Beatles – as well as outfits like the Stone Roses who had themselves already borrowed heavily from earlier bands – were highly influential.

One of the first bands to be associated with the genre were Suede. Vocalist Brett Anderson was highly derivative of 70s glam icon David Bowie, as can be heard on Suede's debut single 'The Drowners' (1993). A creative nadir was reached by arch-traditionalists Ocean Colour Scene, who recreated the British sound of the 60s on their album *Moseley Shoals* (1996), without adding any new ideas or sounds.

Though less backward-looking than many of the Britpop acts, Sheffield band Pulp, with foppish vocalist Jarvis Cocker, made bittersweet observations about provincial England that placed them firmly in the Britpop camp. No overnight sensation, the band beavered away for twelve years before achieving success with the indignant indie disco classic 'Common people', a hit in 1995. The song's lyrics contrast the fantasies of an ignorant rich girl about being poor with the despair and drudgery of the real working classes. The band stirred up controversy on the follow-up single, 'Sorted for E's and wizz', an affectionate satire on the rave culture of the time:

> Oh is this the way they say the future's meant to feel?
> Or just 20,000 people standing in a field.
> And I don't quite understand just what this feeling is.
> But that's okay 'cause we're all sorted out for E's and wizz.
>
> 'Sorted for E's and wizz' (Pulp)

The two bands most closely associated with Britpop, however, are Oasis and Blur. Oasis is centred on permanent members (and brothers) Liam and Noel Gallagher, born in a working-class suburb of Manchester. Famed almost as much for their offstage hell-raising antics and constant bickering as for their music, the brothers were highly influenced by the Beatles, the Sex Pistols and the Smiths. Main vocalist Liam has often likened himself to a cross between the Beatles' Lennon and the Sex Pistols' Rotten. Oasis attempted to fuse the aggressive attitude of punk with the melodic songwriting styles of Lennon and McCartney, and they have often been dismissed as Beatles copyists. Emerging in the dance-music dominated Britain of the early 90s, Oasis were notable in that they were a guitar-driven, no-nonsense rock band, albeit with a heavy England-centric 1960s fixation. Signed by Creation in 1993, they quickly achieved success and media attention by virtue of their pugnacious attitude and familiar-sounding tunes.

Despite being London based, Blur were initially loosely associated with the Madchester scene by virtue of their 1991 'baggy' anthem 'There's no other way'. They subsequently developed a more self-consciously English sound and outlook, collaborating with actor Phil Daniels on the song 'Parklife', a celebration of everyday life in southern England. Blur's southern, middle-class, art-school upbringing put them at odds with arch-rivals Oasis, and there was much public antagonism between the two bands. Ironically it was usually Blur who sang about working-class issues while Oasis occupied themselves with thinly-disguised paeans to drugs and stardom.

Blur's output was more experimental and varied than that of Oasis. The stylistic range covered between the 80s synthpop/disco combination of 'Girls and boys' and the intense, grunge-influenced 'Song 2' is evident. However, their music was less popular outside the UK, especially compared with Oasis, perhaps because of Blur's resolutely British outlook and subject matter. Singer Damon Albarn has since worked on several projects in theatre, world and film music (notably *Monkey: Journey to the West*, a 2007 stage adaptation of a 16th-century Chinese novel) as well as being a member of indie/hip-hop crossover outfit Gorillaz. In 2011 he formed the band Rocketjuice and The Moon with Flea from the Red Hot Chilli Peppers.

1997 brought a change of UK government following eighteen years of Conservative administration. The previous year, a brand of American ice cream called 'Cool Britannia' was introduced in the UK, and this phrase was taken up by the British media as a buzzword to describe the flourishing scene in the British visual arts, fashion and music. Keen to capitalize on this and enhance his 'street-cred', the new Prime Minister, Tony Blair, invited pop-music celebrities, including members of Blur, Oasis and Pulp, to 10 Downing Street.

Two bands not included under the banner of Britpop but who have been influential and popular around the world are Wales's Manic Street Preachers and England's Radiohead. Beginning as Clash look-alikes with slogan-covered shirts, the Manic Street Preachers aroused the interest of the British music press with their blend of punk swagger and stadium glam, as well as energetic live performances, politicized lyrics, frank interviews and attention-grabbing declarations. Initially dismissed as being little more than retro-punk poseurs, the group gained credibility when guitarist Richie James Edwards famously carved the phrase '4 REAL' into his arm with a razor-blade during an interview in 1991. Their debut double-album, *Generation Terrorists* (1992) was pitched somewhere between the Sex Pistols and Guns N' Roses, even allowing the occasional guitar solo (previously frowned on in indie circles) to make an appearance, notably on the anthemic and haunting 'Motorcycle emptiness', a hymn to the dangers of empty consumerism.

Oxford's Radiohead are a different proposition entirely. Starting off as a fairly straight-forward indie-rock outfit, blessed with singer Thom Yorke's vulnerable-sounding, expressive voice, the band had a UK top-ten hit with their grunge-tinged anthem to self-loathing, 'Creep', in 1992. In 1997 their third album, cryptically titled *OK Computer*, showed a marked change of direction barely hinted at in their previous output. It is a complex album both musically and lyrically, with subtle rhythms and complex syncopations helping to create unusual textures and atmospheres. The song 'Paranoid android' established the tone for the album and also for much of Radiohead's later output. It presents an oblique stream-of-consciousness collage of Yorke's experiences in the US, combined with a critique of contemporary America (comparing it to the Roman Empire), the different themes being mirrored in the song's tripartite structure. This relative complexity has led to comparisons with Queen's 'Bohemian rhapsody', and Radiohead have faced accusations of reviving progressive rock, mainly due to the free-form structures, inscrutable lyrics and growing appetite for unusual time signatures in the band's recordings. Despite its challenges, *OK Computer* was a No. 1 album in the UK, spawning three hit singles: 'Karma Police', 'No surprises' and 'Paranoid android'.

In 2000, after a three-year hiatus, tracks from a new album, *Kid A,* were leaked onto the internet. They revealed a fragmented sonic collage that made previous Radiohead releases sound like easy-listening by comparison, and showed a musical complexity rare in the indie and alternative scenes of the time. *Kid A* seemed to capture the pioneering spirit of the Beatles at their most experimental, rather than simply just emulating their sound *à la* Oasis. *Kid A* was successful on both sides of the Atlantic, despite there being no tour, singles or videos to stimulate sales. *Amnesiac* (2001) and *Hail to the Thief* (2003) have continued in a similarly adventurous style, the latter album being named after an anti-Bush slogan during the end of the controversial 2000 presidential election campaign in the US.[6]

DANCE

It was in the 90s that Europe took the foundations of electronic dance music from the USA and forged ahead as the world leader in modern dance music, creating myriad new sub-genres. Trends in dance music chopped and changed at a dizzying rate, with some releases considered passé after only a few weeks. For an analytical, rather than historical, comparison of dance music styles, see Chapter 12.

One of the main differences between dance and the established pop/rock scene was that dance singles were not a vehicle to promote albums, but rather an entity in themselves, with writers and producers often adopting pseudonyms to work on an array of different projects. This way of working, with 12-inch singles issued by a proliferation of little-known acts and producers, ran counter to the traditional, highly recognizable image of the 'pop star', and accusations of 'facelessness' were often levelled at the dance scene.

Rave

By the summer of 1989 the acid-house scene was so popular that promoters were organizing large-scale parties (or 'raves') which often lasted all night. They usually took place in empty warehouses or fields in order to avoid unwanted attention from the police, as large quantities of drugs, especially LSD and Ecstasy, were being consumed. These events grew to an enormous size, as attested by visiting American DJ Frankie Bones. Accustomed to playing in front of a few hundred people in his native country, Bones found himself DJ-ing to crowds of 25,000 people in Britain.

The sound had also changed from the music played at the small London clubs. The jarring pick 'n' mix sound of acid house had been largely replaced by the new sound of 'Italian house'. Full of screaming divas and pounding pianos, the Italian sound is probably best typified by the Black Box hit 'Ride on time' (1989).

Ever since the house-music boom of the late 80s, sampled fragments of vocals were used in place of conventional vocals. Narrative was abandoned, and the vocal element was reduced to a few intense, sampled phrases. The reasons for this were twofold – sampler memory was still limited, making it difficult to sample longer phrases; and such short, catchy phrases sounded great under the effects of Ecstasy.

Raves were often organized via the relatively new mobile-phone network, in an attempt to outmanoeuvre the police. When the link between dance music and drugs became apparent, media attitudes – initially friendly – became antagonistic. Scandalized headlines became the order of the day, reaching fever pitch when a teenage girl died at the Hacienda club while under the effects of Ecstasy. The British police, wise to the rave organizers' tactics, set up the 'Pay Party Unit' to deal with large outdoor events, sounding the death-knell for the big outdoor raves of 1989. Party-goers travelled miles across the country only to find the rave cancelled due to police intervention. Fortuitously, however, licensing laws had been relaxed, allowing clubs to stay open much longer – some until noon the following day – so the emerging rave culture went back to its original clubland roots.

---

[6] 'Hail to the thief, our commander in chief'

Hardcore

The UK rave scene was coming up with its own sound, far removed from the more refined sounds of Chicago and Detroit. The drum-machine rhythms of house and techno were augmented (and often replaced) by sampled hip-hop breakbeats, speeded up to faster, more urgent tempos. These were mixed with the jerky synth rhythms of earlier acid house, resulting in tracks like 'Anasthasia' by T-99 (1991), whereas the influence of piano-dominated Italian house can be heard on a top-ten hit of the same year, 'Playing with knives', by Bizarre Inc. Additionally, vocal samples were tuned up to give a frenetic, helium-like sound on many tracks (for example the Prodigy's 'Everybody in the place'), and the deep, dubby bass found on many hardcore tracks such as Altern 8's 'Infiltrate 202' and DJ Trax's 'We rock the most' was overwhelming when heard on a large PA system. ('Infiltrate 202' actually came with a tongue-in-cheek verbal warning before it started: 'watch ya bass bins I'm telling ya'.)

The Prodigy were one of the biggest dance acts of the 90s, incorporating guitars into their increasingly hard-hitting and menacing sound, as heard on their breakthrough album, *Songs for the Jilted Generation* (1994). They had a UK No. 1 with the single 'Firestarter' in 1996, the video of which had *Top of the Pops* inundated with phone calls from concerned parents of terrified children who had witnessed vocalist Keith Flint's bizarre, punk-derived performance.

Scottish band the Shamen moved in the opposite direction, leaving their indie roots for an increasingly dance-oriented direction, and converting many indie fans to the dance scene. Their album *Entact* (1990) was played in indie and dance clubs alike, due to its combination of electronic sounds, loops and drum machines embedded in a traditional, song-based format. Their uplifting anthem 'Move any mountain' was so popular that *Progeny*, an album containing nothing but different mixes of the song, was released in 1991. *Progeny* also included all the elements of the original track, enabling record buyers to remix the track themselves.

A glut of novelty records such as 'Roobarb and custard' and 'Sesame's treet', which comprised excerpts from children's television theme tunes of the 70s, signalled the end of hardcore as the cutting edge of UK dance music. It subsequently evolved into the sub-genre of 'happy hardcore', whose cheesiness and frenzied, almost undanceable tempos were a turn-off for many. However, hardcore's speeded-up drum loops and increasingly disjointed sound laid the foundations for one of dance music's 90s innovations – jungle.

Jungle, drum'n'bass

Initially a stripped down but rhythmically complex mutation of hardcore, jungle also absorbed elements of dub, especially in respect to the bass line. Its later title of 'drum'n'bass' hints at the genre's key feature – a combination of drum loops and bass lines at a very fast tempo (typically 170 bpm: beats per minute), with the cartoonish vocals and frantic synthesizers of hardcore left out of the formula. Almost entirely a UK genre, jungle had its beginning with releases such as 'Original nuttah' (1994) by Shy FX and vocalist UK Apache (a.k.a. Apachi). The siren-like wail was straight out of hardcore, while the frenzied snare-drum roll, reggae-like bass-line and ragga-style vocal (a feature of early jungle) were definitely something new.

Jungle was soon renamed 'drum'n'bass', and split into numerous sub-genres. Bristol's Roni Size added jazz and hip-hop flavours with his 1997 release *New Forms*, notably on his top-twenty hit 'Brown paper bag'. LTJ Bukem is often credited with inventing 'intelligent drum'n'bass', a more experimental, electronica-infused form, as can be heard on his *Logical Progression* albums.

Another veteran of the hardcore scene, Goldie (so-called because of his gold-plated teeth) was one of drum'n'bass's most high profile figures in the 90s.[7] He evolved a much harder,

---

[7] Apart from DJing and writing music, Goldie has also appeared in such films as *Snatch* and *The World is Not Enough*, and has produced art work for several exhibitions. His many television appearances include work in classical music as both a conductor and composer.

darker sound through his 'Metalheadz' club nights and releases. The haunting and disembodied sound of 'Inner city life', from his album *Timeless*, was a cross-over success when it was re-released in 1995.

Perhaps as a reaction to the increasingly considered and experimental direction pursued by artists such as Size and Bukem, a tougher, no-nonsense style of drum'n'bass known as 'jump up' evolved. Jump up had more of a funky, hip-hop feel, often with half-tempo sections bringing the tempo down to typical hip-hop speeds, as on Amazon 2's 'King of the beats'. The main label for this genre was Urban Takeover, which released the jump up anthem 'Rock the funky beats' by Natural Born Chillers in 1997. The breakbeat loops of drum'n'bass also featured heavily in the 'Nu skool breaks' movement of the late 90s and early 2000s. Nu skool's slower tempo had a funkier feel, often containing elements of electro and techno, as can be heard on 'Kool and deadly' by T-Power, and 'Fibonacci sequence' by BT.

Techno

Manchester's 808 State can lay claim to one of the earliest European techno tracks with their 1988 single 'Cubik'. Its chattering drums and angular robotic synth riff reveal links to the old Detroit sound, bearing comparisons with Juan Atkins's output, but adding a much harder edge.

Taking Detroit's cool, synthetic sound as a starting point, UK artists such as LFO, Orbital and Leftfield added their own brand of British experimentation and eclecticism. Though releasing only a handful of records before splitting up in 1996, LFO have an important place in UK techno history. Their bleepy, dreamy single 'LFO' reached No. 12 in 1990 and did much to promote techno in Britain in the process.

Orbital – brothers Paul and Phil Hartnoll – were one of the mainstays of British techno throughout the 90s. The duo had two early hit singles, the gentle 'Chime' and hard-hitting 'Satan'. The latter's huge metallic riffs sound nearer to Metallica than dance music. Orbital have since concentrated on albums and gigs, trail-blazing a way for other electronic dance acts by playing big outdoor festivals such as Glastonbury and Woodstock 2. Shunning pre-recorded DATs, Orbital have always operated their equipment live, allowing them much more flexibility during performances. They were also one of the first techno acts to incorporate exciting visual effects into their performances. The band split in 2004 and reformed in 2009 to headline the Big Chill festival.

Leftfield's *Leftism* was an important album in that it combined techno with ambient and world music, opening up new sonic possibilities. The album included collaborations with singer Toni Halliday (from indie outfit Curve) and underground veteran John Lydon (Johnny Rotten) in an attempt to shrug off the 'faceless techno bollocks' tag – a tongue-in-cheek T-shirt slogan from the 90s.

Meanwhile, in Belgium, a release by an American was again about to have a massive influence on European dance music, though this time it would be on a European label, R&S. 'Energy flash', a classic by New Yorker Joey Beltram, had its roots in Detroit techno, but it also ushered in the European techno sound of the 90s with its pounding bass drum, analogue squelches and filtering monotone synthesizer riff, the latter also being a precursor to acid techno.

Germany developed a growing appetite for techno. Berlin's 'Love Parade' festival began in 1989, and was a fixture on the dance music calendar during 1989–2003 and again in 2006, with the city taken over by thousands of techno lovers from Germany and abroad. In 2007 it moved to the Rühr region. The festival was permanently cancelled in 2010 after 21 people died, many from suffocation, in an incident near an overcrowded tunnel leading into the festival.

Germany was also home to an important techno label, Tresor, which released so-called 'minimal techno' (a.k.a. 'intelligent techno' to distinguish it from its busier, breakbeat- and sample-laden relatives in the UK) made by both Europeans and Americans such as Detroit's

Jeff Mills and Juan Atkins. The hard and austere sound often comprised only the 'bu tic bu tic' of a Roland drum machine along with a few analogue squelches and rumbles, with no breakbeats or samples present, as heard on tracks like 'Domina' (Maurizio mix) by Domina, and 'Ten four' by Joey Beltram.

Detroit's techno scene was not particularly based around drug-taking, whereas in European clubs taking drugs (especially Ecstasy) was becoming *de rigeur* in the 90s.[8] European techno evolved harder, more psychedelic sounds, which heightened the effects of the drug. Long, drum-free 'breakdown' sections originating from 'trance' (see below) built to an orgiastic climax before the drums piled back in, accompanied by wildly filtering acid-like synths. This combination of acid and techno became known, unsurprisingly, as 'acid techno', and became particularly popular in the UK, 'Access' by DJ Misjah and DJ Tim being a prime example. Its tense breakdown section creates a sense of expectation that is fully realized when an initially innocuous bubbling synth slowly morphs into a screaming, electronic maelstrom accompanied by a pummelling drum loop.

Acid techno was closely linked with the 'free party scene' in Europe. Reminiscent of the free festivals of the 60s, these parties consisted of *ad hoc*, often small-scale squat-based raves. Made possible by donations given on entry, the parties catered for a loose confederation of clubbers, ex-hippies, travellers and 'crusties' (a derogatory term for unkempt, often unemployed, squatters). After the huge three-day Castlemorton party in 1992, the UK government cracked down. The 1994 Criminal Justice Act outlawed gatherings of more than a hundred people at which amplified music 'characterized by the emission of a succession of repetitive beats' was played. This signalled the end of the scene's heyday, forcing punters into legal clubs or abroad to the more tolerant regimes of Thailand and Goa.

Allied to acid techno was 'breakbeat techno', which shunned the 'four-on-the-floor' bass drum pattern of much techno, replacing it with breakbeats and creating a more nu-skool feel. Its finest hour was the surprise UK top-ten hit 'Higher state of consciousness' by Josh Wink (1995), whose hard acid sound is a love letter to the filtering possibilities of the revered TB 303. There were also many examples of cross-fertilization between techno and its close relative house in the 90s, resulting in endless (and often indistinguishable) new genres such as tech house, hard house, handbag and even hardbag.

Trance

Often considered an offshoot of techno, trance had a generally softer, more melodic sound that became popular in the late 90s. The funkier elements of Detroit techno were stripped away, producing a much 'whiter' sound. The first proto-trance track is generally considered to be Lil' Louis' 'French kiss' (1989), whose hypnotic groove was fused with some decidedly over-the-top sexual moans, vying with Donna Summer's 'Love to love you baby' in their blatancy. However, the melodic and harmonic elements present in later trance were not yet in evidence.

It was 'Acperience' (1993) by German outfit Hardfloor that really set the template for trance. The steady tempo and incrementally filtering 303 builds almost imperceptibly to a long, drum-free breakdown section, with a high string pedal added to increase the tension. The end of the breakdown is accompanied by the snare-drum roll that was to become such a cliché in the late 90s.

The trance sound became increasingly popular, supplanting techno, house and drum'n'bass as the most popular dance genre. It was more experimental than house, less threatening than drum'n'bass and more melodic than techno. Robert Miles' melodic and sentimental 'dream house' track 'Children' was a huge hit all over Europe in early 1996 ('dream house' was the name given to a gentle, melodic Italian sub-genre of house). Its constantly

---

[8] 'A 1997 Release survey conducted in nightclubs revealed that 97% of British clubbers had tried drugs, and that just under 90% were planning to take some kind of illicit substance *that evening*.' Reynolds (1998): 423.

off-beat bass line and swirling chords were an important influence on trance over the next few years. The catchy piano melody also opened up new areas (as well as audiences) for trance. Released later the same year, 'Seven days and one week' by French outfit B.B.E. similarly shows the increasingly melodic route trance was taking at the time, and was a massive chart and clubland success.

Trance also started to become more harmonically complex than its predecessors. Cygnus X's 1998 'Orange theme' (released on legendary German trance label Eye Q) was a massive dancefloor hit, and its quasi-classical chord progression and pulsating bass-line had a big influence – evident on tracks such as Ferry Corsten's remix of William Orbit's arrangement of Barber's *Adagio for strings* (1999), in the Morse-code-like rhythms and harmonically-supportive role of the bass line.

Previously much electronic dance music focused on rhythm and timbre rather than melody or harmony, but trance brought the latter two back to the fore. This new sound took off outside the hardcore dance fraternity, and trance ruled many of the clubs that sprang up in the 90s.

One 90s phenomenon was the 'superclubs' – large venues capable of holding 1,000–2,000 clubbers and decked out with podium dancers, entertainers and extravagant light-shows. Sets by internationally famous DJs such as Paul Oakenfold, Pete Tong and Danny Rampling often meant exorbitant entrance fees. These huge venues were an attempt to recreate the 'vibe' of the raves and free party scene in more salubrious surroundings, but ever-increasing admission prices deterred many clubbers, and many such clubs went into decline.

The new, poppier sound of trance became a fixture of both the clubs and the charts in Europe. Artists like Sash! enjoyed hits such as 'Encore un fois' across the continent. Meanwhile, UK outfits such as Faithless and Underworld pursued a less overtly commercial sound within a band-like set-up, and gained widespread cross-over success with tracks like 'Insomnia' and 'Born slippy' (both 1996).

Sticking to a tried and tested formula of off-beat bass lines, long breakdowns and increasingly cheesy melodies, trance became less innovative and more and more formularized. Its popularity ebbed, and it was replaced in the public's affection by the funkier, heavily syncopated sound of 'garage'.

House, R&B, Garage

House continued to evolve throughout the 90s, generating new sub-genres and combining with other genres. Examples include 'filtered house', where whole sections of the track are filtered, an early example being 'Musique' by France's Daft Punk, or the later, more disco-inflected 'Music sounds better with you' by Daft Punk's Thomas Bangalter under the moniker of Stardust. Daft Punk were included on the soundtrack for the Sony PlayStation game *Wipeout 2097*, along with other cutting-edge dance acts such as Photek and the Chemical Brothers. With the introduction of CD-based media for games, many high profile artists have licensed their recordings for game soundtracks, providing an entirely new, and lucrative, source of revenue.

'Hard house' flowered in the late 90s and early 2000s, with a heavier, more underground sound popularized by DJs such as Lisa Lashes and Pete Wardman, setting itself apart from the more commercial sounds of 'handbag house', which was prevalent in the mid-90s. House had also become part of pop's mainstream, with artists including Madonna (on her 1990 hit 'Vogue') incorporating elements of it into their sound.

New York's house and garage scene thrived, making a superstar of the house DJ and remixer Armand Van Helden. Having absorbed hip-hop and electro in his formative years, Van Helden shot to fame in the 90s, remixing artists such as New Order, Jimmy Somerville and most famously singer–songwriter Tori Amos. Van Helden's mix of Amos's 'Professional widow' (1997) took only fragments of the original vocal from the quirky harpsichord-driven original. He drastically increased the tempo and added a funk-derived bass-line and pummelling house loop. The resulting single was a massive worldwide hit.

Subsequently, Van Helden became the remixer everyone wanted to use. The records kept on coming, including his 2009 collaboration with rapper Dizzee Rascal on the No. 1 hit 'Bonkers'.

The term 'R&B' took on a new meaning in the US in the late 80s and 90s. Soul had been combined with the tougher street sounds of hip-hop to produce a new hybrid – R&B (a.k.a. 'urban'). Key elements were soul-influenced, virtuoso vocals (often with close harmonies), and tight, syncopated drum programming. Examples include 'What have you done for me lately' by Janet Jackson (1986), 'No scrubs' by TLC (1999) and 'Bootylicious' by Destiny's Child (2001). The style also took off in the UK with songs like 'Power of a woman' by Eternal (1995).

'Garage' had also begun to mean something different in the UK in the mid-90s. A new sub-genre combined the deep bass of jungle with drum loops of US garage and ragga-style vocals to produce 'Speed Garage' (or simply 'garage'). Early examples include 'Gunman' by 187 Lockdown and 'Rip groove' by Double 99 (1997), featuring the 'tape stop' sound effects, squelchy analogue bass and time-stretched vocals that were to become typical elements of the style. The genre rejected drum'n'bass's increasingly experimental direction, and consequently its more conservative sound became a big hit, initially in London clubs but eventually nationwide. It heralded a return to the aspirational, dressed-up days of disco, with sharp dressing and expensive champagne *de rigeur*.

Ayia Napa, a resort on the island of Cyprus, became the favoured destination for garage lovers. It was here that US R&B was introduced into the mix, adding syncopated rhythms and soulful vocals which made for a smoother sound, as heard on 'There you go (sovereign mix)' by Pink, and 'Why? (Matt 'Jam' Lamont remix)' by Mis-Teeq. Garage also crossed over into mainstream pop with UK hits such as 'Fill me in' and '7 days' by smooth-voiced garage superstar Craig David.

A return to a tougher, more underground sound was made by garage outfit the Streets on their innovative debut album *Original Pirate Material* (2002), where Mike Skinner's skilled MC-ing, well-observed lyrics and avoidance of garage's increasingly clichéd sound helped garage find a new audience. One of the stand-out tracks is the evocative single 'Weak become heroes', a dewy-eyed paean to the lost, all-inclusive vibe of early-90s clubs.

Rap in the 90s

Rap went from strength to strength in the 90s, absorbing elements of different genres, including R&B and house, into its sound. New forms such as the mellow, non-aggressive 'daisy age' rap of De la Soul arrived. Their jazz- and psychedelia-tinged debut album, *Three Feet High and Rising* (1989), was widely praised, suggesting a new way forward for rap. However, they were subsequently eclipsed by the aggressive, angry sound of hardcore and ganster (or 'gangsta') rappers such as Wu-Tang Clan and Master P, as well as Snoop Doggy Dogg, who incorporated a G-funk-inspired, drawling style.

Female rappers came to the fore in the 90s. The most successful and innovative was Missy Elliott. She has always written and performed her own material, and has penned hit songs for such artists as Aaliyah and Mariah Carey. On *Miss E…So Addictive* (2001), she introduced house grooves ('4 my people'),[9] ethnic instruments, and unusual rhythms (on the hit 'Get ur freak on') on one of the freshest and most important rap albums of recent years. All-female rap outfit Salt 'n' Pepa, who had being going since the 80s, reached the height of their popularity in the 90s with the albums *Blacks' Magic* (1990) and *Very Necessary* (1993). They introduced pop and R&B elements into their sound, and addressed issues such as safe sex on 'Let's talk about sex', an idea unthinkable to most male rappers of the time. Rap was also combined with R&B on the Fugees album *The Score*. The smooth grooves, combined with Lauryn Hill's silky voice and their covering of past hits 'Killing me softly' and 'No woman, no cry', were a hit with audiences.

---

[9] House grooves (or loops) are generally a combination of four-on-the-floor bass drum and off-beat hi-hat.

Also no stranger to other artists' music, multi-faceted rap superstar Puff Daddy had a string of hits, many based entirely around samples of other songs. Known for his work as a businessman, A&R man and producer as well as a rapper, Puff Daddy ensured the success of many of his tracks by basing them on established hit songs – tracks like 'Let's dance' by David Bowie (on 'Been around the world') or 'Every breath you take' by the Police (on 'I'll be missing you').

Irish-American rappers House of Pain had more credibility and a massive hit with their rowdy rap crossover hit 'Jump around' in 1992, but could not subsequently match it. In 1999, Eminem shot to fame with the release of the quirky 'My name is', whose surreally violent lyrics endeared him to many a bored teenager. During the 2000s he was rap's biggest star, much to the chagrin of many a black MC.

Ambient, chillout, trip-hop

Brian Eno practically invented the ambient (a.k.a. chillout) genre with albums such as *Discreet Music* (1975) and *Music for airports* (1978), the latter conceived as background music for departure lounges rather than conscious listening, a collage of gentle piano phrases and slowly evolving soundscapes. Chillout as a genre came out of the proliferation of 'chillout' rooms found in clubs in the early 90s, whereby clubbers could take time out from dancing by relaxing on cushions and listening to soft music. It also became the music of choice for many an after-club soiree. The cyclical and non-dramatic sounds of classical minimalist composers such as Terry Riley and Steve Reich also had an influence on its evolution. Leading practitioners were initially the Orb and pop-art pranksters KLF.

Techno-hippies the Orb sampled Steve Reich's *Electric Counterpoint* on the dreamy and mesmeric track 'Little fluffy clouds' (1990). They used dialogue from a US children's TV programme featuring singer–songwriter Rickie Lee Jones to form a narrative – and a title – for the track. Ms Jones was not impressed, and the Orb's record company had to settle out of court, but the track became a touchstone for the ambient scene. They later released the longest single in UK history with 'Blue room', which came in at almost 40 minutes. Their infamous appearance on *Top of the Pops* saw the duo playing chess and waving at the camera while a much truncated edit of the tune played on.

Under the guise of the Timelords, KLF members Bill Drummond and former Orb-member Jimmy Cauty were originally known for novelty records like 'Doctorin' the Tardis' (1988). Two years later, the duo released the ambient classic *Chill Out*. An almost completely beat-free album, *Chill Out* was a pastoral collection of 'found' environmental sounds, distant guitars and occasional interjections of a celestial-sounding choir.

Later exponents of ambient include the iconoclast Richard James (a.k.a. Aphex Twin). *Selected Ambient Works 85–92* (1993) and the darker *Selected Ambient Works, Vol. 2* (1994), though ambient in style, are not necessarily relaxing and can make for decidedly uneasy listening. By the end of the 90s 'chillout' had become big business, with countless chillout compilations on sale in the record shops, including the annual release of the soothing 'Café del Mar' series of albums, named after a famous chillout bar in Ibiza.

'Trip-hop' originated in the west of England (particularly Bristol). The most famous proponents of this shadowy combination of dark and down-tempo hip-hop drum loops, dubby bass and mournful vocals were Portishead and Massive Attack. The slow tempos meant that trip-hop was meant for listening to rather than dancing. Both bands made use of traditional hip-hop techniques such as scratching, whilst often keeping to a more traditional song-based structure.

60s spy-film soundtracks were an influence, especially those of James Bond composer John Barry, as heard on 'Sour times' by Portishead from their claustrophobic and moody debut album *Dummy* (1994). Beth Gibbons' melancholic vocals are set among a collage of creepy cimbalom[10] and twangy, disembodied guitar. '6 underground' by the Sneaker Pimps

---

[10] Stringed instrument from Eastern Europe struck with mallets, producing a metallic sound.

features a harp sample from the Bond film *Goldfinger*. The nostalgia for British pop culture of the 60s invites parallels with Britpop, but trip-hop is characterized by the tense atmosphere of the 'cold war' rather than the exuberance of the 'swinging 60s'.

Massive Attack had a less austere sound, taking more from dub and the club scene, but the songs had a similarly bleak character, as on their lush, string-laden 1991 hit 'Unfinished sympathy' and the dubbier 'Safe from harm', where Shara Nelson's emotive vocals add a more soulful dimension.

Industrial

A term originally applied to experimental electronic bands such as Throbbing Gristle and Cabaret Voltaire, 'industrial' was also used for more dance-based outfits of the late 80s such as Skinny Puppy, Front 242, Nitzer Ebb and KMFDM. These bands had embraced the MIDI revolution and incorporated synthesizers as well as 'found sounds',[11] such as samples of scraping metal. The drums were generally not complex and relied on a heavy, hammering sound, ignoring the funky syncopations of US house and techno. Guitars became more prominent in the early 90s, with acts like Ministry and Nine Inch Nails introducing metal and goth elements into their sound. The combination of hammering drums and heavy guitars plus a little humour is evident on 1000 Homo DJs' exhilarating cover of Black Sabbath's 'Supernaut'. Industrial dance-floor favourite 'Head like a hole' from the album *Pretty Hate Machine* (1989) by Nine Inch Nails showcases Trent Reznor's histrionic voice laid over menacing synthesizers, thrashing guitars and Teutonic-sounding drums. Reznor was industrial's first star, introducing a more melodic, song-oriented style while maintaining the aggressive, distorted sounds typical of the genre. Reznor's work in particular was an influence on the goth/metal sounds and shock-image of Marilyn Manson.

Big beat

The rise of the superclubs in the mid- and late 90s, with dressy door policies, corporate style and overpaid DJs, was to many a corruption of the original, non-exclusive scene of the late-80s clubs. This response, coupled with the numerous new styles that had evolved in the ten years since house and techno first appeared, led to the birth of 'big beat' – a sample-heavy cornucopia of styles, from disco through acid to rock, all held together with a rollicking drum loop, usually hip-hop derived, but harder and bigger.

Big beat happily plundered pop's history, from the organs and 60s surf guitar samples on Psychedeliasmith's 'Give me my Auger back' to a sample from the Who on Fatboy Slim's 'Going out of my head', which also uses the guitar riff from Yvonne Elliman's cover of 'I can't explain'. Big beat was a delirious combination of dance technology and rock's uninhibited Bacchanalian attitude, having more in common with the acid house and hardcore scenes of the late 80s and early 90s than the rather po-faced stance of minimal techno. The drug of choice was alcohol, making for a boisterous and lively atmosphere. This, in conjunction with its 'anyone (with a sampler) can do it' attitude led to comparisons with punk, though there was no specific political ideology or image attached to the scene, simply the pursuit of a good time.

Big beat originated at small clubs such as the Heavenly Sunday Social in London and the Big Beat Boutique in Brighton. The Chemical Brothers were associated with the big beat scene, and became well-known faces at the Heavenly Sunday Social. They put out their first release, the hip-hop/house chimera 'Song to the siren', after borrowing £300 from a friend. It was much admired by DJ Andy Weatherall, who signed them up to his Junior Boys Own label. 'Leave home', the opening track on their debut album *Exit Planet Dust* (1995), has an overdriven bass-guitar riff over a souped-up hip-hop break, adding a hard, more rock-like edge to the track, and instantly distancing the Chemical Brothers from 'pure' dance music.

---

[11] Noises and ambient sounds that are then used in a musical context.

Known for DJ-ing a wide variety of music, the Chemical Brothers had a love of psyche-delia (the Beatles' 'Tomorrow never knows' is their favourite song) that can be heard on *Dig Your Own Hole* (1997). 'Private psychedelic reel' is an epic of sitars, wailing clarinet and filter sweeps, all underpinned by big, trashy drums.

Brighton's Big Beat Boutique was started off by local record label Skint, which became, together with London's Wall of Sound, one of the most important big-beat labels. The opening night of the Big Beat Boutique in April 1996 featured soon-to-be-legendary DJ Fatboy Slim (the big-beat alter ego of Norman Cook) as well as Oasis tour DJ Sean Rowley, emphasizing the cross-genre playlist of the club. Fatboy Slim went on to be the star of the big-beat scene in the UK.

Big beat had a big impact on the UK charts, with the Chemical brothers, Fatboy Slim and the Propellerheads all notching up hits. The combination of dance and rock also won many converts from the indie scene, with big-beat tracks played alongside songs by the Manic Street Preachers and Oasis at indie clubs. The Chemical Brothers utilized the vocal talents of Oasis' Noel Gallagher (on 'Setting sun' and 'Let forever be') and the Verve's Richard Ashcroft (on 'The trip'). Strengthening the bond between big beat and indie brought them success in the more rock-friendly USA, where the album *Dig Your Own Hole* sold 40,000 in its first week of release.

PURE POP

All-boy and all-girl vocal groups enjoyed a revival in the 90s. In the late 80s and early 90s, the US produced a string of boy-bands including New Kids on the Block and Color Me Badd. They performed a blend of pop toughened up by the urban sounds of rap and R&B, alternating between sweet ballads and more up-tempo dance tracks accompanied by choreo-graphed dance moves. Their audience consisted almost entirely of (pre)adolescent girls who adored their air-brushed icons. They were followed by the more solidly R&B and vocally talented Boyz II Men.

In the UK, photogenic bothers Matt and Luke Goss formed the group Bros along with Craig Logan in the late 80s. They adopted sounds and styles similar to those of their US counterparts and had a legion of screaming girl fans. Bros were succeeded by the incredibly successful Take That, who defined the look and sound of 90s boy-bands and spawned endless look- and sound-alikes. They were marketed at young girls and gay men, much as Stock, Aitken and Waterman's output had been in the 80s. Indeed, the group soon incorporated elements of SAW's melodic and hook-laden pop/dance formula into their own songs, as can be heard on 'Relight my fire' (1993). Their habit of performing covers set the tone for the 90s.

Roguish Take That member Robbie Williams left the group in 1995, keen to pursue a solo career. His debut album *Life Thru a Lens* (1997) included the hit ballad 'Angels' and more up-tempo 'Let me entertain you', the latter sounding like a souped–up 'Sympathy for the devil', in keeping with his laddish image. On his follow-up album, *I've Been Expecting You* (1998), he flirted with James Bond imagery, and used a sample of the theme from the Bond film *You Only Live Twice* on his UK No. 1 'Millennium'. The 90s' practice of using old songs as a basis for newer ones, as well as a general love for all things retro, was followed by Williams on 'Supreme', a slightly altered version of Gloria Gaynor's disco hit 'I will survive'.

This lack of innovation and reliance on old songs prompted David Bowie to dismiss the British pop industry, including Robbie Williams and Kylie Minogue, as simply 'cruise ship entertainment'.[12] The immense popularity of the UK (and later US) TV programme *Popstars*, where aspiring singers audition in the hope of being included in a 'manufactured' vocal group, adds credence to Bowie's prophetic criticism.

Kylie Minogue was a major pop icon of 90s Britain. Previously known for her soap-opera career and sugary pop songs with Stock, Aitken and Waterman, Minogue duetted

---

[12] Quoted from www.bbc.co.uk (5 July 2002).

with Australian goth Nick Cave on 'Where the wild flowers grow' and appeared as a temptress in the video for the more mature-sounding 'Confide in me' (1994) in an attempt to shed her innocent image. This process continued with the retro-disco glitz of 'Spinning around' (2000), whose video established her new titillating image. She followed up with a string of hits, culminating with the massively popular dance anthem 'Can't get you out of my head'.

The prodigiously successful Spice Girls performed a lively combination of pop, R&B and dance, taking the world by storm with their philosophy of 'girl power', their own playful brand of feminism. Each member was given a separate image and character, setting them apart from the often indistinguishable members of other girl- and boy-bands.[13] The video for their first single, 'Wannabe' (1996), portrayed the girls as slightly anarchic but fun-loving, an image they retained throughout their career. They enjoyed hit after hit, becoming massive media celebrities. 'Ginger Spice', Geri Halliwell, left in 1998 to pursue a solo career, while the remaining Spice Girls soldiered on till 2001. The members went on to plough their own furrows in the entertainment industry with varying degrees of success. 'Posh Spice', Victoria Adams, found most success, marrying David Beckham and going on to become the ultimate WAG and style icon.

Several female solo singers achieved success in the 90s, notably Christina Aguilera, Britney Spears and Mariah Carey. Like several 'manufactured' singers, Christina Aguilera began her showbusiness career on American children's TV favourite *The Mickey Mouse Club*. *Christina Aguilera* (1999) contained teen-friendly sentimental pop songs with a light R&B/hip-hop feel. She changed her image and direction with *Stripped* (2002), appearing topless on the cover. The track 'Dirty' has a much harder, more urban R&B sound, while her powerful voice is exploited to full effect on the rock track 'Fighter'.

Fellow *Mickey Mouse Club* veteran Britney Spears presented a titillating image from the start of her pop career, famously appearing in a schoolgirl uniform in the video for 'Baby one more time' (1999), a catchy dance-tinged pop song written by Swedish producer and song-writer Max Martin. Spears's subsequent hits 'Crazy' and 'Oops I did it again' stuck to the same formula, sounding like re-writes of her first single. Like Aguilera, Spears opted for a tougher (and increasingly oversubscribed) R&B sound with accompanying sexual imagery, evident on the promo video for 'I'm a slave 4 U', but in doing so she partially alienated her teen fans. The following years saw more hits, but headlines were dominated by her chaotic personal life rather than her music.

Mariah Carey's debut album *Mariah Carey* (1990) was a collection of lightweight poppy R&B tracks and slushy ballads which showcased her vocal ability. An acrobatic singing style, with much use of 'melisma' (where a group of notes is sung on one syllable), became a defining element in her music and that of her peers Beyoncé and Christina Aguilera. Carey wrote her own songs on *Emotions* (1991), though the immature, childlike lyrics earned her criticism from some quarters. *Butterfly*, released later the same year, saw her take a tougher hip-hop/R&B direction, abandoning her relatively squeaky-clean image for a more raunchy look and setting a precedent for Aguilera and Spears. The growing trend for female singers to use sexual imagery to sell their records prompted singer KD Lang to comment:

> You know they are both really good singers. But they are caught in the push to be overly sexy and to sell themselves as objects when it's enough that they are great singers. I feel for them. They're in the grip of the celebrity sex madness that is going on. I'm not a prude, but where do they go from here?

> Interview with Liz Smith in the *New York Post*

It was a good question. Mariah Carey's career turned to a nightmare as she suffered a breakdown during the promotion of her film and soundtrack album *Glitter* (2001). On her

---

[13] Baby-faced Emma B was 'Baby Spice', cheeky red-head Geri was 'Ginger Spice', slinky Victoria was 'Posh Spice', football-mad Mel C was 'Sporty Spice' and mouthy Mel B was inexplicably named 'Scary Spice'.

post-trauma album *Charmbracelet* (2002) Carey reclaimed her former demure image, dropping the tougher sound and seeking to recapture her adult middle-of-the-road fanbase.

NEW TERRITORIES

Pop music has traditionally been dominated by the twin axes of the USA and the UK, but the 90s saw new acts emerging from countries previously not known for their pop output, as well as an infusion of music from ethnic minorities in the more established countries, particularly the UK.

In the 90s and early 2000s, Scandinavia, previously well known only for Abba, produced a variety of successful artists, including Swedish indie-poppers the Cardigans and Norwegian electronic outfit Röyksopp, whose calming mellow sound earned them a number of hit singles in the UK in the early 2000s. Idiosyncratic Icelander Björk emerged as a major figure, and is profiled below.

French dance duo Daft Punk and the more ambient-style Air brought French pop music into the limelight. Air's album *Moon Safari* (1998) blended laid-back 70s disco, progressive rock and swirling synthesizers into a dreamy mosaic of sound, achieving a hit with 'Sexy boy'. Vienna is home to the innovative hip-hop/dub label Klein Records, whose jazzy hip-hop outfit Sofa Surfers released *Encounters* (2002), featuring a guest appearance by Jamaican roots luminary Junior Delgado.

The growth of the South Asian community in the UK, especially in London and Birmingham, has resulted in various fusions of traditional Pakistani and Indian music with Western pop sounds. Bands such as Asian Dub Foundation and Fun Da Mental combine South Asian melodies, rhythms and sounds with those of hip-hop, dub and traditional Western pop instruments. Both bands are strongly political and anti-racist. The critically lauded *Community Music* (2000), by Asian Dub Foundation, combined the above elements with angry guitars, and crossed over to the indie audience.

Originally referring to folk music from the Punjab region, the term 'bhangra' is now more often used to describe the combination of traditional Punjabi string and drum instruments and singing with other elements, such as Hindi film music and Western music. Bhangra emerged in the UK in the 70s, particularly in the Midlands, where young Asians were listening to traditional music from the Punjab as well as Western music and Hindi film music. The dance revolution of the late 80s was a large influence, and hip-hop, reggae and drum'n'bass were absorbed into the style. Fusing the heavy beat of the dhol drum with the theme from the 70s TV programme *Knightrider*, Panjabi MC had a big hit in 2003 with the bhangra song 'Mundian to bach ke'.

While the USA and UK were often over-concerned with their illustrious past, pop music continued to evolve far away in Eastern Asia. Previously labelled mere Western copyists, a growing number of bands from Japan adopted a post-modern smash-and-grab attitude to pop culture. Hugely popular in their home country, Japan's Judy and Mary juxtaposed jazz, languorous pop and squealing punk noise on the genre-defying song 'Music fighter' from their album *Pop Life* (1998), putting many of the efforts of their backward-looking Western counterparts to shame.

Tokyo band Plus-Tech Squeeze Box displayed similarly schizophrenic tendencies on their album *Fakevox* (2000). The track 'Early riser' combines vocals, blistering guitar, cartoon-like sound effects and game-show music into a disorienting, kaleidoscopic sound, fully exploiting the possibilities of digital technology while simultaneously maintaining a heart of pure pop.

Japanese solo artist Cornelius has built up a substantial following in the West, partly due to his stunning live performances which combine musical eclecticism with tightly integrated video projections, resulting in a unique blend of live gig and contemporary video installation.

PROFILES

Björk

Hayley Madden/Rex Features

Björk at the London Palladium, 1998

Brought up on an eclectic diet of lullabies, jazz and pop music, all of which would be a great influence on her, Icelandic songstress Björk knew all the songs from the film *The Sound of Music* before she was three. Her musical leanings evident from early on, she recorded her debut album, *Björk*, at the tender age of eleven and became a child star in her native country. In her teenage years she was involved in numerous bands, including post-punk outfit KUKL, who evolved into the Sugarcubes in 1986. Fronted by the talented and photogenic Björk, they had an unusual sound that soon raised interest outside Iceland, and the band gained an indie following in the UK as well as mainstream success at home.

Björk's trademark oddball lyrics and highly individual vocal style are to be heard on the single 'Birthday' from *Life's Too Good* (1988), which was an indie hit in the UK and US. After 'Birthday' media interest focused more on Björk and less on the rest of the band, creating tension between Björk and maverick co-singer Einar. In 1990 Björk recorded a jazz/swing album with the Icelandic trio Gudmundar Ingólffson. Released only in Iceland, it revealed her passion for music other than pop.

The Sugarcubes disbanded in 1992 and Björk moved to London, arriving in the midst of the thriving dance culture. She began to work with many of dance's well-known figures, including Underworld, Tricky and, more importantly, producer Nellee Hooper, with whom she collaborated on her solo album *Debut* (1993). The relationship proved highly successful, and *Debut* was released to rave reviews. The quirky instrumentation, unusual jazz-like melodies and Björk's unique and powerful voice were unlike anything around at the time. Her eclectic style extended to her dress sense, as she typically combined mountain boots with frocks by leading designers such as Martin Margeira and Hussein Chalayan.

Her much anticipated follow-up album *Post* (1995) offered an even broader canvas of sounds. Björk and Hooper experimented with many genres, from the quasi-industrial opening track 'Army of me' to the chromatic and sophisticated orchestral ballad 'Isobel'. Unusually for the often musically conservative 90s, this highly innovative album was another commercial success in the UK, though it still struggled for mainstream US radio airplay and MTV exposure, despite an array of imaginative and acclaimed promotional videos.

Björk extended her musical boundaries still further on her next album *Homogenic* (1997), where she ditched Hooper in favour of dance luminaries Howie B, Mark Bell from LFO and Mark 'Spike' Stent. The heart-rending, multi-layered ballad 'Unravel' is evocative of Baroque chamber music, while elsewhere lush strings play alongside heavily effect-laden electronic loops and samples on the epic 'Batchelorette' and the emotional 'Joga', Björk's song to her native country.

In 2000 she starred in the film *Dancer in the Dark*. The accompanying soundtrack, *Selmasongs*, showed Björk opting for a dark, at times industrial sound to complement the film's often bleak atmosphere. Björk pursued a more reflective direction on her next album, the fragile and luscious *Vespertine* (2001), where her vocals are often limited to a whisper, giving the delicate and practically drum-free arrangements room to breathe – as on 'Pagan poetry', where her voice is complemented by a harp and what sounds like a multitude of music boxes. With her expressive, individual voice, eclectic outlook and original combinations of acoustic instruments and cutting edge dance music techniques, Björk summed up much of what was best in the music of the 90s.

Norman Cook (Fatboy Slim)

Norman Cook began his pop career playing guitar for left-wing indie-poppers the Housemartins, and also DJ-ing. The band split in 1987, and Cook formed Beats International, with whom he could explore his love of a more dance-oriented music.

Cook landed himself in hot water with Beats International's hit 'Dub be good to me', which used the bass-line from the Clash's 'Guns of Brixton' without crediting it, a situation which Cook has been careful to avoid ever since. Following money problems, a divorce, and a period of depression, he formed the funky retro outfit Freak Power, who had a top-ten hit with 'Turn on, tune in, cop out' in 1995. At the same time he had a solo project, Pizzaman, which had some success. He then began DJ-ing as 'Fatboy Slim' at the Big Beat Boutique in Brighton.

One of Fatboy Slim's early tracks, 'Everybody needs a 303', is typical of much of his heavily sample-derived 'big beat' style. It opens with a cheeky slap-bass riff accompanied by funky breaks and a vocal sample from 'Everybody needs love' by 70s funk singer Edwin Starr. The sound of a distorted TB 303 gradually encroaches on the track until the breakdown, which comprises only the 303 over a chant of 'party party'. Cook then employs his favourite technique of repeating a sample (the Starr sample in this case) at increasingly short intervals, giving a feeling of acceleration, followed by the inevitable reintroduction of the drums and much extended 303 filtering.

His tellingly-titled *Better Living Through Chemistry* (1996) summed up the emerging big-beat style and brought Cook UK recognition and success, while also sparking overseas interest. His reputation as a remixer grew, following the successful remix of Cornershop's 'Brimful of Asha' (1998), where he converted the rather drab original into a bouncy big-beat classic and club favourite, far outselling the original version. Cook's 1998 remix of Wildchild's 'Renegade master' remains one of big beat's crowning achievements,[14] full of filtered, cut-up vocals, riotous hip-hop beats and the most exciting breakdown section of the

---

[14] For an analysis of 'Renegade master' see page 188.

whole genre. Following these releases, Cook became the remixer everyone wanted to use. He remixed Missy Elliot and the Beastie Boys, but famously turned down Madonna.

His second album, *You've Come a Long Way Baby* (1998), brought Cook international fame as an artist in his own right. The supercharged surf nostalgia of 'Rockafeller skank' was a UK top-ten hit, but it was the gospel-tinged single 'Praise you' that delivered his biggest commercial success, its more mellow quality showing a shift from the raucous sound of big beat.

The more relaxed style continued on his third Fatboy Slim album, *Halfway Between the Gutter and the Stars* (2000), where he collaborated with soul diva Macy Gray and funk-bass legend Bootsy Collins. On 'Ya mama', which is full of clamorous guitars, wildly filtering synthesizers and rollicking breaks, Cook showed that he has not completely abandoned big beat. However, the standout track is 'Sunset (bird of prey)', which presents a poem by the Doors' Jim Morrison set to a swirling soundscape of synthesizers and breakbeats.

Eminem

Troubled bad-boy rapper Eminem was born Marshall Mathers in 1972 in St Joseph, Missouri, and moved to a housing project in Detroit at the age of twelve. Raised by his dysfunctional mother in mobile homes in poor working class areas, he had an unhappy childhood. In Detroit he learned how to rap, and by the age of fourteen called himself 'M + M' (after his initials), which became 'Eminem'. He participated in 'rap battles' (contests where rappers improvise, trying to better each other's raps) in an attempt to make his name in what was still very much a black area of music. He rapped for various outfits including controversial Detroit rap sextet D-12, whose gritty and disturbing raps profoundly influenced his own style.

Following lukewarm reviews of his first album *Infinite* (1996), Eminem went through a barrage of personal problems and, increasingly reliant on drugs and alcohol, attempted suicide. All the above presaged the cartoonish brutality and nightmare-like qualities of Eminem's alter ego, Slim Shady. Taking material from his own turbulent life, Eminem made Slim Shady a vehicle for an increasingly dark and disquieting style. On 'Just the two of us', from *The Slim Shady EP* (1997), Eminem serenades his daughter while her murdered mother lies in the boot (trunk) of their car.

Eminem gained worldwide recognition after hooking up with rapper and producer Dr. Dre. The Dre-produced *The Slim Shady LP* (1999) contained the massive hit 'My name is'. The track's blackly humorous and disturbing lyrics found an instant audience of teenage boys who lapped up the bleak and violent imagery. His lyrics paralleled the outlook of many emerging nu-metal bands of the time, such as Limp Bizkit and Slipknot, and simultaneously embodied the fears of liberal America.

Eminem rerecorded 'Just the two of us' as '97 Bonnie and Clyde' on *The Slim Shady LP*. His woman-slaying theme continued on the album's cover, which features what appears to be a woman's legs hanging limply out of an open car boot while Eminem gazes moodily onto a river. The combination of Dre's imaginative production with Eminem's highly skilled rapping and controversial lyrics made the album a huge hit, and he became the first credible white solo rapper to achieve mainstream success.

His next album, the disturbing *The Marshall Mathers LP* (2000), sold almost two million copies in seven days. The album opens with 'Kill you', a vitriolic attack on his mother. The harrowing 'Kim' is another attack, this time on his estranged wife. The obsession with death and murder continues on 'Stan', a fictional account of an obsessive fan who kills himself by driving into a river with his pregnant girlfriend trapped in the car boot. To great effect, the chorus skilfully employs the haunting verse from 'Thank you', by Dido.

Controversial words and incidents have guaranteed Eminem constant media scrutiny. He duetted with Elton John at the Grammy awards ceremony in 2001, in an attempt to play down accusations of homophobia, raised by the lyrics of 'Kill you'. Eminem also starred in the 2002 film *8 mile*, which was loosely based on his experiences as a young rapper in Detroit. His 2002 album *The Eminem Show* explores new avenues, including traditional singing, and is both musically and lyrically a more complex proposition than its predecessor. His frustration with the state of the nation is evident on the raps 'White America' and the bizarre waltz-time track 'Square dance', in which he targets racism, hypocrisy and the Bush administration.

FURTHER LISTENING

Metallica *Metallica* (1991)
Thrash metal titans Metallica became hugely successful with this album, finding new audiences with a succession of big singles, the occasional orchestral ballad and MTV-friendly videos. Despite the grunge revolution, this album set the precedent for the wide-scale success of heavy music in the mainstream in the late 90s.

Steve Vai *Fire Garden* (1996)
Virtuosic playing from guitar hero Steve Vai.

Alanis Morissette *Jagged Little Pill* (1995)
Former child star Morissette reinvented herself as the queen of angst-fuelled anthemic 'alternative' pop with this massively successful album.

Janet Jackson *Janet* (1993)
This album demonstrates her slick R&B and contains the single 'That's the way love goes', which occupied the top of the US charts for eight weeks.

The White Stripes *White Blood Cells* (2001)
With the charts choked by nu-metal, Eminem and plodding R&B, unlikely success came to Detroit's Jack and Meg White, a guitar and drums duo playing stripped down, catchy, blues-based songs with surprisingly convincing attitude and flair.

Faith No More *Angel Dust* (1992)
FNM were influential in bringing together rock and rap as it mutated into nu-metal, bringing an eclectic, subversive and often brilliant mixture of pop melody, Lionel Richie, funk and thrash metal to this varied and somewhat odd album.

Beck *Odelay* (1996)
Wunderkind Beck Hansen managed to summarize the 90s 'alternative' boom with this dazzling assimilation of every style going: hip-hop, country, jazz, rock, grunge, metal, blues and more. The post-modern effortlessly accomplished with breezy slacker cool.

Cypress Hill *Black Sunday* (1992)
Cypress Hill's blend of cannabis-promoting lyrics and spooky, laid-back music helped them find a big audience among 'alternative' rock fans, joining the Lollapalooza circus and influencing much 90s hip-hop production.

Jay-Z *The Blueprint* (2001)
With ruthlessly fluent rhymes over heavy funk and soul samples, Jay-Z was a dominating force in late 90s hip-hop.

Jeff Buckley *Grace* (1994)
A raw and emotional work, *Grace* is Jeff Buckley's only studio album. It features what many consider to be the definitive version of the Leonard Cohen song 'Hallelujah', along with the powerful 'Lilac wine' and the rock ballad 'Grace'. Like his father, the singer-songwriter Tim Buckley, Jeff Buckley died tragically early.

Moby *Play* (1999)
Accessible electronic music from this New York DJ, singer-songwriter and performer. Several tracks, including 'Natural blues' and 'Why does my heart feel so bad?', are based on samples taken from vintage blues and gospel music. Moby made all the tracks available on commercial licence from the outset, and most songs are familiar from films or advertisements.

Primus *Tales from the Punchbowl* (1995)
This bizarre album from San Francisco band Primus is hard to categorize. Its quirky surrealism, with song titles such as 'Wynona's big brown beaver' and 'Year of the parrot', falls somewhere between Captain Beefheart, King Crimson and Rush, all underpinned by the elaborate, sometimes funky bass lines of Les Claypool. In 1996 Primus composed the theme song to the animated television programme *South Park*.

chapter

8

Toby Bricheno, Ben Kaye and Jessica Winterson

2000s

The 2000s saw a fragmentation of musical styles but little in terms of new movements or genres outside of dance music, where two new genres, grime and dubstep, emerged. Female artists, both solo and all-girl groups, grew increasingly dominant in the pop world with acts such as Beyoncé, Adele, Amy Winehouse, Girls Aloud, Sugababes, Katy Perry and Lady Gaga achieving worldwide commercial success in a variety of genres.

Retromania

The shadow of the 1980s loomed large in the 2000s for two reasons: many of the artists had grown up listening to music of the 1980s via their parents and elder siblings, plus the decade was just about distant enough to have gained a patina of nostalgia for the younger musicians who had not experienced it first-hand – 'borrowed nostalgia for the unremembered 80s' as LCD Soundsystem's James Murphy put it so succinctly in the 2002 debut single 'Losing my edge'.

Some music was so referential to the 1980s that it became a virtual pastiche: the carefully-studied electropop of the Knife, the neo-New Romanticism of White Lies, even the previously reviled stadium rock pomp of Simple Minds had a resurgence, as can be heard on Glasvegas's second album *Euphoric Heartbreak* (2011) and the song 'Still life' (2011) by the Horrors.

In his critically lauded book *Retromania* (2011), music journalist Simon Reynolds deals with the lack of innovation and curator-like plundering of past styles prevalent in the first decade of this century:

> Many of the 2000s' most commercially prominent trends involved recycling: the garage-punk resurgence of The White Stripes, The Hives, The Vines, Jet et al.; the vintage-soul style of Amy Winehouse, Duffy, Adele and the other white Brit females who pass for black American lady singers from the sixties; eighties synth-pop-inspired femmes such as Little Boots and Lady Gaga.
>
> *Retromania*, Simon Reynolds pub. By Faber and Faber 2011

The eclectic songwriter Sufjan Stevens also bemoaned the lack of innovation:

> There are great bands today – I love White Stripes, I love The Raconteurs, but it's a museum piece. They are channeling the ghosts of that era – The Who, punk rock, the Sex Pistols, whatever. It's been done.
>
> Ibid.

In a turn of events aided and abetted by the all-pervading internet and its instant access to music from every era, innovation somehow dropped out of fashion. Rather than the invention of entirely new genres, fragmentation and a fusing of existing styles became a hallmark of the 2000s.

A considerable amount of cross pollination occurred between pop, dance, R&B and hip-hop, from hip-hop acts like Outkast (with their hit 'Hey ya') to female artists such as Rihanna and Nicki Minaj.

The focus for much alternative music was on North America: from the polished but innovative R&B of Beyoncé, the unhinged art-rock of the Yeah Yeah Yeahs, the gritty punk funk of LCD Soundsystem, the sensuous 'Hollywood sadcore' of Lana Del Rey, or the cross-genre eclecticism of Dan Deacon – the 2000s belonged to the US.

POP

Whilst the unadventurous stadium rock of Foo Fighters and the conservative, indie-by-numbers of Snow Patrol and Coldplay (whose collaboration with dance diva Rihanna on 'Princess of China' is arguably their most innovative release this century) remained popular, mainstream artists such as Beyoncé proved more musically daring. The bouncing rhythms, child-like call and response vocals of the verse and the surprisingly ominous bass line of the chorus of her hit single 'Single ladies (put a ring on it)' inspired contemporary composer Mark-Anthony Turnage to quote the song extensively in his orchestral work *Hammered Out* in 2010.

Madonna and her legacy

Madonna's popularity continued throughout the 2000s. Her 2005 album *Confessions on a Dance Floor* sold 12 million copies and was a worldwide hit, taking the No. 1 slot in 40 countries and earning her a place in the 2007 Guinness Book of Records. It yielded the disco-influenced hit single 'Hung up', whose chorus is based around a sample of Abba's 1979 hit 'Gimme! Gimme! Gimme! (A man after midnight)'.

Most importantly, Madonna was a huge influence on an array of female artists who rose to popularity in the 2000s, especially in terms of image, sexuality and self-determination. Gwen Stefani, Katy Perry, Pink and Rihanna have all expressed admiration. Self-styled hip-hop superstar Nicki Minaj and uncompromising English singer M.I.A. willingly appeared as pom-pom-waving cheerleaders in the video for 'Give me all your luvin' (as well as guesting on the track itself), illustrating the respect that Madonna is accorded by the rising stars of the next generation.

The BRIT school and its female alumni

The BRIT school, situated in Croydon in South London, was founded in 1991 by Mark Featherstone-Witty, who was inspired by Alan Parker's 80s film *Fame* to create a secondary school specializing in the performing arts. Former students include Adele, Amy Winehouse and Jessie J, all talented singers who have gone on to achieve considerable success (Adele's album *21* has sold more than 27 million copies at the time of writing), but none of whom were particularly innovative.

Amy Winehouse

Despite only completing two albums in her short life, *Frank* and *Back to Black*, Winehouse made an indelible mark on the history of pop in the 2000s and was credited with paving the way for other soulful but arguably less talented British singers such as Adele and Duffy. Even pop doyenne Lady Gaga credited Winehouse with paving the way for her stellar success.

The jazzy pop of Winehouse's 2003 debut album *Frank* was well received but produced no hit singles. Her collaboration with producer Mark Ronson on her second album *Back to Black*, released in 2006, resulted in a poppier sound that showcased her distinctive husky

Rex Features

Amy Winehouse at the Isle of Wight Festival, 2007

contralto voice and was highly reminiscent of Motown 60s girl groups, fused with hip-hop beats, a streetwise attitude and unflinchingly honest lyrics. It received both critical and commercial success and yielded a string of hits, including 'Rehab', 'Back to black' and 'You know I'm no good'. Following the troubled singer's untimely death from alcohol poisoning in July 2011, *Back to Black* became a best-selling album in the UK. An album of unreleased tracks and demos, *Lioness: Hidden Treasures*, was released in December 2011, with a share of the profits going to the Amy Winehouse Foundation for addiction, set up by her family.

Winehouse's uncompromising autobiographical lyrics, rebellious and often drug-fuelled behaviour and outlandish image (combining 60s beehive hair and numerous tattoos) marked her out as a maverick and provided respite from the clean-cut acts offered up by the reality TV shows of the time such as *Pop Idol* and *X Factor*.

Adele

Shortly after graduating from the BRIT school in 2006, Adele was discovered by XL recordings after a friend posted a clip of her singing on MySpace. More mainstream than Amy Winehouse, the Tottenham-born singer-songwriter conquered the world with her show-stopping voice. On her albums *19* and *21*, tear-jerking ballads and more up-tempo, bluesy, gospel–influenced numbers proved a popular combination. 'Someone like you' (2010) – simple but powerfully affecting, with her emotive voice backed only by an acoustic piano – was her first No. 1 single in the UK, and became her second US hit following 'Rolling in the deep' earlier the same year. In the autumn of 2011, Adele cancelled two tours due to damaged vocal cords. Following laser microsurgery she made a comeback at the 2012 Grammy awards where she won in every category that she was nominated – six in all. In 2012 she sang the theme tune to the James Bond film *Skyfall,* topping the US charts and winning an Oscar in the process. Her adept songwriting and big bluesy voice earned her an array of celebrity fans from Madonna to stadium rockers such as Dave Grohl and even veteran punk rocker J. J. Burnel of the Stranglers.

Bohemian female pop

From the male-dominated UK indie scene, a handful of female artists emerged in the 2000s with something different to offer, taking their influences from alternative female vocalists such as Siouxsie Sioux, Björk, PJ Harvey and Kate Bush.

Florence Welch of Florence and the Machine has described her onstage image as 'Lady of Shalott meets Ophelia, mixed with scary gothic bat lady', putting her firmly in the canon of English eccentrics. Whilst her 2008 debut single 'Kiss with a fist' owed something to the garage blues-punk of the White Stripes, her style has since become increasingly epic, notably with the thundering anthem 'No light, no light' from the 2011 hit album *Ceremonials.* The rather more wistful Natasha Khan (better known as Bat For Lashes) has drawn comparisons with Kate Bush, as evidenced on tracks such as 'All your gold' from her delicate and under-stated 2012 album *The Haunted Man.* Perhaps her most intriguing song is the exquisitely atmospheric 'What's a girl to do', which draws equally on 60s girl groups, film soundtracks and hip-hop, as it tells a mournful tale of the end of desire.

One of the most inventive female artists of the 2000s was pop chameleon Alison Goldfrapp. In conjunction with band member Will Gregory she veered from the John Barry-esque soundscapes of *Felt Mountain* via the stomping electro pop of *Black Cherry* (with the synth-glam stomp of 'Strict machine', one of the defining songs of the decade) to the neo-disco of 'Ride a white horse' from their third album *Supernature* (2005) and the psychedelic folk of *Seventh Tree* (2008). Goldfrapp arrived a little late to the 80s revival party with the disappointing follow-up album *Head First* (2010).

Lana Del Rey – an American original

In her own words a 'self-styled gangsta Nancy Sinatra' Lana Del Rey (real name Elizabeth Woolridge Grant) arrived fully formed and seemingly out of nowhere with her hit 'Video games' in 2011. A stylistically mixed drum-less, string-drenched ballad, it was a perfect vehicle for Del Rey's smoky contralto croon. The internet, especially YouTube, was instrumental in her success. Del Rey's self-made video featured webcam footage intercut with archive clips, skateboarders, anonymous home video, and a drunken celebrity at the mercy of the paparazzi. This kaleidoscope of atmospheric but narrative-free stream of consciousness went viral and resulted in her first hit, reaching the top ten in various European countries. Del Rey's subsequent album *Born to Die* (2012) continued her melancholic orchestral style, and was a worldwide hit.

Reality TV

In the 2000s a new range of TV programmes appeared, in the form of a glorified karaoke competition with contestants simply singing straightforward renditions of well-known songs before a panel of judges. Essentially these programmes were a development from 1970s talent shows such as *New Faces* and *Opportunity Knocks*, with the added drama of a soap-opera style documentary, as cameras followed the varying fortunes of the hopefuls on a weekly basis.

In 2001, ITV began screening *Popstars*, a weekly talent show (based on the New Zealand show of the same name), whereby singers of varying degrees of technical ability sang before a panel of judges, with the more successful participants progressing to the next round. Week by week, singers were eliminated at the behest of the judges until only a handful remained. The final five participants were then assembled into the vocal group Hear'say, who enjoyed chart success before splitting up after 18 months. The five runners-up formed Liberty X and ironically enjoyed greater success and longevity than the winners.

Spice Girls manager and music svengali Simon Fuller created a similar show, *Pop Idol*, with one crucial difference: viewers were encouraged to vote on who stayed in the show via premium phone lines and texts. This feature proved immensely popular, as well as highly lucrative. *Popstars The Rivals* accordingly adopted the audience-voting feature for its second series in 2002. The eventual winners of this series, Girls Aloud, went on to become the 'most successful reality TV group' of all time (*Guinness Book of Records* 2007). Girls Aloud hold the current UK chart record for the most consecutive top-ten singles (including 'Sound of the underground' and 'The promise') by a female outfit. Renowned indie outfit Arctic Monkeys covered one of their hits, 'Love machine', on BBC Radio 1's *Live Lounge*.

The second series of *Pop Idol* became one of ITV's most profitable shows. Outspoken *Pop Idol* judge Simon Cowell decided to start a similar show in which he owned all the publishing rights, and created the *X Factor* in 2004. Its close similarity to *Pop Idol* led to a legal dispute, which was eventually settled out of court. *X Factor* became an instant hit and enjoyed continuous success – Series 6 had a peak audience of almost 20 million in the UK and the show spawned a worldwide franchise. By September 2012 artists appearing on the *X Factor* had made 29 No. 1 singles, dominating the UK charts. The show generated widespread criticism for its relentless commercialism and lining of Cowell's pockets. This culminated in a successful Facebook campaign in Christmas 2009 to prevent *X Factor* from reaching the No. 1 slot by urging people to buy 'Killing in the name' by Rage Against The Machine.

UK indie

The 2000s continued in much the same vein as the nineties. Indie and rock produced little innovation but continued, with few exceptions, to look backwards with increased intensity. Indeed, the conservative and bland UK indie scene earned itself the moniker 'Landfill Indie'.[1]

New Rave

New Rave was allegedly born out of a pun on 'New Wave' and described as a 'joke that went too far' by one of the most celebrated new rave acts, Klaxons. Alongside Shitdisco and New Young Pony Club, these were some of the key bands of this mid-2000s genre. However, the movement is sometimes cited as being purely a media construct, initiated by the *NME* to prop up falling sales by inventing a 'scene', as the bands included were stylistically disparate.

New Rave had little musically in common with 80s rave; instead, there was a strong new-wave influence. However, this didn't stop many of its fans sporting glow sticks and fluorescent clothing that was more commonly associated with the rave scene. New Rave was stylistically loose, with a traditional indie band line-up of drums, bass and guitar and the occasional keyboard or sample – as for example in 'Atlantis to Interzone' by Klaxons. The frenetic supercharged funk of 'I know Kung Fu' by Shitdisco and the stripped-down 80s groove of 'Ice cream' by New Young Pony Club show the breadth of styles that were incorporated in the genre.

Four bands

Aside from New Rave, there was little in terms of a 'scene' in UK indie and indeed the term 'indie' became less meaningful in the twenty-first century – were Coldplay indie or merely contemporary AOR? From this increasingly fragmented genre, four stylistically differing bands are considered below.

Franz Ferdinand, a Scottish band named after Archduke Franz Ferdinand, whose assassination precipitated World War 1, was a major band of the 2000s. Their preference for single

---

[1] www.guardian.co.uk/music/2009/jan/17/florence-and-the-machine-indie
www.huffingtonpost.co.uk/django-wylie/requiem-for-a-scene-i-mis_b_2101767.html

notes over chords and funk-like rhythms gave them an angular, stark sound reminiscent of 80s post-punk acts such as Gang of Four. Their second single, 'Take me out', with its dramatic tempo change and strident guitars, became a big indie hit in 2004, as was 'Do you want to' the following year.

Leeds' Kaiser Chiefs were similarly 80s-influenced but drew more on new wave bands, particularly the Jam, as can be heard on their hits 'I predict a riot' (2004) and 'Every day I love you less and less' (2005). Their often humorous lyrics and melodic hooks (and the boundless energy of frontman Ricky Wilson) also recalled 80s ska/pop band Madness.

Likewise, the Libertines drew strongly on their English roots and owed much to the 60s guitar pop of the Kinks as well as the more chaotic and raucous sounds of the Buzzcocks and the Sex Pistols. Frontmen Carl Barat and Pete Doherty were renowned for their close but often fraught relationship; their incessant infighting was frequently influenced by Doherty's prodigious drug intake and erratic behaviour. The noisy and boisterous guitar-driven sound in songs such as 'Don't look back into the sun' (2003) and 'Can't stand me now' (2004) can be heard as an influence in later bands of the decade, particularly in the early work of Arctic Monkeys.

Equally influenced by English bands, Kasabian had a harder, rockier sound, reminiscent of Oasis, combined with electronics and funky, baggy-like Madchester beats, particularly on tracks like 'Underdog' from their 2009 album *West Ryder Pauper Lunatic Asylum* and 'Days are forgotten' from *Velociraptor!* (2011). Their football-loving, laddish attitude alienated some, but hits such as 'Fire' (which features some inventive time-signature swapping) and the almost disco-esque 'Where did all the love go?' showed their more inventive side.

North American indie

The White Stripes became increasingly popular through the decade, and spawned a host of bass-less bands in the process, while retaining a raw and gritty sound showcasing Jack White's guitar pyrotechnics. Their major label debut was *Elephant* (2003), which produced perhaps their most instantly recognizable hit, 'Seven nation army'. The band broke up in 2011, and multi-instrumentalist White enjoyed continued success with the Dead Weather (as a drummer) and the Raconteurs. In 2012, White released his first solo album, *Blunderbuss*, which, though stylistically broader in scope than the White Stripes, was less inventive, sounding positively retrogressive when set alongside his earlier work.

One-time White Stripes support band the Yeah Yeah Yeahs made a huge impact on the 2000s. The electrifying art-rock of their debut album *Fever To Tell* (2003) combined the charismatic, occasionally unhinged vocals of Karen O with Nick Zinner's powerful and endlessly inventive guitar work – as heard on 'Date with the night', 'Y control' and especially 'Maps'. Their style evolved throughout the decade, with a strong 80s influence evident on the more electronic, dance-orientated *It's Blitz!* (2009). Their earlier aggressive style and newer electronic direction and pop sensibility combined very effectively on the 2009 hit 'Zero'.

Fronted by multi-instrumentalist and pop music scholar James Murphy, New York's LCD Soundsystem took a post-modernist approach – plundering but never aping pop music's extensive back catalogue. This mixing and matching of styles resulted in some highly inventive music. One of the most striking examples is 'Movement' from their eclectic, eponymously-titled debut album, which segues suddenly from a pounding electronic dance groove into thrashy garage rock more reminiscent of the Stooges. Murphy became known for his acerbic lyrics and distinctive singing style, often being compared to Mark E. Smith from the Fall. Both influences are evident on the 2002 single, 'Losing my edge', in which Murphy narrates a chronologically and geographically improbable list of pivotal moments in musical history at which he was present. Along with fellow New York outfit the Rapture, whose mutated funk song 'House of jealous lovers' was cited as one of the most important songs of the decade by influential blog Pitchfork, LCD Soundsystem established New York as a focus for innovative fusions of dance and indie in the 2000s.

Arcade Fire, from Canada, were an influential indie act. 'Rebellion (lies)', from their debut album *Funeral* (2004), became – with its chiming piano, driving guitars and impassioned vocals – a blueprint for much of the indie of the decade. Their already large sound (featuring orchestral and folk instruments alongside the traditional drums, bass and guitar) increased further with the addition of orchestra, pipe organ and choir on the follow-up *Neon Bible* (2007), which featured the anthemic single 'No cars go'. Their third album, *The Suburbs* (2012), added commercial success to critical acclaim.

Eclectic American eccentrics

A breed of experimental bands and artists appeared in the US in the 2000s, clustered around the east coast of the United States. Happy to mix acoustic, electric and electronic sound sources, their innovative approach was a far cry from the more careerist bands on the other side of the Atlantic.

New York band Liars take a highly eclectic approach, veering between disjointed psychedelic disco on 'There's always room on the broom' (2004), blistering angst-rock in 'Plaster casts of everything' from *Liars* (2007), to ambient electronica on 'The exact colour of doubt' from *WIXIW* (2012). Experimental psychedelic outfit Animal Collective from Baltimore likewise use a range of influences: everything from the American psychedelia of Mercury Rev and Flaming Lips to the experimental music of György Ligeti. They often mix 'found' sounds with acoustic instruments, electronics and samplers, and have a generally lo-fi approach. One of their most affecting and accessible songs, 'My girl', from their breakthrough album *Merriweather Post Pavilion* (2009), is awash with cascading synthesizer arpeggios and uplifting chanted vocals. To get a taste of them at their most experimental, listen to the three-minute feedback howl 'Untitled' from their debut album *Spirit They've Gone Spirit They've Vanished* (2003), or the disorientating but joyous 'We tigers' or 'Who could win a rabbit' from *Sung Tongs* (2004).

Also working out of Baltimore, Dan Deacon's most recent album, *America* (2012) is similarly eclectic, ranging from the bruising electronics of 'Guildford Avenue bridge' (which owes as much to minimalist composer Steve Reich as to popular music), via the joyous Animal Collective-like romp 'True Thrush' to the final four-movement electronic/orchestral suite of 'USA'.

Further afield

After showing much promise in the 90s and early 2000s, the Japanese scene, possibly due to the ever-increasing pervasiveness of the internet and the levelling of popular culture that has followed in its wake, unfortunately lost a lot of its unique flavour.

In mainland northern Europe, electronic music continued to flourish. Already established acts like Air and Daft Punk continued to thrive, with the latter continuing to broaden stylistically, providing the combined orchestral/electronic soundtrack for *Tron: Legacy* in 2010. Fellow French duo Justice combined disco, hip-hop, techno and rock to make a punchy cut-up sound, as on their masterful remix of 'The fallen' by Franz Ferdinand, released in 2006. In Berlin, the stylistically similar Boys Noize, aka Alexander Ridha, produced a comparably tough and funky sound on the album *Oi Oi Oi* (2007). An interesting conflation of their two styles can be heard on the Boys Noize remix of Justice's 'Phantom part II' from the same year. Belgian indie/dance outfit Soulwax became known both for their own music, such as 'NY Excuse' (featuring guest vocals by Nancy Whang of LCD Soundsystem) from their 2005 album *Any Minute Now*, and for their many remixes, which include a remarkable garage rock version of Kylie Minogue's 'Can't get you out of my head' from the album *Most of the Remixes* (2007).

Further north, cementing Iceland's reputation for punching above its weight in the wake of the Sugarcubes and Björk, were Sigur Rós from Reykjavík. The angelic falsetto of lead singer Jonsi (singing in a mixture of Icelandic and nonsense language 'vonlenska'), combined with bowed guitars and orchestral instruments to make a ethereal but often epic sound, as heard on 'Sæglópur' from their 2005 hit album *Takk*. Their most well-known song, the uplifting 'Hoppipolla' from the same album, featured in innumerable television programmes and adverts. Their latest and most ambient-sounding album *Valtari* (2012) often blurs the boundaries between popular and contemporary music, as heard in the use of choir on the spine-tingling 'Varuo'.

M.I.A. (real name Mathangi 'Maya' Arulpragasam) spent her early childhood in Sri Lanka. Her father was a Tamil political activist, and she experienced at first hand the terrors of the Sri Lankan civil war before moving to London aged 10. Her upbringing is reflected in her music: she combines myriad genres from so-called 'world music' to hip-hop, grime and electro. *Rolling Stone* named her one of eight artists who defined the 2000s decade. Her early single, 'Galang' (2003), combined lolloping global beats with a squelchy filtered bass line and received critical acclaim. M.I.A.'s breakthrough hit, however, was the down-tempo 'Paper planes' released in 2008. It was written in collaboration with Diplo and used a sample of 'Straight to hell' by the Clash, who received a writing credit. The patchwork fusion of guitars and beats was enlivened by controversial political lyrics and a sing-song melody.

In Brazil, CSS, from São Paulo, were most well known for their genre-hopping indie/dance hit 'Let's make love and listen to death from above', from their debut album *Cansei De Ser Sexy* (2005). The album shows influences from the 1980s, (most notably Tom Tom Club) but combines retro-pop sensibilities with guitar-fuelled aggression in 'Alala'. US dance supremo and remixer Diplo produced a CD (and later documentary) *Favela On Blast*, documenting the rise of *baile* funk (aka *funk carioca* or 'Rio funk', a dance genre born in Rio de Janeiro), which influenced an increasing number of artists including M.I.A. (on 'Bucky done gun'). He collaborated with rapper Pantera Os Danadinhos on the heavily baile-influenced (and supremely funky) 'Percao' (2004).

PROFILES

Lady Gaga

One of the best-selling female artists of all time, Lady Gaga is regularly compared to Madonna, whom she openly admires: 'There is really no one that is a more adoring and loving Madonna fan than me. I am the hugest fan personally and professionally' (*Rolling Stone*), 'I don't want to sound presumptuous, but I've made it my goal to revolutionize pop music. The last revolution was launched by Madonna 25 years ago' (*Daily Record*). The claim appears rather overstated; while there is no denying her popularity and commercial success, she falls far short of revolutionary. Gaga is more innovative and daring visually than musically, and there is something of a mismatch between her outlandish image, arty pretensions and unoriginal, unadventurous Europop/dance sound: low art masquerading as high art.

One example is the video for her hit 'Born this way', which begins with nearly three minutes of dramatic imagery and quasi-mythic musing on good and evil, set to Bernard Hermann's evocative music from Hitchcock's *Vertigo*, before segueing into what could best be described as a close copy of Madonna's feel-good anthem 'Express Yourself'. Madonna herself commented 'that sounds very familiar … It felt reductive',[2] and subsequently performed a live 'mash-up' combining both songs and culminating with the refrain 'she's not me' on her MDNA tour in 2012. Neil McCormick, music critic of the *Daily Telegraph*, described 'Born this way' as '[basically] a reworking of Madonna's "Express yourself" with a touch of "Vogue", which is a bit too much Madonna for someone who is trying to establish her own identity as the, er, new Madonna.' Though singles since 'Born this way' have not charted as highly as previously, Gaga continues to enjoy worldwide success.

---

[2] MTV.com

Rihanna

Rihanna has named Madonna as her idol and biggest influence. She even went so far as to say that she wishes to be the 'black Madonna'.[3] She has certainly taken a leaf out of Madonna's book with her sexually-charged performances and promotional videos. Her Caribbean roots are evident on the rhythms of her debut single, 'Pon de replay' from 2005, which also shows how her vocals were influenced by R&B and, in particular, by Beyoncé. 'SOS', released the following year, showed a much more synth-orientated style, paving the way for the increasingly Euro sound of 'Only girl in the world', and 'S&M'. Rihanna's biggest hit, 'Umbrella', was originally offered to Britney Spears but rejected, as Spears already had enough material for her next album. 'Umbrella' went on to become one of the best-selling singles of all time.

Beyoncé

A member of the successful girl group Destiny's Child, Beyoncé released her solo album, *Dangerously in Love*, in 2003, with her powerful and versatile voice making her one of the biggest stars of R&B in the 2000s. Her trademark vocal acrobatics and use of melisma is heard on the Destiny's Child song 'Emotion', while 'Run the world (girls)' showcases her expertise at vocal harmonization.

Arctic Monkeys

The Arctic Monkeys shot to fame in 2005. Singer Alex Turner and drummer Matt Helders both studied music technology at Barnsley College. In 2003, the band began gigging around Sheffield, giving out free demo CDs at gigs; their local following developed and some of their tracks were file-shared by fans. Soon they commanded a fierce online following, and were able to play a series of small but sold-out shows across the country. A meteoric rise to fame followed, and their first single, 'I bet you look good on the dancefloor' (2005), went straight to No. 1. At the time of its release, their first album, *Whatever People Say I Am That's What I'm Not* (2006), became the fastest selling British debut album of all time.

Because of these successes, the band is often credited as a catalyst for a new way for music to be consumed. They continued to eschew typical commercial channels, and chose to sign to the (then) relatively small independent record label Domino Records.

Alex Turner has a direct and articulate lyrical style, citing the punk poet John Cooper Clarke as an influence. This is especially apparent in their first album, in which he makes eloquent observations around the general theme of nightlife. Other influences range from the Smiths to Nick Cave and David Bowie.

A faster, heavier follow-up album, *Favourite Worst Nightmare* (2007), was vibrant, adventurous and full of new ideas. Josh Homme, of Queens of the Stone Age, co-produced their third album, *Humbug*, much of which was recorded in America. The Arctic Monkeys have had a major impact on the UK indie music scene – arguably the most influential British band since Oasis a decade before.

DANCE

The splintering of dance music styles that began in the 1990s did not stop in the 2000s. Countless subgenres and fusions emerged, such as the glitchy, off-kilter variant of house known as fidget house, and liquid drum'n'bass – so named because it absorbed elements of house and disco, resulting in a more ambient sound that fans could listen to at home, as well as in the club. This was driven in part by an explosion in the number of dance music internet

---

[3] Beverly Smith, 'The Good, the Bad, the Rihanna', *Paper*, 13 July 2007

blogs and forums which catered for increasingly niche genres. By the end of the decade, the culture of swapping the latest white-label underground vinyl[4] was replaced, first by record-able CDs and then by MP3 downloads. From their introduction early in the decade, CDJs[5] have allowed up-and-coming producers to play their music at nightclubs without having to get their records pressed to vinyl. However, despite the greater exposure now available to underground productions, the dance music scene has managed to remove one of the criti-cisms previously levelled at it: it is no longer a starless genre. International DJs such as David Guetta, Daft Punk and Deadmau5 have emerged into the mainstream, both as artists in their own right, and remixing and producing some of pop's biggest artists.

House and Techno

House continued its dominance of the mainstream dance market throughout the 2000s. Electro-house gradually pushed out trance and progressive house to become the most popular dance genre. The first sounds of electro-house were heard in the late 90s and early 2000s. An early example is Mr Oizo's 'Flatbeat', a bonus track from his experimental techno album, *Analog Worms Attack* (1999), which was popularized when it was used by Levi's to advertise their jeans in a television advertisement. The track's squeaks and bleeps, laid over a four-on-the-floor drum beat and resonant analogue bass riff, would set the template for the genre – a template closely followed by Benny Benassi on his 2002 release 'Satisfaction'. This track makes use of side-chain compression, a technique used to lower the volume of the rest of the track at each kick drum hit, creating a pumping sound which brings the beat to the fore and adds energy to the track to get the dance floor jumping. The developing sound exploded in 2006 with two big releases: first Tocadisco's remix of the Egg's track 'Walking away' and, secondly, Bodyrox's 'Yeah yeah' – the latter making extensive use of glide[6] on its layered synth parts (a technique which would become a feature of many tracks in the genre).

An offshoot of the electro sound in the middle of the decade created what internet bloggers began to call fidget house, pioneered in the UK by DJ and producer Dave Taylor aka Switch. The style makes use of short vocal samples and snippets of sound, big rave synth stabs and wild pitch-bent bass lines. Many of the releases in this field came in the form of remixes of current indie and pop songs. Switch's remix of the Futureheads' 'Worry about it later' takes a small section of the original's vocal line and builds a track around it, chopping the sample almost beyond recognition. Artists such as Hervé, Jack Beats and the Italian duo Crookers would take the genre further, later incorporating the wobble bass sound developed in dubstep (see page 132).

Bass-heavy house music reached its extreme with bassline house. The sound takes elements from 90s speed garage, with pitched-up vocals, combined with grime style MC-ing, a four-on-the-floor house drum beat, and a prominent and heavy bass line. Although influ-enced by the grime and dubstep coming out of London early in the decade, bassline house emerged from Sheffield, in the north of England. The 2007 bass-line track 'Heartbroken' by T2 and Jodie Aysha was one of the first in the genre to achieve commercial success. The track begins with Jodie Aysha's high-pitched vocals and synthesized strings, before the bass drop[7] which introduces the four-on-the-floor beat, and a bass line, typical of the genre, which

---

[4] Limited number vinyl test pressings, usually having only a plain white label with a handwritten title, used by producers to see how their tracks are received before deciding if they are worthy of larger general release.

[5] A compact disc player that DJs can use in a similar way to a vinyl turntable, see Dance Music Technology, pages 157–9.

[6] Glide is a function available on many synthesizers (sometimes labelled portamento) it creates a slide or glissando between two pitches.

[7] In dance music the drop is usually preceded by a build-up section, crescendo or filter sweep, switching from a sonically rich texture to a stripped back sound featuring only the percussion and bass parts.

glides up and down octaves. Just as bassline house was garnering mainstream interest, the genre imploded. The bass-line scene had been centred around the Sheffield nightclub Niche, which became increasing popular by promoting bass-line nights and providing a space for up-and-coming producers and DJs to play their music. However, with that popularity came gang violence, leading to its closure in 2007.

House and electro-house now permeate much of the pop market, the likes of Rihanna and Lady Gaga following the lead of Madonna in the 90s and incorporating elements of the house sound into their own styles. Rihanna's 'We found love' (2011), produced by Scottish electro-house DJ and songwriter Calvin Harris, plays like a conventional house track, with a 128 bpm four-on-the-floor beat and typical house structure. The connection between pop and house has not been a one-way street: mainstream house producers David Guetta and the Swedish House Mafia (a house supergroup comprising Steve Angello, Sebastian Ingrosso and Axwell) have been very successful in the later part of the decade by incorporating pop vocals into their tracks. Their highly polished house productions are designed as much for radio play as for the clubs, with many releases featuring a catchy sing-along chorus.

After the success of acts such as Orbital and Underworld in the 90s, techno moved back towards the underground in the 2000s. From the genre's conception in Detroit in the 1980s, Germany has since become techno's new home. The scene centres around clubs such as the Berghain in Berlin, an enormous dance floor in a disused power plant, with club nights that frequently span an entire weekend. The club's own label Ostgut Tonträger has released tracks from the nightclub's resident DJs, André Galluzzi and Ben Klock. Klock's 2007 release 'Czeslawa' on the Ostgut Tonträger label is typical of the Berghain sound: minimal and yet heavy with a deep pounding bass drum. If there are still superstars in the techno scene, then Sven Väth could be so considered: with a career spanning nearly 30 years, Väth is owner of the Cocoon brand, which includes a record label, nightclubs in Frankfurt and Ibiza, and an outdoor techno festival in Leeds. Väth is famed for his 12-hour-long endurance DJ set. His own sound incorporates trance and tech-house, as can be heard on his 2002 album *Fire*. The music of another stalwart of techno, Richie Hawtin, has closely followed the trajectory of the genre as a whole. Originally producing techno in the Detroit mould in the early 90s, Hawtin became one of the main proponents of the minimal movement of the late 90s and 2000s before moving to Berlin in 2004. Releasing under the moniker Plastikman, Hawtin has produced a number of conceptual albums, such as *Closer* (2003) – an album, more suited to the armchair listener than a nightclub, which has allowed Hawtin to stretch the boundaries of techno, creating abstract and minimal rolling and evolving soundscapes.

Hip-hop

Following the decline of G-Funk and the more aggressive forms of gangsta rap, hip-hop has diversified tremendously. This was thanks, in part, to a return to the mellower hip-hop popularized in the early 1990s by acts such as De La Soul. In the UK, this renaissance has been led by independent record label Ninja Tune, launching the careers of many artists including Mr Scruff and Roots Manuva. Ninja Tune paved the way for an approach to hip-hop production and sampling that embraced many different genres. J Dilla led the equivalent revolution stateside, largely posthumously. East/West Coast rivalry and amateur gun slinging is no longer such a defining feature of hip-hop. This is not to say that it is without its disputes – most of rap's biggest stars continue to air their lyrically-enhanced dirty laundry (Jay-Z and Nas have a famously long-running feud, for example). With several economic crises from the turn of the millennium, it is no surprise to see a rejuvenation of ferociously articulate political hip-hop. Names such as Akala, Lowkey and Immortal Technique are gradually emerging from the underground, suggesting that hip-hop may still be the genre most concerned with the underprivileged. Further innovations in technology and the impact of electronic dance music on hip-hop have also contributed to its unrivalled rise in popularity worldwide.

Despite all this, since the 1990s the genre has often faced accusations that it can no longer live up to the early 'classic' rap songs of Wu-Tang Clan or Public Enemy, because it has lost its political potency. Rather, it is argued, hip-hop has been subsumed into a commodified form that exploits its early black roots of resistance in the interests of making money for overwhelmingly white entrepreneurs. Snoop Dog, 50 Cent and So Solid Crew may throw themselves up as obvious examples of this, but the two current kings of hip-hop, Jay-Z and Kanye West, can alone blur the lines of this argument. Jay-Z was born poor into the housing projects of Brooklyn, New York and, now worth hundreds of millions of dollars, embodies the modern rags-to-riches story. Yet his charity work and skilful use of language demand that a portrayal of him as little more than a salesman for commodity capitalism is resisted. In turn, self-proclaimed genius Kanye West, arrogance aside, also commands respect. A notable turning point for hip-hop came in 2007 when 50 Cent, a protégé of Eminem, lost out in a sales battle with his third album *Curtis*, to Kanye's *Graduation*, released on the same day. With *Graduation*, Kanye produced a more reflective, anthemic style of hip-hop. His legacy will also include his ability to blur the line between samples and songs in which he often uses large chunks of old soul records.

The late 2000s has seen an increasing number of hip-hop artists beginning to rise from the underground to produce tracks with a political potency approaching that of Billie Holiday's protest song 'Strange fruit'. Akala, Lowkey and Immortal Technique are three examples and have much in common, each artist explicitly seeking to break down the culture of cliché and stereotype that they feel has begun to smother the genre. Railing against the two-dimensional emphasis on cash and 'hoes' (whores), each expresses injustices in carefully constructed yet seamlessly flowing lyrics.

Akala and Lowkey show that, in the twenty-first century, posting a YouTube video can be a social and political act. Their freestyle 'Fire in the Booth' sessions for Radio 1 DJ Charlie Sloth have each clocked up around a million views and demonstrate what can make hip-hop so powerful in its message, musicality and intelligence. Akala's third album *Doublethink* (2010) is partly a concept album inspired by classic novels of dystopian fiction – a far cry from 50 Cent's 'look baby this is simple, you can't see, you fuckin' with me, you fuckin' with a P I M P'. Lowkey also focuses on controversial issues, although his staunch pro-Palestinian stance has led to his music being ignored by large sections of the media. Nonetheless, his second solo album *Soundtrack to the Struggle* (2011) was released to wide critical acclaim, charting at No. 1 in the UK hip-hop charts. Lowkey worked with his American peer Immortal Technique on their single 'Voice of the voiceless' (2009), a defiant song about racism and war that warns: 'Detain my body, but you can't imprison my mind, If it's my time I'll probably die with my fist in the sky'. Immortal Technique honed his rapping skills in jail and, following a decade-long rise, his uncanny ability to make the complex seem simple has garnered great respect for him as a rapper in the USA – the birthplace of hip-hop.

As global capitalism continues to pit the powerful against the rest, this style of hip-hop increasingly commands attention, not as a niche sub-genre, but as an invaluable critique. Following the remarkable self-reinvention of Plan B from rapper, then soul-singing charmer, 2012 saw Britain's first mainstream political protest song in 30 years. As a searing critique of post-riots Britain, Plan B's song 'Ill manors' saw him demanding, across the major airways and in the high street shops: 'Oi! What you looking at you little rich boy?! We're poor round here, run home and lock your door!'

Just as in the 1990s (if not more so), hip-hop continues to absorb the influences of other genres without prejudice, and advances in technology remain crucial to its trajectory. As Auto-Tune became more widely accepted,[8] it allowed some artists, who previously only rapped, to sing. This technology was first used in hip-hop by Florida-born T-Pain on his

---

[8] Auto-Tune is an audio processor which enables pitch correction. It was created by Antares Audio Technologies in 1997 and was famously first used to produce the altered vocal effects on Cher's 1998 hit 'Believe'.

album *Rappa Ternt Sanga* (2005) – a dialectal spelling of 'rapper turned singer'. Just as T-Pain openly alludes to his use of Auto-Tune, in 2008 Kanye West made a major musical departure with his album *808s & Heartbreak*, where he makes extensive use of the technology – allowing him to sing bitter lyrics about the trials and tribulations of love in an over-processed robotic style on top of tribal-influenced beats programmed on a Roland TR-808 drum machine.

The electronic dance music scene has had a two-fold influence on hip-hop. On the one hand, producers such as Timbaland and the Neptunes showcase an exciting and experimental side of hip-hop that uses techno-like sounds and riffs, double-time beats and off-kilter electronic funk. On the other hand (and to the chagrin of many die-hard hip-hop fans), hip-hop's convergence with pop music has seen less emphasis on the words in order to get the tracks popular on the dance floor (arguably a profit-motivated concern). This popularization of hip-hop, in which the poetry and content of the lyrics become less important, is exemplified by the successful group Black Eyed Peas. 'I gotta feeling', produced by French house DJ David Guetta, has a four-on-the-floor drum beat, catchy chorus and simple singalong party lyrics ('I gotta feeling that tonight's gonna be a good night' being pretty much the sum total).

J Dilla, whose life was cut short at 32, is now universally respected in the hip-hop community. His final album, the instrumental *Donuts* (2006), was released only days before his death. Raised on jazz, and also known as Jay Dee, his musical lineage was strong, with an opera singer for a mother and a bassist for a father. He emerged from the mid-90s underground hip-hop scene in Detroit, producing tracks for many of the hip-hop greats: Common, Busta Rhymes, the Roots, the Pharcyde and A Tribe Called Quest. From the early 2000s his solo career began to take off, but in 2006 he died from the incurable blood disease Lupus. His legacy continues to inform contemporary hip-hop. Tributes and tracks continue to be released posthumously. One such example is *Dillagence*. This was released by Busta Rhymes (a long-time friend and one of Dilla's most passionate supporters) as a free download in 2007, and features his rapping over previously unreleased tracks produced by Dilla.

Many female rappers came to the fore in the 80s and 90s: Salt-N-Pepa, Missy Elliot, Lauryn Hill, to name but a few. Women in hip-hop remain significant, and in 2002 Ms Dynamite (Akala's older sister) beat hip-hop and garage outfits the Roots and the Streets to win the prestigious Mercury Music Prize. As hip-hop's reach continues to extend internationally, fellow UK female MC M.I.A. has also gained credibility. 'Galang' (2003: see also page 124) incorporates elements from her Sri Lankan roots with dancehall and jungle. In 2011, American rapper Azealia Banks shot to fame after she topped the indie-fashion magazine *NME*'s 'cool list'. A talented rapper, Banks now takes the reins as a more contemporary Missy Elliot.

If further evidence were needed to highlight the extent of hip-hop's influence, the embracing of the genre in Barack Obama's 2008 presidential campaign fits the bill. Support for Obama came from many artists, including Jay-Z, Outkast, Nas and LL Cool J. This support is felt to have been crucial to his success, enabling him to reach a section of the voting population who may not have previously voted, or felt they were not part of the system. Nas even released a track entitled 'Black President' which begins with a sample from Obama's 'Yes We Can' speech and ends with a prophetic announcement of Obama's election into office. Yet, speaking in 2012, Nas commented 'I'm supposed to love Barack Obama being a black man as president. I'm glad I lived to see it – the flipside is, after we get over that, it's back to the politics, and it's something which doesn't have time for people'. There has been further backlash from the hip-hop community following Obama's first few years in office, with many rappers feeling that he had failed to take up the many issues facing black people in the US. In his 2011 song 'Obama Nation', Lowkey raps 'It's over – people wake up from the dream now – Nobel Peace Prize, Jay-Z on speed dial, the substance within, not the colour of your skin – Are you the puppeteer or the puppet on the string?' Perhaps significantly, when Obama's 2012 campaign released its song playlist, there was not one rap song on it.

So, although it may be possible to find examples of the so-called degeneration of hip-hop, the debate cannot easily be polarized. Lowkey's 'diss' of Jay-Z and his resistance to the political mainstream show that hip-hop remains a free voice that has not forgotten its roots in the blues as the voice of resistance. It may simultaneously degrade and enrich a society, but its words can often legitimately take their place in what could be regarded as poetry. Furthermore, the popularity of the genre shows that hip-hop is not just a phase. At its best, it can be a lifestyle.

Grime

With many parallels to the American hip-hop movement of the 80s, grime has been a way for London's young black and ethnic minorities to find their voice and define their own culture. In doing so, they were able to shake off many of the Americanisms that had been adopted by their UK hip-hop predecessors. Taking the darker aspects of UK garage into new territories, grime draws influence from both hip-hop and dancehall, with most tracks featuring MCs. Grime artists let their London accents come through strongly in their MC-ing, which is usually delivered at a high energy level and tempo. Generally around 140 bpm, grime features dark and sporadic bass stabs over syncopated broken beats; the melodically constricted bass lines are often repeated by synthesized strings a third, fifth or an octave above.

Largely disowned by the UK garage scene, much early grime was not released through record labels in the traditional way; instead it operated as an underground scene with a do-it-yourself punk ethos. Artists made their name by whatever means possible, MC-ing over their productions at raves, getting radio play on local pirate stations, or recording their MC battles – DVDs of which were swapped, or sold at local record shops. As well as being important in the early development of dubstep, London-based pirate radio station Rinse FM also provided a platform for grime artists to air their own sound.

The main proponents of early grime were the members of the grime crews Roll Deep, set up by the self-proclaimed father of grime, Richard Kylea Cowie (aka Wiley), and Ruff Sqwad, whose lead member Tinchy Stryder would later go on to mainstream solo success. Ruff Sqwad's 'Tings in boots', self-released on white label in 2003, epitomizes the early genre. The rough production and upfront bass-sound almost swallow the gang vocals, which themselves distort – highlighting the naivety of the recording, as the rappers deliver their rhymes ever more furiously. In 2003, grime was briefly propelled into the mainstream when Dizzee Rascal's *Boy in Da Corner* was released to wide critical acclaim. His lyrics, delivered in a unique fast-paced and high-pitched style, and with an added twist of dark humour, speak of the difficulties of life growing up in an East London council estate with greater honesty and intelligence than that of many of his peers. The production utilizes synth and percussion sounds which are often left raw, without further effects or processing – the focus is on the drums and bass, making the music danceable despite its disjointed rhythms.

Despite the stand-out success of Dizzee Rascal, for most of the decade grime remained largely an underground scene, with only a handful of artists achieving wider recognition. This has been attributed in part to its association with crime and gang culture, which led to criticisms from commentators and government officials. In a 2003 radio interview after the killing of two black teenagers caught up in a dispute between rival gangs, then Culture Minister Kim Howells spoke of black British rappers, saying: 'It is a big cultural problem. Lyrics don't kill people but they don't half enhance the fare we get from videos and films. It has created a culture where killing is almost a fashion accessory.' This led to a backlash of criticism, with the Minister being labelled as racist. By the end of the decade, a number of grime artists had finally broken through into the mainstream. Tracks such as Tinchy Stryder's 'Take me out' were big hits in the UK, although his style had to soften considerably in order to appeal to the wider audience.

Drum'n'bass

The drum'n'bass scene continues to thrive, and some of the biggest names from the 1990s are still going strong – Roni Size, Goldie and LTJ Bukem, for example – but new names, styles and subgenres are constantly popping up. In the 1990s, it was almost entirely a UK genre, but it has now established itself worldwide, with some countries developing their own sound. The Brazilian Sambass genre, for example, combines drum'n'bass rhythms with influences from Latin American music. The roots of drum'n'bass still lie in the UK scene, however, and its trajectory can be followed from there.

If trance supplanted drum'n'bass as the most popular dance genre during the 1990s, then garage can be said to have taken the limelight at the turn of the millennium. This was possibly thanks in part to the increasingly dark sound of drum'n'bass – led by artists such as Dom and Roland, Konflict and Bad Company. These artists released tracks that lacked the commercial appeal of Roni Size and Goldie (who had dominated the genre during the 1990s). Instead, their sound took inspiration from the raw and caustic elements of early jungle and drum'n'bass, and became known as techstep. In 1998, two pioneers of the techstep sound, Ed Rush and Optical, co-produced the album *Wormhole*, which is now widely regarded as a classic, genre-changing album. This important subgenre is now led by artists including Noisia, Spor, Black Sun Empire and Klute.

Despite media declarations that drum'n'bass was dead, the early 2000s saw a revival of the original sound and a drive to bring back the fun to drum'n'bass. This was seen in the chart success of artists such as Andy C with 'Body rock' (2002), and Shy FX with 'Shake ur body' (2002). This mainstream success marked the resurgence of the 'jump-up' style of drum'n'bass. A new wave of artists such as DJ Zinc, Hype and Dillinja took the bouncing bass lines from the first generation of jump-up, but added edgy production, three-tier bass lines (high, mid and low) and wobble sounds to give jump-up a new and easily recognizable sound, (as in, for example, 'Twist em out' by Dillinja).

In 2003, two acts formed that were to change the face of drum'n'bass forever. Chase and Status, and their Australian counterparts Pendulum, began careers that would see them break into the mainstream on a scale not achieved by any drum'n'bass DJ or producer before them. Chase and Status's original releases, such as their 2006 'Duppy man', which used vocals from reggae superstar Capleton, were at first well received by the drum'n'bass scene. Now more likely to work with pop superstars such as Rihanna, they are often accused of 'selling out', and have a sound more reminiscent of club/dance music. Pendulum moved from Australia to London specifically to submerge themselves in the home of drum'n'bass. In 2006 they released *Hold Your Colour*, which had a cross-genre appeal that gave them worldwide fame. In the 1990s, drum'n'bass might have been largely defined as an electronic genre in which the only live element was the DJ's selection and mixing of tracks. From around 2008, Pendulum and Chase and Status spearheaded a new wave of drum'n'bass in live performance, using electric, electronic and acoustic instruments played by musicians on stage. However, they were not the first live drum'n'bass act of note. Following the release of their album *Billion Dollar Gravy* in 2003, London Elektricity toured as a live band. They produce a unique sound, combining elements of drum'n'bass with soulful jazzy singing, funky rhythms, tight bass lines and virtuosic drumming from Jungle Drummer, aka Chris Polglase.

Since setting up the RAM Records label in 1992, Andy C has been a pioneering force in drum'n'bass, launching the careers of Chase and Status, and Subfocus, amongst others. He is also one of the world's most respected DJs, specializing in energetic sets, fast mixing and multiple 'drops'. In 2012, Andy C premiered his own live show, using state-of-the-art technology and playing across three decks in a huge stage structure.

Although drum'n'bass is still released on 12″ vinyls, releasing online for download is now a popular option. This is supported by a strong online presence for fans, with many dedicated internet radio stations (to some extent replacing pirate radio stations) and communities. Drum&bassarena and Dogs on Acid are the two most popular online forums, with a significant rivalry between the two. Drawing on the genre's roots in reggae and hip-hop, DJs are often accompanied by one or more MCs when playing out. Although MCs don't generally receive the same level of recognition as DJs and producers, well-known and respected MCs include Dynamite MC, MC Conrad, Skibadee and Stamina. Liquid, or 'intelligent' drum'n'bass, continues to be popular – with nights that are sometimes marketed as being MC free. Hospital Records, which started in 1996, continues to lead the liquid drum'n'bass movement, with popular artists High Contrast, Cyantific, Logistics, and Camo and Krooked signed up.

The drum'n'bass scene is now very diverse and it is difficult to pinpoint any one subgenre as the dominant style. The genre continues to absorb elements from a wide range of styles, although the original influences are often still evident with, for instance, many tracks continuing to use ragga vocals. Testament to the enduring popularity and credibility of drum'n'bass is the way in which subsequent genres such as grime and dubstep use it as one of their major reference points.

Dubstep

One of the most notable developments in the 2000s dance music scene has been dubstep. This term was initially used to describe a sound that was a fusion of bass-driven and effect-laden dub with the syncopated half-time drum patterns of two-step garage. As the genre has developed, it has drawn influences from a much wider spectrum of music, taking stylistic cues from genres as diverse as nu-metal and bhangra, and has spawned its own subgenres such as the sonically aggressive American-influenced brostep.

Dubstep is typified by its use of sub-bass (frequencies below 60Hz) and, in particular, wobble bass – a sound created by applying a low-frequency oscillator (LFO) to modulate the filter cut-off frequency, or other bass synthesizer parameters such as amplitude, to give a rhythmic element to a sustained note. The rate of the oscillation is often set such that it creates a triplet or duplet rhythm. Wobble bass is central to Crissy Criss's 2008 release 'Soap dodger': the same bass line is repeated throughout the track with the interest coming from the variations in the LFO rate and depth. Dubstep drum patterns often have a half-time feel, with the snare generally only sounding on the third beat – and with a tempo of around 140 bpm, it has led many to think of dubstep as slowed down drum'n'bass. The patterns are usually syncopated and often swung,[9] leading those dancing to dubstep to adopt the skank, a dance previously seen in ska and reggae dancehalls, performed by moving from one leg to the other in a running motion with alternating bent-elbow fist-punches.

The dubstep sound was pioneered by a loose collective of underground producers, DJs and club promoters in London in the early 2000s. The club night Forward (FWD>>) was catering for an increasingly dark strain of UK garage, focusing on sub-bass sounds that had to be felt as much as heard. Forward also had a radio show on Rinse FM hosted by Kode9. It was through these early shows and nights that artists Kode9, Hatcha, Skream and Youngsta developed the sound.

Although as early as 2003, artists such as Distance and Digital Mistikz were getting radio play on John Peel's BBC Radio 1 show, the genre was still very niche. The release of Skream's 'Midnight request line' in 2005 was a watershed moment, and hinted at the possibility of dubstep's wider appeal. Unlike the pared-back, dark garage sound that preceded it in much early dubstep, 'Midnight request line' takes a more melodic approach, also changing key half way through, giving a sense of progression that was often lacking in early dubstep releases. In 2009, the Skream remix which appeared as the B-side for La Roux's 'In for the kill', made it onto BBC Radio 1's daytime playlist. It was around this time that dubstep began to split

---

[9] A beat is swung by shifting certain hits slightly behind or ahead of the beat to give the percussion a certain groove. In dance music, the technique is often used to give a more natural feel to a programmed beat.

into different styles, with subgenres taking similar trajectories to those found in drum'n'bass. Producers Caspa and Rusko were creating more light-hearted tracks influenced by jump-up, suitable for the nightclub main room: their 2007 release 'Mr Chips' features samples from the 1990s TV game show *Catchphrase*, used to offset the squelching envelope-filtered bass line that drives the track. Meanwhile, Bristol artist Joker and fellow Bristolian Pinch were producing a more chilled-out strain of dubstep. Pinch's 2007 album *Underwater Dancehall* draws heavily on Jamaican dancehall and also brings influences from non-western music. The stand-out track 'Qawwali' features samples of a harmonium, and the Pakistani Sufi singer Nusrat Fateh Ali Khan.

In 2011, dubstep entered the mainstream and went international. American artist Rihanna's album *Rated R* features three tracks that have strong dubstep influences, and Britney Spears released the track 'Hold it against me', which features an extended dubstep breakdown. American producer Skrillex's take on the jump-up drum'n'bass-influenced sounds of Rusko has since flooded the UK charts. Skrillex's productions, which fall under the slightly derogatory term 'brostep', take the focus away from the sub-bass and place more emphasis on the mid-range, using layered synthesizers and extensive filtering to sculpt the aggressive and wild textures. His track 'Bangarang', released in 2011, is far removed from the original UK sound. Drawing influence from his time in an emo-rock band, From First to Last, it features guitar riffs and a straighter rock beat than most dubstep, along with chopped-up vocal samples and his trademark aggressive synths. Despite achieving mainstream success, his jarring sounds have alienated a lot of dubstep's fans and producers, with internet bloggers and forums accusing him of selling out the genre.

PROFILES

Dizzee Rascal

Dizzee Rascal, born Dylan Kwabena Mills in 1984, has had a remarkable career. He began MC-ing on pirate radio stations, became a major proponent of grime music, and is now an internationally-successful pop musician. He was raised by his mother in East London and has Ghanaian and Nigerian ancestry. He was a disruptive and often violent teenager and was expelled from school several times. Despite this, he began making music on a school computer as a teenager, with support from a favourite teacher, Tim Smith, who said of him, 'He knew what he wanted to achieve and he worked quickly. He was noticeably better than the others because his music had a clear structure and pattern – an amazing balance between rhythm, bass and melody'.

Along with prolific music producer and rapper Wiley, he was a founding member of the grime collective Roll Deep Crew in 2002. Roll Deep Crew has also been the springboard for the careers of other successful artists, including the singer Tinchy Stryder.

Dizzee Rascal's breakthrough album, and most significant musical contribution to date, is his 2003 album *Boy in Da Corner*. He wrote and produced the album himself at the age of 18, and its enormous popularity marked a brief entrance of grime into the musical mainstream. The album draws on a multitude of genres, including dancehall, ragga and drum'n'bass. Dizzee Rascal raps grimy battle rhythms over the top, detailing his experience of life as a teenager in London housing estates. The same year, he founded his own record label, Dirtee Stank, on which he continues to release his own material as well as signing less well-known artists.

Since the success of *Boy in Da Corner*, Dizzee Rascal has eschewed grime in order to focus on mainstream popular music, and has now released several commercially successful albums, including *Maths + English* (2007) and *Tongue n' Cheek* (2009). His musical collaborations are diverse, and he has worked with, amongst others, the Arctic Monkeys, Shakira and Calvin Harris. On 'Bonkers', one of his biggest hit singles, he worked with the American dance producer Armand Van Helden.

The Streets

In 2002, Mike Skinner signed a five-album record deal with his band the Streets. Skinner had a unique take on garage, combining steady and sparse production with an honest lyrical style that was new to the genre. This gave the band an unexpected mass appeal but also brought some enmity from the established garage scene.

Working in fast-food restaurants to support himself, Skinner began making his own music as a teenager. Growing up in Birmingham, he found it difficult to relate to the guns, champagne and money-focused lyrics of American rap and British garage. *Original Pirate Material*, released in 2002 and featuring amusing rhymes that relate directly to the culture Skinner saw around him, was extremely popular. It gave the band a widely varied audience and a number of hit singles. 'Let's push things forward' expresses Skinner's views on the music industry, capturing the album's general philosophy.

2004 saw the release of the second album, *A Grand Don't Come For Free*, and includes many of the Streets' biggest singles. It is a concept album written from a first-person perspective, detailing the trials and tribulations of everyday life and losing, and then finding, a grand. The chipper lead single, 'Fit but you know it', said to be written about a celebrity girlfriend, displays Skinner's wit.

In the 2000s, Mike Skinner and his long-time collaborator Ted Mayhem launched an independent record label, The Beats Recordings, that helped to launch the careers of Professor Green, the Mitchell Brothers and Example. In 2011, the Streets fulfilled their recording contract, allowing Skinner to concentrate on film and other music projects.

FURTHER LISTENING

MGMT *Oracular Spectacular* (2007)
An intriguing, if occasionally sprawling album from the psychedelic US duo which produced the hit singles 'Time to pretend' and 'Kids', the latter used (without the band's permission) by French politician Nicholas Sarkozy's UMP party. After initially offering a paltry one Euro in compensation, the UMP finally settled out of court for a considerably larger sum, which was then donated to charity by MGMT.

Keane *Hopes and Fears* (2004)
Tuneful, anodyne and guitar-less indie album, with angelic vocals by lead vocalist Tom Chaplin. It proved immensely popular, and is typical of the unchallenging, carefully crafted, easy-on–the-ear UK indie of much of the 2000s.

Outkast *Speakerboxxx/The Love Below* (2003)
This Grammy award-winning album (the first and only Grammy for a hip-hop outfit) by the Georgia-based duo was a double solo album split between the Southern hip-hop of Boi on *Speakerboxxx* and the more genre-hopping styles of Andre 3000 on *The Love Below*. It spawned two hit singles, 'Hey ya' and 'The love below'.

Plan B *The Defamation of Strickland Banks* (2010)
A radical departure from Plan B's grime roots, this Motown-influenced concept album is based around the fictional story of a singer, Strickland Banks, who is wrongfully accused of rape and sent to prison. The hit single 'She said' showcased Plan B's crooning falsetto soul voice very effectively.

The XX *xx* (2009)
Critically-acclaimed on its release, the stripped-back and restrained indie pop of *xx* also has traces of soul and hip-hop in its makeup, making it one of the more original albums of the decade.

Antony and the Johnsons *I am a bird now* (2005)
Lead singer Antony Hegarty's extraordinary and unmistakable voice propelled him to stardom in the middle of the 2000s. The affecting piano ballad 'Hope there's someone' makes an interesting contrast to Adele's more mainstream approach – especially the distinctly avant-garde middle section.

The Killers *Hot Fuss* (2004)
Though hailing from Las Vegas, indie rock outfit the Killers betrayed a strong British influence on their debut album, as heard on their anthemic hit singles 'Somebody told me', 'Mr. Brightside' and 'All these things I've done'.

The Klaxons *Myths of the Near Future* (2007)
With a rock-based sound that draws on other influences, such as 1990s rave culture, the Klaxons are often cited as the figurehead for the 'New Rave' genre that briefly saw an army of fans dressed in neon and brandishing glow sticks.

DANCE

Erol Alkan *Disco 2006* (2007)
Originally given away with the January edition of *Mixmag* in 2007, *Disco 2006* became an electro classic. Mixed by indie-kid Erol Alkan, it includes his genre-defining remix of Justice's 'Waters of Nazareth'.

Kitsuné Tabloid *Compiled and Mixed by Digitalism* (2008)
The French electronic music and fashion label Kitsuné promotes a variety of electro musicians with their Kitsuné Tabloid mixes. This compilation, by German production and DJ duo Digitalism, helped to boost the careers of Calvin Harris, Hercules and Love Affair, and Late of the Pier.

Ivan Smagghe *Death Disco* (2004)
French DJ and producer Ivan Smagghe's *Death Disco* showcases the kind of subversive electro that defies pigeonholing.

Buraka Som Sistema *Black Diamond* (2008)
Hailing from Portugal, this dance music project fuses techno beats with the kuduro genre born in Angola in the 1980s. The single 'Sound of Kuduro' features rapping from M.I.A.

Daft Punk *Musique Vol. 1 1993–2005* (2006)
The hugely popular electro-house duo Daft Punk have enjoyed enduring success since the early 1990s. This compilation showcases the best tracks from their three studio albums to date.

Plastikman *Kompilation* (2010)
Plastikman is the pseudonym of Richie Hawtin, a pioneer of the Detroit techno sound in the early 2000s. *Kompilation* is an education in minimal techno and gives an insight into the sounds Hawtin deems most important from his long career.

Akala *Doublethink* (2010)
The title of English rapper Akala's third album *Doublethink* makes reference to George Orwell's classic political novel *Nineteen Eighty-Four*.

Lowkey *Soundtrack to the Struggle* (2011)
Lowkey's second and final album controversially covers many political issues, including the conflict in Israel/Palestine.

Dead Prez *Let's Get Free* (2000)
This American hip-hop duo's album was released to widespread critical acclaim and features one of their most famous songs, 'Hip-Hop'.

Andy C *Nightlife* (2002)
Andy C's Nightlife mixes are hugely anticipated in drum'n'bass and this, his first, has become a stand-out classic of the genre.

Calyx & TeeBee *Anatomy* (2007)
This London-based production team's first album is representative of the dark side of drum'n'bass.

chapter

9

Julia Winterson

The History of Recording

Pop music is unthinkable without technology. Technology is central to the way that it is created, played, amplified, distributed and consumed. The term 'unplugged' is sometimes used for acoustic music, especially as played by musicians who normally use the full panoply of amplification. But if the plug really were pulled out, then we would not, in most circumstances, be able to hear the instruments, there would be no CD, internet or radio, and we would not be able to see performances on television or film. Today's dance music would not exist in any form.

Chapters 9, 10 and 11 present an overview of the most significant developments in music technology. They show some of the ways in which these advances have helped to fashion pop music, and how in turn pop music has influenced the way in which music technology has developed.

For a chronological list of music technology developments see pages 161–4.

THE HISTORY OF RECORDING

The early days of sound recording

The earliest developments in sound recording began well over a hundred years ago. In 1877 Thomas Edison made the first recording of a human voice with the words 'Mary had a little lamb'. Edison worked on the principle that sound creates vibrations and therefore vibrations create sound. He spoke into the horn of a hand-cranked machine which captured the vibrations of his voice by means of a diaphragm with a needle attached. The needle recorded the vibrations by indenting them onto a continuously grooved, revolving metal cylinder wrapped in tin foil. The sound could then be played back. The following year he was granted a patent for his new invention – the **phonograph**.

In 1885 Chichester Bell and Charles Tainter invented a second type of phonograph – the **graphophone**. This used wax-coated cylinders scored with vertical-cut grooves. 1887 saw the third and ultimately most successful recording system, Emile Berliner's **gramophone**, which used a flat disc engraved with a lateral-cut groove. It was manually rotated and had a two-minute capacity. Berliner was the first to mass-produce hard rubber vulcanite copies (later replaced by shellac[1]) from a zinc master disc through a straightforward stamping process. Neither the graphophone nor the cylinder phonograph was able to mass-produce copies, and by 1910 the gramophone had the upper hand and was in widespread use.

---

[1] Shellac was made from lac, a transparent resin produced by scale insects, found on twigs. This was then melted into fragile thin plates. It was phased out with the introduction of new plastics after World War II and replaced by vinyl.

The first records had two significant limitations. Firstly, because they were played back at the rapid speed of 78 rpm (revolutions per minute) they could only store a few minutes of sound. Secondly, it was difficult to reproduce the more extreme frequencies – the very high and the very low.[2] Double bass parts were sometimes doubled up on a tuba to make them audible.

To begin with, record companies concentrated on classical music, but eventually they began to realize that there were advantages to recording popular music. For one thing, the more strident sounds of popular music suited the sound better – the scratchy quality seemed to matter less – and for another, there was more money to be made from it. In 1917 the first jazz record, 'Livery stable blues' and 'Original Dixieland one-step', was recorded by the all-white Original Dixieland Jazz (or Jass) Band from New Orleans. It sold a million copies – and the gramophone's popularity increased still further.

Throughout the various developments in music technology, two recurring themes emerge. The first is the way in which several major developments were originally conceived for industries other than the music business, and the second is the way in which musicians have used music technology in ways unintended by the manufacturers. The introduction of electrical recording using **microphones** is a good example of both. Microphones were originally developed for use in the telephone and broadcasting industries, but from 1925 onwards they began to be used in recording studios – with immediate impact on the shape and style of popular music, particularly on singing styles. Microphones helped the voice to be heard over the jazz bands and swing orchestras in vogue at the time, but recording artists soon discovered that 'mikes' also allowed them to sing softly. This offered a new emotional intimacy, and Bing Crosby was one of the first to exploit it. The introduction of the microphone led directly to a new style of singing known as 'crooning', with the microphone held close to the singer's mouth. Microphones also shaped the music in other ways: the increased frequency-range of the electrical process meant that the string bass could be more easily heard, and it soon replaced the tuba.

The dissemination of pop music was further enhanced through the **radio**. In the 1920s the sound quality of radio was superior to that of records, and during the Great Depression, when money was short, radio was seen as an attractive alternative to buying records. Record sales went down sharply, and for a while the recording industry slumped. However, the industry managed to survive, and picked up as the Depression lifted. Radio stations began to play records more frequently, and by the late 1930s the industry was booming.

Juke-boxes were also proliferating. The juke-box craze of the late 1930s saw a major upturn in the record market as young people danced to the swing-band sounds of Benny Goodman and Glenn Miller. This popularity boomed further during the 1940s as bobbysoxers fainted to the sounds of Frank Sinatra.[3]

War of the speeds

By the 1940s microphones had an increased frequency-range, but the sound quality of records was still quite low, often sounding tinny. It was also clearly a disadvantage for records to be so limited in capacity; a shellac record could store a mere five minutes of sound per side at the most, which meant that a fifty-minute symphony would fill five discs. These came in brown-paper sleeves inside leather-bound cases known as albums – a term still commonly used. Experiments had been going on for years to try to discover a way of allowing uninterrupted listening, and during the late 1940s new technologies, which had been developed during the war, finally led the way forward. In 1948 Columbia Records introduced the 12-inch 33⅓-rpm microgroove LP (Long Playing) vinylite record with a 23-

---

[2] Frequency is the number of times per second that a sound wave (or other type of wave) oscillates. The higher the frequency of a sound, the higher is the pitch.

[3] Bobbysoxxers was a name used for white American teenage girls at the time.

minute capacity per side. As a result, a full symphony could be recorded on one disc – though to play it required an LP adaptor, made by the Philco Corporation and costing $29.95.

Meanwhile RCA Victor had developed seven-inch 45-rpm 'singles' which were easily stackable in jukeboxes, and in 1949 they introduced the seven-inch 45-rpm microgroove EP (Extended Play) vinylite record and player. The EP was developed as a rival to the LP, and for a while RCA and Columbia were in fierce competition, vying for the dominant record speed. Consumers were forced to decide on one size and speed of record, or buy two record players; understandably they held back, waiting to see how the battle would work out. Later in 1949, Capitol became the first major label to support all three recording speeds of 78, 45 and 33⅓ rpm. The war of the speeds was finally resolved in 1951 when RCA and CBS began to manufacture records at both 33⅓ and 45, and multi-speed record players went into widespread production. LPs established themselves in the classical market, but singles (or 45s) became the preferred format for popular music.

At this stage, records still used monophonic sound (**mono**), transmitted through one channel. When the left and right channels were recorded on opposite sides of the groove, and two or more loudspeakers were used, the result was stereophonic sound (**stereo**), which had a more natural sound and added a three-dimensional effect. In 1958 a world standard for stereo records was established and the first stereo recordings were available on vinyl. However, it was some time before all recordings were released in stereo. Although the first Beatles records were recorded in stereo, their first vinyl releases were mono. The availability of records in stereo led to an upsurge of interest from 'hi-fi' (high fidelity) enthusiasts, who soon began to assemble linked chains of equipment – turntables, amplifiers, stereo speakers – to play back these new recordings at home.

Sixties style: the Dansette record player, 1965

David Magnus/Rex Features

Magnetic tape recording

Experiments in magnetic tape recording had been taking place in Germany since the late 1920s. During the 1930s a method was devised to record magnetic pulses onto plastic-based tape coated in iron oxide. The 1935 Berlin Radio Fair saw the first public demonstration of the BASF/AEG **Magnetophone**, which recorded and played back magnetic tape. It was originally conceived as a business device for recording dictation, but in 1936 the first BASF/AEG music recording was made. This was of a live orchestral concert conducted by Sir Thomas Beecham.

In the next few years there were several developments in tape technology. The German BASF corporation achieved an increased frequency range, approaching that used by records. The 3M company (Minnesota Mining and Manufacturing) pioneered the development of high-quality magnetic tape in the United States, and Ampex began to manufacture professional tape recorders. These tape machines were soon put to general use in radio and film as well as record production. Bing Crosby was one of the first to exploit their potential when he became dissatisfied with the conventional recording techniques of the time.[4] In order to ensure 'perfect' performances, he insisted that his radio programmes be pre-recorded. NBC were reluctant to use the new tape machines, and as a result Bing moved to ABC, taking with him the new Magnetophones to tape his shows.

It was not possible to edit early records. If a mistake was made in the performance the recording process had to start again. Tape recording not only offered an alternative to recording on disc, it also meant that recorded sound could be edited. Several takes of a piece could be made in the studio and then edited or 'spliced' later on without the performers needing to be there. Seamless splice editing meant that producers could use the best material from a number of takes and put it together as the final product. The advantages of magnetic tape could not be ignored. Eventually the recording quality of magnetic tape matched that of the direct recording process, and in 1949 high-fidelity magnetic tape became the industry standard.

Multi-track recording

Tape technology introduced new possibilities in sound recording, and from the 1950s producers and engineers, performers and composers, all began to experiment with the new-found potential. For example, the echo effect began to be exploited in pop music;[5] one of its first uses was on Elvis Presley's 'Heartbreak Hotel'.

The American guitarist Les Paul had been experimenting with recording techniques since the 1930s.[6] He was introduced to the tape recorder by Bing Crosby, and soon began making guitar and voice recordings with his wife, the singer Mary Ford. Multi-track recording techniques began to be used in professional recordings in the 1950s, when a third track would be added to the two tracks of the professional stereo recorder. The extra track could be used to isolate and enhance the voice of the singer against the orchestral backing, and this technique was used to good effect with pop singers such as Nat King Cole and Frank Sinatra.

During the early 1960s four-track recorders were available, and the technology they offered was soon integral to the pop sound. Until then 'studio recording' was usually little more than the reproduction of live performances, with bands arriving at the studio to record

---

[4] Bing Crosby was one of the first artists to have been created through the record and film industries, and by 1960 he had gone on to sell more than 200 million records (including 'White Christmas', which was for many years the best-selling record of all time).

[5] On a reel-to-reel recorder with separate record and playback heads, an echo effect can be produced by recording with the playback volume turned up. The microphone picks up the signal just recorded and repeats it at diminishing volume.

[6] The multi-talented Les Paul (b.1916) also developed the solid body electric guitar which was produced for him by the instrument company Gibson. He has also been credited with the design of the first eight-track tape recorder.

their previously composed and rehearsed material. Multi-tracking opened up new possibilities, and experienced producers were able to add their technological skill and editorial precision to the artistic process. One of the first to produce his own distinct sound was Phil Spector. He pioneered a unique sound – the 'wall of sound' – with bands such as the Ronettes, using echo, tape loops and multi-layering.

George Martin used many imaginative production skills on the Beatles' records, culminating in the 'concept album' of 1967, *Sergeant Pepper's Lonely Hearts Club Band*. For example, 'Being for the benefit of Mr Kite' makes much use of **overdubbing**, tape splicing, and effects produced by changing the speed of tapes. At the end of the second side, a hidden track was placed on the runout groove. The album set a new standard in the public's audio expectations. Joni Mitchell's albums of the late 1960s and early 70s use overdubbing to record multiple harmony parts from the recording of her single voice. Track capacity expanded rapidly from the late 60s, from four to eight, sixteen and then twenty-four tracks. This offered enormous possibilities for the control and layering of sounds. Effects such as panning (where sound sweeps from one speaker to the other),[7] and phasing (a whooshing effect),[8] and also the use of synthesizers to create new sonic landscapes, all originated around this time and were rapidly adopted by studios around the world.

The use of the multi-track studio soon became part of the compositional process. Bands who could afford studio time would no longer arrive with pre-rehearsed material, but would often spend months in the studio, experimenting, composing and recording as they went along. Jimi Hendrix, for example, had his own studio in New York, Electric Lady, where he was free to create new sounds.

The multi-track studio soon began to use a wide range of technical equipment – tape recorders, microphones, mixing console, monitors and signal processors. More recently, digital samplers, synthesizers and computers have been added. Individual voices and instruments are recorded one by one, and are later combined (or stripped away) in the final mix. Mixing has come to be regarded as an expert task, using specialist engineers.

Increasingly from the 1970s, pop musicians began to invest large sums of money in buying their own studios, where they would be free to experiment. An understanding of basic music technology increasingly became a necessary part of the pop musician's skills. During the 80s manufacturers began to design low-cost multi-track equipment for the home studio market. The Tascam Portastudio, for example, integrated the tape recorder and mixer functions in a single device for the amateur recording market. With such simplified equipment, bands were able to produce demo tapes. By the mid-1990s digital multi-track recorders had become available at modest prices, and the sound quality of some home recording equipment was able to match that found in commercial studios.

In the 1940s the idea of using pre-recorded tapes as the basis of contemporary art music had begun in France. The composer Pierre Schaeffer experimented with making musical collages using natural and man-made sounds. The sounds were recorded, and the tapes then processed in different ways: at different speeds; forwards and backwards; spliced; looped; superimposed. This transformed the sounds dramatically, producing previously unheard timbres and effects. To describe this collage technique, Schaeffer coined the term **musique concrète**. Many of the same techniques were to be used twenty years later by George Martin and the Beatles, particularly on *Sergeant Pepper's Lonely Hearts Club Band* and their double album of 1968, *The Beatles* (often called the 'White Album').

Many of the developments in electronic music during the 1950s were made in the field of avant-garde classical music. In 1951 the French broadcasting authority opened its first electronic music studio, with several of France's eminent composers working there, including Messiaen and Boulez. In the same year studios were established in Cologne (at West German

---

[7] Panning is the technique of shifting a sound within the stereo field so that it appears to move from one loudspeaker to another. It can be heard on 'Crosstown traffic' by Jimi Hendrix.

[8] Phasing is an effect using slight delay, whereby a copy of the input sound lags fractionally behind the original sound. It can be heard on the Small Faces' 'Itchycoo Park'.

Radio, WDR, where the composer Stockhausen worked) and New York (the Columbia-Princeton Electronic Music Center). Studios began to look beyond 'real' (conventionally-created) sounds, and instead used oscillators, amplifiers and other signal-processing devices to generate sounds electronically. Stockhausen's *Gesang der Jünglinge* (1956), which combines the sound of the human voice with pure electronic sound, bridged the gap between electronic music and musique concrète. The BBC Radiophonic Workshop opened in London in 1958, and in 1963 produced a particularly well-known piece of electronic music – the theme for the television series *Dr Who*. Some of these developments paved the way for subsequent synthesizer technology, and other uses of electronics in pop music.

The home tape market

Since the late 1940s, hi-fi enthusiasts were able to make recordings at home using **reel-to-reel tape**. The machines were large and cumbersome, and the tape had to be manually threaded. The recording industry began to look for a way of producing magnetic tapes and machines that would be more commercially viable. This led to compact **audio cassette** machines using high-quality BASF polyester ⅛-inch tape, which were sold for the first time in 1964. They were originally intended by Philips, the manufacturers, as dictation machines; the huge demand for blank tape to be used for personal music recording was unanticipated.

Soon afterwards, **eight-track cartridges** appeared, and from 1966 many cars were fitted with cartridge players. The cassette versus cartridge battle was on. Blank tapes, pre-recorded tapes and cassette decks were all more freely available than cartridges, which had the added disadvantage of being substantially larger than the pocket-size cassette tapes. Then in 1969 Dolby Noise Reduction was introduced for cassette tapes, eliminating much superfluous hiss. Cassette players soon dominated the car market, and eight-track cartridges were consigned to history.

In 1979 Sony introduced the pocket-size TPS-L2 **Walkman** portable audio-cassette player, which soon became very popular. The market for portable personal music players has grown to huge proportions. In 1983 more pre-recorded audio cassettes (236 million) were sold than LPs, and at the beginning of the twenty-first century cassettes continue to be widely used across the globe.

Piracy has been a constant headache to the recording industry, and cassettes made this much easier. The simplest type of piracy involved borrowing an LP or CD and recording it onto a blank tape, either for personal use or on a commercial scale. Illegal profits could also be made from the recording of live concerts. These recordings were known as '**bootlegs**', and were able to command inflated prices if the material appealed to collectors – which was particularly the case with certain artists, for example Bob Dylan, the Rolling Stones or Bruce Springsteen. These illegal practices presented a major legal and technological challenge to the record industry, which had waged a long campaign against infringement of copyright, and it began to take a toll on record sales in the 1970s.

Compact discs

The system of recording in use before the 1980s was known as **analogue recording**. There is a description above of how Edison's phonograph scratched a wave-shape onto a cylinder. This wave can be described as an analogue wave because the recorded signal is stored in patterns which correspond with (or are analogous to) the waveforms of the original sound.

When CDs were invented, the new method of **digital recording** converted the master recording into digital information, by analysing the analogue wave into a stream of numbers. These numbers are then stored – for instance on magnetic tape or on a computer disk – and can be copied and turned back into sound. As long as they are not corrupted, they will not lose any of the original quality. This means that in theory the recorded sound can be perfectly reproduced – although in reality some of the quality is lost through, for example, the use of playback systems.

The first digital audio five-inch CD discs went on sale in 1982. In the early life of the CD, some vinyl purists argued that the sound of CDs was inferior, and criticized it for being too sterile. In comparison with vinyl records and audio cassettes, however, CDs had the advantages of being relatively robust and of making simple track-hopping possible.

Once the CD format had been properly adopted, the record industry was quick to drop the production of new LPs, and soon capitalized on the new market by producing CDs which were re-issues of the vinyl back catalogue. In 1988, for the first time, CD sales surpassed LP sales, leaving CD and cassette as the two dominant formats. Vinyl records still survive among some hi-fi enthusiasts, and their use is also widespread within DJ practice, where turntables originally made possible the techniques of 'mixing' and 'scratching'.

Exploitation of digital technology has been rapid in the ensuing years. There is no clear line of evolution, and development has been ad hoc – though much influenced in turn by the recording industry's fear of piracy and by consumer demand. Many systems have developed; some have flourished, but others disappeared almost as soon as they had arrived on the market.

Once consumers became accustomed to the perfection of digital music playback, they demanded the ability to record digitally as well. In 1987 Digital Audio Tape (**DAT**) tapes and players using helical-scan technology[9] were introduced. The quality of sound was very high, and at one point seemed to threaten the supremacy of the CD. However, protracted trade wrangles over digital-audio copy protection scuppered DAT's chances of becoming popular with consumers.[10]

A further important development, however, was the introduction by Sony of the **writeable CD** in 1992. With major implications for the computer industry, this also presented further copyright problems to the music industry, by making high-quality copying easy.

Sony developed the **MiniDisc** in 1991. MiniDisc equipment records digital-audio data onto discs using Magneto Optical technology.[11] There were many selling points for MiniDisc. Because the process does not require any physical contact between the laser/recording heads and the disc itself, the disc does not wear out even with repeated writings. The cartridge acts as a protection for the disc, which can't become scratched like a CD or tangled like a tape. The sound quality is high, tracks can be edited, and song searching is facilitated through title inputting. The pre-recorded MiniDisc flopped on its introduction in the early 1990s, but the recordable version became very popular later in the decade, when it was reinvented as the sophisticated alternative to the (now ancient) audio cassette. It was well suited to home recording and playback using a MiniDisc Walkman.

In the early days of rock 'n' roll, several songs were recorded in one session – all live in the studio. For instance, on 2 July 1956 Elvis Presley, with his vocal group the Jordanaires and five backing musicians, recorded three songs: 'Hound dog', 'Don't be cruel' and 'Anyway you want me'. 'Hound dog' and 'Don't be cruel' were coupled together, and became one of the biggest-selling singles. Compare this with another huge Elvis hit which appeared 46 years later (and 25 years after Elvis's death). In 2002 Elvis's two-minute song 'A little less conversation' was remixed and expanded into a six-minute version by JXL. The remix opens with the original guitar riff and drums, but then explodes into something much more contemporary. In this Elvis recording the contribution of the musicians was little more than raw material which, through the use of technology, was manipulated, transformed and re-composed in the studio.

---

[9] Helical scan is a way of recording information onto magnetic tape using a spinning read/write head. It began in the VCR world and was first used to record television programmes in the 1960s.

[10] Measures were taken to prevent unauthorized duplication of copyright material. In 1990 decks started appearing for the consumer market with SCMS, which allows one to make a digital copy from a digital master, but which prevents one from copying that copy. There is no law requiring SCMS; it was implemented voluntarily by the manufacturers.

[11] The process involves a laser head heating up the recording spot at a very high temperature while the recording head uses positive and negative magnetic signals to write audio data patterns.

So what of the future? Fear of the technological unknown has often been the cause of delays in potential advances and new devices. Just as NBC were reluctant to let Bing Crosby use the new tape machines in his radio broadcasts of the 1940s, the recording industry continues to struggle to find a way of dealing with the widespread practice of downloading recordings from the internet. Since the demise of free peer-to-peer ('P2P') applications such as Kazaa and Napster, BitTorrent – a method of getting files by downloading from many users at the same time – has increased in popularity. In 2012 the UK courts ordered internet service providers (ISPs) to block popular BitTorrent directory Pirate Bay, to prevent UK users from visiting the site, which had 43 million downloads in the first six months of 2012 in the UK alone.

Recording on the move has become increasingly common. The popularity of the iPod, iPhone and iPad has seen a range of applications with multi-track recording and sampling capabilities. Microphones made specifically for Apple products by well-established audio companies (such as Tascam and Shure) are also available, as are adaptors that make it possible to plug a guitar directly into an iPhone.

In 2009, the 88, an indie band from Los Angeles, recorded an entire song on an iPhone using Sonoma Wire Works' FourTrack app, a feat which only a few years earlier would have been the stuff of science fiction. Later that same year, New York duo Nuclear O'Reilly recorded and produced the first ever album on the iPhone, using Intua's BeatMaker software.

Apple's highly affordable sequencing and recording application, GarageBand, has been a big hit on the iTunes app store. Complete with virtual guitar effects boxes, amplifiers and even video tutorials on learning to play instruments, it is essentially a cut-down of their flagship Logic Pro software, which along with Pro Tools dominates the pro audio recording market at the time of writing.

chapter
10

Toby Bricheno and Julia Winterson

Electronic Instruments

Early electronic instruments

Electronic instruments have been with us for a long time: it is more than a century since Thaddeus Cahill invented the **telharmonium**. In 1898 Cahill was granted a patent for the 'Art and Apparatus for Generating and Distributing Music Electrically'. This instrument, a massive bank of rotary generators and telephone receivers, was designed to transmit sound over telephone wires, and was played from a keyboard. This was before the invention of amplifiers and loudspeakers, which would have provided a more effective means for the sound to be heard. The telharmonium was exhibited in New York in 1906, but it weighed 200 tons, interfered with the normal telephone service, and was soon abandoned.

In 1920 Leon Thérémin invented the 'aetherophone' (later called the **thérémin**). It works on the basis of oscillating electric currents which are amplified and played through a loud-speaker.[1] The thérémin has a radio antenna to control dynamics, and a rod projecting from the side to control the pitch. It is played by moving the hands around the antenna, producing an ethereal, almost vocal sound much used in film music to create eerie atmospheres. It has also been used on a number of pop music recordings, the most famous being 'Good vibrations' by the Beach Boys.

One of the first electronic keyboard instruments, the **ondes martenot**, was invented by the French musician Maurice Martenot in 1928. Like the thérémin, it uses oscillated sounds, but has a range of five octaves and a variety of tone colours. One of its characteristics is its ability to swoop above and across other sounds, using a mechanical device which can slide the pitch continuously in sweeping glissandi. The pure amplified sound is similar to that of the thérémin. It was quickly taken up by classical composers and is still played in concerts today.[2]

The telharmonium, thérémin and ondes martenot are all **monophonic** instruments – they can only play one note at a time. In 1933 the first electronic keyboard instrument capable of playing more than one note at a time (**polyphonic**) went on the market. This was the **Hammond organ**. It uses revolving discs spinning in a magnetic field to produce simple electronic waveforms that can be used in combination to produce a variety of tone colours. It soon became very popular in cinemas, theatres and dance bands, and can be heard in many pop songs of the 1960s and 1970s.

In 1963 the first **mellotron** was built. This instrument was an early sample player, using tape loops. It was based on a simple idea by which each key set a length of tape in motion, playing back whatever was recorded on the tape. It was a complicated instrument to master:

---

[1] The instrument uses oscillators to produce beat notes (or beat frequencies). Two notes of slightly different pitch are played together, producing a beating sound with a certain warbling quality.

[2] The ondes martenot is prominent in the ten-movement *Turangalîla-symphonie* by the composer Olivier Messiaen.

the left-hand keyboard played different rhythms and accompaniments, while the right-hand keyboard played lead-lines or chords. The unique sounds of the mellotron meant that it rapidly became a huge success, and was used by many bands, including the Beatles, Led Zeppelin and the Rolling Stones. Examples of its use in the 1960s include Brian Auger and Julie Driscoll's 'This wheel's on fire'. The mellotron was central to the music of certain bands such as King Crimson and the Moody Blues. It can be likened to an early synthesizer, in that it was a keyboard instrument which re-created the sound of other instruments. But whereas a true synthesizer produces synthetic sounds by electronic means, the mellotron played recordings of authentic instrumental sounds.

The electric guitar

More than any other instrument, the electric guitar defines the tone and character of popular music. It has inspired entirely new types of music. In the early twentieth century, the acoustic guitar was already an important instrument in blues and jazz, but by the 1920s guitarists in jazz bands found it increasingly difficult to be heard over the drums and powerful brass sections. In an attempt to overcome this, cone-shaped metal resonators were attached to the body of the guitar, but this had limited success; a better solution was required.

In Los Angeles in the late 1920s George Beauchamp developed the principle of the guitar amplification, using horseshoe magnets and wound copper coil. Six 'pole pieces' (metal grub screws) concentrated the magnetic field under each of the six strings of a steel guitar.[3] The vibration-frequency occuring in the string – equivalent to the pitch of the note being played – generated a corresponding electrical voltage in the coil. This method of 'picking up' the vibration of the strings led to the electromagnetic device being referred to as a 'pickup'.

Beauchamp's first guitar to incorporate the pickup featured a round body with a long thin neck, and was aptly nicknamed the 'frying pan'. It was the world's first truly electric guitar, but it was played in the lap, not in the upright position we are accustomed to today. Beauchamp and his friend Adolf Rickenbacker set up what later became the Electro String Company to manufacture the 'frying pan'.[4] Hawaiian-style steel players enthusiastically endorsed it.

The first person to produce an electric guitar designed to be played in a sitting or standing position (often referred to as 'Spanish' style) was another American, Lloyd Loar. He was an acoustical engineer for the **Gibson** company, which at that time was mainly known for making mandolins. In 1933 Loar created a company called Vivitone, which manufactured an electric Spanish-style guitar. Loar's company foundered, but Gibson took an interest in his ideas, and in 1936 produced the ES150, the world's first successful Spanish-style electric guitar. 'ES' stood for 'Electro Spanish', and the '150' referred to its selling price of $150. The ES150 shortly produced its first virtuoso, jazz legend Charlie Christian. His name became so linked with the ES150 that even today this model is often referred to as the 'Charlie Christian'.

Despite the success of the hollow-bodied ES150, its main flaw was unwanted **feedback**. Feedback occurs when the amplified sound of the guitar coming out through the speakers is picked up again by the guitar pickups, resulting in a sonic loop and creating a howling, wailing sound.[5] In 1946 American guitarist **Les Paul** came up with the idea of making a solid-bodied guitar, which greatly reduced the feedback problem. He used a solid piece of pine, and gave the guitar its nickname: 'The Log'.

---

[3] Often called a 'Hawaiian steel', a steel guitar is played seated, held flat on the lap or on a stand, as opposed to being held against the body.

[4] The name 'Rickenbacker' is nowadays associated with the Beatles, and also with the jangly guitar sound of the Byrds. Rickenbacker is also a major manufacturer of bass guitars, especially the 4000 series, favoured by bass players in bands such as U2 and Motorhead.

[5] Guitar feedback has been a popular feature since the 1960s, when players including the Who's Pete Townshend, and Jimi Hendrix employed it specifically for its unruly character.

In the late 1940s, in Anaheim, California, an inventor called **Leo Fender** was also working on a solid-bodied electric guitar, and by 1951 the Fender Broadcaster was available. It was soon renamed Telecaster due to brand-name problems (Gretsch were already producing a drum kit named 'Broadcaster'), and became the first solid-bodied Spanish-style electric guitar to be commercially produced.

Jazz musicians did not favour the Telecaster's bright, twangy sound, preferring the more mellow tones of Gibson's ES series. However, the Telecaster became popular with young country and blues players, and emerged as the world's premier rock 'n' roll guitar, remaining popular to this day. Fender produced two other revolutionary instruments – the Precision bass in 1951, and the Stratocaster guitar in 1954 (later played by Jimi Hendrix). Late-50s and early-60s designs such as the Fender Jazzmaster and Jaguar enjoyed a revival in the 1990s with bands including Nirvana and My Bloody Valentine.

Fender's 'Precision' bass guitar was the first successful solution to the need for an amplified bass to compete with the volume of large drum-kits and amplified guitars. Modelled in part upon Fender's Telecaster shape, and tuned like a double bass, it was a pioneering instrument. By the end of the decade rock 'n' roll bass players had begun to make the switch from double bass to bass guitar. Elvis Presley's bassist, Bill Black, played the electric version on 'Jailhouse rock' (1957), and soon the bass guitar (by Fender and then a rapid succession of other manufacturers) had become the standard bass instrument in pop. Other bass innovators included Paul McCartney with the Beatles, the Who's John Entwistle, James Jamerson (who played on countless sessions for Motown in the 1960s), Larry Graham, Bernard Edwards from Chic, and Flea from the Red Hot Chilli Peppers.

In the light of Fender's success, Gibson's president, Ted McCarty, reworked Les Paul's solid-bodied design. Gibson launched the Les Paul model in 1952, which featured the warm-sounding P90 pickup. Five years later the classic 1957 Les Paul was introduced, featuring a new type of pickup – the 'Humbucking' pickup.[6]

The 1957 Les Paul had a less twangy tone and higher output than its Fender rivals, making it easier to produce the distorted rock guitar sound that has been popular since the 1960s. This thicker tone, coupled with a long sustain, brought the Les Paul guitar unparalleled success. Over the years it has remained the quintessential rock guitar, notably associated with Jimmy Page of Led Zeppelin. The high-quality electric guitars produced by Fender and Gibson during the 1950s and early 1960s are today viewed as collectors' items, and command very high prices.

The Gibson and Fender models have proved to be the lasting basis for a range of further developments in guitar design, which have come about in response to the demands of leading guitarists. By the 1980s a 'superstrat' design was being sold by companies such as Jackson/Charvel and Ibanez, mainly aimed at the showmanship and virtuosity of hard rock guitarists such as Steve Vai. These guitars increased the range of the instruments, expanding the neck to a full two-octave range, reducing the action (the distance between the strings and the fretboard) to facilitate the speed of playing and tapping techniques (see footnote on page 78), and adding a locking tremolo system that allowed wild pitch-bends while maintaining the tuning of the guitar. Other innovations include higher-output pickups, the addition of a seventh, lower string, and the unorthodox design of Parker's 'Fly' guitar, with a Piezo transducer and graphite construction.

In 2002 the Variax modelling guitar was launched by Line 6. It offered the sounds of an entire guitar collection in a single instrument, attempting to reproduce the sounds of many guitars such as vintage Les Pauls and Stratocasters, as well as acoustic guitars and electric sitars.

Despite the many technological advances since their introduction, Gibson and Fender designs remain immensely popular, and are still the instruments of choice for many guitarists.

---

[6] Single-coil pickups, as found on the ES150 and many Fender models, were susceptible to hum and electrical interference. To address this problem, Gibson produced a new pickup which combined two coils wired in parallel and out of phase. This new configuration was very effective at getting rid of hum – hence the name 'Humbucker'.

Guitar amplification

As soon as electric guitars were invented, they required amplification. The role of the amp is to take the guitar's signal and make it audible by boosting it enough to drive a speaker. The evolution of guitar amplification is essentially the response of manufacturers to the guitarist's desire for more volume and power.

Fender's early amps (known as 'Woodies', due to their wooden construction) became popular in the late 1940s. The most famous Fender amp was 'The Twin' which used two 12-inch speakers. Most amplifiers at this time combined an amplifier and speaker in one box. The most famous incarnation of the Twin was the 'Blackface Twin' (so named because of its black control panel), first introduced in 1963 and popular ever since for its warm sound. Fender also produced the 'Bassman' amp in 1952 to partner its new electric bass, the Precision. The Bassman was to become highly influential in the design of future amps for guitar (as opposed to bass).

In London in the early 1960s **Jim Marshall** was running a musical instrument shop. After making his own PA system and bass amplifiers,[7] he decided to embark on the design and manufacture of guitar amps. Many guitarists liked the Fender amps but wanted a more powerful and exciting sound. Marshall looked at the amps of the time for inspiration, especially the Fender Bassman. His first 50-watt model incorporated four 12-inch speakers in a cabinet, immediately creating a much bigger sound. Further, the valves used by Marshall distorted much more quickly and easily than those in the Fender amps.[8] In 1965 Pete Townshend of the Who asked Marshall to build a more powerful amp. Marshall obliged with a 100-watt head.[9] This amplifier proved very popular and was used by, among others, Jimi Hendrix. Since their introduction, Marshall amps have been associated with a powerful, distorted guitar sound and are much favoured by rock bands including Nirvana, Green Day and Blur.

Unlike the amplifier in a hi-fi system, which is designed to amplify the music as clearly and purely as possible, most guitar amplifiers are designed so that guitarists can control the level of **distortion** of their sound. Guitarists have been experimenting with distortion for many years. As far back as 1951 Sam Phillips is said to have stuffed wads of paper down the back of an amp to create the buzzy guitar sound on Jackie Brenston's 'Rocket 88'. Dave Davies, lead guitarist with the Kinks, created his distinctive sound by taking the output of one amplifier into the input of his Vox AC30 combo, thereby boosting the signal and overdriving the Vox.[10] He also slashed the speaker cones with a razor blade to further distort his guitar. A good example of this sound can be heard in the 1964 Kinks hit 'You really got me'.

The late 1960s saw the psychedelic era and hippy culture. Pop musicians began to look for new sounds. Electronic instruments and effects provided the ideal swirling and ethereal soundtrack for the hippy movement, reflecting the hallucinogenic effects of mind-bending drugs. During the 1960s distorted sound became increasingly popular, and distortion pedals known as **fuzzboxes** appeared in an attempt to gain even more distorted tones and to achieve distortion at a lower volume. In the late 1970s the addition of a master volume control on Marshall amps enabled lower volume distortion by having separate volumes for the input and output valves.

In the 1970s an American company, Mesa Boogie, used Fender amps as a starting point for their own designs. Their first amp combined a 'souped up' Fender Bassman amp with a Fender Princeton speaker cabinet. Mesa Boogie amps have often been described as a cross between Fender and Marshall amps in terms of sound. They are very popular; Mesa Boogie endorsers have included Limp Bizkit, Blink 182, R.E.M., Radiohead and Santana.

---

[7] PA stands for 'public address' i.e. the speakers the audience hears at a gig.

[8] Amplifier distortion occurs when the valves are overdriven by the amplifier, causing an aggressive, ragged sound used on many rock records from the early 60s to the present day.

[9] A head is a common term for an amplifier without an inbuilt speaker.

[10] The English-made AC30 generated a mildly distorted sound, still popular with contemporary guitarists.

After the distortion pedal or fuzzbox became available, guitarists searched for increasingly novel effects. The **wah wah pedal** continuously varies the tone of the guitar. It is often played rhythmically, and is famously used in Isaac Hayes' theme music to the 70s film *Shaft*, and by Jimi Hendrix on 'Voodoo chile (slight return)'.

During the 1940s Les Paul built his own **echo effects** units, and tape-based **echo pedals** (such as Watkins' Copycat) were around from the 1960s; but echo effects became really popular in the 1980s with the advent of digital technology and consequently digital delay (a digital version of the echo pedal). U2's guitarist, the Edge, has often incorporated delay pedals as part of his style, e.g. in 'Pride (in the name of love)'.

A **flanger** works by mixing the original sound with a very slightly delayed version, resulting in a whooshing, jet-like effect. **Phasing** is a similar effect, producing a gentler, sweeping sound. Effects such as these have been employed by guitarists such as Robert Smith of the Cure ('A forest', 1980) and David Gilmour with Pink Floyd (for example, on 'Run like hell' on *The Wall*, 1980). In the early 1990s Digitech introduced the **whammy pedal**, which enabled the guitarist to bend the pitch of the instrument up or down two octaves, or alternatively to play a self-harmonizing line. A good example of this effect can be found in the guitar solo by Tom Morello in 'Killing in the name' by Rage Against the Machine.

The birth of MIDI in the 1980s eventually enabled guitarists to control synthesizers and other MIDI instruments via a guitar fitted with a MIDI pickup. The guitar synthesizer has been a limited success, the best-known examples being Roland's GR series.

Other instruments

The advent of MIDI brought about a host of innovations in other instruments as well, based upon existing acoustic models but now using the new technology. Various different types of MIDI controller became popular for a short time in the 80s, for instance the AKAI EWI (electronic wind instrument), used on albums by Paul Simon, Paul McCartney and others. A more lasting impact has been made by the use of electronic drum pads, played like a regular drum kit but used to trigger whatever patches are required. Roland's V-Drums, launched in 1997, are a particularly sophisticated contemporary example, allowing a drummer to choose and manipulate the sounds of hundreds of different drum kits or recall the sound of classic drum machines. Sometimes pads are used in conjunction with acoustic drums to allow samples to be triggered in live performance. This is a long way from the early electronic drum kits, pioneered by Simmons in the early 1980s, famous for their hexagonal pads and synthetic sound.

Synthesizers

Synthesizers are at the forefront of music technology today, and can be heard in film and classical music as well as pop music. The basic concept is that an electronically generated signal is processed, resulting in a unique sound which cannot be duplicated by conventional instruments.

A **synthesizer** is a device that generates sounds electronically.[11] The classic synthesizer uses a technique called 'subtractive synthesis'. This is so called because a raw wave-form (such as a sawtooth wave) is used as a starting point. Its inherent sound is rather buzzy and uninteresting, so the sound is 'sculpted' by shaping and filtering, 'subtracting' from the basic wave-form. A basic synthesizer is made up of four elements: oscillators, filters, envelopes and modulators. Even though few synthesizers nowadays are analogue, these core elements of synthesizers remain fundamentally the same.

Oscillators provide the sound sources for the instrument. In the 1960s and 70s the sound sources were analogue wave-forms. As synthesis evolved, the analogue wave-forms were

---

[11] Synthesizer comes from the word 'synthesis', which means putting together parts or elements to form a whole.

gradually replaced by samples of basic wave-forms or of actual instruments (as in the Korg Trinity), or by mathematically modelled reproductions of wave-forms (via the process of 'physical modelling') as in the Clavia Nord Lead. An analogue oscillator is referred to as a 'VCO' (voltage controlled oscillator).

A **filter** shapes the tone of the sound, e.g. making it bright or dull. The type of filter used greatly influences the overall sound of a synthesizer. Moog filters are known for their warm and 'fat' sound. In older synthesizers, filters were analogue, and are often referred to as VCFs (voltage controlled filters).

The term **envelope** refers to the dynamic shape of a sound. An envelope commonly has four parameters known collectively as ADSR (attack, decay, sustain, release).

- **Attack** – how long the sound takes to reach maximum. A piano's attack is fast, while a violin's attack can be very slow.
- **Decay** – how quickly the sound decays from maximum to the 'sustain' level.
- **Sustain** – the continuing level of loudness while the finger remains on the keyboard.
- **Release** – how long the sound takes to decay to silence after the key is released.

There is normally one ADSR envelope for the amplifier section (or VCA), which can be used to shape the overall volume, and one for the filter (or VCF), which works the same way but affects the tone instead.

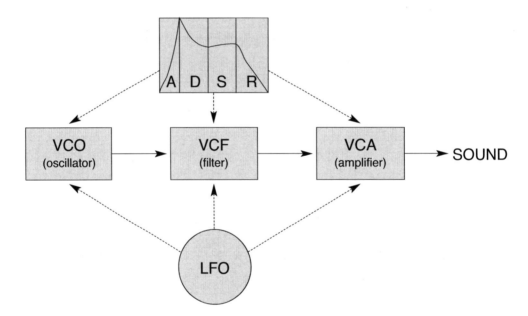

Modulation most commonly uses an LFO (low frequency oscillator), which does not make an audible sound itself but can be used to alter or 'modulate' the oscillator (or whatever sound source is being used). This causes variations in pitch, often used to mimic vibrato. The LFO can also modulate the filter, causing changes in tone quality (e.g. a slow 'sweeping' effect that is often heard in dance music). Additionally, the LFO can modulate the amplifier section, often to create rapid changes in volume, resulting in a tremolo effect. The ADSR envelope can also be utilized to modulate the oscillator(s), filter and amplifier.

The earliest synthesizers were **modular**, i.e. they were not made in a self-contained unit but in separate modules (such as VCO, VCF, etc.), connected together by cables. The connections between cables were patched together, and a particular sound was known as a **patch** – a term which is still in use today to describe the individual sounds stored in a synthesizer's memory. In 1955 the first synthesizer was developed at the RCA studios in New York. Using valve-based technology, it was programmed by punched paper tape. It was huge and very expensive, occupying a whole room. Robert A Moog developed a smaller transistorized synthesizer, the **Moog modular**, which became available to order in 1965. This meant that electronic music could be created more easily, although the machine was still cumbersome and not really suited to live performance. The introduction of the smaller and more afford-able **Minimoog** in 1969 saw the birth of the first truly portable integrated synthesizer. It was also much simpler to use, as no patch cords were needed. The Moog synthesizer could produce a wide range of sounds which could not be created on conventional instruments. In 1968, Walter Carlos recorded a collection of J S Bach's keyboard and orchestral pieces played on the Moog. The album, *Switched on Bach*, sold more than a million copies and brought electronic music to a wider audience.

At the same time in England, EMS (Electronic Music Studios) were also manufacturing small, portable synthesizers. Their most famous instrument was the **VCS3**, which was very popular with British psychedelic bands as well as with the BBC's Radiophonic Workshop (it was used extensively on the *Doctor Who* theme). Its keyboard was separate from the main synthesizer, so it could not be described as truly integrated. The VCS3 was a highly flexible but eccentric instrument, with extensive patching capabilities that allowed a great variety of sounds to be generated. However the Minimoog's 'fat' sound and ease of use made it the more popular synthesizer.

The drawbacks of the older analogue synthesizers were that polyphony (the number of notes playable at one time) was very limited, and tuning stability was generally poor. In the late 1970s synthesizers with digital oscillators (DCOs) began to be produced. Their tuning stability was a vast improvement over their analogue predecessors. One of the earliest DCO synthesizers was EDP's Wasp, first produced in 1978.

In the early 1980s **FM (frequency modulation) synthesis** arrived. This worked by additive synthesis – which, as its name implies, *combines* sine waves, rather than starting off with a raw waveform and 'sculpting' it as in subtractive synthesis. Probably the most famous FM synthesizer was Yamaha's DX7, first produced in 1983. FM synthesis was very good at reproducing sounds such as electric pianos and brass, but its often hard and metallic sounds were less successful at reproducing richer timbres such as strings.

In 1987 Roland brought out the D-50, which used memory-hungry samples of real instruments for the short, attack part of the sound, combined with more traditional synthesis for the much longer remaining portion. This system was known as S+S or **sample and synthesis**. It resulted in richer timbres that were quite realistic in their attempts to reproduce acoustic sounds.

As memory became cheaper and processors faster, many synthesizers began to have large numbers of samples on board, which could be processed through filters and special effects to produce complex, as well as realistic, sounds.

At the beginning of the twenty-first century, 'physical modelling', also known as **virtual synthesis**, was developed. In a traditional synthesizer, different parts of the circuit board form the oscillator, filter, etc. Virtual modelling synthesizers are derived from mathematical models of 'real-world' sounds, or of analogue sythesizers, which are then recreated inside the virtual synthesizer's software. A virtual synthesizer may attempt to recreate an old analogue synthesizer, including the distinctive way that the components of that particular synthesizer react with each other. Or it may take an acoustic instrument as a starting point. The Yamaha AN1X and Clavia Nord Modular are early examples of hardware virtual synthesizers. Many virtual synthesis instruments are software-only, e.g. Propellerheads' Reason, and Native Instruments' Reaktor.

ELECTRONIC INSTRUMENTS IN THE TWENTY-FIRST CENTURY

From the 1950s to the 80s, musicians would often modify or use their electric and electronic instruments and amplification in innovative ways: using the Fender Bassman, intended as a bass amplifier, for guitar because of its overdriven sound; ripping the speaker cones of amplifiers to get a more distorted sound; 'scratching' records on turntables; using the Roland TB-303 as a screaming resonant synth rather than as a bass-player substitute as intended by the manufacturer; and overdriving the mixing desk to get a more aggressive kick drum sound from a Roland TR-909.

In the twenty-first century, as technology has become faster, more powerful and more affordable, it has become more difficult to use it in ways not already envisioned by the manufacturers. Instead, a plethora of virtual instruments and sampled-based versions of acoustic instruments has appeared. The most innovative developments are the weird and wonderful hardware sound generators/sequencers such as Korg's Kaoss pad, Yamaha's Tenori-On and the truly amazing Reactable, whereby blocks inscribed with pictograms are placed and manipulated on a glass table top. Their motions and symbols are tracked by a camera under the table-top, and are used to affect various parameters of the Reactable's sound generators such as tempo, filter cutoff, LFO speed and so on. The Tenori-On and Reactable have been extensively used by UK electro-pop artist Little Boots and idiosyncratic Icelandic artist Björk respectively. It is worth noting that all three have now been ported to Apple's mobile devices as software applications, with the Reactable selling more than a million units at the time of writing.

A development that began in the 1990s was computer-based modular sound generators, virtual versions of the modular synthesizers of the 60s and 70s. Hardware versions have enjoyed a revival in the twenty-first century, with many new modular models being manufactured.

Native Instruments' Reaktor software is a modular sound generator and manipulation tool for Mac and PC that allows users to design their own instruments, samplers, sound effects and sequencers as well as altering any of the instruments in its library in myriad ways. Instruments, samplers and so on created by other users can be downloaded online.

The more complex Max/MSP software is a graphical environment for audio, visual and multimedia applications, and uses the Max visual programming language. Radiohead's Jonny Greenwood uses Max/MSP while playing live to achieve the unique 'stuttering' guitar solo on the band's live renditions of 'Airbag' from *OK Computer*.

Virtual instruments and simulators

In recent years highly realistic emulations of orchestral, ethnic and popular music instruments, including many models of classic synthesizers such as the Arp Odyssey and Moog's Minimoog, have become available. Good examples from these three genres are Platinum Orchestra, Ra, and Ministry of Rock by East/West. The comprehensive bass instrument Trillian and the highly versatile Omnisphere by Spectrasonics, along with the vast selection of purely orchestral instruments provided by Vienna Symphonic Library, illustrate the breadth of what is available.

Just as there are virtual instruments, there are also virtual guitar amplifiers that simulate or 'model' the sound of famous guitar amps such as Fender and Marshall. Native Instruments' Guitar Rig, AmpliTube by IK Multimedia, and the Amp Designer that comes with Apple's Logic Pro software are all noteworthy.

In terms of what the future holds, there is a definite trend (in all branches of technology) to make the interface between musician and instrument ever more transparent. This is elegantly illustrated by the highly tactile Reactable, which though powerful and complex, in use is reminiscent of a child at play with blocks, and a far cry from the earlier image of electronic instruments as a forbidding array of arcane knobs and sliders and inscrutable LCD displays.

Toby Bricheno and Ben Kaye

Digital Technology

Digital technology opened up the way for a host of new developments in music. These were not confined to the realm of digital music playback, which was discussed in the previous chapter. The introduction of MIDI in 1983 had huge implications both for pop musicians and for consumers, opening up a new range of creative possibilities. Today's musician is able to produce an entire song from start to finish with only a computer and a microphone. In 2009 a whole album was made on an iPhone.

MIDI

MIDI (Musical Instrument Digital Interface) is a digital system for connecting electronic instruments so that they can be used simultaneously and in conjunction with each other. MIDI control signals (such as note on/off each time a key is pressed or released) are sent as messages down a MIDI cable in the form of numeric data.[1] This enables a musician to draw on the capabilities of several electronic instruments by operating only one to which all the others are connected.

MIDI also provides the means for electronic instruments to communicate with computers – which can then send, store and process MIDI data. This is central to the function of a **sequencer**: a device for inputting, editing, storing and playing back data from a musical performance. It records many details of a performance – such as duration, pitch and rhythm – which can then be edited.

There are different types of sequencer: some are built into a keyboard, some take the form of computer software, and some form stand-alone units, although these are becoming much less common.[2] The musical data is represented in different ways according to the type of sequencer – graphically, numerically or as conventional music notation. The most popular software sequencers in pop and dance music are Emagic's 'Logic Audio' and Steinberg's 'Cubase Audio'. Both programs are also capable of recording sound, as well as incorporating samplers and sound-shaping 'plug-in' effects such as compression, reverb or phasing. It has been possible since the early years of the twenty-first century to record and mix a song using one of these programs on a PC or Apple Mac.

---

[1] This became possible when manufacturers agreed a common system which allowed electronic instruments to control and communicate with each other. This took the form of a set of standards for hardware connections, and for messages which could then be relayed between devices.

[2] For example the Roland MC-500, used on stage by the Pet Shop Boys among others.

Sampling

Digital technology led to the development of the first **samplers** in the 1980s. A sampler is a device that can take any sound that is put into it, process it and play it back. A **sample** is a digitally recorded fragment of sound taken from a pre-existing source for use in a new one: it could be a drum rhythm, a keyboard phrase or a whole section of a song, the Queen's speech or the sound of a vacuum cleaner, or indeed anything.

There are basically two applications for sampler technology within popular music. The first is in the digital reproduction of one instrument's timbres for playback by another instrument. Typical examples might be sampled brass or string instrument sounds. This type of sampling technology was designed to make studio recording cheaper; the necessity to hire an orchestra is eliminated if the sound of orchestral instruments can be copied accurately enough by a digital device. Similarly, a drum machine might use samples of real drums, to give a realistic drum sound without having to hire a session drummer.

The other application of sampler technology is in the field of dance music, such as drum'n'bass, where the sampler is the essential element. Starting with a fast beat – around 160 bpm (beats per minute) – drum'n'bass tracks are created by adding layers of sampled sound. These elements may then have live instruments and vocals added.

Digital samples of existing records are also used as the basis for new ones. Often the sample will be of a rhythm-section part, e.g. a bass-line or drum beat, looped as the foundation for a track.[3] Some songs have lifted a sizeable proportion of one track to make a new one.[4] Thus sampled sounds are as much a part of the modern producer's arsenal as synthesizers and sequencers, with the history of recorded pop music an ever-growing resource for the creation of new records.

Sampler technology

The sampler takes 'snapshots' (like film frames) of the sound. These are then converted to a stream of numbers, i.e. digitally recorded. The number of snapshots taken per second is known as the 'sample rate'. The higher the sample rate, the better the finished sample. To get a really faithful impression of a sound, 44,100 snapshots are taken per second. When the stored sample is triggered, these snapshots are played back in order, giving a smooth reproduction of the original sound, like film frames in a cinema projector.

Bit resolution is also important in determining the quality of a sample. The incoming sound is measured (or quantized) against a series of numbers; the higher the resolution, the more numbers are used. The accuracy of the final sample is dependent on the number of **bits** used to represent the height of the wave-form (amplitude). It is rather like the image resolution of a computer monitor – higher resolutions give a clearer image on your monitor. In the same way, the higher the resolution, the higher the sound definition and the closer to the original the sample will sound. For example, how much a sampled cello sounds like a real one will depend on the level of resolution. Most samplers have a bit resolution of at least 16 bits and some as high as 24.

The first commercially available sampler was the Australian Fairlight CMI (computer musical instrument), which went into production in 1979. Comprising a monitor with light-pen, two keyboards and the computer itself, the Fairlight was capable of sequencing and synthesizing as well as sampling. Such revolutionary technology came at a high price; the original Series 1 went on sale at £18,000, with Series 3 selling at around £60,000. The only customers able to afford such high prices were large studios and pop stars. Peter Gabriel bought a Fairlight, and introduced his friend Kate Bush to this new technology. One of the

---

[3] For instance A Tribe called Quest's 'Can I kick it?' (1989), which samples the bass from Lou Reed's 'Walk on the wild side' (1972).

[4] For instance Puff Daddy's 'I'll be missing you', which not only samples the verse sections of the Police's 'Every breath you take' but also adopts the vocal melody, with altered lyrics.

earliest examples of the use of a Fairlight is the cello part on 'Army dreamers' by Kate Bush in 1980. The Fairlight is also featured on 'Shock the monkey' by Peter Gabriel in 1982, and was used extensively on 'Close to the edit' by the Art of Noise in 1984.

New England Digital's Synclavier was another expensive instrument, again aimed at wealthy musicians and studios. Its most famous incarnation was the Synclavier II. Lighter and more portable than the Fairlight, the Synclavier was also capable of FM synthesis and had a built-in sequencer.[5]

Another American company, Emu, saw the potential in sampling, and produced the Emulator Sampler in 1981. The Emulator did not feature the synthesis or sequencing functions of the Fairlight or Synclavier, but it was much cheaper, retailing at just under $8,000. Stevie Wonder was so impressed that he bought serial number 001. In 1985 the MIDI-equipped 8-bit Ensoniq Mirage was introduced, probably the first sampler within the budget of the average musician. Its list price was $1,695. It featured 144K of internal RAM and a five-octave velocity-sensitive keyboard, as well as a small sequencer. Two of the most desirable and innovative features of the Mirage were the five-stage VCA and VCF envelopes and low pass filter, recalling the sound-shaping capabilities of older synthesizers. Such features later became standard on all samplers.

In Japan in 1986, AKAI launched what was to become the workhorse of the sampling world – the S900. For its time it had superior 12-bit resolution and also a maximum 63 seconds of sample time. It also had many editing options and ten audio outputs. Its reasonable price and ease of use ensured its success. Everyone from Vangelis to Fatboy Slim used the S900. AKAI retained its sampler blueprint for many years. In 1988 the stereo 16-bit S1000 became the new benchmark. Its graphical wave-form display made editing far easier and more accurate. S1000 users also had the option of 'timestretching' a sample – a process discussed below (page 128). The S1000 was, if anything, even more popular than the S900, and was itself followed by the industry standard sampler of the 1990s, the S3200 XL, which offered a larger memory plus a more comprehensive filtering section.

In the early 1990s a new type of sampler emerged, the software sampler. This ran as a program within a computer. The use of a large computer monitor, as opposed to the small screen found on hardware samplers, made editing much easier. It was now possible to run a sampler alongside sequencing and audio software, all on one machine, which proved especially convenient when saving information. The fact that no new hardware was required made software samplers particularly affordable.

One problem often associated with sampling concerns the copyright of the original sample. In order to obtain permission to use a sample in a new song, both the master recording rights (usually owned by the record company) and the underlying copyright in the sampled composition (usually owned by the songwriter or the songwriter's publishing company) need to be negotiated and cleared in advance of any release. In 1990 Vanilla Ice sampled the main riff from David Bowie and Queen's 'Under pressure' without asking permission. They also failed to credit the writers on the recording. The case never went to trial, but was allegedly settled out of court.

The Verve sampled the string arrangement from the Rolling Stones' 'The last time' on their 1997 hit 'Bittersweet Symphony'. Although the Verve credited the writers, one-time Stones manager Allan Klein eventually received a 100% royalty on the Verve song. Rubbing salt in the wound, Klein then licensed the track to Nike for use in a trainer advert. When 'Bittersweet Symphony' was nominated for a Grammy award, Mick Jagger and Keith Richards were named as the writers. In the light of this case, artists are now far more wary about sampling work without first obtaining the writer's permission. In return, the writer of the sampled work usually receives a percentage of royalties from the resulting track. Having work sampled can sometimes revive a career. For example, Armand Van Helden sampled

---

[5] **FM (frequency modulation) synthesis** or additive synthesis worked by combining sine waves, rather than starting off with a raw waveform and 'sculpting' it as in subtractive synthesis.

Gary Numan's 'Cars' on 'Koochy', and another Numan track, 'Are "friends" electric' was used as a basis for the 2002 Sugababes hit 'Freak like me'. As a result, Numan's popularity increased and attracted a new generation of listeners.

Drum machines

These are special units containing drum sounds and a sequencer, allowing the user to program drum sequences which can then be played back. The first drum machines were used mainly as accompaniments for electronic-organ players. They had a small number of pre-set rhythms and could not be programmed. The earliest to have programmable rhythms were the Roland CR and TR series, which both used analogue synthesis.

Later drum machines started to use digital samples to make the sounds (today the majority of drum machines are sample-based). The first sample-based drum machine, the Linn LM-1,[6] appeared in 1979. With its digital samples it sounded much more realistic than its analogue contemporaries such as the Roland TR-808.[7] However, such cutting-edge technology came with a high price-tag – the LM-1 sold for $5000. It was superseded by the Linndrum,[8] which was marginally less expensive and had samples of crash and ride cymbals that were missing on the original machine. The Linndrum was used on many hits of the early to mid-80s.

In 1988 Alesis introduced the HR-16,[9] which was the first affordable drum machine using digital technology. It was eventually superseded in 1991 by the Alesis SR-61 which had amazing longevity and is still manufactured more than 20 years later. However, like hardware samplers, hardware drum machines have been almost entirely replaced by software equivalents and emulations. For example, FXpansion's Geist offers much more than a conventional drum machine: it is muti-timbral, has the ability to sample and resample, and can also slice up loops in the manner of Propellerheads' Recycle. It works either as a standalone unit (generally for live use) or integrated into a DAW (digital audio workstation) such as Logic Pro or Pro Tools.

Computers and music

In late 1985 **Atari** released the ST home computer. It was the first computer to have MIDI sockets as standard, and software sequencers written for the Atari soon followed. With sequencing software (unlike its hardware counterpart), it was possible to see on screen all the different parts that made up the arrangement. Editing was also much easier on a software sequencer because of the various editing options available. These ranged from conventional notation to the popular 'piano roll' grid notation, which has since become standard on most sequencers.

The Atari was eventually superseded by the small, relatively cheap PCs (IBM-compatible personal computers) and Apple Macs that have been widely used since the mid-1990s. Meanwhile, computer processors were getting faster and computer memory becoming increasingly cheap. With the introduction of Cubase Audio and Logic Audio for the PC and Apple Mac in the mid-1990s, it became possible to record MIDI information and audio onto one machine. As the processor became still faster, internal effects such as reverb and delay became viable, as well as a greater number of tracks. The affordable DAW (digital audio workstation) had arrived. With the introduction of CDRs (recordable CDs) it became possible to write, sequence, record, mix and produce a finished CD master on one machine. At the same time, software synthesizers and virtual-modelling guitar amplifier modules such as the Pod and V-amp became ever more popular.

---

[6] As used on Prince's 'When doves cry' (1984).

[7] Notable users include Bomb the Bass, The Prodigy, Faithless and the Manchester group 808 State.

[8] As used on Peter Gabriel's 'Shock the monkey' (1982).

[9] As used by the band Orbital.

As well as being able to record and process sounds digitally, modern computers have still further applications in music. With the right software the computer user can create music notation of publishable quality, control and edit performance data using MIDI, or send music files around the globe on the internet. With the introduction of Elastic Audio by Pro Tools (and subsequently Logic Pro's Flex Time), users were able to quantize audio in much the same way as MIDI can be quantized. Endless creative possibilities have been opened up.

Computer memory was relatively small in the early days of PCs, and audio files took up large amounts of space. This meant that any storage or transmission of sound was severely restricted. However, over the last thirty years computer memory has increased greatly, and in the mid-1990s **MP3**, as it became known, demonstrated a way of compressing audio data.[10] MP3 is a file format that is able to compress audio files to a fraction of their size while maintaining a reasonable quality of sound. Through its use, audio files can be stored and transmitted more easily over the internet. MP3 was soon unofficially recognized as a way of sharing music over the internet – with major pirating implications. Some of the larger sites were prosecuted in 1996, but the informal and fast-moving nature of the internet has proved problematic for any kind of copyright control. At the time of writing, the recording industry is still trying to get to grips with this difficult issue.

Dance music technology

Of all the genres of popular music, dance music has had the closest relationship with technology. The innovative sounds in modern dance music stem from Western innovators using Japanese music technology in ways probably not envisaged by the manufacturers.

The use of the turntable as a musical instrument goes back to 1938 when the avant-garde American composer John Cage experimented with the sliding notes produced by changing turntable speeds in his piece *Imaginary Landscape No. 1*.

In the late 1960s, Jamaican-inspired DJ Kool Herc came up with a technique which extended non-vocal sections of songs by placing two identical copies of a record on two turntables and starting one as the other came to the end of the instrumental section. Herc's rhythmic chanting over these passages was a precursor to rap. The technique of switching between turntables was termed 'hip-hopping', and later shortened to 'hip-hop'. It was later refined by the DJ Grandmaster Flash to create 'breakbeats' – the drum/percussion 'breaks' between vocal sections.

The introduction of the SL1200 turntable in 1973 by Japanese company Technics had a big impact on the dance scene. In the mid-1970s two New York DJs, Afrika Bambaataa and Grand Wizard Theodore, discovered that records played on the SL1200 quickly returned to their original speed after being pushed back and forth by hand. This technique came to be known as 'scratching' and, coupled with the constant speed of the SL1200's sturdy motor, established the turntable as a musical instrument, or **turntablism**. In the late 1970s Technics upgraded the SL1200, adding a pitch control which enabled the user to speed up or slow down records. This feature enabled two records of roughly similar speeds to be matched or 'beat matched' in tempo. As a result, songs could be mixed seamlessly together with no change in tempo. Because this was easier to achieve on sections without vocals, many 12-inch mixes begin and end with a drum or percussion section to facilitate mixing.

Roland introduced the CR78, the world's first programmable drum machine, in 1979; it can be heard on Phil Collins' song 'In the air tonight'. However, it was not until the arrival of the TR808 in 1980 that Roland captured the interest of the emerging dance scene in the United States. As the drum sounds were synthesized, the TR808 did not sound like a real drummer, but its sounds could easily be manipulated. The bass drum pitch and 'decay' were adjustable, a feature which proved very popular among dance musicians. The TR808's deep booming bass-drum can still be heard on many hip-hop and R&B recordings today. In the early 1980s American DJ Frankie Knuckles began playing records over a drum machine. This

---

[10] MP3 stands for Moving Picture Experts Group (MPEG) 1, Layer 3.

was an historical moment for dance music, as it brought turntables and electronic instruments together in what was to prove a fruitful relationship.

In 1982 and 1983 Roland introduced two machines that would have an enormous influence on dance music, the TB303 and the TR909. The TB303 (or transistor bass) was designed as a substitute bass player, and included a simple sequencer. Because it was a synthesizer, it did not sound like a real bass guitar and was discontinued in 1985. However, in Chicago in the late 1980s DJs Pierre, Spanky and Herb Jackson experimented with the 303's filter and decay controls while a bass line was playing, rather than leaving them set as was intended by the manufacturers. The resulting squelching, morphing and somewhat piercing sound was used on what is generally agreed to be the first ever acid house record, 'Acid trax', recorded under the name of Phuture.

If a 303 is put through a distortion box the effect becomes still more aggressive. This helped to define the sound of acid techno in the early 1990s. The 303 has been used on countless records; notable appearances include Josh Wink's 'Higher state of consciousness', and Fatboy Slim's 'Everybody needs a 303'. The rather fiddly step-time programming system[11] led easily to errors when inputting – inadvertently resulting in the odd discordant notes and unusual rhythms which became a feature of acid house music.

In 1983 came the **TR909**. It was only in production for one year, with approximately 10,000 being made, but later it became Roland's most celebrated drum machine. This machine is often credited for the birth of **house music**. It was programmed in a similar way to the TR808 and TB303. As on the 808, all the main drum sounds (apart from crash and hi-hat, which were 6-bit samples) were synthesized. The most distinctive sounds of the 909 were the powerful bass drum, aggressive snare drum and hard metallic hi-hats. It has been used on just about every house record ever made, and also on many trance and techno tracks. Both the TR909 and TB303 began to command ever larger amounts of money as acid house and techno became increasingly popular. Original 909s and 303s became scarce and expensive, and with Roland showing no signs of resuming production, many later hardware synthesizers and drum machines attempted to reproduce their sounds.

In 1997 the Swedish company Propellerheads introduced the Rebirth software, which was effectively two 303s and an 808 in one program. Rebirth was an instant success and has since been upgraded to include the TR909. Roland responded by producing the MC series of Grooveboxes, a combination of the TR series drum machines and the 303. While Roland have long been associated with synthesis and drum machines, another Japanese company, AKAI, has been synonymous with affordable sampling in dance music since they launched the S900 in 1986. AKAI samplers were used by practically everyone involved in dance music, but their later models, the Z4 and Z8 released in 2002, despite being very powerful, sold poorly and sounded the death knell for the hardware sampler. Envisaging that samplers would be used to replace conventional instruments, AKAI provided samples of flutes, pianos, etc. with their machines. In dance music, however, samplers were mainly used to sample vocals, drum loops and sound effects. Rather as DJ Kool Herc had extended instrumental sections using turntables, musicians began to search their record collections for drum or percussion-only sections that could be used as a drum loop or break. The TB303 and the Roland drum machines were also heavily sampled. Drum sounds, with their short durations, were particularly suitable for the early samplers' small memory. Much dance music would never have existed were it not for the sampler; for example, jungle came about when breakbeats were played back at a higher pitch in the sampler, thereby increasing the tempo.

The introduction of stereo samplers such as the AKAI S1000 (and previously of the mono S950) gave users the option of 'timestretching' a sample, a process whereby the duration of a sample can be altered without changing the pitch, or the pitch without changing the tempo. This is very useful, for example, when a drum loop is not at the exact tempo of a song, or when a pitched sample is in the wrong key. In extreme cases the effects can be bizarre and have been much exploited in dance music, for example in 'Rip groove' by Double 99.

---

[11] A method whereby rhythms and pitches are input manually rather than played in real time.

In the 1990s samplers became increasingly complex and powerful, with more extensive filtering options. In this respect they became more like synthesizers. The 'low pass filter' or LPF, a common feature on many samplers, has often been used to slowly filter up entire tracks. Indeed, a sub-genre was created in the mid/late 1990s called 'filtered house'; good examples include Daft Punk's 'Musique' and 'One more time'.

Until the introduction of Pioneer's CDJ-1000 in 2001, DJs still mixed records in essentially the same manner as that developed in the 1970s. The CDJ allowed DJs to manipulate the pitch and tempo of a CD in a similar way to vinyl, but with the digital technology came a host of new capabilities. The tempo could now be adjusted without affecting the pitch, a BPM readout and waveform display made beat matching a far simpler task, allowing DJs to focus more attention on being creative with their mixes. Accurate cue points[12] and looping meant that DJs could now mix at any point of a track without having to wait for the mix-in/mix out sections.

The laptop DJ also appeared in the early 2000s. Since Native Instrument's Traktor was released in 2000, a number of software houses developed applications that allow music to be mixed on a computer. Traktor is entirely software-based, but is best used with a midi controller, whereas Serato Audio Research's Scratch Live (often just referred to as Serato) makes use of traditional vinyl turntables by playing a special vinyl disc containing time code. Both offer the DJ features such as sync, where tracks are locked together at a given tempo, along with looping capability and a number of effects. Ableton Live, although not originally designed as DJ software, allows tracks to be dissected and then reassembled live; this functionality, along with its built-in synthesizers, samplers and effects, allows DJs not only to mix but effectively to remix tracks on the fly.

Project studios and home recording

Up until the introduction of the cassette-based portable studio, recording almost always meant hiring an expensive commercial studio by the hour. Creating multi-track recordings at home involved either buying a bulky and costly four-track reel-to-reel recorder and separate mixing desk, or embracing the time-honoured method of recording one instrument (or vocal) onto one cassette and then playing or singing along while recording the combined results onto another cassette recorder. This always resulted in a drastic drop in quality.

In 1981 the arrival of Tascam's Portastudio changed all of this. It was compact, relatively affordable, had an integrated mixer, and used cheap, easily obtainable cassette tapes. It could record up to four separate tracks. Additionally, up to three tracks could be recorded and then 'bounced' together onto one track,[13] thereby freeing up tracks.

Machines similar to the Portastudio quickly followed from other manufacturers. The era of affordable, convenient home recording had finally arrived. And if a hardware MIDI sequencer was used, it was possible to synchronize MIDI equipment with the cassette-based portable studio by using a synchronization code recorded on one of the four tracks. However, the resulting music still needed to be transferred onto either ¼-inch reel-to-reel tape or a standard cassette in order to be played elsewhere.

By the 1990s the introduction of digital technology had a big impact on recording. The arrival of the Alesis ADAT digital eight-track recorder in 1996 brought high-quality digital recording to the small studio. Tape hiss (one of the banes of analogue recording) was virtually eliminated, and the frequency range was much improved.[14] The finished stereo mix was usually recorded onto a DAT cassette (see page 163), resulting in a high-quality master.

---

[12] A cue point in DJing is where you want a song, or section of a song, to start.

[13] A procedure whereby the outputs of various tracks are combined onto a different track, enabling the original tracks to be erased.

[14] Frequency range, from the lowest to the highest frequency a device can produce, equates to pitch range, also from lowest to highest.

Although the ADAT was digital, it was still tape-based – and therefore time consuming to locate a particular section of a song, because the machine had to fast-forward or rewind. The arrival of hard-disk recording gave virtually instant access to any part of songs recorded on it. It also enabled 'cut and paste' editing, whereby tracks could be chopped up and rearranged, allowing performances to be compiled from various takes with ease. Because editing was non-destructive, if the resulting edit was not to one's liking, it could be 'undone', a procedure previously impossible with analogue tape machines.

The accessibility of professional-quality sound recording technology for home studio use has had a remarkable effect upon the creation of pop music in recent years. In 2001, Daniel Bedingfield scored a No. 1 with 'Gotta get thru this', created using Making Wave's Audio 2 software at his home studio; and famously Moby created his *Play* album (1999) at home in New York.

Portable and home studios are still evolving – the increasing power of laptops and introduction of recording applications to the iPad and iPhone has made recording truly mobile. Digital technologies will continue to affect the way we create, play, amplify, distribute and consume music.

A CHRONOLOGY OF MUSIC TECHNOLOGY

1877   Thomas Edison made the first recording of a human voice with the words 'Mary had a little lamb'. A year later he was granted a patent for his tinfoil cylinder phonograph.

1885   Chichester Bell and Charles Tainter were granted a patent on a phonograph that they called the Graphophone. This used wax-coated cylinders scored with vertical-cut grooves.

1887   Emile Berliner was granted a patent for his Gramophone, which used a flat disc engraved with a lateral-cut groove.

1889   Louis Glass of Pacific Phonograph Company created the first version of the juke box.

1896   Emile Berliner patented the flat recording disc.

1897   Shellac discs replaced vulcanite.

1898   Thaddeus Cahill was granted a patent for his Telharmonium, the first electronic instrument.

1917   The first jazz record, 'Livery stable blues', was recorded by the Original Dixieland Jass Band from New Orleans.

1920   Lev (Leon) Thérémin invented the thérémin, an electonic instrument which works by oscillating electric currents that are amplified and played through a loudspeaker.

1925   Microphones were first used in recording studios.

1926   Bing Crosby began to use the new microphones developed by Bell Labs that encouraged the 'crooner' sound when held close to the singer's mouth.

   The British Broadcasting Company (BBC) came into being, becoming the British Broadcasting Corporation in 1927.

1927   The BBC Music Department was created.

   The first successful sound film, *The Jazz Singer*, appeared with a soundtrack on gramophone records

1928   One of the first successful electronic keyboard instruments, the ondes martenot, was invented by Maurice Martenot.

1931   AEG began to construct the first magnetic tape recorders.

1932   BASF joined with AEG to develop magnetic tape recording. By 1934 BASF was able to manufacture reels of plastic-based tape.

   The first commercially successful electric guitar, the so-called 'Frying Pan' was developed and marketed by George Beauchamp and Adolph Rickenbacker.

1933   The Hammond organ was invented.

   Lloyd Loar began to manufacture his electric Spanish-style guitar.

1935   AEG built and demonstrated the first Magnetophone tape recorder.

1936   The first BASF/AEG tape recording was made. This was of a live concert conducted by Sir Thomas Beecham.

   Gibson produced the ES150, the world's first successful Spanish-style electric guitar.

1938   American composer John Cage experimented with sliding notes produced by changing turntable speeds in his piece *Imaginary Landscape No. 1*.

1946   American guitarist Les Paul made the first solid-bodied guitar, nicknamed 'The Log'.

1947   Bing Crosby moved to ABC, where Magnetophones were used to tape his new shows.

1948   Columbia Records introduced the first 12-inch 33⅓-rpm microgroove LP vinylite records, with a 23-minute per side capacity.

1949   RCA Victor introduced the 7-inch 45-rpm microgroove EP vinylite record and player.

Capitol became the first major label to support all three recording speeds of 78, 45 and 33⅓ rpm.

High-fidelity magnetic tape became the standard.

1951   The French broadcasting authority opened its first electronic music studio in Paris. Studios were also established in Cologne (at West German Radio) and New York (the Columbia-Princeton Electronic Music Center).

The war of the speeds ended when RCA and CBS began to manufacture records at both 33⅓-rpm and 45-rpm, and multi-speed record players went into widespread production.

1951   Leo Fender's Fender Broadcaster became available, later renamed the Telecaster. The Fender Precision bass also appeared this year.

1952   Gibson launched the first Les Paul model guitar.

1954   The first Fender Stratocaster appeared.

1955   The first synthesizer was developed at the RCA studios in New York.

1957   The classic 1957 Les Paul was introduced, featuring a new type of pickup – the 'Humbucking' pickup.

1958   The first stereo LPs were sold.

The BBC Radiophonic Workshop opened.

1963   Philips demonstrated its first compact audio cassette using high-quality BASF polyester ⅛-inch tape.

The BBC Radiophonic Workshop produced one of the best-known pieces of electronic music ever – the theme for *Dr Who*.

The first Mellotron was built – an early sample player, using tape loops.

1964   Compact audio cassette machines using high-quality BASF polyester ⅛-inch tape were sold for the first time.

1965   Robert A Moog developed a transistorized synthesizer, the Moog modular, the first commercially available Moog.

1966   8-track stereo cartridge tape players were developed.

1967   The Beatles recorded *Sergeant Pepper's Lonely Hearts Club Band* with producer George Martin.

1968   Walter Carlos recorded a collection of J S Bach's music played on the Moog. The album, *Switched on Bach*, sold more than a million copies.

1969   Dolby Noise Reduction was introduced for pre-recorded tapes.

The first truly portable integrated synthesizer, the Minimoog, was introduced.

1973   Japanese company Technics introduced the SL1200 turntable.

1979   Sony introduced the pocket-sized TPS-L2 Walkman portable audio-cassette player.

The first commercially available sampler – the Australian Fairlight CMI (computer musical instrument) – went into production.

The first sample-based drum machine, the Linn LM-1 appeared.

1980   Roland introduced the TR808 programmable drum machine.

1981   MTV was launched.

Tascam introduced the Portastudio, which could record up to four separate tracks.

1982   The first digital audio 5-inch CD discs went on sale.

Roland introduced the TB303 (transistor bass), which went on to have an enormous influence on dance music.

1983   MIDI (Musical Instrument Digital Interface) was introduced.

More pre-recorded audio cassettes (236 million) were sold than LPs.

Roland introduced the TR909 drum machine, often credited for the birth of house music.

Yamaha introduced the DX7 FM synthesizer.

1985   Sony and Philips produced the standard for Compact Disc Read Only Memory (CD-ROM) computer discs that would use the same laser technology as the audio CD.

The MIDI-equipped 8-bit Ensoniq Mirage was introduced.

Atari released the ST home computer.

1986   Dolby SR was introduced.

AKAI launched the S900 sampler.

1987   Apple introduced the Mac II.

DAT (Digital Audio Tape) players were introduced.

Roland brought out the D-50 synthesizer using the sample and synthesis system.

1988   CD sales surpassed LP sales for the first time.

AKAI launched the 16-bit S1000, a popular sampler with 'time-stretching' function available.

1990   Sony introduced the writeable CD.

1991   Sony developed the MiniDisc.

1992   Sony announced multimedia CD-ROMs.

MP3 was introduced – a computer digital file format enabling audio files to be greatly reduced in size and transmitted over the internet.

1994   DVD was introduced, with a much larger data capacity than a CD.

1995   The first virtual analogue synthesizer, the Clavia Nord, was introduced.

1996   DVD players were first sold

The first MiniDisc multitracks were introduced.

The Alesis ADAT digital 8-track recorder brought high quality digital recording to the small studio.

1997   MP3.com was founded in November by Michael Robertson.

1999   Napster software was introduced, increasing access to music over the internet.

2000   Native Instrument's Traktor was released, allowing music to be mixed on a computer.

2001   Apple Inc. released the first iPod, a portable digital music player and storage device.

The first version of BitTorrent was introduced, making it possible to distribute large amounts of data over the internet, and for many users to download files at the same time (peer-to-peer file sharing).

The Pioneer CDJ-1000 was introduced, enabling DJs to manipulate the pitch and tempo of a CD in a similar way to vinyl.

The first version of Ableton Live was introduced, allowing DJs to mix and remix tracks live.

2002   The Variax modelling guitar was launched by Line 6, offering the sounds of an entire guitar collection in a single instrument.

2003   The social networking site MySpace was founded.

2004   Serato Audio Research introduced the vinyl emulation software Scratch Live, allowing DJs to manipulate and playback digital audio files using traditional vinyl turntables.

2005   The US-based video-sharing website YouTube was launched, offering access to a huge number of music videos.

2006   'Crazy' by Gnarls Barkley was the UK's first No. 1 single based on download sales alone.

2007   Apple Inc. introduced the first iPhone – a smartphone incorporating a digital media player.

2008   Spotify, the music streaming service, was launched, offering access to a vast library of music. In July 2012 it reported 15 million active users worldwide.

2009   Los Angeles indie band the 88 recorded an entire song on an iPhone using Sonoma Wire Works' FourTrack application.

New Yorkers Nuclear O'Reilly recorded an entire album on the iPhone using Intua's BeatMaker software.

Julia Winterson, Toby Bricheno and Peter Nickol

Style and Structure

It is beyond the scope of this book to describe all the styles, or analyse all the structures, that make pop music what it is. In this chapter we take some examples, with the intention of showing how certain basic structures have been used and re-used with many different stylistic colourings, at the same time explaining some of the common terminology used to describe pop music. At the end of the chapter there is a glossary of relevant musical terms.

FROM BLUES TO ROCK 'N' ROLL

Blues: the 12-bar chord structure

The blues laid the foundation for pop music. Most, although not all, blues are built on the **12-bar blues** form. There are three phrases, each taking four bars. The 12-bar pattern is repeated for each **verse** of the song. The most common chord structure uses three chords and follows the pattern below (the example is given in the key of A).

Phrase 1	A (tonic)	A (tonic)	A (tonic)	A (tonic)
Phrase 2	D (subdominant)	D (subdominant)	A (tonic)	A (tonic)
Phrase 3	E (dominant)	D (subdominant) or E (dominant)	A (tonic)	A (tonic)

If we use roman numerals instead of letter-names for chord symbols, the chart works for any key.

    I = tonic (or key-note)
    IV = subdominant (the chord on the fourth note of the scale)
    V = dominant (the chord on the fifth note of the scale)

Now we write the 12-bar chart as follows:

Phrase 1	I	I	I	I
Phrase 2	IV	IV	I	I
Phrase 3	V	IV or V	I	I

Many variations on the above structure have been developed:
- Bar 2 often has chord IV in place of chord I.
- Bar 12 often has chord V in place of chord I. This gives the verse a natural tendency to lead into the next verse, since chord V (the dominant) tends to lead to chord I (the tonic or key-note).

Blues chords are often played as **7th chords** rather than straight major chords.

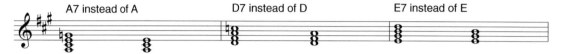

The chart may then be presented as follows:

I7	I7	I7	I7
IV7	IV7	I7	I7
V7	IV7 or V7	I7	I7

Blues: the lyric structure

Normally the text of the second phrase is a repeat of the first; then the third phrase represents an advance or response – a punchline, even – relative to what came before. Here are two examples:

> The mean old hangman is waitin' to tighten up that noose
> The mean old hangman is waitin' to tighten up that noose
> Lord I'm so scared, I'm tremblin' in my shoes.
>
> Blind Lemon Jefferson 'Hangman's blues' (1928)

> Hey now mama, don't take your daughter away from me
> Hey now mama, don't take your daughter away from me
> I've been raising her since a baby, and she mean the world to me.
>
> Little George Sueref 'Don't take your daughter' (2000)

In verse 3 of 'Don't take your daughter', Little George Sueref packs a lot of text into the first line of the verse, using **stop time** (the accompaniments stops except for a short, sharp chord on the first beat of each bar) to highlight the words. For another example of stop time, listen to 'I'm leavin' you' by Howlin' Wolf (1959).[1]

Not all blues follow the standard lyric structure. In 'WPA blues' by Casey Bill Weldon (1936) the first line is extended from 4 to 8 bars, all on the tonic chord, to allow a longer verse. Lines 2 and 3 then take on more the character of a refrain or chorus.[2]

Typically the words of a blues song are concentrated in the first half of each line, allowing a guitar (or other instrument) break or fill before the next line.

The 'blues scale'

The 'blues scale' is not a precise series – rather a way of describing the notes blues musicians play. Compared with the major scale (see below), certain notes, known as **blue notes**, are flattened – commonly the 3rd, 5th or 7th. They may be flattened by a semitone, or 'bent' by a smaller interval.

---

[1] Included in Winterson (2000).

[2] Included in Winterson (2002a), with a chart showing the lyric and chord structure.

In any one song, the 3rd may be flattened for some of the time and not for the remainder. Sometimes the flattened 3rd is found in the melody while at the same time the major 3rd is present in the backing (e.g. within the guitar solo in 'Rock around the clock' – see page 169 for more about this song). This results in an ambiguity between major and minor, so that the song is not felt to be in either – a feature also found in British and American folk music.

The following scales demonstrate these relationships:

Scale of A major

Scale of A minor

The minor scale takes several different forms. Here, the 3rd, 6th and 7th are all flattened.

Minor pentatonic scale

Like the minor scale above, this contains the flat 3rd and 7th. The pentatonic scale is widely found in folk music.

Blues scale

It would be misleading to print a 'given' form of blues scale, though some guitar tutor books show it as the minor pentatonic with the flattened fifth added. Blues players may use any version or combination of the above scales – but almost certainly with the 'blue notes' featuring or emphasized.

Typical elements of blues style

Certain patterns and **riffs** are typical of the blues style. For instance, the pattern below, playable on the piano (left hand), would be repeated through the song, with the same shape being built on the different chords of the 12-bar blues. The time signature, C, indicates 'common time', which is 4/4, or four crotchet beats in each bar. This pattern includes both the major and minor third.

The next example is a typical walking bass-line, ending with a **turnaround**. A turnaround is a sequence of chords or a melodic twist, played at the end of one section to provide a smooth transition into the next section.

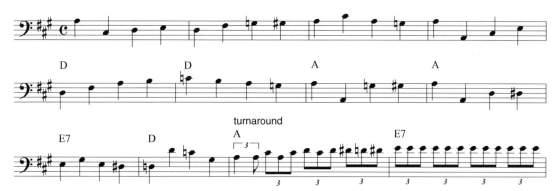

Here is another typical turnaround figure, e.g. for guitar. This one is in the key of E.

1950s dance-hall band blues (a.k.a. rhythm and blues or R&B – see Chapters 2 and 3) was one of the foundations of rock 'n' roll. The drum-kit style, with the offbeat stressed by the snare drum to give an insistent **backbeat**, became typical of rock music. (See page 171 for a key to the drum notation.)

Much R&B had a strong, pounding pulse with a triplet feel. The bass line would often repeat the same note – the root of the chord:

A typical R&B piano part would reinforce this triplet or 12/8 feel:

Listen to artists such as Fats Domino, B B King or John Mayall for examples.

Rock 'n' roll

Much that was called rock 'n' roll in 1955 was just the same as the R&B of a few years earlier, but generally it was up-tempo with a strong backbeat. Here is a typical drum rhythm:

Sometimes rock 'n' roll featured the following piano figuration, often heard in the music of Fats Domino and Jerry Lee Lewis:

Or this Little Richard style piano:

Chuck Berry developed a distinctive style of guitar-playing which has since been much copied.

Here are two more typical rock 'n' roll figures:

Bass lines:

Bo Diddley popularized a distinctive rhythm, possibly owing something to African origins, which was subsequently picked up by others – e.g. Buddy Holly in 'Not fade away', the Who in 'Magic bus', and Bruce Springsteen in 'She's the one'. It is sometimes known as the 'Bo Diddley beat' or 'shave and a haircut, two bits' (words which match the rhythm of the phrase). It was first heard in his 1955 hit 'Bo Diddley'.

'Rock around the clock' – Bill Haley and the Comets (1954)

This rock 'n' roll song is based on a 12-bar blues progression which is repeated throughout the song. The song itself is not 'bluesy', but is music for dancing; there is no let-up in the pace and drive of the record. All the verses follow the same pattern, with contrast being provided by a hard-edged guitar solo between verses 2 and 3, and later a rhythmic riff played by the horn section and guitar between verses 4 and 5.[3]

The song starts with the famous **intro**, which builds up tension by setting the words 'One, two, three o'clock, four o'clock, rock' etc. on a rising arpeggio.

For rock 'n' roll this record was a landmark, but its instrumentation and style were essentially that of dance-hall R&B, with these features:

- Simple riffing horn accompaniments in the same rhythm as the guitar
- A walking bass with a 'slapped', percussive sound, giving a slight country tinge
- Characteristic drum sound – continuous rhythm on the rim of the snare drum, marked with big accents on the full head of the drum
- A typical chromatic blues turnaround to finish the song

CD timing	
0:00	INTRO
0:12	VERSE 1
0:27	VERSE 2
0:43	GUITAR SOLO
0:59	VERSE 3
1:15	VERSE 4
1:31	HORN RIFF
1:46	VERSE 5
2:00	ENDING

[3] In pop the term 'horn section' refers to the wind and brass section – most often saxophones and trumpets, also sometimes trombones – rather than 'horns' in the classical sense of French horns.

Later style-patterns: R&B, soul, funk, disco, reggae, punk

Different styles are identified by their various musical characteristics: instrumentation, chord progressions, rhythms, characteristic riffs and guitar patterns, all contribute to the overall feel of the music. Even the **tempo** may be significant; part of the urgency of punk stems from its fast speed, whereas the slower tempo of reggae helps to give it a laid-back feel.

The examples below show some typical drum and guitar patterns. They are not templates, less still formulas, but they illustrate how different elements can contribute to the general flavour of a given style.

50s vocal group R&B
Typical bass line:

Many songs were built round the I VI IV V I chord sequence, in the 50s and early 60s. Examples include 'Sh-boom' (the Chords, 1954), 'Stand by me' (Ben E King, 1961) and 'Every beat of my heart' (Gladys Knight and the Pips, 1961). I VI II V I was a close variant.

Turnaround:

60s soul
Motown-style bass line (the cross-head note is damped):

Drum part:

Funk
Drum loop:

Guitar pattern:

Bass line:

Disco
Drum part:

Bass line:

Reggae
Bass line:

Typical guitar pattern, very muted and clicky, with upstrokes on the guitar giving emphasis to the top notes of the chord:

Drum pattern:

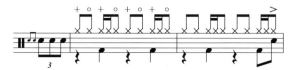

Punk
Drums:

Guitar power-chord riff, likely to be doubled in the bass:

Drum notation key

──────────────────── ◄─ hi-hat   + = closed hi-hat, o = open hi-hat
──────────────────── ◄─ snare drum
──────────────────── ◄─ bass drum

SONG STRUCTURES: CASE STUDIES

Broadly speaking, the structure of any piece of music relies on a balance between repetition and contrast. A great song is usually shaped by the way that the structure and harmony lead from one section to the next, building and releasing tension and anticipating the next chorus or main riff. Likewise, songs can take surprising twists or use particular quirks to take the listener in an unexpected direction, building further interest and excitement.

Over the next few pages several songs have been analysed, covering a cross-section of styles. We have tried to choose easily-obtainable recordings, as the charts and accompanying comments are intended to be considered while actually listening to the music.

CD timings are shown on the charts. These can help greatly when following the structure of a song, but different compilation-releases of the same recording may differ slightly in the timings displayed.

'Maybe baby' – Buddy Holly and the Crickets (1958)

0:00	INTRO (based on verse)
0:14	VERSE 1
0:28	VERSE 2
0:42	MIDDLE EIGHT
0:56	VERSE 1 (repeat)
1:10	Instrumental (based on verse)
1:24	MIDDLE EIGHT
1:38	VERSE 1 (repeat)
1:52	ENDING

Form: Intro A A B A A B A

The pattern of
        verse – verse – middle 8 – verse
derives from the **AABA** song form, sometimes called the 32-bar song form (where each section has eight bars, and the B section is called the 'middle eight'). This was widely used for Tin Pan Alley and show songs, and sometimes in country songs. Two examples are 'I got rhythm' by George Gershwin and 'Over the rainbow' by Harold Arlen.[4]

From the 60s onwards songs have adopted more extended structures, but often with an element of AABA form contained within them. The general principle of having a contrasting middle or bridge section, and what it achieves musically, applies in many situations – as we will see in the next few pages.

The term **middle eight** is often used for such a contrasting section, even if it is not eight bars long. It will often have a different arrangement of instruments, and be in a different key or use different chords from the verse or A section. The lyrics often have a different mood or angle from the rest of the song. In 'Maybe baby' the middle eight moves to the subdominant chord, D.

Another feature of the song is the strong use of **close harmony** in the backing vocals, especially in the instrumental verse.

[4] Strictly speaking, it is the *choruses* of 'I got rhythm' and 'Over the rainbow' that exemplify so well the A A B A form. The verses of those songs, as with many Tin Pan Alley or show songs, are comparatively rarely heard.

'I want to hold your hand' – the Beatles (1963)

0:00	INTRO
0:07	VERSE 1
0:22	CHORUS
0:29	VERSE 2
0:48	CHORUS
0:50	MIDDLE EIGHT
	LINK
1:10	VERSE
1:26	CHORUS
1:33	MIDDLE EIGHT
	LINK
1:53	VERSE
2:08	CHORUS
2:15	ENDING

The structure of this song is very similar to that of 'Maybe baby' – A A B A B A – but with the important ingredient of a **chorus** after each verse. This sort of form can be heard in countless songs from a wide variety of musical styles. The chorus is almost always the catchiest, most distinctive part of a song, and usually contains the title-line.

The middle-eight section, which (as in 'Maybe baby') moves to the subdominant, is expanded by a three-bar link, building tension back to the verse – and breaking with the conventional four- or eight-bar phrase lengths.

The instrumentation of two guitars, bass and drums is a basic pop blueprint, whether for the Beatles, the Rolling Stones, AC/DC or Oasis.

Details to note:
- Handclaps distinctively augment the drums.
- The rhythm-guitar parts are in a style typically associated with Chuck Berry.
- There are typical Beatles vocal harmonies throughout.
- Paul McCartney adds a bass-guitar fill to the end of the lines in the verses, helping the harmony I – V – VI – III7 to flow.
- The middle eight is marked by a shift in guitar strumming, and by the drummer's hi-hat being closed. The music is tighter and more controlled, which suits the changing sentiment in the lyrics. Lead guitar accents, and the opening of the hi-hat, build through the repeated line at the end of this section into the last verse.
- A big drum-kit fill leads to the last chorus.
- At the very end a dramatic climax is provided by accented triplets as a final build up of energy.

'Waterloo sunset' – the Kinks (1967)

Time	Section	Lyrics
0:00	INTRO	
0:10	GTR MELODY	
0:20	VERSE 1 (A)	Dirty old river, must you keep rolling, flowing into the night
0:27	(A)	People so busy, makes me feel dizzy, taxi light shines so bright
0:38	(B)	But I don't need no friends
0:47	(A)	As long as I gaze on Waterloo sunset, I am in paradise
0:56	MIDDLE EIGHT	Every day I look at the world from my window But chilly, chilly is evening time, Waterloo sunset's fine
1:18	VERSE 2	Terry meets Julie, at Waterloo Station, every Friday night
1:27		But I am so lazy, don't want to wander, I stay at home at night
1:36		But I don't feel afraid
1:45		As long as I gaze on Waterloo sunset, I am in paradise
1:54	MIDDLE EIGHT	Every day I look at the world from my window But chilly, chilly is evening time - Waterloo sunset's fine
2:16	VERSE 3	Millions of people swarming like flies round Waterloo underground
2:25		But Terry and Julie cross over the river where they feel safe and sound
2:34		And they don't need no friends
2:42		As long as they gaze on Waterloo sunset, they are in paradise
2:52	GTR MELODY	
2:58	CODA to fade	Waterloo sunset's fine

'Waterloo sunset' reflects the evolution of pop music from 1963 to 1967. In 'Maybe baby' and 'I want to hold your hand', the verse is very short – hardly more than a few words, a vehicle for a catchy tune – and verse 1 is repeated after the middle eight. 'Waterloo sunset' is a different proposition, with a longer lyric that progresses through the song, painting a picture, telling a story. It is more 'poetic', more expressive, more carefully written. (The Beatles, of course, were doing the same thing by 1967.)

The verse is itself in miniature AABA form. The song does not really have a chorus, but the fourth line of the verse functions as a sort of chorus, carrying a crucial repeated line of text (subtly varied in verse 3).

Other points to note:
- The **intro**: a rhythmic guitar figure played on one note along with a descending bass. It returns at the end of the middle eight, helping to lead back to the verse.

- After the intro but before the singer comes in, the guitar plays the main tune, line A of the verse. It does so again in a corresponding position at the end of the song: after verse 3 but before the coda.
- The shape of the melody in the A section of the verse: a distinctive opening phrase, which then keeps its shape but moves down to a different pitch – and then moves down again, slightly altered. This shape, in its different forms, is repeated many times through the song.
- The B line of the verse: a contrast melodically and harmonically.
- The middle eight: again, new material for further contrast, and a new perspective lyrically.
- The **coda** or ending. In 'Maybe baby' the coda is an extra repeat of the last line, and the same happens in 'I want to hold your hand', with the accented triplet rhythm adding a flourish. In 'Waterloo sunset' the coda is more extensive: the guitar rhythm from the intro reappears, this time reinforced by the bass staying on one note (the dominant). The singer and backing vocals overlap as they build up and then fade, singing 'Waterloo sunset's fine…'.
- Backing vocals, as in 'Maybe baby' and 'I want to hold your hand', occur through the song. They echo the words of the singer, or sing 'oo's and 'sha la la's.
- **Guitar licks** – short solo phrases – can be heard at the end of some of the sung phrases, for example after the words 'flowing into the night' and 'light shines so bright' in the first verse, echoing the shape of the main tune. **Drum fills** can also be heard, for example at 'And they don't need no friends' in verse 3. A **fill** is a short decorative passage that embellishes or punctuates a repeated pattern.

'You've got a friend' – James Taylor (1971)

This song, written by Carole King, is in the singer–songwriter style associated with introspective, thoughtful lyrics and expression. It has quite involved, jazz-influenced harmonies. The sound is generally gentle, with unobtrusive percussion. Notable features include:
- The intro hook (0:00). A **hook** is a short, catchy melodic or rhythmic idea (in this case melodic), designed to be instantly memorable.
- The ornate bass guitar fill at 0:07.
- Finger-picked guitar fills, e.g. at 0:27.
- The descending figure leading into the chorus (0:47).
- The singer's gospel-inflected ornamentation of the melody at 2:05.
- From the second chorus (2:20 onwards), the backing vocals (performed with Joni Mitchell) create some interesting harmonies, starting (on the word 'call') at an unusual interval – a major seventh above the bass.
- The coda repeats the melodic intro hook, combining it with the title phrase.

'You've got a friend'

0:00	INTRO
0:10	VERSE 1
0:30	
0:51	CHORUS
1:29	INTRO
1:38	VERSE 2
2:00	
2:20	CHORUS
2:57	MIDDLE EIGHT (10 bars)
3:24	CHORUS
4:01	CODA (Intro, repeated)

0:00	GTR INTRO
0:09	HORNS
0:17	VERSE 1
0:34	CHORUS
0:51	VERSE 2
1:08	CHORUS
1:25	VERSE 3
1:43	CHORUS
2:00	MIDDLE 8
2:11	INTRO, new key
2:19	CHORUS to fade

'Soul man' – Sam and Dave (1967)

This song is a good example of the Atlantic/Stax soul sound, with a horn section around the core rhythm-unit of guitar, bass and drums.

The form follows a verse–chorus–middle-eight pattern, with a guitar intro and a catchy hook at the end of the chorus. Three verses and choruses are heard before the middle eight, which is used to change key. The intro is repeated in the new key, and then the chorus melody is repeated to fade over the verse grooves. Changing key for the repeated chorus at the end of a song is a trick often used by songwriters, from soul hits like this to mainstream pop.

'Trenchtown rock' – Bob Marley and the Wailers (1970)

Trench Town is the shantytown district of Kingston where the Wailers lived. The song has an uplifting message of relief from that existence through the joy of music.

This song has a verse–chorus form. There are two long middle sections, which provide contrast through the shift to minor chords and the blocks of semi-improvised vocals.

0:00	INTRO
0:09	VERSE 1
0:28	CHORUS
0:54	MIDDLE SECTION
1:26	INTRO repeat
1:32	VERSE 2
2:52	CHORUS
2:18	MIDDLE SECTION
2:49	INTRO to fade

The instrumentation for 'Trenchtown rock' is limited to drums, bass, guitar and percussion (which is very low in the mix). The overall **texture** is very percussive; the choppy, edgy guitar is more rhythmic than melodic, and the drum-kit part is punctuated by fills on the snare drum (as heard at the very beginning of the song) which contrast with the subtler rim shots heard throughout. The backing vocals are important as the main source of harmonic coloration, providing a warm backing for the lead vocal. With almost no melodic decoration from the band, there is room for scat-type improvisation, especially in the middle sections.

Typical reggae features:
- The music is dominated by a low, full bass-guitar sound, playing a line based on roots and fifths.
- The bass drum falls on beats 2 and 4 of the bar.
- The rim of the snare is used most of the time, except for particular accents.
- The intro fill is a characteristic figure.
- The sparse, percussive off-beat guitar often plays in up-strokes, which accent the top notes of the chord.
- Chord progressions are straightforward and repetitive.
- A general sense of musical economy pervades the song; an effective sound is created through the sparse, economic deployment of limited forces.
- Tempo: laid back.

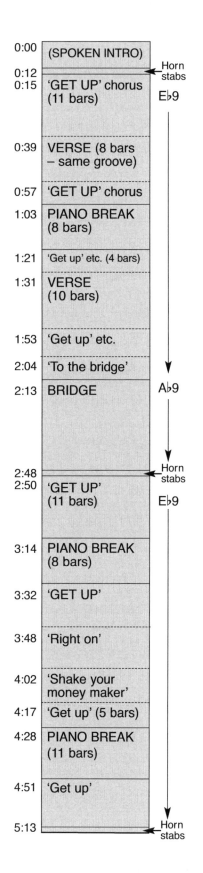

Time	Section	Chord
0:00	(SPOKEN INTRO)	
0:12		Horn stabs
0:15	'GET UP' chorus (11 bars)	E♭9
0:39	VERSE (8 bars – same groove)	
0:57	'GET UP' chorus	
1:03	PIANO BREAK (8 bars)	
1:21	'Get up' etc. (4 bars)	
1:31	VERSE (10 bars)	
1:53	'Get up' etc.	
2:04	'To the bridge'	
2:13	BRIDGE	A♭9
2:48		Horn stabs
2:50	'GET UP' (11 bars)	E♭9
3:14	PIANO BREAK (8 bars)	
3:32	'GET UP'	
3:48	'Right on'	
4:02	'Shake your money maker'	
4:17	'Get up' (5 bars)	
4:28	PIANO BREAK (11 bars)	
4:51	'Get up'	
5:13		Horn stabs

'Get up (I feel like being a) sex machine' – James Brown (1970)

This James Brown hit still has verses and choruses, and a bridge (see below), but the structure is much looser than that of a conventional song. The chorus is hardly different from the verse; the vital element here is the **groove** (a long section where the same rhythm parts repeat), on a single chord (E♭9), over which the verses and call-and-response choruses are heard.

As can be clearly heard, the sections are cued by James Brown himself; for instance we can hear him calling in the bridge section, which shifts to a different chord (A♭9). Because the form is dictated by the singer, there are sections of uneven length (e.g. the first chorus, which is 11 bars). There is a piano riff, heard several times, and horn 'stabs' which are heard at the beginning, middle and end.

The **bridge** in this song works more like the middle eight of a conventional song, providing a contrasting section rather than a linking passage.

The song relies upon the work of the rhythm section – guitar, bass and drums. The drum beat is a good example of the kind of funk beat which was later sampled in much hip-hop. The guitarist plays the same clipped pattern throughout. The bass line is more varied – each bar is a slight variation on a basic rhythm pattern, with busier fills as the song progresses.

Other instruments are used with remarkable economy. The horns (sax and trumpet) enter only for the three rounds of stabs heard at the beginning, middle and end of the song. The piano plays only for its eight-bar breaks (the first at 1:03, the last stretched to 11 bars).

0:00	INTRO
0:04	VERSE GROOVE (instrumental) (8 bars)
0:18	CHORUS (8 bars)
0:34	VERSE 1 (16 bars)
1:03	CHORUS (8 bars)
1:18	VERSE 2 (16 bars)
1:47	CHORUS (8 bars)
2:02	MIDDLE EIGHT (9 bars)
2:19	VERSE 2 (repeat) (16 bars)
2:50	CHORUS (repeat to fade)

'Disco inferno' – the Traamps (1976)

'Disco inferno' is a disco classic. Many of the essential elements of disco can be heard, including the **four-on-the-floor** drumbeat, the hedonistic lyrics, and the lush instrumentation which includes strings and horns.

The song is essentially groove-based, but follows a verse–chorus structure, with a striking intro and a middle eight. It begins with a crashing cymbal, a flurry of violins, and a driving descending line which gathers momentum into a verse groove dominated by clavinet (an electronic keyboard instrument) and bass. This works to grab the attention (and hopefully fill the dance floor).

The first vocal entry is the chorus – starting the song with the catchiest section is a common device.

Each first chord of the verses and choruses is 'pushed', brought forward to the last quaver (eighth-note) of the previous bar, so that it anticipates the main beat – a common funk-derived syncopation.

The verse is based on a single-chord groove (Cm7) which contrasts with the descending chords of the chorus.

The middle eight provides contrast and relative instability. A sudden thinning out of the texture in bar 7 increases the tension, which is then wound up even more by the cutting in of a two-bar link, accompanied by a descending figure reminiscent of the intro. The return to the verse groove takes on extra momentum because of this build-up.

'Holidays in the sun' – the Sex Pistols (1977)

The verse–chorus structure extends to punk (and to hard rock, metal and grunge). This song is the vicious opener to the album *Never Mind the Bollocks*. It is a good example of the energy that fuelled the Sex Pistols.

The song has quite an involved form: basically riff-based, with verse–chorus–middle-eight, but also with added sections of just the main riff, plus an extension or bridge after the middle eight, and a guitar solo.

0:00	INTRO
0:19	MAIN RIFF
0:33	VERSE
0:46	CHORUS
0:59	MAIN RIFF
1:14	VERSE
1:26	CHORUS
1:39	MAIN RIFF
1:52	MIDDLE EIGHT
2:06	EXTENSION OR BRIDGE
2:19	GUITAR SOLO
2:30	CHORUS
2:45	MAIN RIFF: repeat to end

0:00   The intro, with the taped sound of marching feet, blends into sustained guitar chords. The tempo here is slightly slower than the following riff.

0:19   A violent drum outburst introduces the main riff.

0:33   In contrast to the main riff, the verses are accompanied by tighter, chugging guitar and drums, with a fill between each vocal line. The drums alternate between ride/crash cymbals and hi-hat, depending upon the sound and feel required.

0:46   The chorus is fortified by shouted backing vocals.

0:59   The guitar riff is as important as the vocals, and the climax of the chorus precedes the return of that riff each time.

1:39   Added lead-guitar fills augment the riff here, and then cut through more clearly in the middle eight (01:53).

2:06   Following the middle eight comes this section: a less distinct eight bars, with chaotic, spoken ad libs.

2:19   The guitar solo is about as direct as is possible: one repeated, continuous phrase. No frills here.

2:45   The long final section of the main riff is embellished by spoken, stream-of-bile vocals and a general sense of snowballing energy.

0:00	INTRO
0:25	VERSE 1
0:33	(voice enters after 4 bars each time)
0:50	BRIDGE
1:06	CHORUS
1:31	LINK RIFF
1:39	VERSE 2
2:04	BRIDGE
2:20	CHORUS
2:44	LINK RIFF
2:53	GTR SOLO (= verse)
3:09	(= bridge)
3:25	VERSE 3
3:49	BRIDGE
4:06	CHORUS
4:30	CODA (extension)
4.46	FINAL CHORD RINGS

'Smells like teen spirit' – Nirvana (1991)

'Smells like teen spirit' uses basically the same root progression F – B♭ – A♭ – D♭ throughout; the structure is primarily defined by differences in instrumentation and dynamic. The pattern of quiet verses building to loud, powerful choruses can be found in many of Nirvana's songs (and in those of their imitators). The vocal melody in the chorus is essentially the same as the guitar riff; the guitar is as important as the vocals for this song.

An important device found in lots of heavy guitar music can be heard in the intro, where a riff is played by a single guitar before being repeated by the whole band. This builds tremendous tension and excitement, so that all the energy is released when the riff kicks in.

This song uses bridges to build up to the release of the chorus. A big snare drum fill marks the arrival of the chorus riff each time. After choruses 1 and 2 there is a brief, different link-riff, standing out from the rest of the texture.

After the second link-riff there is an instrumental verse, with the guitar playing the melody from the verse and bridge, leading to a final vocal verse. This is given variety by removing the two-note guitar hook heard in the previous verses, so that the bass-line comes to the fore below the sustained feedback from the solo.

0:00	INTRO
0:15	VERSE 1
0:49	CHORUS
1:07	VERSE 2 (i)
1:15	VERSE 2 (ii)
1:33	CHORUS
1:51	VERSE 3
2:25	CHORUS
2:43	INSTRUMENTAL BREAK
3:00	VERSE 4
	ENDING/fade

'Bring the noise' – Public Enemy (1987)

This is an example of Public Enemy's urgent **rap** style. Rapping is basically rhythmical, rhyming semi-spoken recitation. In this song the lead vocal is augmented by another member of the group, who doubles the last word of some lines, adding spoken ad libs and answering phrases. The dynamic set-up between two or more rappers (for instance, the Beastie Boys or Wu-Tang Clan) is an important part of Hip-hop music. Most solo rap stars, such as Eminem, have one or more other rappers on stage with them, doubling or answering alternate lines.

Despite its ferocious musical barrage of samples and programmed beats, this song holds onto a verse–chorus structure, with an anthemic shout-along chorus. There is even an instrumental middle eight, before the final verse.

Each line of the chorus is answered with **scratching**: percussive manipulation of a record on a turntable, backwards and forwards against the needle in sync with the fader on the DJ's mixer. The music is a collage of sirens, squeals, sampled horns and synths, and a mixture of programmed (drum-machine) drums and samples.

The second verse is in two parts. Initially there is a four-bar break, using a sample from James Brown's 'Funky drummer', albeit with the addition of programmed double bass-drums (also heard at the very beginning of the song). The second half of the verse returns to a similar backing to other verses; the contrast with the first section provides urgency and excitement to push the song forwards.

This song is typical of the politically charged aggression of Public Enemy's 80s hip-hop. Many of their trademarks can be heard here – rhetoric-filled lyrics, sloganeering, James Brown-inspired samples, and a musical backdrop bordering on cacophony.

0:00	Section 1 INTRO VERSE 1 CHORUS 1 VERSE 2 CHORUS 2
1:58	Section 2 BRIDGE GUITAR SOLO
3:34	Section 3 CHORAL PASSAGE
5:36	Section 4 SECTION 2 REPRISE (heavy) GUITAR SOLO REPRISE

'Paranoid Android' – Radiohead (1997)

'Paranoid Android' is taken from Radiohead's 1997 album *OK Computer*. The esoteric lyrics and Thom Yorke's eerie vocals are typical of Radiohead's music. Jonny Greenwood's guitar work uses a mix of clean and distorted sounds with bends, pitch shift, whammy pedal and pedal-based filter effects – all part of the characteristic Radiohead sound. The song was originally 15 minutes long, but was cut down to its present almost 6½ minutes after touring. Due to its complexity and markedly differing sections it is often compared to 'Bohemian Rhapsody' by Queen.

'Paranoid Android' is a complex song which changes tempo several times and shifts between two time signatures: 4/4 and 7/8. It has an unusual song structure, very different from the usual verse/chorus of a classic pop song. There are four discrete sections, composed by different members of the band, with only the guitar solo recurring. Additionally the song modulates (changes key) several times.

It opens in 4/4 at a moderate speed, with an acoustic guitar playing in C minor, then alternating C minor and G minor chords over an ominous bass line with a prominent and somewhat discordant E natural.

Section 2 opens in 4/4 in A minor, then moves into a 7/8 passage in modal C. The texture becomes more dense with the addition of heavily distorted guitars at 2:45. The subsequent intense guitar solo is followed by a unison A, rather suggesting an F major tonality.

The song returns to 4/4 and slows down for section 3, which opens in C minor and then moves into D minor with an almost classical style choral accompaniment.

Section 4 returns to the tempo and texture of the second section and modulates back to C minor, switching between 7/8 and 4/4 as previously. The closing bars feature a variant of the heavily distorted guitar solo from section 2, and an unexpected abrupt ending.

0:00	INTRO
0:11	VERSE 1
0:32	BRIDGE
0:42	CHORUS
1:03	VERSE 2
1:23	BRIDGE
1:34	CHORUS
1:54	INTRO (repeat)
2:05	MIDDLE EIGHT (verse variant)
2:25	CHORUS VARIANT
2:46	CHORUS
3:06	CHORUS

'Baby one more time' – Britney Spears (1999)

This song is an example of the slickly produced mainstream 'pure pop' of the 90s. Its appeal is based on small catchy elements in the tune and lyric, and on musical hooks such as the three-note piano riff first heard at the very beginning.

A bridge section links each verse to the chorus that follows.

The middle eight reiterates the same harmony which has been used for the verses and choruses, but the instrumentation reduces to arpeggiated piano, changing the mood of the song completely for eight bars by dropping the rhythm section.

The repeats of the chorus towards the end are cleverly constructed: a variant at 2:25, the original chorus at 2:46, and a combination of the two at 3:06.

Other things to listen for:
*   Britney Spears is multi-tracked as backing vocals, accompanying herself in the bridge.
*   Synth strings are added for a dramatic 'orchestra hit' in the chorus.
*   In the second verse a pulsing eighth-note synthesizer pattern and more backing harmonies are added.

0:00	INTRO
0:20	VERSE 1
0:39	BRIDGE
0:59	CHORUS
1:19	4-BAR LINK
1:28	VERSE 2
1:48	BRIDGE
2:07	CHORUS
2:27	LINK
2:37	Spoken two bars
2:42	MIDDLE EIGHT (vocal harmonies)
3:01	CHORUS (repeat to fade)

'Independent women Pt 1' – Destiny's Child (2001)

This is an example of contemporary R&B/pop. Key features:
- soul-styled, semi-improvised vocals
- an economical, funky riff, heard through most of the song
- stuttering staccato programmed drums and bass
- a neat vocal hook at the beginning, where the singer begins several lines with 'Question: ...'
- call-and-response vocals
- disco-influenced strings

The riff and overall texture are consistent, but the verse, bridge and chorus are distinguished melodically and harmonically. These are the chord structures:

Verse	I	I	I	I	I	I	I	I
Bridge	IV	I	IV	I	IV	I	IV	V
Chorus	I	I	I	I	IV	I	IV	I

Each repeated chorus includes increasingly virtuosic vocal performances, both in the elaboration of the lead line and the added harmonies – a key aspect of R&B.

The middle eight is harmonically similar to the chorus, but has a strikingly different texture. The riff stops, giving way to *a cappella* vocal harmonies plus gospel-like wordless vocal improvisation.

0:00	INTRO
0:34	CHORUS
0:54	VERSE 1
1:29	CHORUS
1:46	VERSE 2
2:18	CHORUS
2:37	OUTRO

'Crazy' – Gnarls Barkley (2006)

Gnarls Barkley is a musical collaboration between singer Cee-Lo Green and artist/producer Danger Mouse. 'Crazy' is taken from their 2006 debut album *St. Elsewhere*. It owes much of its musical inspiration to the song 'Last Man Standing', which features in the 1968 spaghetti western *Viva! Django*. Parts of its melody and chord structure are used in 'Crazy', and, perhaps most notably, the one-bar drum rhythm –

– which is repeated throughout most of the song.

'Crazy' could be described as a fusion of soul and contemporary R&B. It has a strong 1960s soul flavour, powered by Cee-Lo's dynamic falsetto vocals with an R&B influence heard in the melismatic vocal line and use of synthesized strings.

There are several melismatic passages, where a group of notes is sung on one syllable. The word 'possibly' at the end of the chorus, for example, is sung over thirteen notes:

The song, which is in 4/4 and a minor key, follows a fairly conventional verse/chorus structure. The only departure from the norm is the extended intro – which, although it incorporates elements of the verse melody and chord structure, is suitably different.

0:00	Jay-Z rapping
0:11	Jay-Z rap verse
0:34	Rihanna VERSE 1
0:57	CHORUS
1:41	VERSE 2
2:03	CHORUS
2:47	BRIDGE
3:11	CHORUS
3:52	OUTRO
	(fade)

'Umbrella' – Rihanna (2007)

Rihanna was born in Barbados. At the age of 16 she moved to the USA where, following an audition with Jay-Z, she was signed to his label, Def Jam Recordings. 'Umbrella' is from her 2007 album *Good Girl Gone Bad*.

'Umbrella' is in 4/4 in a minor key. It could be described as R&B pop. It opens with a rap verse by Jay-Z and then follows the absolutely classic intro—verse—chorus—verse—chorus—bridge—chorus—outro format. Its most distinctive feature is the simple catchy hook on the syllables '-el-la' and 'eh' at the end of the choruses.

The vocals have a narrow range of less than an octave. The verse melody illustrates a classic pop device: a repetitive melody (mainly three notes) is supported by changing chords to provide colour and variety. The chorus melody uses another standard pop device: a descending melodic sequence where the same short pattern is restated at a lower pitch

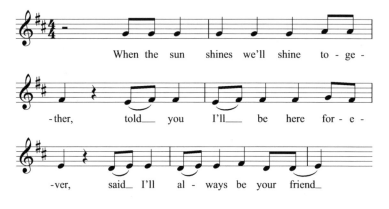

The contrast between verse and chorus is heightened by the chorus having a more major feel; the opening chords form a plagal cadence (IV–I) in the relative major.

Notice how the texture thins dramatically in the bridge; most of the drums and some of the synthesizers, especially the deeper ones, drop out. This device is often heard in dance music, so that just before the final chorus the reintroduction of bass frequencies from drums and synthesizers adds extra impact.

'She said' – Plan B (2010)

'She said' is taken from the concept album *The Defamation of Strickland Bank*. It is a narrative song telling the story of a character who is wrongfully accused of rape and is imprisoned, and is an interesting mix of retro soul and rap. Falsetto singing is used, in marked contrast to Plan B's earlier tougher-sounding hip-hop-influenced output.

The soul influence can be heard in Plan B's crooning falsetto vocals, with sustained notes on the strings and a horn section (saxophones, trombone, trumpet, flugelhorn). 'She said' is in E minor and uses swung rhythms. Plan B has an unusually wide vocal range; the vocal here spans more than two octaves.

Structurally it follows a variant of the classic intro—verse—chorus—verse—chorus—bridge—chorus—outro formula, with the intro leading straight into a chorus and also reappearing before the final chorus.

0:00 **INTRO**	
0:13 **CHORUS**	
0:46 **VERSE**	
1:25 **CHORUS**	
1:51 **BRIDGE/RAP**	
2:34 **RE-INTRO**	
2:40 **CHORUS**	
3:06 **OUTRO**	

0:00 **Intro** The song opens with a lo-fi sample of clapping and a vocal version of the bass line before drums and bass enter at 0:06. At 0:12 a chromatic string flurry leads us into the chorus; this motif reappears throughout the song.

0:13 **Chorus** Strings enter along with horn stabs. Snare drum rhythm enters at 0:40.

0:46 **Verse** The vocal line continues with the same soul-like feel as the chorus. The accompaniment features prominent strings and an electric guitar playing off the beat.

1:25 **Chorus**

1:51 **Bridge/rap** This section – a complex rhythmic rap – contrasts with the chorus and the verse. The horn section drops out for the rap, leaving just the drums and strings for the simple rhythmic backing.

2:34 **Re-intro**
2:40 **Chorus**

3:06 **Outro** An extension of the chorus. Most instruments drop out, leaving rhythm guitar and bass. At 3:18 the drums re-enter, ending the song with a flourish.

DANCE MUSIC

'Renegade Master' (Fatboy Slim Old Skool Mix) – Wildchild (1998)

This track is composed entirely of samples, with no synthesizers or live performances. The uses of breakbeats show the influence of hip-hop on big beat. The entire track is on the chord of C, interest being generated by timbre and rhythm rather than harmony and melody.

Structure
The track has five main sections, in a structure that is common in much dance music:

Mix in
Main section
Breakdown
Reprise of main section
Mix out

time	section	bar
0:00	MIX IN (32 bars)	
1:02	MAIN SECTION (84 bars)	33
3:44	BREAKDOWN (36 bars)	117
4:53	REPRISE OF MAIN SECTION (16 bars)	153
5:24	MIX OUT (18 bars)	169

Mix in (32 bars)
This unpitched, rhythm-oriented section gives the DJ up to 32 bars to mix the track in over the previous one, before the bass guitar enters at bar 33, setting the tonality of the track – which may clash with that of the previous record.

The heavy bass drum on the downbeat of bar 1 provides a handy reference point for the DJ, helping to find the first beat of the track quickly when cueing it up.

Main section (84 bars)
The various elements that make up the track – vocal, drums, bass, guitar sample, sax stab sample, vocal sample ('jump'), scratches and squeals – are combined in different ways, with instruments often dropping in and out of the mix. There are brief drum and vocal-only episodes which help to break up the structure. In these episodes the vocal is variously looped, cut-up and re-triggered, a technique typical of Fatboy Slim's style.

Breakdown (36 bars)
All the instruments drop out and the vocal is heard alone. The vocal is gradually filtered down, dulling its sound until it becomes almost inaudible. At bar 129 it begins to filter back up again, and is joined by the other instruments, initially a loop and the guitar sample. The texture thickens as more and more instruments enter. The entire track gains a feeling of acceleration as the rhythms of the individual instruments speed up, another hallmark of Fatboy Slim's technique.

Reprise of main section (16 bars)
This is a truncated version of the main section. Here the main loop powers back in, releasing the tension that was built up in the breakdown.

Mix out (18 bars)
The tonal elements are dropped out of the mix, leaving only the rhythmic vocal samples and drums, providing the DJ with an ideal opportunity to mix into the next track.

0:00	MIX IN (16 bars)	
		bar
0:27	MAIN SECTION (77 bars)	17
2:37	BREAKDOWN (52 bars)	93
4:06	REPRISE/ CLIMAX (96 bars)	145
6:49	MIX OUT (8 bars)	241

'Access' (1995) – DJ Misjah and DJ Tim

Every pitched note in 'Access' (apart from the breakdown vocal samples) is an A, placing even greater importance on rhythm and timbre to sustain interest than in 'Renegade master'. 'Access' incorporates synthesizers and artificial drum sounds, resulting in a sonic world very different from Fatboy Slim's mix.

The track is based round the immense tension created in the breakdown section and then released in the climactic reprise. Even more than in 'Renegade master', the different sections are not clearly delineated but seem to grow out of each other, unlike the verses and choruses of a typical pop song. Also note the 'four-on-the-floor' bass drum pattern, typical of most house and techno.

Structure
'Access' has the same five-section structure as Fatboy Slim's mix of 'Renegade master'.

Mix in (16 bars)
The track starts off with drums only, to facilitate mixing.

Main section (77 bars)
The track's signature synthesizer pulse enters, and the texture progressively thickens with the addition of new elements, such as bass synth. Additional interest is created through instruments dropping in and out of the mix, especially the heavy drum-loop, much as in 'Renegade master'. A high string **pedal note** (introduced at bar 77) and snare-drum roll (bar 85) add tension, and are often used in dance music to indicate an imminent breakdown section.

Breakdown (52 bars)
The track drops down to just strings and disembodied vocal samples. The synth pulse is then reintroduced to keep a sense of tempo, and is followed by a muted synthesizer riff which gradually filters up, accompanied by a snare-drum roll to increase the tension. In 'Renegade master' the acceleration of the instruments and vocal achieve a similar effect.

Reprise of main section (96 bars)
This is the climax of the track. Note the relative length of this section compared with the corresponding part of 'Renegade Master'. The raucous sound of the filtering synthesizer makes this more than a simple reprise, and is a key feature of the acid techno style. The section is broken up by one-bar vocal pauses, and a drumless episode (bars 177–193).

Mix out (8 bars)
This short ending, comprising drums only, gives the DJ an opportunity to mix easily into the next track.

'I luv U' – Dizzee Rascal (2003)

'I luv U' is the debut single from Dizzee Rascal's *Boy in da Corner*, and is an example of grime. There are at least three versions available. The one used here lasts 3:30 and includes the final flute section/tempo change. The female vocals are provided by Jeanine Jacques.

The song tackles the subject of underage sex and pregnancy with witty, often dark, word play – 'Yo, If that girl knows where you stay that's poor, some whore banging on your door, what for? Pregnant? What're you talking about this for, fifteen, she's underage, that's raw.'

It has a relentless pace, with the machine-gun rattle of Rascal's rapping and a barrage of disjointed rhythms from raw synth and percussion sounds. The opening 'I luv U' female vocal sample becomes increasingly retriggered and syncopated. In terms of arrangement, note how the kick and bass synth are constantly dropped in and out of the mix, giving a very 'choppy' feel. There is an uneasy semitone movement in the typically minimal bass line; the lack of supporting harmony also adds to the sparse and uncompromising sound. The only melodic elements (until the outro) are the disquieting synthesizers in the female (chorus) section. Note the abrupt and jarring change of tempo at 2:30.

As the American music critic Sasha Frere-Jones wrote in the New Yorker, '...grime sounds as if it had been made for a boxing gym, one where the fighters have a lot of punching to do but not much room to move'.
(http://www.newyorker.com/archive/2005/03/21/050321crmu_music#ixzz2KWElumj7)

0:00	I luv U (vocal sample)
0:22	Yo, If that girl knows where you stay that's poor…
0:51	CHORUS boy/girl
1:04	Alright, she's a bad girl, I'm a buss doe…
1:33	CHORUS boy/girl
2:00	Listen, I like your girl so you better look after your girl…
2:30	FINAL SECTION – FLUTE SOUNDS

'Midnight request line' – Skream (2005)

'Midnight request line' is an example of early dubstep and is made up of repeated loops and layers of loops. The deep bass is highly reminiscent of dub, and is distinct from the 'wobble bass' of later dubstep. The track is in C minor and the alternating C/Eb B/D intervals in the arpeggio give it a somewhat eerie feel. The track is in binary form (in two sections), structured by the alternating C/B/C and F/E/F bass lines.

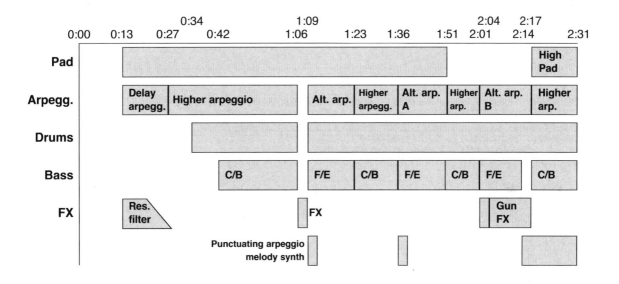

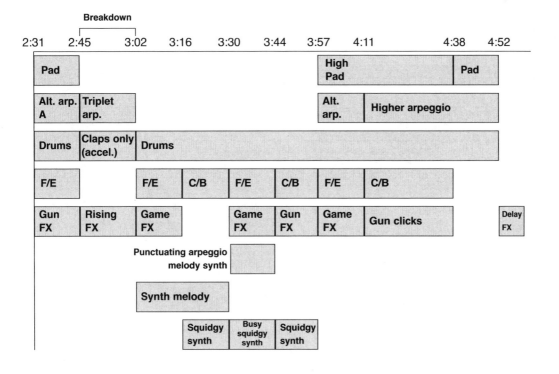

'Bangarang' – Skrillex (2011)

The song is named after the 'Bangarang' battle cry of the lost boys in Steven Spielberg's *Hook*. It uses forceful layered synthesizers, samples and filtering to create an aggressive barrage of sounds, combined with guitar riffs, a rock beat and the chopped up vocals from rapper Sirah. 'Bangarang' is often quoted as an example of brostep, a sub-genre of dubstep. However, compare 'Bangarang' with 'Midnight request line' by Skream: the distinctive dubstep snare drum on beat 3 is completely absent here, as is the deep dub-like bass line. It owes more to earlier dance music, for example 'Poison' by the Prodigy, despite its more aggressive sound. It is made up of short sections, each repeating a one- or two-bar loop. Though the sounds are contemporary, the breakdown at 2:14 and subsequent climactic build-up is typical of much dance music going as far back as the early 1990s.

0:00	Guitar intro
0:10	SECTION A – voices enter with: Shout to all my lost boys Sh-sh-sh-sh-sh-sh-shout to all my lost boys [etc: x4]
0:29	SECTION B New section heralded with word 'Bangarang'. [Loop x 4]
1:04	SECTION A [Loop x 2]
1:21	SECTION C Cut-up bass and short aggressive samples
1:56	SECTION D (BRIDGE) New section starting with word 'Bangarang'
2:14	SECTION E (BREAKDOWN and BUILDUP) Dynamic drops, voices drop out [Loop x 4]
2:31	Guitar enters and dynamic builds up
2:47	SECTION C
3:05	SECTION B
3:23	Vocal outro 'They say I lost my marbles, but I got these beats banging out the back of my toy car, Aye yo! I'm eating Fun Dip right now, not giving a fuck' [slowing, pitch dropping at end]

Dance music styles

There are many different styles of dance music, and these are being added to all the time. Here are the defining characteristics of some of the main ones since the 1990s.

Bassline house
◇ Uses a prominent heavy bass line and pitched-up vocals, combined with grime style MC-ing and a four-on-the-floor house drum-beat.
◇ Tempo: generally around 135–140 bpm (beats per minute)
◇ **Example** 'Heartbroken' by T2 and Jodie Aysha.

Big beat
◇ A heavily sample-oriented combination of hip-hop breaks and rock 'n' roll sensibilities with modern dance sonorities.
◇ Tempo: generally around 100–140 bpm
◇ **Examples**
'Renegade master' by Wildchild (Fatboy Slim old skool mix)
'Leave home' by the Chemical Brothers

Dubstep
◇ Dubstep is typified by its use of sub-bass, particularly 'wobble bass', and often uses the snare sounding on the third beat.
◇ Tempo: generally around 140 bpm
◇ Variants: Brostep
◇ **Examples**
'Soap dodger' by Crissy Criss
'Midnight request line' by Skream

Electro house
◇ Layered synth parts, squeaks and bleeps, laid over a four-on-the-floor drum beat with a resonant analogue bass riff.
◇ Tempo: generally around 120–130 bpm
◇ **Examples**
'Satisfaction' by Benny Benassi
'Walking away' by Tocadisco
'Yeah yeah' by Bodyrox

Fidget house
◇ An offshoot of electro house, it uses short vocal samples and snippets of sound, big rave synth stabs and wild pitch-bent bass lines. Tracks are often remixes of current indie and pop songs.
◇ Tempo: generally around 120–130 bpm
◇ **Example** Switch's remix of the Futureheads' 'Worry about it later'

Grime
◇ High energy MC-ing accompanied by dark and sporadic bass stabs over syncopated broken beats. Simple bass lines are often repeated by synthesized strings a third, fifth or an octave above
◇ Tempo: generally around 140 bpm
◇ **Examples**
'Tings in boots' by Ruff Sqwad
Boy in Da Corner by Dizzee Rascal
'Take me out' by Tinchy Stryder

Hardcore
◇ A frenetic offshoot of acid house, with much use of breakbeats and samples.
◇ Tempo: generally around 120–145 bpm
◇ Variants: happy hardcore
◇ **Example** 'Everybody in the place' by the Prodigy

House
◇ Features four-on-the-floor bass drum and off-beat hi-hat patterns. It is more sample-oriented than synthesizer-oriented. It may include vocals, or vocal samples, which are often soul-influenced.
◇ Tempo: generally around 120 bpm
◇ Variants: acid house, handbag house, hard house, tech house, deep house, garage
◇ **Examples**
Chicago house: 'Love can't turn around' by Jesse Saunders and Farley 'Jackmaster' Funk
Acid house: 'Oochy koochy' by Baby Ford
90s house: 'Professional widow' by Tori Amos (Armand van Helden remix), 'Short dick man' by 20 Fingers featuring Gillette

Jump-up
◇ Energetic drum'n'bass with bouncing bass lines, edgy production, three-tier bass lines (high, mid and low), and wobble sounds.
◇ Tempo: generally around 160–180 bpm
◇ **Examples**
'Twist em out' by Dillinja
'Body rock' by Andy C
'Shake ur body' by Shy FX

Jungle/drum'n'bass
◇ Uses speeded-up hip-hop breaks, and often consists of little other than a drum loop and a heavy bass line (hence 'drum'n'bass').
◇ Tempo: generally around 170 bpm
◇ Variants: jazzy drum'n'bass, hardstep, techstep, jump up (see separate entry)
◇ **Examples**
Nightlife by Andy C
Anatomy by Calyx & TeeBee
Jungle: 'Original nuttah' by UK Apache and Shy FX
Jazzy drum'n'bass: 'Brown paper bag' by Roni Size
Jump up drum'n'bass: 'Rock the funky beats' by Natural Born Chillers
Techstep: *Wormhole* co-produced by Ed Rush and Optical

Rap/hip-hop
◇ Originally based on loops of 70s funk and disco, though often programmed loops are used. Accompanied by rhythmic 'rap' vocal.
◇ Tempo: generally around 90–110 bpm
◇ Variants: gangsta rap, West Coast rap
◇ **Examples**
'Straight outta Compton' by N.W.A.
'My name is' by Eminem
Reasonable Doubt and *The Blueprint* by Jay-Z
Graduation by Kanye West
Donuts by J Dilla

Speed garage
◇ Comprises house loops combined with deep synthesized bass lines, which are derived from drum'n'bass.
◇ Tempo: generally around 120 bpm
◇ Variants: UK garage
◇ **Examples**
Speed garage: 'Rip groove' by Double 99
UK Garage: 'Why?' by Mis-Teeq (Matt 'Jam' Lamont remix)

Techno
◇ More synthesizer-oriented than house, but shares similar drum patterns. There is generally little or no chord movement.
◇ Tempo: generally around 120–140 bpm
◇ Variants: acid techno, minimal techno
◇ **Examples**
Detroit techno: 'No UFOs' by Model 500
Acid techno: 'Access' by DJ Misjah and DJ Tim
Minimal techno: 'Ten four' by Joey Beltram
The Berghain sound: 'Czeslawa' by Ben Klock, *Fire* by Sven Väth, *Closer* by Plastikman

Trance
◇ An offshoot of techno, with more emphasis on harmony, and very synthesizer-oriented.
◇ Tempo: generally around 120–150 bpm
◇ Variants: epic trance, commercial trance
◇ **Examples**
'Orange theme' by Cygnus X
Commercial trance: 'Seven days and one week' by B.B.E.

Trip-hop
◇ Dark and dreamy fusion of mellow hip-hop breaks with experimental instrumental textures. Often uses sung as opposed to 'rapped' vocal.
◇ Tempo: generally around 60–100 bpm
◇ **Example**: 'Sour times' by Portishead

AN A–Z OF STYLE AND STRUCTURE

A cappella	Vocal harmonies, without instrumental accompaniment
Arpeggio	A spread chord with the notes played singly, upwards or downwards
Auto-Tune	An audio processor that enables pitch correction
Backbeat	The rhythmic emphasis on beats 2 and 4 within a four-beat bar. Many rock drum patterns are based around the kick (bass) drum played on beats 1 and 3 with the snare drum sounding the backbeat on beats 2 and 4.
Ballad	A slow and usually romantic song with a wide, expressive melody and vocal delivery
Beat	The underlying pulse
bpm	Beats per minute
Break	Most instruments suddenly stop playing, with one instrument (or singer) continuing alone. A break usually occurs for just a bar or two.
Breakbeat	In dance music, the drum/percussion 'break' between vocal sections. The word 'break' is often substituted.
Breakdown	The section of a dance track where sounds drop out in order to create tension as they build up again
Bridge	A short passage that links two different sections. Sometimes the middle eight of a song is referred to as the bridge. Musicians may call a contrasting section the bridge or middle eight.
Cadence	A point of repose at the end of a phrase, usually harmonized by two chords
Call and response	A soloist sings a phrase, and (typically) a larger group responds with an answering phrase. It is also known as question and answer. It is especially prevalent in gospel-influenced soul and R&B. Use of the term may also be extended to parallel situations, for instance when an instrument 'answers' a singer's phrases, or two instruments alternate in a question-and-answer manner.
Chord	The simultaneous sounding of two or more notes
Chorus	A setting of the refrain of the lyrics, often containing the title words of the song. The chorus usually returns several times, and is likely to be the 'catchiest' part of the song.
Chromatic	Pitches outside the prevailing key and its scale
Close harmony	When the intervals between two or more voices are small (close together)
Coda	A concluding section
Decoration	Embellishment of a melody or rhythm
Dominant	The fifth note of a key. Also, the name of the chord built on the fifth degree of the scale, indicated by the symbol V.
Drum fill	A short decorative embellishment of an otherwise repeating drum pattern, often used as 'punctuation', marking a change from one section to another
Dynamics	Varying degrees of loud and soft
Feedback	Electrical interference between a sound and the amplified version of that sound coming from a speaker. Typically used by guitarists to produce a loud, wailing effect.
Fill	See also **drum fill**. A fill is a short decorative passage. It may be used to fill a gap, or to cover bare beats during solo portions of the music. Fills are often played at the end of a vocal line, before the next line starts.
Four on the floor	A bass-drum style often found in disco. The bass drum plays on all four beats of the 4/4 bar.
Groove	A repeated rhythmic pattern and 'feel', usually designed for dancing. It will

probably be the main rhythm of a record, and may run right through the track.

Hi-hat	A pair of cymbals on a stand, operated by a foot-pedal. A regular part of the drum kit.
Hook	A short catchy melodic idea designed to be instantly memorable
Horn section	The wind and brass section of a rock band – all the instruments that are blown
Instrumental	A solo section, often improvised, usually based on the chords of the verse or chorus
Interval	The difference in pitch between any two notes
Intro	The opening section of a song. It could be a repeated riff, a few strummed guitar chords, or one of the main melodies.
Key signature	In music notation, a set of sharps or flats to be observed by the player reading from the score. It shows the key of the music.
Lick	A short solo
Loop	A section or sample repeated over and over again, often rhythmic in nature
Melisma	A vocal style where more than one note is sung to a syllable, frequently found in contemporary R&B
Middle eight	A contrasting section in the middle of a song (not necessarily eight bars long), often with different arrangement of instruments, and/or different chords. The words may also have a different subject. Sometimes the middle eight of a song is referred to as the **bridge**.
Mix in	The opening section of a dance track, where the DJ mixes the previous track into the new one
Mixing	The blending together of separate audio tracks
Mix out	The closing section of a dance track, where the DJ starts to mix in the next track
Modulation	The process of changing key
Motif	A short fragment or idea, which may be repeated, or used again but in an altered form
Pedal note	A sustained or repeated note sounded against changing harmonies
Pentatonic scale	A five-note scale
Pitch	How high or low a note is, or specifically what note it is (A, B, C, etc.)
Power chord	A powerful, heavy guitar chord, often played with distortion, often only containing the root and fifth
Reprise	The return of a section of music
Riff	A short, repeated melodic pattern, often forming the background to a solo or vocal line, or to a whole song. It is usually 1–4 bars long. It may be heard at different pitches to fit in with the harmony and may also change its shape slightly.
Root	The note upon which a triad or chord is built
Sample	A digitally recorded fragment of sound, newly recorded or taken from a pre-existing source for use in a new one
Scat singing	Singing nonsense syllables, rather than words. Mainly a jazz singer's technique; the singer is effectively functioning as an instrumentalist.
Scratching	A DJ (disc jockey) moves a record back and forth on a turntable to create a rhythmic, percussive sound.
Sequence	The immediate repetition of a motif or phrase in the same part but at a different pitch
Semitone	Half a tone, usually the smallest interval in Western music

Stab	An accented single note or chord
Stop time	The accompaniment is reduced to a stab on the first beat of each bar, leaving the vocalist (or, especially in jazz, instrumental soloist) otherwise unaccompanied for a short passage. The change of texture creates a dramatic contrast, relieved when the full accompaniment resumes.
Subdominant	The fourth note of a key. Also, the name of the chord built on the fourth degree of the scale, indicated by the symbol IV.
Syncopation	When offbeat notes are accented
Tempo	The speed of the underlying beat, sometimes shown precisely by 'bpm' (beats per minute)
Texture	The overall picture of the sound: how many layers there are, whether dense or sparse, whether chords or single notes, whether continuous or spaced out. It is a difficult term to define, but is an important musical quality.
Timbre	Instrumental colour, the quality that makes one sound (e.g. a steel-stringed guitar) different from another (e.g. a nylon-stringed guitar)
Time signature	In music notation, two numbers on a stave, one above the other. The upper number indicates the number of beats per bar, and the lower number indicates the time-value of the beat.
Tonic	The first note of a key. Also, the name of the chord built on the first degree of the scale, indicated by the symbol I.
Turnaround	The final part of a section, in which the melody or chords prepare for the next section
Verse	A section of melody which is repeated each time with different words. Along with the chorus (with which it may alternate), one of the most important 'building blocks' of a song.
Vocoder	A device that treats vocal sound, sometimes making it seem artificial or robotic
Walking bass	A steady melodic bass-line that 'walks' along, marking all four beats of the bar and thereby serving a rhythmic as well as harmonic function. It usually mixes arpeggio-type movement with scale-type movement, and often hits the root note of the chord on the first beat of the bar.

chapter
13

Toby Bricheno and Julia Winterson

The Music Business

The first years of the twenty-first century witnessed revolutionary changes in the music business. Ever-evolving advances in digital music technology transformed nearly every aspect of the industry from recording to distribution, consumption to performance, formats to promotion. Coupled with the meteoric rise in downloading, both legal and illegal, and the burgeoning popularity of social networking sites, this has meant that few areas of the industry have been unaffected.

The seeds of the revolution were sown in the closing years of the twentieth century. The introduction of MP3 in 1992 meant that audio files could be easily distributed across the internet. In 1999 the pioneering peer-to-peer network Napster was introduced, leading to the free exchange of music files encoded in MP3 format. Copyright law provides that a person must have permission to make a copyrighted work available for download on the internet. Doing so without permission of the copyright owner (in this case, the record label) is against the law. Napster soon ran into legal difficulties over copyright infringement and was forced to close down in 2001. However, the floodgates were opened, threats of legal action from the music industry failed to stem the flow and, very soon, file sharing music sites (both legal and illegal) proliferated.

The first MP3 player for the mass market was introduced in 1998, the Rio Diamond PMP300. The MP3 compression format resulted in much smaller data volumes with little discernible loss in sound quality. Its key advantage was its storage technology, which made CDs seem bulky in comparison. The demand for MP3 players reached its peak in 2007 when 43.5 million devices were sold in the EU, outstripping the sales of CD players fourfold. However, the recent trend towards multi-function devices means that demand is dropping as more devices such as mobile phones are able to play back MP3 files – a good illustration of how quickly the market for high-tech products can change in the twenty-first century.

To begin with, online file sharers made MP3 popular. The commercial music industry was forced to embrace MP3, owing to rampant piracy and the increasing popularity of hardware devices such as the iPod. At the same time bandwidths increased, as did access to computer networks. Increased internet speeds made it practicable to stream music and video[1] live over the internet from sites such as YouTube and services such as Spotify, last.fm and Grooveshark. Some services, for example YouTube, are completely free, some are subscription based, and others offer both free and subscription options. Music users, by means of YouTube, Spotify and file sharing, have become accustomed to getting music for nothing or very little. All this has led to a paradigm shift in the way that consumers store music and, partly as a consequence of this, CD sales have plummeted. The 2011 report of the British record industry's trade association, the British Phonographic Industry (BPI), illustrates this

---

[1] To transmit (data) in real time, so that the user can begin listening/watching the content before it has all been completely sent.

well.[2] The BPI found that between 2005 and 2010 total UK sales of CDs almost halved, falling from £1707 million to £870 million, and the average retail price of a CD fell from £10.84 to £7.55.

Digital piracy too has taken its toll on the music industry worldwide. Between 2000 and 2011, global recorded music sales (including both physical products and downloads) fell from around £23 billion to around £10 billion:[3] a fall of 57%. Some countries fared worse than others, with United States music industry revenue falling by 72% from roughly £9 billion to just over £2.5 billion.

At the same time as the sale of CDs was decreasing, the amount of spending on downloaded albums was gradually increasing. In 2010 in the UK, retail spending on digital albums increased by 23% to £146m with more than 56.5m digital albums having been sold since the format launched in 2006. By this time the format accounted for one in six of all albums sold in the UK.

Thanks to streaming, consumers were able to be more selective in choosing the music they purchased. As a result people were buying the individual songs they liked rather than buying the whole album. In 2006 the UK recorded its first number one single based on download sales alone with 'Crazy' from Gnarls Barkley. Sales of singles in the UK have since increased 12% year-on-year, with downloads representing 98.7% of all singles sales in 2011. Downloads are not generally as profitable to the music industry as physical products, and although singles sales are healthy they do not usually generate significant profits for record companies who look to album sales to recoup the investments they have made in up-and-coming artists.

These dramatic shifts in revenue distribution changed the balance of power in the music industry. As consumers turned to online stores and streaming services while sales of physical formats fell, many high street record shops went to the wall. Tower Records closed its doors in 2006, followed a couple of years later by Virgin Megastores; in 2009 two of the best known UK music retailers – Woolworths and Zavvi – collapsed. In order to survive, record companies and artists had to diversify.

DIVERSIFICATION

British music companies had to reinvent their businesses for the digital age by marketing and promoting their music through every channel available. In 2011, the BPI found that revenues from music synchronization, '360 degree' artist deals, concerts, music-related TV production, broadcasting and public performance had grown and accounted for a fifth (20.5%) of record industry trade turnover. The back catalogues of record companies also took on an increasing significance.

Live performances

The old glory days of outdoor music festivals had been in the 1960s and 1970s, climaxing in Jimi Hendrix's appearance at the Isle of Wight in 1970, with a crowd of over half a million. In the ensuing years, the festival scene, with a few exceptions, died down, but the first few years of the twenty-first century witnessed a major revival. In order to compensate for declining recording revenues, much more money was invested in live performances, with a burgeoning of outdoor music festivals and concerts. Between 2005 and 2010, the UK market grew strongly with sales up by 69% and admissions up by 29%. The number of music festivals in the UK now hovers around the 700 mark.

One of the biggest and oldest festivals, Glastonbury, mushroomed in size. Somerset farmer Michael Eavis organized the first festival in 1970 when 1500 people bought tickets for £1. By 2011 the festival was a massive venture. It had multiplied in size a hundredfold

---

[2] THE BPI Annual Yearbook 2011

[3] International Federation of the Phonographic Industry (IFPI) 2012 Recorded Music Sales report

and required an extensive infrastructure in terms of accommodation, security, transport, water and power supply, not to mention television coverage. Tickets by then were £195. Other festivals, such as Reading, came out of the doldrums with tickets regularly selling out in less than two hours in the 2000s. The biggest dance festival, Creamfields, is now a huge enterprise, staging events across Europe, South America and most recently the United Arab Emirates. The twenty-first century boom in festivals took place across the world and catered for all musical tastes.

360 degree deals

In 2002 Robbie Williams signed a massive £80 million deal with EMI, giving them a stake in his entire career including touring and merchandising. This was the first much-publicised contract of what became known as 360 degree or multiple-rights deals. Labels take a percentage from all angles (hence the name). Under such contracts, record labels receive a percentage of the earnings from all of an artist's activities rather than just record sales. This could include concert revenue, merchandise sales, endorsement deals and ringtones. In exchange, the labels usually commit to promoting the artist for a longer period of time and to developing new opportunities in an almost managerial capacity. The American live events company Live Nation has famously signed million-dollar 360 degree deals with, amongst others, Jay-Z, U2 and Madonna. Madonna received more than $100 million in exchange for three albums and the exclusive rights to promote her concerts and to market her merchandise. U2's deal with Live Nation gave them the right to handle their digital distribution, merchandise, and branding rights for the next 12 years.

Such deals are not without controversy – some argue that we are now in the age of managers and venture capitalists and that there is a danger that the industry will become less and less about the music, with musicians in danger of losing any creative control. Nevertheless, 360 degree deals are becoming increasingly common in major label contracts.

Back catalogues

Record companies have always made a certain amount of their revenue through their back catalogue (albums which were originally released more than 18 months before) and have relied on re-mastered recordings and compilations through their quiet periods. However, these sales are taking on increasing significance within the embattled music industry where record labels can struggle to make money on new artists. In the US, the first half of 2012 brought sales of 76.6 million back catalogue albums as opposed to 73.9 million current albums.

Dealing with the tried and tested, rather than the new and speculative, gives more dependable returns on marketing investment. As a result record labels are on the lookout for hidden gems and classic tracks to exploit anniversaries, the new generations of fans, and the demand for well-packaged collectable re-releases. The search facility of streaming sites means that it has never been easier to explore music from any era. This, combined with a frustration with the lack of originality of new acts and a desire to hear the 'real deal', meant that record companies were able to exploit their back catalogue more effectively.

STREAMING

At the time of writing, two of the most popular streaming services are Spotify and YouTube. Spotify, based in Sweden, was launched in 2008 and offers free access to a vast library of music supported by radio-style advertising, along with an ad-free, fixed-fee subscription service. In July 2012 it reported 15 million active users worldwide including four million paying subscribers.[4]

---

[4] http://business.time.com/2012/08/16/spotify-is-growing-but-the-idea-of-music-ownership-is-holding-it-back/

YouTube is a US-based video-sharing website owned by Google, allowing registered users to upload videos and have them hosted free of charge. A huge number of music videos are available to view, with some posted by individuals and some by record companies. According to the *Wall Street Journal*, in 2012 nearly two thirds of US teenagers used YouTube as the way they listened to music, in preference to Spotify, iTunes or CDs. With YouTube, unlike Spotify, video is supported, and there are myriad free applications available to download the videos onto computer. It appears that physical ownership of music, even as just a file on a computer, is still seen as a desirable thing, especially when it is free.

YouTube has played a part in launching the careers of some major stars, notably Canadian teen-pop superstar Justin Bieber, who shot to fame after his bedroom performances singing Chris Brown, Usher and Ne-Yo hits were posted on YouTube and subsequently stumbled upon by talent manager Scooter Braun. Braun shrewdly played the homemade, lo-fi quality of the YouTube videos to his advantage,[5] and Bieber's management have continued to use YouTube as an important marketing tool. The prospect of an angel–faced white Canadian boy singing black American R&B has proved immensely popular with young teenage girls, with the visual aspect of YouTube playing a large role in his success. By the time of his first single, 'One time', he had 40 million subscribers.[6] In 2010 the video to 'Baby' became the most watched (but also the most 'disliked') video ever on YouTube. 'Gangnam style', by idiosyncratic and highly exuberant South Korean artist PSY, went viral in August 2012 solely on its YouTube video, sparking a global dance craze and many parody videos in the process. In a few months it became the first video to be viewed more than a billion times. The idea of a song sung in Korean being a worldwide hit is inconceivable without the presence of YouTube.

Streaming services are not without their problems for the music industry. They have been criticized frequently by artists for the small amounts of revenue they receive from streams. This is clearly illustrated in David McCandless' Information is Beautiful chart 'How much do music artists earn online?'[7] Composer Ellen Shipley, who wrote 'I drive myself crazy' for 'N Sync, received only $4.31 for 333,000 YouTube streams. 'I can't even buy a pizza for that,' she remarked.[8] Record labels and artists are also unhappy with the way that music videos, expensive to produce, are being screened on YouTube for free and then earning large sums in advertising revenue. As a consequence, a number of high-profile artists and bands such as the Beatles, AC/DC, Taylor Swift and Coldplay have refused to let some or all of their music be streamed.

The death of the printed music press and the rise of the blog

The heyday of the British music press was in the second half of the twentieth century. The *New Musical Express*, popularly known as *NME* and published weekly since 1952, developed a tradition of serious rock journalism, recruiting young writers such as Stuart Maconie, Paul Morley, Danny Baker, Mary Anne Hobbs and Steve Lamacq. In its prime, its influence on the British music scene was considerable. It created the first UK singles chart, gave the Sex Pistols their first music press coverage, coined the term Britpop, and even, through staff writers such as Tony Parsons and Julie Burchill, helped to develop a new and irreverent style of journalism. For many years the *NME* and its sister music weekly *Melody Maker*, provided important exposure for both new and established artists.

The two music papers developed a long-standing and intense rivalry, but in 2000, because of low sales, the two merged. The circulation of this, the UK's sole surviving weekly music

---

[5] In an interview with the *New York Times* he commented on his strategy: 'Justin, sing like there's no one in the room. But let's not use expensive cameras. We'll give it to kids, let them do the work, so that they feel like it's theirs.'

[6] http://www.azcentral.com/thingstodo/music/articles/2010/03/19/20100319justin-bieber-billboard.html

[7] http://www.informationisbeautiful.net/2010/how-much-do-music-artists-earn-online/

[8] http://www.guardian.co.uk/media/2012/oct/10/music-streaming-songwriters-youtube-pandora

newspaper, fell steadily from 2003 onwards, shedding 66% of sales in the eight years from 2003 to 2011. However, the online version, created in 1996, is currently the world's biggest standalone music site, with more than 7 million users per month.

This clearly illustrates the dominance of the internet over traditional methods of dissemination, with 'physical' media, such as CDs, being replaced by MP3s and printed media being supplanted by websites and blogs. The advantages of the internet over hard copy are easy to see. No printed magazine can hope to achieve the potential readership offered by the internet. Furthermore, news can be updated instantly and articles can carry audio and video content and support more reader interaction.

Since 2009 *NME* has been under the editorship of Krissi Murison, who ran a series of retrospective covers: 'Young fans really love these covers; our focus groups get really excited when it's the Smiths or John Lennon. You used to be really limited in what you could listen to, but now you have access to everything – young readers don't think chronologically about music.'[9] These sentiments echo the popularity of magazines such as *Mojo* and *Q*, which sprang up to cater to older fans' nostalgia and younger fans discovering 'classic rock' for the first time.

In part, the music press had acted as gatekeepers of the music industry, arbiters of taste who picked out artists that they felt would be, or deserved to be, successful. Along with the recording and publishing companies they decided who was worthy of being exposed to a wider audience. Digital technology and the internet have meant that the music of anybody and everybody can easily be made available to the public. Now there are new gatekeepers or, as some would argue, none. Music consumers decide what is worthy of their time, attention and money. As music critic Paul Morley said, 'In the past there were 150 rock critics, now there are 17 million'. The music press is losing its influence, especially in discovering new talent. In 2012 Ollie Jacob, co-founder of leftfield pop label Memphis Industries, stated that many young bands have eschewed the music press for websites and blogs such as Pitchfork, Stereogum or Gorilla vs. Bear. 'I don't think any of them would go to NME.com to find a band.'[10]

The music business has a complex structure encompassing many roles, both creative and otherwise. The following pages look at the main areas of the music business and the various roles within it – as shown in the chart on page 205.

Music, like any other industry, generates many supporting roles – secretary, accountant and so on – and an administrative role can be a good way of entering the industry. However, this sort of job does not often lead to a creative position, e.g. performer or remixer. With this in mind, we will focus here on roles unique to the music business.

CREATIVE ROLES

These are people involved with writing and performing music.

Band member
◇ Performing musician and integral part of band.
◇ May or may not be involved in the writing process.
◇ Traditionally was usually a singer, guitarist, bassist, drummer or keyboard player, but these days may just as often be a DJ or programmer (see below).
◇ Skills/attributes:
  • Proficiency on chosen instrument, or characterful singing voice
  • Individual style
  • Charisma and distinctive looks if a front person
  • Works well as member of a team

---

[9] 'As the NME nears its 60th birthday, has its influence in music world waned?' Michael Hann, the *Guardian*, 28 February 2012

[10] Ibid

Solo artist
◇ Almost always a singer.
◇ Often does not write his or her own material, but relies instead on a songwriter.
◇ Skills/attributes:
  • As for a band member, but with greater emphasis on looks, style and marketability
  • Drive, ambition and confidence

Songwriter
◇ Composes the song.
◇ Sometimes performs, but alternatively may write songs for other bands and solo artists to record and perform.
◇ Skills/attributes:
  • Competent musician
  • Musically creative
  • High self-motivation, happy to work alone

DJ/remixer
◇ Often starts out as a DJ, later taking on the more creative role of a remixer. A remixer takes the individual elements of a song (vocal, bass-line, guitar parts, etc.) and discards some of these parts, combining the remaining elements with new ideas (often new bass lines and drum parts). The result is usually a new, often longer, song structure.
◇ Skills/attributes:
  • In-depth knowledge of production techniques
  • An interest in keeping up to date with latest developments in music technology
  • Familiarity with various contemporary musical styles; a good ear

Programmer
◇ Well versed in contemporary music technology such as samplers, digital audio work-stations, etc., a programmer helps to add a modern, often dance-oriented edge to a song. The role is often similar to that of a remixer, with the emphasis more on complementing the existing song rather than changing it dramatically.
◇ Skills/attributes:
  • Encyclopaedic knowledge of music technology
  • Ability to work efficiently alone, often under pressure

RECORDING ROLES

People involved with recording the artists' music.

Producer
◇ Responsible for controlling the overall sound and artistic direction of the recording.
◇ Also responsible for making sure that it is 'on schedule' and 'on budget'.
◇ May or may not be directly involved with actually recording the band/artist to tape or hard disk. If actively involved with the recording and mixing process, is often referred to as a 'producer/engineer'.
◇ Skills/attributes:
  • Ability to deal diplomatically yet decisively with band members, record companies and managers alike
  • Ability to coax optimum performances from artists
  • A thorough working knowledge of the recording studio and recording techniques
  • Willingness to work unsocial hours
  • Ability to concentrate for extended periods of time

KEY ROLES AND ORGANIZATIONS

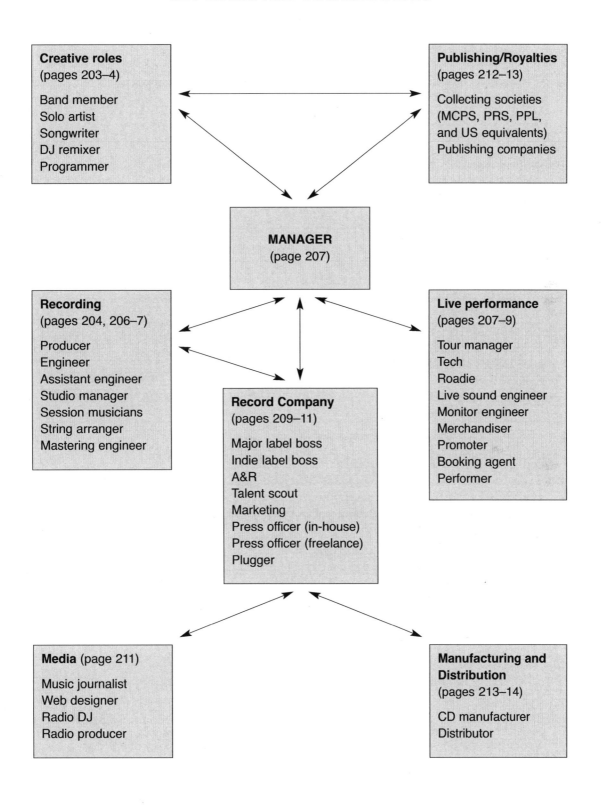

Creative roles
(pages 203–4)

Band member
Solo artist
Songwriter
DJ remixer
Programmer

Publishing/Royalties
(pages 212–13)

Collecting societies
(MCPS, PRS, PPL,
and US equivalents)
Publishing companies

MANAGER
(page 207)

Recording
(pages 204, 206–7)

Producer
Engineer
Assistant engineer
Studio manager
Session musicians
String arranger
Mastering engineer

Live performance
(pages 207–9)

Tour manager
Tech
Roadie
Live sound engineer
Monitor engineer
Merchandiser
Promoter
Booking agent
Performer

Record Company
(pages 209–11)

Major label boss
Indie label boss
A&R
Talent scout
Marketing
Press officer (in-house)
Press officer (freelance)
Plugger

Media (page 211)

Music journalist
Web designer
Radio DJ
Radio producer

**Manufacturing and
Distribution**
(pages 213–14)

CD manufacturer
Distributor

Engineer

◇ Responsible for shaping and committing the sounds of the band/artist to tape or hard disk. However, unlike the producer, the engineer generally has little or no artistic influence.

◇ In low-budget recording sessions, some bands forgo the extra expense of a producer and work cooperatively with an engineer instead.

◇ Skills/attributes:
- In-depth technical knowledge of recording equipment and techniques
- Substantial hands-on experience
- Willingness to work long unsocial hours
- A calm and professional manner in often difficult situations

Assistant engineer

◇ Also referred to as a 'tape op', although nowadays tape is becoming something of a rarity.

◇ Assists the engineer, keeps track of the mixes, and more often than not makes the tea! Generally considered the lowest rung of the studio ladder, and as the first step towards a career as an engineer or producer.

◇ Skills/attributes:
- Attentive and efficient
- Happy to work long unsocial hours
- Interested in music technology

Studio manager

◇ Responsible for keeping a commercial studio properly maintained, and for booking in clients (i.e. bands and record companies).

◇ Skills/attributes:
- Highly organized and efficient
- Good communicator
- Good numeracy

Session musician

◇ Technically competent musician, paid either hourly or per session to come into a studio and, usually, to play or sing a pre-determined part.

◇ Often works with solo artists who do not have a permanent band but need live musicians when recording.

◇ Sometimes hired because a band member's recorded part is not up to scratch!

◇ Skills/attributes:
- Highly proficient on their chosen instrument
- Ability to read music useful
- Wide knowledge of various musical styles
- Calm under pressure

Mastering engineer

◇ After a song has been recorded and mixed into stereo by the producer and engineer, this final mix is given to a mastering engineer, who usually compresses it (i.e. optimizes the loudness) and applies some final equalization (or EQ). To compile an album, he/she then puts the song in order with other songs on a 'PQ master' on U-matic tape (or comparable process) to present to the CD manufacturing company, also referred to as the 'pressing plant'.

◇ Skills/attributes:
- Thorough and up-to-date knowledge of mastering procedures
- Ability to concentrate for long periods of time

String arranger
◇ Often from a classical music background.
◇ Responsible for composing and/or arranging an accompanying string part for a song.
◇ Skills/attributes:
  • Excellent working knowledge of orchestral and string scoring
  • Ability to work to very short deadlines
  • Conducting skills are very useful

MANAGER

The manager acts as a buffer between the band/artist and the rest of the music business. As can be seen from the diagram (page 205) it is a pivotal role. On behalf of the band/artist, the manager liaises as appropriate with the record company, producer, tour manager, the media, etc. For doing this he/she takes around 20% of the band/artist's income.
◇ Skills/attributes:
  • Excellent communicator
  • Diplomatic and tactful yet assertive
  • Good head for business
  • Strong networking skills
  • Comfortable dealing with crises and unexpected situations
  • Solid negotiating skills

LIVE PERFORMANCE ROLES

These people are responsible for the organization and smooth running of a concert or gig.

Tour manager ('TM')
◇ Responsible for organizing and overseeing the transport, accommodation, staff, budget and itinerary for a tour, and for making sure that the band/artist is in the right place at the right time.
◇ Skills/attributes:
  • Strong coordinating/organizing skills
  • Diplomatic but firm manner
  • Quick thinker, calm under pressure
  • Strong negotiating and numeracy skills
  • Willingness to travel away from home for extended periods

Instrument technician ('tech')
◇ Ensures that the instrument they are responsible for (e.g. guitar, bass, drums, keyboards, etc.) is functioning correctly between and during gigs. If a guitarist breaks a string on stage, it is the guitar tech's job to provide a replacement guitar immediately.
◇ Skills/attributes:
  • Thorough technical knowledge of their chosen instrument and accessories
  • Playing ability very useful
  • Quick thinker, cool under pressure

Roadie

◇ Depending on the size and complexity of the gig, roadies are responsible for transporting, setting up and dismantling the artist's equipment, lighting and PA system at gigs. It is a very physical job, entailing much heavy lifting.

◇ The roadie often doubles up as a tech in lower budget tours or gigs.

◇ Skills/attributes:
  - Physical strength and stamina are a high priority for 'humping gear'
  - Happy to work as part of a team
  - Willingness to work unsocial hours away from home for lengthy periods

Live sound engineer (a.k.a. front-of-house engineer)

◇ Responsible for the sound the audience hears during the gig. Balances the instruments with the singer(s), using a mixing desk. The mixed sound is then projected to the audience via the PA system. If the sound engineer is employed by a venue, rather than a band, they are known as a 'house engineer'.

◇ Skills/attributes:
  - Thorough working knowledge of PA equipment
  - Excellent hearing, a good ear for music
  - Ability to improvise solutions under pressure

Monitor engineer

◇ Responsible for the sound the band hears on stage. The sounds of the vocals and instruments are combined by the monitor engineer and relayed to the band via onstage speakers known as 'monitors'. It's an important job, because if the band cannot hear what they are doing, then they are likely to give a poor performance.

◇ Skills/attributes:
  - Sound knowledge of monitoring equipment
  - Calm, professional manner

Merchandiser

◇ Concerned with the design, manufacturing and selling of the band's merchandise (T-shirts, posters, memorabilia, etc.). In smaller outfits, the band may deal with design and manufacture, while the merchandiser simply sells the product, often from a stall at gigs.

◇ Skills/attributes:
  - Visual flair
  - Ability to work to tight deadlines if manufacturing
  - Personable nature if working at gigs

Promoter

◇ Responsible for letting the public know about their band/artist's gigs, usually by flyposting, leafleting, and advertising in listings magazines, newspapers and on the radio.

◇ Organizes printing of tickets.

◇ Liaises with the tour manager over venue organization.

◇ Collects and distributes monies once the gig has ended ('settling the show').

◇ In smaller operations the 'venue promoter' looks after one venue only, and indeed may be responsible for just one night per week at a set venue. At smaller venues the bands may share promotional duties with the venue promoter.

◇ Skills/attributes:
  - Thorough knowledge of the contemporary music scene
  - Excellent organizational skills
  - Numerate
  - Good communicator

Booking agent
◇ Organizes tours and one-off gigs, often in conjunction with the release of an album or single.
◇ Scouts around for new live bands to represent.
◇ Usually takes a fee of around 10% for their services.
◇ Skills/attributes:
  - Thorough knowledge of the contemporary music scene
  - Ability to evaluate new or up-and-coming bands

Performer
◇ See also under CREATIVE ROLES (pages 203–4)
◇ Many types of musician, including backing musicians, functions bands, residency bands (e.g. hotels, cruise ships) and tribute bands, perform wholly or mainly non-original material.
◇ Backing musicians are technically adept, generally hired solely for touring.
◇ Many functions bands play mainly hits or well-known songs in a wide range of styles.
◇ Skills/attributes:
  - Excellent technical ability
  - Top-quality equipment if an instrumentalist
  - Calm and professional manner
  - Stylish if a singer
  - Adaptability

RECORD COMPANY ROLES

The record company represents the band/artist through their recordings. They advance money against prospective royalties and are responsible for organizing recordings, exploiting and promoting them, and making sure that the recordings are available in shops to buy. Once a band/artist signs a record contract, any recordings of songs made during the term of that contract belong to the record company.

A&R
◇ A&R stands for 'artists and repertoire', and is a term derived from the early days of record companies, when members of the A&R department would select specific songs (or repertoire) for an artist to record.
◇ These days the A&R person's main responsibility is to find and sign artists to their record label. They may also help to develop and build a 'buzz' around them.
◇ They are also the record company's main point of contact for the artist and manager.
◇ The A&R person is usually involved in deciding which songs should be released.
◇ They are often responsible for selecting the producer for a project.
◇ Skills/attributes:
  - In-depth knowledge of current musical trends
  - Ability to work under pressure
  - Strong instinct for what will sell

Talent scout (a.k.a. Junior A&R)
◇ Their job is to keep an eye out for unknown or little-known bands. This is done by listening to unsolicited demos and checking out small gigs. They then report back to the main A&R person or team.
◇ Skills/attributes:
  - Commitment to discovering new talent
  - Concentration and decisiveness when judging material
  - An instinct for recognizing the 'next big thing'

Marketing and Promotions

◇ Responsible for targeting recordings at specific groups of consumers.
◇ Controls and coordinates design of artwork and packaging.
◇ Chooses the format of a release, e.g. CD or vinyl.
◇ In charge of TV, press and radio, online and digital (new media) advertising campaigns. Essentially makes sure that the target audience is aware of the release.
◇ Skills/attributes:
  • Creative and visual flair, with an eye for a novel idea
  • Strong organizational and communication skills
  • Good working knowledge of the advertising industry
  • Team player

Press officer

◇ These normally operate in-house at a major label, whereas indie labels usually hire a freelance press officer.
◇ Supplies the press with information and promotional material regarding gigs, tours and releases. The aim is to 'up the profile' of the band/artist, i.e. create as much publicity as possible about them.
◇ Skills/attributes:
  • Excellent command of English
  • Solid copywriting and proofreading skills
  • Good communication and organizational ability
  • Strong networking skills
  • Up to date with the current music scene
  • Ability to work to tight deadlines

Plugger

◇ Their sole purpose is to persuade DJs and radio producers to play the records of the artists they represent. Radio stations often have playlists typically listed as A, B and C. Records on the A list are played repeatedly on the station throughout the day. B-list records are played frequently, C-list records on a less regular basis. It is the plugger's aim to get his or her records onto one of these lists – ideally onto the A list. A TV plugger's work is along the same lines.
◇ Skills/attributes:
  • Persuasive personality
  • Strong communication skills
  • Knowledge of current musical trends

Major label boss

◇ Steers the artistic direction of a label, receiving advice from A&R, marketing, etc. on which acts to sign, keep or drop.
◇ Ultimately responsible for the financial health of the label.
◇ Often answerable to another, higher, executive in the corporation.
◇ Skills/attributes:
  • Willing to take overall responsibility for the label
  • Ability to listen and communicate at all levels
  • Ability to delegate
  • Sound financial acumen
  • Decisiveness
  • An instinct for what will sell
  • Creative vision

Indie label boss
◇ Performs the same function as a major label boss. In addition, often fulfils the roles of A&R person, marketing department, etc., depending on the size of the label. Generally answerable to no one, as indie labels traditionally operate independently of other companies.
◇ Skills/attributes:
  • As for a major label boss, with the added ability to switch between roles as necessary
  • In touch with the current music scene
  • Strong persuasive skills

MEDIA ROLES

Radio producer
◇ Controls the overall style and content of a radio programme.
◇ Responsible for compiling the show's playlists, sometimes in collaboration with the radio DJ.
◇ Skills/attributes:
  • Working knowledge of radio broadcasting equipment and procedures
  • In touch with the tastes of the target audience
  • Delegating skills

Radio DJ
◇ Responsible for playing the songs on air.
◇ Also for links and interviews throughout the programme.
◇ Generally, the more the commercial and mainstream a show is, the less influence the DJ has over what is played.
◇ Skills/attributes:
  • Clear and confident speaking voice
  • In-depth knowledge of their chosen genre
  • In touch with the tastes of the target audience
  • Familiarity with broadcasting equipment and procedures
  • Individual style and creativity is desirable

Music journalist
◇ May be either a staff writer (employed by one particular publication) or freelance (contributing to various publications).
◇ Writes articles and reviews for websites, newspaper music sections and the music press.
◇ Does interviews, and writes them up for publication.
◇ Often receives demos from unsigned bands, and goes to local venues to discover up-and-coming talent.
◇ Skills/attributes:
  • Communication and networking skills
  • Excellent command of the written word
  • Creative flair
  • Inquiring nature

Web designer
◇ Responsible for designing and maintaining a website. Usually commissioned and paid for by the artist's record label.
◇ Skills/attributes:
  • Thorough understanding of web programming languages
  • Background in IT desirable
  • Eye for good design

PUBLISHING AND ROYALTIES

Whenever a record is manufactured, or when a song is played on the radio or TV, money is payable by law to the songwriter(s). Such sums are referred to as 'royalties'. There are two copyrights in any one song – the music itself (a musical work) and the lyrics (a literary work). The term 'copyright' refers to the exclusive rights of the author or creator of an original work, including the right to copy, distribute and adapt that work. These rights can be licensed, transferred and/or assigned. Copyright protects original literary, musical and artistic works, sound recordings, films, broadcasts and the typographical arrangement of a published edition. The legal framework for copyright in the UK is the Copyright, Designs and Patents Act 1988. As well as the copyright in the song, there is also a separate copyright in the recording of the song.

In Britain, PRS for Music (formerly the Performing Right Society) collects money on behalf of songwriters and publishers. Performance royalties are due whenever copyright music, live or recorded, is broadcast or played in public. MCPS sits under PRS for Music, and licenses the 'mechanical' (reproduction) rights and pays the mechanical royalties. Mechanical royalties are generated from the recording of music, and the reproduction of recordings, whether on CDs, DVDs, videos or any other format, or as digital downloads. Similar or equivalent organizations – called 'collecting societies' – exist in the USA and in many other countries.

MCPS (Mechanical-Copyright Protection Society)
The MCPS is the British organization that acts on behalf of its writer and publisher members, negotiating agreements with those who wish to record music, and distributing the mechanical royalties. The MCPS also ensures that writers and publishers get a royalty when their music is used in a film or advert. This is known as a 'synchronization fee'.

PRS for Music; ASCAP, BMI
PRS is the British organization administering the collection and distribution of performance royalties. The US equivalents are ASCAP (American Society of Composers, Authors and Publishers) and BMI (Broadcast Music, Inc.). All three are membership associations of composers, songwriters, lyricists, and music publishers. They collect money from TV, radio companies, internet sites, pubs, clubs and other venues that play music, whether live or recorded; and they distribute the royalties to their members.

MCPS and PRS royalties are payable to people who actually had a part in *writing* the music, and to their publishers, not to those who only performed it.

PPL (Phonographic Performance Ltd)
The PPL collects royalties on behalf of record companies and their performing artists. Any artist who has played on a recording will receive these royalties, whether or not they were involved in the writing process. (Again, this describes the British model.)

Music publisher
A publisher deals with the administration of copyrights on behalf of a writer: protecting, registering and exploiting copyrights, issuing licences, and collecting and distributing royalties from the collecting agencies (in Britain, PRS and MCPS). It may also print songs as sheet music, or license them for inclusion in printed anthologies. Further royalties accrue through sales of the printed music. Just as a record company signs up a singer or group, the music publishing company signs up a songwriter for a given number of years, usually paying an advance which is set against future royalties. All songs that are written during the agreed period (or term) are administered and controlled by the publisher, either by way of assignment of copyright or by exclusive licence.

◇ Skills/attributes:
  - Legal training
  - Administration and business affairs skills
  - Communication and PR skills
  - Accounting skills
  - Knowledge of current musical trends
  - An instinct for what will sell

MANUFACTURING AND DISTRIBUTION

CD manufacturer
◇ Responsible for making duplicates of the CD. After receiving the PQ master from the mastering engineer the manufacturer makes a 'glass master' from which all copies of the CD are produced.
◇ Skills/attributes:
  - Ability to work under pressure and to tight deadlines

Distributor
◇ The distributor is the link between the record company and the retail shops. After the recording has been mastered and manufactured, it is the distributor's job to get the product into the shops. Major labels generally have their own distribution network while indie labels tend to use independent distribution companies.
◇ Skills/attributes:
  - Strong organizational skills
  - Self-motivated with persuasive selling ability
  - Team player
  - Good communication skills
  - Instinct for what will sell

Digital distribution
The availability of music as data files, rather than as CDs, has significantly reduced the costs of distribution because record companies are not faced with the problem of physical space. Most companies also sell music through online distributors and music stores such as iTunes, Spotify and Amazon, where customers download from the internet straight to their own home. While many high street record shops and chains have gone out of business, digital distribution has helped to revitalise the singles market.

MAJOR LABELS

In the early days of the music business, record labels were set up by large companies such as Columbia and Victor. Nowadays approximately 70% of music in the world market is released on one of three major labels (known as the Big Three): Sony Music Entertainment, Universal Music Group, and Warner Music Group. The acts these labels represent are generally aimed at the mass market or 'mainstream'.

Major labels (often referred to as 'majors') are large companies with various departments such as A&R, Marketing and Distribution, working in conjunction with one another. As the majors are multi-national companies, with offices all over the world, they are able to promote and distribute their music worldwide.

The main advantage for an artist on a major label is that more money is available to promote them on a worldwide network. However, such huge investment means that the major-label artist is expected to sell a large number of records. An artist will soon find their contract terminated if their sales do not measure up to the label's expectations.

INDIE LABELS

Traditionally indie labels are known for introducing new and innovative artists, who tend to enjoy greater artistic control than their major-label counterparts. Indie labels tend to specialize in 'niche' markets such as guitar bands, reggae, drum'n'bass, etc. As their financial resources are much more limited then the majors, they employ fewer people. And as they do not have international offices, indie labels license their recordings to foreign record companies in order to sell their product abroad.

Some indie labels collaborate with majors. The indie label signs and records the artist but relies on a major label to manufacture, market and distribute the finished product. The artist is perceived as belonging to a small indie label, thus gaining 'credibility' (and qualifying their releases for inclusion in the independent charts), while simultaneously receiving the support of a major label's infrastructure. Some indie labels rely on a major label solely for distribution purposes. In return for their involvement, the major label usually receives a share of sales of the product. Occasionally major labels gain part-control of the indie label with which they are collaborating.

Some of the smallest independent labels are run as a one-person venture. Working from home and armed with a telephone line and an internet connection, this individual takes on the role of label manager, A&R, marketing and so on. There are very limited funds available for the artist involved in such a set up, but the pressure to sell is also reduced. As a result many indie-label artists are able to experiment musically, which can result in more radical, innovative releases.

PUTTING ON A GIG (INDIE BAND)

These comments are specifically aimed at anyone who wants to promote their music by playing live. Some pointers are given on how to achieve this, and what to expect.

◇   For most small gigs, bands approach the venue promoter directly. Before you contact the promoter check through their website to make sure that they are what you are looking for in terms of the type of music and audience numbers.

◇   Send the promoter an email including the name of your band, genre of music, your social networking or website link, a brief description and biog with gigging experience, plus your contact details. Aim for short snappy sentences that will make the reader want to listen to the demo.

◇   The promoter may ask for demos. Always put the strongest song first (and on your website or social networking site). Promoters receive a large number of demo tapes, and if the first song does not appeal to them, they will not listen to the rest of the demo.

◇   You may be given an option for what time your band will go on stage (i.e. headline, bottom support, etc.). Be wary of immediately opting for the headline slot, especially if you are unsure of how large an audience you will bring. If you headline a gig and fail to pull a large enough audience, the promoter will be unlikely to consider you for any future gigs.

◇   Before the gig make sure that you are well-rehearsed and check that all your equipment is in good working order. Turn up on time, know which songs you are going to play, don't waste time in the sound check, enjoy yourself and don't panic if anything goes wrong.

◇ Besides asking your family and friends to come and watch you play, the traditional way to promote your gig is to design a flyer, and leaflet or 'fly' outside similar venues, clubs, etc. when people enter or leave. Try to ensure the flyer gives an impression of the sort of music your band plays – and do not forget the obvious details such as date, time, place and how much it will cost to get in.

◇ On the day of the gig have flyers for your next gig ready to hand out. It is a good idea to have a mailing list available at the gig, so that interested people can leave their contact details in order to find out about future gigs or releases.

◇ You might want to produce and sell your demos at gigs – this is a good way to create interest and generate revenue for the band.

◇ If you do not have a large audience, it is not a good idea to gig too frequently, e.g. more than once every six weeks. Friends quickly tire of being coerced into watching you play every fortnight!

PUTTING ON A GIG (MAJOR LABEL VERSION)

Major-label artists generally tour or gig only when they have a release to promote, as gigs often lose money. Tours are more common than one-off gigs.

◇ The artist's manager first meets with a booking agent to discuss the style and genre of the artist, their pulling power (i.e. how many people will pay to see them) and so on. The booking agent then puts together a package of suitable gigs and dates, in consultation with the artist's manager and tour manager. He or she contacts the promoters of the chosen venues, sorts out details such as the band's requirements, and negotiates a fee for hiring the venue.

◇ The promoter arranges for tickets to be printed, and publicizes the gig via the internet, music press, newspapers, flyposting, and leafleting at gigs ('flying'). Tickets for major gigs are usually sold via ticket agencies and sometimes at the venue itself.

◇ The merchandiser designs and organizes the manufacture of T-shirts, posters, and other memorabilia.

◇ Major-label acts often supply their own PA and lighting rig. This is known as a 'full production show'.

◇ Once the gig is over, the tour manager receives the band's fee (less venue hire, etc.) from the promoter. This is sometimes known as 'settling the show'.

Bibliography

The books listed here include those to which reference is made in the text, as well as a number of others which readers may find useful, chosen to cover a wide range of popular music styles.

Adams, S. (1999) *Jazz: a Crash Course* London: Simon & Schuster

Bennett, A. (2000) *Popular music and youth culture: music, identity and place* Basingstoke: Palgrave

Boyd, J. (2006) *White Bicycles – Making Music in the 1960s* London: Serpent's Tail

Britten, A. (2009) *Working in the music industry* Oxford: How To Books

Broughton, F. and Brewster, B. (2006) *Last night a DJ saved my life: 100 years of the disc jockey* London: Headline Book Publishing

Byrne, D. (2012) *How music works* Edinburgh: Canongate

Calcutt, A. (2000) *Brit Cult: an A – Z of British Pop Culture* London: Prion Books

Clarke, S. (1980) *Jah Music* London: Heinemann Educational

Denselow, R. (1990) *When the Music's Over: the Story of Political Pop* London: Faber and Faber

Frith, S., Straw, W. & Street, J. (Ed) (2001) *The Cambridge Companion to Pop and Rock* Cambridge: Cambridge University Press

Gillett, C. (1996) *The Sound of the City* New York: Da Capo Press

Jones, L. (1963) *Blues People* New York: William Morrow & Co

Lee, E. (1982) *Folksong & Music Hall* London: Routledge and Kegan Paul

MacDonald, I. (2008) *Revolution in the Head: the Beatles' Records and the Sixties* London: Vintage

Malone, B. C. (2010) *Country Music, U.S.A.* Austin: University of Texas Press

McNeil, L. & McCain, G. (1997) *Please Kill Me: the Uncensored Oral History of Punk* London: Abacus

Mellers, W. (2011) *Music in a New Found Land: Themes and Developments in the History of American Music* New Jersey: Transaction Publishers

Mellers, W. (1973) *Twilight of the Gods: the Beatles in Retrospect* London: Faber & Faber

Melly, G. (2008) *Revolt into Style: The Pop Arts in Britain* London: Faber and Faber

Merwe, P. van der (1989) *Origins of the Popular Style* Oxford: Oxford University Press

Millar, B. (1971) *The Drifters* London: Studio Vista

Milner, G. (2009) *Perfecting Sound Forever: the Story of Recorded Music* London: Granta Publications

O'Brien, L. (2012) *She Bop: the Definitive History of Women in Popular Music* London: Jawbone Press

Oliver, P. (1997) *The Story of the Blues* London: Pimlico

Reynolds, S. (2007) *Bring the Noise* London: Faber and Faber

Reynolds, S. (2011) *Retromania: Pop Culture's Addiction to its Own Past* London: Faber and Faber

Rogers, D. (1982) *Rock 'n' Roll* London: Routledge and Kegan Paul

Russell, T. (1970) *Blacks, Whites and Blues* London: Studio Vista

Scaduto, A. (1972) *Bob Dylan* London: W. H. Allen & Co

Shelton, R. (1986) *No Direction Home* London: Hodder & Stoughton

Shepherd, J. (1982) *Tin Pan Alley* London: Routledge and Kegan Paul

Smith, S. J. and Richards, M. (2009) *How to Make it in Music* London: Dennis Publishing

Vincent, R. (1995) *Funk: the Music, the People, and the Rhythm of the One* New York: St Martin's Press

Vulliamy, G. (1982) *Jazz & Blues* London: Routledge and Kegan Paul

Williams, R. (2003) *Phil Spector Out of his Head* London: Omnibus Press

Websites
www.artscouncil.org.uk
www.prsformusic.com
www.allmusic.com

Index of Artists

Producers, remixers, DJs, MCs and classical composers are included here. Authors and instrument-designers are listed in the General Index. Page-numbers in **bold** refer to profiles or principal entries.

Index of Titles

Album titles are in *italics*. Films and TV programmes are listed in the General Index. Page numbers in **bold** refer to analyses in Chapter 11.

General Index

Where there are multiple entries, principal ones are shown in **bold**.